Cataloging and Classification
An Introduction

McGRAW-HILL SERIES IN LIBRARY EDUCATION

Jean Key Gates, Consulting Editor
University of South Florida

Cataloging and Classification
An Introduction

Lois Mai Chan
University of Kentucky

McGraw-Hill Book Company
New York   St. Louis   San Francisco   Auckland   Bogotá
Hamburg   London   Madrid   Mexico   Montreal
New Delhi   Panama   Paris   São Paulo   Singapore
Sydney   Tokyo   Toronto

Cataloging and Classification: An Introduction

10 11 12   BRBBRB   89

This book was set in Palatino by Graphic Technique, Inc. The editors
were Richard R. Wright and Susan Gamer; the design was done by Caliber
Design Planning; the production supervisor was Rosann E. Raspini.

C I P

Library of Congress Cataloging in Publication Data

Chan, Lois Mai.
    Cataloging and classification.

    (McGraw-Hill series in library education)
    Bibliography: p.
    Includes index.
    1. Cataloging.   2.   Classification—Books.   I.   Title.
Z693.C437   025.3   80-15695
ISBN 0-07-010498-0

To
S. K., J. M., and S. Y.

Contents

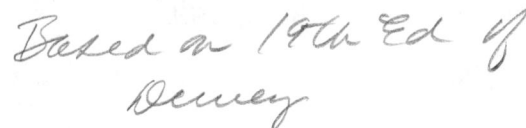 

Based on 19th Ed of Dewey (handwritten)

PART THREE   Subject Cataloging

PART FOUR   Classification

Preface

This book is intended as an introductory text to cataloging and classification for use in a beginning course. The scope is the analysis and presentation of library materials—both book-form and nonbook materials. Emphasis is on the three basic processes in the organization of library materials: descriptive cataloging, subject cataloging, and classification. In each part, emphasis is placed first on the historical development and the principles, which are considered essential to the understanding of cataloging and classification. Discussion and examples of provisions in the basic tools are then presented in order to illustrate the operations of cataloging and classification.

Each part begins with a list of background readings designed to help the student gain an overview of the subject to be presented. For those who wish to pursue the subject in greater depth, a list of further readings is included.

In recent years, cataloging and classification have been rapidly changing fields. In this book, an attempt has been made to reflect current practice. In descriptive cataloging, the second edition of *Anglo-American Cataloguing Rules* is used as the basis. Discussion of subject cataloging is based on the ninth edition of *Library of Congress Subject Headings* and the eleventh edition of the *Sears List of Subject Headings*. A brief discussion of PRECIS, the system used for subject indexing of books in the *British National Bibliography*, is also included. For classification, discussion and examples are based on the nineteenth full edition and the eleventh abridged edition of the *Dewey Decimal Classification* and the most recent editions of the *Library of Congress Classification* schedules. It should be pointed out that this text is intended to be an aid in the study of these operations and the basic tools and should not be used in place of the cataloging and classification tools. In other words, one cannot classify a document without using a classification scheme. Likewise, one should not attempt to prepare a bibliographic description of an item without resorting to the *Anglo-American Cataloguing Rules*. Therefore, the discussion concentrates on the essence of the rules, and no attempt is made to replicate or reproduce the cataloging rules in the text.

In Parts Three and Four, the chapters on the individual subject headings systems and classification schemes have been designed so that they may be used as a whole or selectively. For example, Chapter 9, on the *Sears List of Subject Headings*, may be used without first studying Chapter 8, on the *Library of Congress Subject Headings;* and in Chapter 12, the sections on the abridged edition of *Dewey* can be used without the sections on the full edition. As a result, certain overlapping discussions or repetitions of similar points occur in these chapters. This method was used because certain library science programs are designed for specific types of libraries—e.g., school libraries—in which not all systems of subject cataloging or classification are covered.

The author is indebted to many individuals for their assistance in the preparation of this book: John Phillip Comaromi, Doralyn Hickey, and John D. Byrum for reading parts or all of the manuscript; Barbara B. Mabry, Barbara A. Van Nostrand, and Shirley DeSimone for proofreading; and Patricia A. Boyle, Melda Fuller, and Celia Smith for typing the manuscript.

Lois Mai Chan

Cataloging and Classification
An Introduction

PART ONE

Introduction

BACKGROUND READING

Horner, John. *Cataloguing.* London: Association of Assistant Librarians, 1970. Chap. 2.

Prospects for Change in Bibliographic Control. Abraham Bookstein, Herman H. Fussler, Helen F. Schmierer, eds. Chicago: University of Chicago Press, 1977.

FURTHER READING

Davinson, Donald. *Bibliographic Control.* London: Clive Bingley; Hamden, Conn.: Linnet Books, 1975. Chap. 2.

Freedman, Maurice J. "Automated Network Catalog Products and Services." *Journal of Library Automation,* **9**:145–155, June 1976.

Rather, John C. "The Future of Catalog Control in the Library of Congress." *Journal of Academic Librarianship,* **1**:4–7, May 1975.

CHAPTER 1

Bibliographic Records and Library Materials

BIBLIOGRAPHIC CONTROL

The term *bibliographic control* refers to the operation by which recorded information is organized or arranged and thereby made readily retrievable. Indexing, cataloging, and classification are some of the ways to achieve bibliographic control.

BIBLIOGRAPHIC RECORDS

The most common devices of bibliographic control are files or lists called *bibliographic records*. Bibliographies, indexes, and catalogs are the most common types of bibliographic records.

CATALOGS

The bibliographic records of a library collection are generally contained in a file called a *catalog*. The catalog serves the purpose of communicating briefly the essential facts about the documents in the collection. These essential facts include a bibliographic description giving the identification, publication (issue), and physical characteristics of the document; subject headings which state succinctly the subject content of the document; and a call number (consisting of the classification number based on the subject content and a book number based on the author, the title, or both) which indicates the location of the document in the collection. The information provided in the catalog allows a user to identify particular items in the collection or to select relevant items for specific purposes.

Forms of Catalogs

Library catalogs appear in various physical forms. The predominant types—the book catalog, the card catalog, the computerized catalog, and the microform catalog—are discussed below.

Book catalog

The book catalog is a list in book form of the holdings of a particular library collection or a group of collections. The cataloging records are displayed in page format. This is the oldest form of library catalog. The items may be recorded by handwriting as in a manuscript catalog, by a printing process, or by typing. The oldest manuscript catalog goes back as far as the Pinakes compiled by Callimachus for the Alexandrian library. The book-form catalog was the predominant form of library catalog until the late nineteenth century, when the idea of the card catalog began to spread.

The major disadvantage of the book catalog in the early days was the difficulty and cost of updating. It was difficult to revise and susceptible to wear and tear. The major advantages were portability and the possibility of multiple copies.

From the late nineteenth century until the 1960s, the card catalog became the dominant form of catalog in American libraries. Book catalogs continued to be issued in small numbers.

Beginning in the 1960s, there has been a renewed interest in the book catalog, as a result of advances in technology and equipment related to book-catalog production. These included the availability of a high-speed sequential card camera and of a 120-character print chain for computers, and improvement in offset printing methods.

Card catalog

In this type of catalog, cataloging entries are recorded on 3 by 5 cards, one entry per card. When the card catalog was introduced, its advantage in the ease of updating was immediately perceived. Libraries in the United States began adopting this format. The Library of Congress printed-card service, begun in 1901, contributed to the widespread use of the card catalog. For nearly a century, the card catalog has been the predominant form of bibliographic record in American libraries.

Automated or computerized cataloging records[1]

An automated or computerized catalog contains records in machine-readable form. Cataloging records are transformed into a format which is recognizable to the computer. When the records stored in the computer can be retrieved instantly, it is called an *on-line catalog*. The

---

[1]Cf. Maurice J. Freedman. "Automated Network Catalog Products and Services." *Journal of Library Automation,* 9:145-155, June 1976.

usual mode of display in an on-line catalog is through the cathode-ray-tube (CRT) terminal. In this mode, individual cataloging records or parts thereof are called by means of search keys and displayed instantly on a television-like screen. Many of the terminals are accompanied by printers, which may be used to print out desired items.

The machine-readable cataloging records may also be stored on magnetic tapes, which can be used for various purposes. A cumulated file of machine-readable records is called a data base. Examples of cataloging data bases are the MARC (machine-readable cataloging) data base, which contains records processed by the Library of Congress (LC), and the data bases of various networks such as OCLC (formerly the Ohio College Library Center), RLIN (Research Libraries Information Network) or BALLOTS (Stanford University's "bibliographic automation of large library operations using a time-sharing system"), and WLN (Washington Library Network), which contain cataloging records contributed by participating libraries in addition to the LC MARC records.

In the 1970s, because of the increasing cost of maintaining a card catalog and the physical deterioration of catalog cards, many large research libraries contemplated an alternative to the card catalog. The Library of Congress announced its plans to close the existing card catalog in 1981 and to rely on the on-line automated catalog for bibliographic retrieval. Many large research libraries are or will be following the same course. Libraries that do not have the facilities or resources to switch to an automated catalog are considering continued use of the card catalog or are exploring other alternatives. Some of these alternatives are discussed below.

Line-printer-produced catalog card or printout

Many member libraries of large networks such as OCLC, RLIN (BALLOTS), and WLN have used the networks' data bases for reproducing cataloging records. Catalog cards and printouts are produced by means of the line printer from machine-readable records. Many large book vendors, such as Bro-Dart and Blackwell North America, provide line-printed catalog cards. In recent years, the Library of Congress has also been producing printed cards from MARC records.

Computer-produced photocomposed book catalog

Records in a computerized data base may be converted into the book form by means of photocomposition. Many public libraries in recent years have converted to the computer-produced book catalogs. The advantages are that copies of the book catalog can be produced for all the branches so that each branch can have a record of the holdings of the entire system. Copies of the card catalog cannot be so readily or economically reproduced.

Once the machine-readable cataloging records have been converted to the book form, all the disadvantages of the book catalog, such as inhospitality to corrections, changes, and additions, are present.

The photocomposition device differs from the line printer in that the former can handle a multiplicity of alphabets and type fonts, while the latter is limited to a single alphabet. In the photocomposition or electronic composition process, the digital information is converted to graphic arts or letterpress-quality images.

Microform catalog

A microform catalog contains cataloging records in microimage and requires the use of a microform reader for viewing. There are various media for the microform catalog, such as microfilm (continuous negative), microcard (positive), and microfiche (negative).

As a variant of the book catalog, the microform catalog has the advantage of economy in duplication. Once a microform catalog is produced, it is much cheaper to duplicate than a book catalog.

A microform catalog may be produced by photographing book catalogs. A more recent method is to produce a microform catalog directly from machine-readable records. This method is called *computer-output microform* (COM). The COM device converts the digital information contained on the computer-generated magnetic tape into print displayed on microform. Thus, the recent advances in micrographics have been combined with the technology of the computer in catalog production, resulting in lower costs and more efficient updating.

The microform catalog carries the primary advantage of book catalogs—portability—to an extreme. Some academic institutions, such as the Georgia Tech Library, have reproduced all their catalogs on microfiche, updated with cumulated supplements produced by COM. This device enables every academic and research department on campus to possess a copy of the entire library catalog, a luxury unthinkable before the development of micrographics.

The major disadvantage of the COM catalog occurs at the use stage. The requirement of a microform reader, the handling of the fiche or film, and the display image tend to create a psychological barrier to the user.

Nonetheless, in recent years, the microform catalog has been playing an increasingly important role in bibliographic control. In the plan of the Library of Congress to close the card catalog and switch to the computerized or on-line catalog, the microform catalog is considered to be one of the most viable back-up devices to supplement and complement the machine-readable data base. For many other libraries, because of the cost in card catalog maintenance on the one hand and the rising costs of printing and paper in the case of the book catalog, the COM catalog is becoming perhaps the most practical alternative.

Organization of Cataloging Entries

In a catalog, individual bibliographic entries are organized into a coherent file. Two predominant methods of organizing the entries are the systematic or classified arrangement and the alphabetical arrangement.

In a classified catalog, the entries are arranged according to a certain system of classification, resulting in subject collocation. This is the older form of catalog arrangement. This form of catalog as a public tool has become all but extinct in American libraries. However, as a working tool for catalogers, this form is still extant in the shelflist usually located in the cataloging department.

In an alphabetical, or dictionary, catalog, entries are organized in alphabetical sequence without regard to subject relationship. This form was introduced in the latter part of the nineteenth century and has since become the predominant form of catalog arrangement in American libraries. Further discussion of the dictionary catalog will appear in Chapter 7.

Elements in Cataloging Records

Regardless of the format or type of display, cataloging records normally contain the following elements: bibliographic description, subject headings or indexing terms, and a call number. Each of the elements is presented according to certain standard tools such as the Anglo-American Cataloguing Rules and the Dewey Decimal Classification. The following chapters provide details with regard to the tools and the creation of cataloging records.

TYPES OF LIBRARY MATERIAL

For the purpose of bibliographic description, the following types of library materials have been identified:

Books, pamphlets, and printed sheets

Cartographic materials
Manuscripts
Music
Sound recordings
Motion pictures and videorecordings
Graphic materials
Machine-readable data files
Three-dimensional artefacts and realia
Microforms
Serials

For definitions of these terms, see *Anglo-American Cataloguing Rules*[2] (2d ed., pp. 563–572), and the Glossary of this book.

[2] *Anglo-American Cataloguing Rules*. 2d ed. Prepared by the American Library Association, the British Library, the Canadian Committee on Cataloguing, the Library Association, the Library of Congress. Michael Gorman and Paul W. Winkler, eds. Chicago: American Library Association, 1978.

PART TWO

Descriptive Cataloging

BASIC TOOL

Anglo-American Cataloguing Rules. 2d ed. Prepared by the American Library Association, the British Library, the Canadian Committee on Cataloguing, the Library Association, the Library of Congress. Michael Gorman and Paul W. Winkler, eds. Chicago: American Library Association, 1978.

BACKGROUND READING

"AACR 2: Background and Summary." *Library of Congress Information Bulletin,* **47**:640–652, October 20, 1978.

Dunkin, Paul S. *Cataloging U.S.A.* Chicago: American Library Association, 1969. Chaps. 3–4.

Gorman, Michael. "The Anglo-American Cataloguing Rules, Second Edition." *Library Resources and Technical Services,* **22**:209–226, Summer 1978.

Henderson, Kathryn Luther. "'Treated with a Degree of Uniformity and Common Sense': Descriptive Cataloging in the United States—1876–1975." *Library Trends,* **25**:227–271, July 1976.

International Conference on Cataloguing Principles, Paris, 1961. "Statement of Principles." *Report of International Conference on Cataloguing Principles.* A. H. Chaplin and Dorothy Anderson, eds. London: Organizing Committee of the International Conference on Cataloguing Principles, National Central Library, 1963. Pp. 91–96.

FURTHER READING

Cutter, Charles A. *Rules for a Dictionary Catalog.* 4th ed. Washington, D.C.: Government Printing Office, 1904. Republished, London: The Library Association, 1953. (First published under the title *Rules for a Printed Dictionary Catalogue* in 1876.)

Horner, John. *Cataloguing*. London: Association of Assistant Librarians, 1970. Chaps. 3–7.

Hunter, Eric. *AACR 2: An Introduction to the Second Edition of Anglo-American Cataloguing Rules*. London: Clive Bingley; Hamden, Conn.: Linnet Books, 1979. (A programmed text.)

Kelm, Carol R. "The Historical Development of the Second Edition of *Anglo-American Cataloguing Rules*." *Library Resources and Technical Services,* **22**:22–33, Winter 1976.

Lubetzky, Seymour. *Cataloging Rules and Principles: A Critique of the ALA Rules for Entry and a Proposed Design for Their Revision*. Washington, D.C.: Library of Congress, 1953.

Needham, C. D. *Organizing Knowledge in Libraries: An Introduction to Information Retrieval*. 2d ed. London: Andre Deutsch, 1971. Chaps. 1–3.

Osborn, Andrew D. "The Crisis in Cataloging." *Library Quarterly,* **11**:393–411, October 1941.

Painter, Ann F., ed. *Reader in Classification and Descriptive Cataloging*. Washington, D.C.: Microcard Editions, 1972. Pt. II, Descriptive Cataloging.

Richmond, Phyllis A. "AACR 2—A Review Article." *Journal of Academic Librarianship*, **6** (1), 30–37, March 1980.

Simonton, Wesley. "An Introduction to AACR 2." *Library Resources and Technical Services*, **23**:321–339, Summer 1979.

Weintraub, D. Kathryn. "AACR 2: A Review Article." *Library Quarterly*, **49**:435–443, October 1979.

CHAPTER 2
Development of Cataloging Codes

The term cataloging refers to the process of preparing entries for a catalog. Descriptive cataloging means providing bibliographic information on cataloging records exclusive of subject representation. In other words, descriptive cataloging includes the presentation of bibliographic description and the determination of access points by means of names and titles.

In the early days of library service, cataloging was largely an individual activity for each library. Each library constructed its own catalog in a way deemed most suitable for its purposes. Bibliographic records were presented in forms and styles that varied from library to library.

Gradually, librarians realized the advantages of cooperation among libraries and standardization of practice. The need for codification of cataloging practice became apparent. Compatibility of cataloging records in the catalogs of different libraries facilitates services to users who move from library to library. It enables library cooperation and economizes library operations through centralized or cooperative cataloging.

Since the middle of the nineteenth century, a series of cataloging codes have been developed. Each new code sought to improve on the preceding ones. The earlier codes represent mostly efforts of individuals, and the later ones are results of corporate undertakings. Following is a brief discussion of the development of the codes.

BRITISH MUSEUM CATALOGUING RULES

Panizzi, Sir Anthony, et al. "Rules for the Compilation of the Catalogue." *Catalogue of Printed Books in the British Museum.* London: British Museum. Printed by order of the trustees, 1841. Vol. 1, pp. v–ix.

British Museum. Department of Printed Books. *Rules for Compiling the Catalogues of Printed Books, Maps and Music in the British Museum.* Rev. ed. London: British Museum. Printed by order of the trustees, 1936.

The British Museum Cataloguing Rules (BM) also known as Panizzi's ninety-one rules, were developed in 1839 as a guide for the compilation of the British Museum catalogs. It reflects the functions of these particular catalogs as inventory lists and finding lists.

It is considered to be the first major cataloging code and has influenced later codes.

JEWETT'S RULES

> Jewett, Charles C. *Smithsonian Report on the Construction of Catalogs of Libraries, and Their Publication by Means of Separate, Stereotyped Titles, with Rules and Examples.* 2d ed. Washington, D.C.: Smithsonian Institution, 1853. Reprinted, Ann Arbor, Mich.: University Microfilms, 1961.

Jewett's code contains thirty-three rules largely based on Panizzi's rules. Jewett's discussion of subject headings represents the earliest attempt at codifying subject headings practice.

Jewett was noted for his proposal of centralized and cooperative cataloging by means of a union catalog which would provide "stereotyped" cataloging entries for all libraries.

CUTTER'S RULES

> Cutter, Charles Ammi. *Rules for a Dictionary Catalog.* 4th ed. Rewritten. Washington, D.C.: Government Printing Office, 1904. Republished, London: The Library Association, 1953.

The first edition appeared in 1876 with the title *Rules for a Printed Dictionary Catalogue,* which formed Part II of the U.S. Bureau of Education Publication, *Public Libraries in the United States.*

It contains 369 rules covering descriptive cataloging, subject headings, and filing.

Cutter's purpose was to "investigate what might be called the first principles of cataloging;" because of this, his code has had greater influence on subsequent codes than any other work in the area of cataloging. It became the basis for the dictionary catalog, which was to take over the form of catalogs in general libraries in the United States.

It contains the well-known statement of the objects of the catalog and the means for attaining them (p. 12):

Objects
1. To enable a person to find a book of which either
   a. the author ⎫
   b. the title   ⎬ is known
   c. the subject ⎭
2. To show what the library has:
   d. by a given author
   e. on a given subject
   f. in a given kind of literature
3. To assist in the choice of a book:
   g. as to its edition (bibliographically)
   h. as to its character (literary or topical).

Means
1. Author entry with the necessary references (for a and d).
2. Title entry or title reference (for b).
3. Subject entry, cross-references, and classed subject table (for c and e).
4. Form entry and language entry (for f).
5. Giving edition and imprint, with notes when necessary (for g)
6. Notes (for h).

The essence of this statement is still discernible in the present Anglo-American cataloging code.

AA 1908

> American Library Association. *Catalog Rules: Author and Title Entries.* American ed. Chicago: American Library Association, 1908.

AA 1908 represented the first joint effort between the American and the British librarians in developing a cataloging code. However, the two groups did not reach full agreement on all details and the code was published in two editions (English and American).

AA 1908 reflected the influence of previous codes—BM, Cutter—and, to a large extent, current practice of the Library of Congress, which had begun distributing printed cards in 1901.

AA 1908 owed a great deal to Cutter's rules. However, it had excluded Cutter's statements of objects and means. The rules for subject headings were also omitted. The major aim of the code was to meet the "requirements of larger libraries of a scholarly character." To a large extent, this statement set the tone of the subsequent codes, which have been drawn up primarily to respond to the needs of large research libraries. The needs of smaller libraries are only occasionally recognized in the provision of alternative rules.

PRUSSIAN INSTRUCTIONS

> *The Prussian Instructions: Rules for the Alphabetical Catalogs of the Prussian Libraries.* Translated from the 2d ed., authorized August 10, 1908, with an introduction and notes by Andrew D. Osborn. Ann Arbor, Mich.: University of Michigan Press, 1938.

Originally developed as a standardized system of cataloging for Prussian libraries, the Prussian Instructions (PI) were adopted by many libraries in Germanic and Scandinavian countries.

The rules reflect two major differences in cataloging between the Germanic and the Anglo-American traditions. PI prescribes grammatical rather than mechanical title. For title entries, the entry word is the first grammatically independent word of the title instead of the first word of the title disregarding an article. The second difference lies in the fact that PI did not recognize corporate authorship.

VATICAN CODE

> Vatican Library. *Rules for the Catalog of Printed Books.* Translated from the 2d Italian ed. by the Very Rev. Thomas J. Shanahan, Victor A. Schaefer, and Constantin T. Vesselowsky. Wyllis E. Wright, ed. Chicago: American Library Association, 1948. (3d ed. in Italian appeared in 1949.)

The rules were developed for the purpose of compiling a general catalog of printed books in the Vatican Library after its reorganization in the 1920s. The persons responsible were either Americans or American-trained librarians. Therefore, American influence and bias are evident. It has been called an "international code with a definite American bias."[1] Its significance for American librarians lies in the fact that for many years, the Vatican code was, as Wright states in the foreword to the English translation, "the most complete statement of American cataloging practice."

---

[1]K. G. B. Bakewell. *A Manual of Cataloguing Practice.* Oxford: Pergamon Press, 1972. P. 32.

Probably the most comprehensive and best-structured code at the time, the Vatican code contains rules for entry, description, subject headings, and filing, with ample examples throughout.

ALA DRAFT (1941)

> American Library Association. *ALA Catalog Rules: Author and Title Entries.* Preliminary American 2d ed. Chicago: American Library Association, 1941.

During the early 1930s, there was a general feeling of the need for a revised ALA cataloging code. A Catalog Code Revision Committee under the American Library Association was established for this purpose. Its intention to cooperate with the Library Association of Great Britain and other national library associations was not fully realized because of the eruption of the Second World War.

The draft code was completed in 1941. The 88-page pamphlet *AA 1908* had blossomed into a 408-page document. The reason for the elaboration, as stated in the preface, was the need for standardization required by centralized and cooperative cataloging. The committee felt that elaborate and precise detail was the means to accomplish this end. The code consists of two parts, one dealing with entry and headings, the other with description. Again, the rules for subject headings were omitted.

The 1941 draft code was dealt a heavy blow in June 1941 by Andrew D. Osborn's article entitled "The Crisis in Cataloging."[2] Osborn criticized the code for attempting to provide a rule for every situation or question that may come up, an approach he referred to as "legalistic." The consequence, Osborne maintained, was unnecessary multiplication of rules.

LIBRARY OF CONGRESS DESCRIPTIVE CATALOGING RULES (1949)

> Library of Congress. *Rules for Descriptive Cataloging in the Library of Congress Adopted by the American Library Association.* Washington, D.C.: Library of Congress, 1949.

Because of the extensive use of Library of Congress printed catalog cards by libraries in the United States, the need was felt for the

---

[2]Andrew D. Osborn. "The Crisis in Cataloging." *Library Quarterly,* **11**:393–411, October 1941.

publication of the Library of Congress (LC) rules, which were not totally compatible with the ALA rules.

In 1946, the Library of Congress published its *Studies of Descriptive Cataloging: A Report to the Librarian of Congress by the Director of the Processing Department*, which advocated simplification of cataloging details. On the basis of the principles (which are reminiscent of Cutter's "objects") and the recommendations in the report, the Library of Congress proceeded to complete the work on the rules for description. A preliminary edition appeared in 1947, and a final edition in 1949 (LC 1949).

The rules cover description only, which is mainly that part of the cataloging entry following the heading. Many types of materials are considered: monographs, serials, maps, relief models, globes and atlases, music, facsimiles, photocopies and microfilms, and incunabula. *

AMERICAN LIBRARY ASSOCIATION RULES 1949

> American Library Association. *ALA Cataloging Rules for Author and Title Entries*. 2d ed. Clara Beetle, ed. Chicago: American Library Association, 1949.

Since the Library of Congress was revising its rules for description, the American Library Association decided to omit that portion of the rules from the 1941 draft and include only the rules for entry and heading in the ALA rules. This decision was made partly because individual libraries had been following LC practice (owing to the availability of LC printed cards) and partly because that portion of ALA 1941 had not been very well received. As a result, the 1949 rules (ALA 1949) cover entry and heading only, and must be used in conjunction with LC 1949.

ALA 1949 and LC 1949 served as the standards for descriptive cataloging for American libraries until the appearance of the Anglo-American Cataloging Rules in 1967.

The criticism of Osborn did not seem to have a great deal of effect on ALA 1949, for the rules in this code, in the opinion of many, are as pedantic, elaborate, and often arbitrary, as those in the preliminary edition of 1941.

ANGLO-AMERICAN CATALOGING RULES

> *Anglo-American Cataloging Rules*. Prepared by the American Library Association, the Library of Congress, the Library Association, and the Canadian Library Association. North

American text. Chicago: American Library Association, 1967. Reprinted in 1970 with supplement of additions and changes.

The strongest criticism of ALA 1949 was voiced by Seymour Lubetzky, whose *Cataloging Rules and Principles*[3] provided a thorough and penetrating analysis of ALA 1949 and proved to be the most important document for subsequent development in the field of descriptive cataloging. Lubetzky criticized ALA 1949 for being unnecessarily long and confusing because it provided duplicate and overlapping rules to meet identical conditions. Related rules were scattered, he maintained, and there was a lack of logical arrangement and organization of the rules.

Lubetzky's work is divided into three parts. Part I presents a detailed analysis of specific rules in ALA 1949. Part II takes up the question of the "corporate complex," again providing a perceptive analysis of the confusion regarding corporate authorship in existing codes, condemning ALA 1949 for many unnecessary rules such as those distinguishing between kinds of corporate bodies. In Part 3, Design for a Code, Lubetzky sets forth two objectives: "(1) to enable the user of the catalog to determine readily whether or not the library has the book he wants; (2) to reveal to the user of the catalog, under one form of the author's name, what works the library has by a given author and what editions or translations of a given work."

Lubetzky's report was received favorably, and another ALA Catalog Code Revision Committee, with Wyllis Wright as the chairman, was established for the purpose of drafting a new code. In 1956, Lubetzky was appointed the editor of the new code.

In 1960, Lubetzky's *Code of Cataloging Rules, Author and Title Entry: An Unfinished Draft*[4] appeared. It begins with the statement of the objectives, followed by specific rules developed on the basis of these objectives. Although not completed, the draft code gives indication of what can be accomplished by basing specific rules on basic principles. One major departure from previous codes is the determination of entry based on the conditions of authorship rather than on types of work.

Lubetzky's work was both exciting and frightening to those involved in cataloging. It presaged a new era for cataloging, yet many were worried about the cost such drastic changes would incur. The latter concern was to become a major force in the ensuing code revision work.

[3]Seymour Lubetzky. *Cataloging Rules and Principles.* Washington, D.C.: Library of Congress, 1953.

[4]Seymour Lubetzky. *Code of Cataloging Rules, Author and Title Entry: An Unfinished Draft.* Chicago: American Library Association, 1960.

In 1961, one of the most important events in the evolution of cataloging codes took place. An International Conference on Cataloguing Principles was held in Paris, October 9-18, 1961, with delegations from fifty-three countries and twelve international organizations. The discussion of principles of cataloging was based on a draft statement of principles circulated before the meeting.

As a result of the conference, a statement of principles which has become known as the "Paris Statement" or the "Paris Principles" was issued. It drew heavily upon Lubetzky's draft code of 1960. The scope is limited to the choice of entry and the forms of headings only. It opens with a statement of the functions of the catalog, which represents a restatement of Lubetzky's and Cutter's objectives. The principles that follow rest logically on these objectives and are stated in specific terms in considerable detail.

The Paris Statement represented a great step forward toward international agreement. One frequently cited feature of this document is its endorsement of corporate entry and natural, rather than grammatical, arrangement of title, which removes the major differences between the Anglo-American and the Germanic traditions of cataloging (see discussion on page 14).

Lubetzky resigned as editor of the new code in 1962 and was succeeded by C. Sumner Spalding. Code revision proceeded on the basis of the work already done under Lubetzky and the Paris Principles. Cooperation between the American and British Library associations was also initiated.

Time and again, the concern for the cost of change caused compromises. The most notorious example was the retention of the practice (appearing as rules 98 and 99) of entering certain corporate bodies under the names of places—a drastic departure from the Paris Principles of entering corporate bodies directly under their names. On this point and certain other points the American and the British committees could not reach complete agreement. This disagreement entailed the publication of two separate texts of the Anglo-American Cataloging Rules (AACR), the North American text and the British text, a fact since lamented by many.

It was decided that the new code should include rules for both entry and description.

Since the Paris Principles deal with the problems of entry and headings only and there were no international guidelines for the development of the rules for description, LC 1949 was used as the basis for Chapters 6 and 7 for description of monographs and serials, as well as for the rules for cataloging nonbook material.

The new code (AACR) appeared in 1967 and was received with mixed feelings. The logical arrangement and its emphasis on the conditions of authorship rather than on types of work were considered to be a great improvement over the previous codes. Some critics lamented the compromises made because of practical considerations.

Implementation of the new rules was quite a different matter from theoretical considerations. The major problem was how to reconcile the conflicts between existing entries in the catalog and new entries prepared according to the new rules without incurring prohibitive costs. It would be extremely expensive to revise existing headings in the catalog in accordance with the new code. The Library of Congress adopted the policy of superimposition. Although the rules for entry and description were to be followed in cataloging all works new to its collection, the rules for headings for persons and corporate bodies were to be applied only to headings being established for the first time. Headings previously established according to former codes continued to be used in cataloging new works. Libraries around the country, on the whole, adopted a similar policy.

In the next two or three years, the application of the new code proved that some of the rules were ambiguous and a few others not satisfactory. A supplement of additions and changes was issued in 1970 and appeared in later printings of the code. Changes occurring after 1970 were announced in *Cataloging Service.*[5]

From the beginning, complete adherence to AACR, even with all its compromises, proved to be hard and slow. Because of practical difficulties, the Library of Congress had to hold back in certain areas, particularly in implementing the rule for successive entry for serial publications which have undergone a change of title or a change of corporate body which is used as the main entry. Complete adoption of this rule came in 1971. Also, the notorious rules 98 and 99 for entering certain corporate bodies under names of places were, respectively, revised and deleted from AACR in 1974.

Since the appearance of the Paris Principles, many other cataloging codes have been revised or developed according to their provisions, notably the German code (Regeln für die alphabetische Katalogisierung (RAK)), the Swedish code, and the Danish code. The RAK represents a major revolution in cataloging in that, for the first time, the concept of corporate authorship was introduced and the mechanical, rather than grammatical, title was accepted.

INTERNATIONAL STANDARD BIBLIOGRAPHIC DESCRIPTION

International Federation of Library Associations. *ISBD (M): International Standard Bibliographic Description for Monographic*

---

[5] A serial publication issued by the Library of Congress. The title was changed to *Cataloging Service Bulletin* in 1978.

Publications. 1st standard ed. London: IFLA Committee on Cataloguing, 1974.

International Federation of Library Associations. *ISBD (S): International Standard Bibliographic Description for Serials.* Recommended by the Joint Working Group on the International Standard Bibliographic Description for Serials set up by the IFLA Committee on Cataloguing and the IFLA Committee on Serial Publications. London: IFLA Committee on Cataloguing, 1974.

The next step toward greater international agreement after the Paris Conference was taken at the International Meeting of Cataloguing Experts held in Copenhagen in 1969. At this meeting, an International Working Party was established with the purpose of developing a standard order and content for the description of monographic material. A document entitled *International Standard Bibliographic Description (for Single Volume and Multi-Volume Monographic Publications)* (ISBD) was issued in 1971. In the following years, this format was accepted and adopted by many national bibliographies. Again, in the course of its applications, many ambiguities and a lack of details in some areas were brought out. These were discussed at the International Federation of Library Associations (IFLA) conference held in Grenoble in 1973. After this conference, two documents were published: *ISBD(M)* and *ISBD (S).*

The objectives of the new format are threefold:

> first, that records produced in one country or by the users of one language can be easily understood in other countries and by the users of other languages; second, that the records produced in each country can be integrated into files or lists of various kinds containing also records from other countries; and third, that records in written or printed form can be converted into machine-readable form with the minimum of editing.[6]

To fulfill these requirements, the order of bibliographic elements to be presented on a record was standardized and a special punctuation pattern distinguishing these elements was prescribed.

ANGLO-AMERICAN CATALOGING RULES: CHAPTERS 6, 12, and 14, REVISED

Anglo-American Cataloging Rules: North American Text.
Chapter 6: Separately Published Monographs. Chicago: American Library Association, 1974.

---

[6]International Federation of Library Associations. *ISBD(M).* 1st standard ed. London: IFLA Committee on Cataloguing, 1974. P. vii.

Anglo-American Cataloging Rules: North American Text.
Chapter 12 Revised: Audiovisual Media and Special Instructional
Materials. Chicago: American Library Association, 1975.

Anglo-American Cataloging Rules: North American Text.
Chapter 14 Revised: Sound Recordings. Chicago: American Library
Association, 1976.

In order to adopt the ISBD in this country, its provisions must be incorporated into the cataloging rules. After the publication of the 1971 edition of ISBD(M), the Library of Congress, upon the request of the American Library Association, undertook the preparation of a revised version of Chapter 6 of AACR. The revision, completed in the summer of 1974, following the publication of the first standard edition of ISBD(M), was published as a separate pamphlet by the American Library Association. The Library of Congress began implementation in September 1974, followed by the libraries around the country. The prescribed punctuation gave the cataloging entry a completely new look. The revised format represented yet another giant step toward international standardization.

The revised Chapter 6 was followed by *Chapter 12 Revised* (1975) for audiovisual media and special instructional materials and *Chapter 14 Revised* (1976) for sound recordings.

AACR 2 (1978)

Anglo-American Cataloguing Rules. 2d ed. Chicago: American
Library Association, 1978.

By 1973, it was considered that the appropriate time had come for an overhaul of the Anglo-American cataloging code. Certain significant developments since the publication of AACR in 1967 pointed to the desirability of a revision.[7] First, rapid progress toward the formulation of international standards for the description of monographs, serials, and other media indicated the need to redraft the AACR provisions for bibliographic description so that the code would facilitate the effort to promote the international exchange of bibliographic data. Second, the rules for nonbook materials in AACR had been considered inadequate from the beginning, a situation which resulted in the proliferation of various cataloging codes for nonbook materials. Only a complete revision of AACR rules for nonprint media could provide the standardization needed in this area. Third, the points of divergence between the separate North American and British texts

---

[7]"AACR 2: Background and Summary." *Library of Congress Information Bulletin,* **37**:640, October 20, 1978.

of AACR had been gradually reconciled, leading to the prospect of a unified code. Furthermore, there had been numerous piecemeal revisions and changes in AACR since 1967, which rendered the code rather inconvenient to use. Finally, the announced intention of the Library of Congress to abandon the policy of superimposition and to close its card catalogs contributed to the momentum toward the decision to produce the second edition.

Universal Bibliographic Control

One major consideration in the revision of AACR was the ideal of universal bibliographic control (UBC). This ideal, which was the theme of the thirty-ninth International Federation of Library Associations (IFLA) meeting in 1973, was adopted as a goal for the ultimate international cooperation. The basic idea is to have each document cataloged only once, as near to the source of publication as possible, and to make basic bibliographic data on all publications issued in all countries universally and promptly available, in a form which is internationally acceptable.[8] In 1974, IFLA established an International Office for UBC with Dorothy Anderson as director.

The fact that such a dream was even conceivable was due to the recent encouraging developments towards international cooperation and standardization in the field of cataloging. The Paris Conference and the International Meeting of Cataloguing Experts in Copenhagen were two milestones on the road toward achieving the goal of UBC. The standards and agreements produced by these conferences played an important role in the revision of the *Anglo-American Cataloguing Rules.*

Work began in 1974 toward the preparation of the second edition of AACR. A Joint Steering Committee for Revision of AACR was formed with representatives from the United States, Britain, and Canada. The objectives of the revision were defined on the outset: to reconcile in a single text the North American and the British texts including official changes since 1967 and to consider for inclusion amendments and changes and work currently in process, with attention paid to international interests. Work on the revision began in early 1975. Paul W. Winkler was appointed editor, with Michael Gorman from Britain serving as associate editor. The five authors were designated: the American Library Association, the British Library, the Canadian Committee on Cataloguing, the (British) Library Association, and the Library of Congress.

In the revision, the Joint Steering Committee decided to conform

---

[8]Dorothy Anderson. *Universal Bibliographic Control: A Long Term Policy—A Plan for Action.* Munich: Verlag Dokumentation, Pullach, 1974. P. 11.

to international agreements and standards, particularly the Paris Principles and the ISBD.

In early 1977, a draft code was completed and a Draft Review Program was begun. In the United States, the library-related organizations and the ALA units concerned were contacted. In Canada and the United Kingdom, an effort was also made to obtain additional reactions to the draft.

The Draft Review Program resulted in a compilation of over 1,000 pages of comments. These were considered and, wherever appropriate, incorporated into the final draft. The code was published in 1978.

The Anglo-American Cataloguing Rules (2d ed.) is divided into two parts: (1) description, and (2) headings, uniform titles, and references. Part One is based on the *International Standard Bibliographic Description* (ISBD) for general materials and those for special types of material. Part Two is based on the Paris Principles.

Options

AACR 2 contains a number of options, indicated by "Optional addition," "Alternative rule," or "Optionally . . . " These allow individual libraries or cataloging agencies to make decisions based on individual considerations in cases where more than one provision are equally valid. The Library of Congress has examined these options and published its decisions. Libraries using LC cataloging data will most likely conform to Library of Congress practice. A list of the AACR 2 "Options to Be Followed by the Library of Congress" is included in Appendix A of this book.

CHAPTER 3

Description

Part 1 of *Anglo-American Cataloguing Rules* contains rules on the description of library materials. The description presents bibliographic and physical characteristics of the material being described. In most cases, the description needs a heading or uniform title added to it before it is used as a catalog entry.

INTERNATIONAL STANDARD BIBLIOGRAPHIC DESCRIPTION (ISBD)

The International Standard Bibliographic Description for Monographic Publications, ISBD(M), developed by the International Federation of Library Associations (IFLA) and published in 1974, served as the basis for rules of description of monographic materials in AACR 2. In 1975, the General International Standard Bibliographical Description, ISBD(G), was developed by agreement between JSCAACR[1] representatives, members of the IFLA Committee on Cataloguing, and chairmen of IFLA's specialized ISBD working groups (see Table 3-1). The ISBD(G) serves as a single framework for the description of all types of publications in all types of media, thereby ensuring a uniform approach in bibliographic description.

The ISBD(G) was incorporated into AACR 2 as the general framework for bibliographic description (Chapter 1 of AACR 2). It contains rules applicable to all types of materials. Chapters 2–13 provide rules for the description of specific types of materials. Each of the chapters in Part 1 may be used alone or in combination with one or more of the other chapters. For example, rule 1.4F in Chapter 1 deals with date of publication, distribution, etc., and all subsequent chapters refer the reader to this rule for instruction in describing this element. When specific types of material require unique treatment of a particular element, the appropriate chapter for the specific type of material must be consulted for more substantial direction because the general chapter provides only brief guidance. The rules in these chapters have been numbered with a mnemonic device to facilitate use. For example, rule 1.5 deals with physical description area, and so

---

[1]Joint Steering Committee for the Revision of AACR.

TABLE 3-1   The ISBD(G)

Area	Prescribed Preceding (or Enclosing) Punctuation for Elements		Element
Note: Each area, other than the first, is preceded by a point, space, dash, space (. —).			
1. Title and statement of responsibility area		1.1	Title proper
	[]	1.2	General material designation
	=	1.3	Parallel title
	:	1.4	Other title information
		1.5	Statements of responsibility
	/		First statement
	;		Subsequent statement
2. Edition area		2.1	Edition statement
	=	2.2	Parallel edition statement
		2.3	Statements of responsibility relating to the edition
	/		First Statement
	;		Subsequent statement
	,	2.4	Additional edition statement
		2.5	Statements of responsibility following an additional edition statement
	/		First statement
	;		Subsequent statement
3. Material (or type of publication) specific details area			
4. Publication, distribution, etc., area		4.1	Place of publication, distribution, etc.
			First place
	;		Subsequent place
	:	4.2	Name of publisher, distributor, etc.

(Continued)

TABLE 3-1 (Continued)

Area	Prescribed Preceding (or Enclosing) Punctuation for Elements		Element
	[]	4.3	Statement of function of publisher, distributor, etc.
4. Publication, distribution, etc., area	,	4.4	Date of publication, distribution, etc.
	(	4.5	Place of manufacture
	:	4.6	Name of manufacturer
	,)	4.7	Date of manufacture
5. Physical description area		5.1	Specific material designation and extent of item
	:	5.2	Other physical details
	;	5.3	Dimensions of item
	+	5.4	Accompanying material statement
6. Series area		6.1	Title proper of series
	=	6.2	Parallel title of series
Note: A series statement is enclosed by parentheses. When there are two or more series statements, each is enclosed by parentheses.	:	6.3	Other title information of series
		6.4	Statements of responsibility relating to the series
	/		First statement
	;		Subsequent statement
	,	6.5	International Standard Serial Number of series
	;	6.6	Numbering within series
	.	6.7	Enumeration and/or title of subseries
	=	6.8	Parallel title of subseries
	:	6.9	Other title information of subseries
		6.10	Statements of responsibility relating to the subseries
	/		First statement
	;		Subsequent statement

(Continued)

TABLE 3-1 (Continued)

Area	Prescribed Preceding (or Enclosing) Punctuation for Elements	Element
6. Series area		6.11 International Standard Serial Number of sub-series
	;	6.12 Numbering within subseries
7. Note area		
8. Standard number (or alternative) and terms of availability area		8.1 Standard number (or alternative)
	=	8.2 Key title
	:	8.3 Terms of availability and/or price
	( )	8.4 Qualification (in varying positions)

SOURCE: International Federation of Library Associations. Working Group on the General International Bibliographic Description. *ISBD(G): General International Standard Bibliographic Description: Annotated Text.* London: IFLA International Office for UBC, 1977.

do rules 2.5 (for books), 3.5 (for cartographic materials), 4.5 (for manuscripts), and so on.

As stated in the introduction to AACR 2, in choosing the appropriate chapter or chapters to be used in cataloging a particular document, the cataloger should start with the physical form of the item being cataloged, not the original or any previous form in which the work has been published. For example, a monographic publication in microform should be described according to the rules in Chapter 11 (for microforms), augmented by those in Chapter 2 (for books, etc.), and Chapter 1 (general rules) when required.

SOURCES OF INFORMATION

AACR 2 specifies sources of information to be used in describing a publication; in the case of a printed monograph, for example, such sources include the title page, the verso of the title page, etc. Of these, the source of bibliographic data to be given first preference as the source from which a bibliographic description is prepared is called the *chief source of information.* The rules identify a chief source of information for each type of material.

TABLE 3-2   Chief Sources of Information

Type of Material	Source
Books, pamphlets, and printed sheets	Title page
Cartographic materials	a. Cartographic item itself
	b. Container or case, the cradle and stand of a globe, etc.
Manuscripts	Title page
	Colophon
Music	Title page
Sound recordings	
Disc	Label
Tape (open reel-to-reel)	Reel and label
Tape cassette	Cassette and label
Tape cartridge	Cartridge and label
Roll	Label
Sound recording on film	Container and label
Motion pictures and videorecordings	Film itself and its container (if integral part of item)
Graphic materials	Item itself including any labels and the container
Machine-readable data files	Internal user label
Three-dimensional artefacts and realia	Object itself with any accompanying textual material and container
Microforms	Title frame
Serials (printed)	Title page

Table 3-2 lists chief sources of information for different types of materials.

In each chapter of AACR 2, prescribed sources of information for individual bibliographic areas are enumerated. Information taken from sources other than the prescribed ones is enclosed in brackets.

Examples of chief sources of information with corresponding bibliographic descriptions are shown in Figures 3-1 to 3-16.

RELIGION IN EDUCATION

AN ANNOTATED BIBLIOGRAPHY

COMPILED BY
JOSEPH POLITELLA

Kent State University

Kent, Ohio

Religion in Education

Copyright 1956, American Association of Colleges for Teacher Education

First Edition

Library of Congress Catalog Card Number: 56-11992

AMERICAN ASSOCIATION OF COLLEGES FOR
TEACHER EDUCATION
11 ELM ST.
ONEONTA, NEW YORK

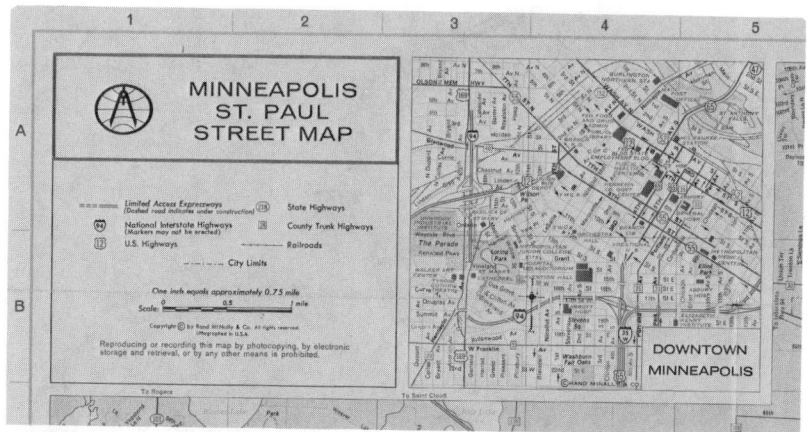

FIGURE 3-2 Part of a map.

> Minneapolis-St. Paul street map [map]. — Scale
> [1:47,520]. — [Chicago?] : Rand McNally, [197-]
> 1 map : col. ; 91X 65 cm.
> Insets: Downtown Minneapolis ; Downtown St. Paul ;
> Minneapolis-St. Paul and vicinity.

FIGURE 3-1 *Opposite page:* Title page and verso of a book.

> Politella, Joseph, 1910–
> Religion in education [text] : an annotated bibliography /
> compiled by Joseph Politella. — 1st ed. — Oneonta, N. Y.
> (11 Elm St., Oneonta, N. Y.) : American Association of Colleges
> for Teacher Education, c1956.
> x, 90 p. ; 23 cm.
> Includes indexes.
> I. Title.

(a)

FIGURE 3-3 *Above:* (a) Labels on sound disc; *opposite page:* (b) front and back cover of slipcase.

Eliot, T.S. (Thomas Stearns), 1888–1965.
The waste land/and other poems [sound recording] / read by
T.S. Eliot. — New York : Caedmon, c1971.
1 sound disc (48 min.) : $33^1/_3$ rpm, microgroove, mono. ; 12 in.
Contents: The waste land (complete) (26 min.)— The hollow men
(4 min.)—Journey of the Magi from the Ariel poems (2 min.)—
La figlia che piange (1 min.) —Landscapes: New Hampshire, Virginia,
Usk, Rannoch by Glencoe, Cape Ann (4 min.) —Morning at the
window (1 min.) —Difficulties of a statesman from Coriolan (3 min.)
—Sweeney among the nightingales (2 min.) —Whispers of immor-
tality (2 min.) —Macavity: the mystery cat (3 min.)
I. Title.

/FOR STEREO OR MONAURAL PHONOGRAPHS/

The Waste Land /and Other Poems
read by T. S. ELIOT

CAEDMON
TC 1326

SIDE 1	TIMING
The Waste Land (complete)	25:35

SIDE 2	
1. The Hollow Men	4:20
2. Journey of the Magi from the *Ariel Poems*	2:27
3. La Figlia che Piange	1:22

	TIMING
4. Landscapes: New Hampshire, Virginia, Usk, Rannoch by Glencoe, Cape Ann	3:50
5. Morning at the Window	:37
6. Difficulties of a Statesman from *Coriolan*	3:20
7. Sweeney Among the Nightingales	1:54
8. Whispers of Immortality	1:43
9. Macavity: the Mystery Cat	3:25

HE MUST CREATE, Wordsworth said, speaking of the authentic poet, the taste by which he is to be enjoyed. And Keats, addressing himself to the problem of influence, to the poet's struggle to free himself from the past, reached a corollary conclusion: that which is creative must create itself. And such was the effort, the *agon*, as he would have called it, of the first half of T. S. Eliot's career, which includes all the poems on this record, among them some of the finest as well as the most famous which he wrote. The second half of Eliot's career was another kind of struggle, the struggle in which the poet is always engaged to *hold off* the culture which would assimilate him, which would deprive him of precisely that singular voice which it is his obligation and hope—and which it has been his reward—to raise.

Eliot, then, in his long, reticent and glorious career, articulates two of the three phases in the life of a poet's work, which it is the work of his life to achieve: the phase of scandal and the phase of scripture (in the first phase, whatever he says is likely to be discounted because he has said it, and in the second or scriptural phase, whatever he says is likely to be accredited because he has said it). The third phase in the life of a poet's work generally begins only after his death and after a certain nimbus—sulfurous or celestial—has ceased to aureole his figure among us. It is the phase in which, at last, we may read what a poet says without the extensions of scandal or scripture; in which his poems are merely poems, language identical to itself as we have already and always known it, but restored to us on the other side of death.

My own generation, which after World War II began reading Eliot's poems with the querulous reverence of baby pelicans seeking nourishment from a rather single-breasted mother, had never known much about the thirty years during which Eliot was derided, parioded and—worst of all—packaged as everything wrong with "modern poetry" (the public at large welcomes what it regards as pedantry in order that it may reject it). Indeed by the time I was puzzling through that chaste, yellow-jacketed copy of the *Collected Poems* which contains all the work on this record, reading *The Waste Land*, (symbolically enough) on the now-discontinued day-train taking me to college from Shaker Heights to Morningside Heights, Eliot was no longer a joke, a target, or even a scarecrow. He was— and alas was to become for me— a *subject*. How eagerly we passed around the one copy of poor Miss Weston's *From Ritual to Romance* we could swipe from the Columbia Library (this was before the days of paperbacks, whose initial mission, it now appears, was to provide precisely the reading-list necessary for an understanding, or at least a check-out, of all Eliot's references). How industriously we looked up all those hard words, found translations of all those foreign languages,

filled in our margins with the provenance of all those "unacknowledged" quotations! We were scholiasts, and would have been as shocked as any medieval monk glossing his Aquinas (if anyone had suggested (no one did) that the poems were written by a man who needed to write them for himself, speaking out of a solitude, into a solitude.

It was during this period of scholasticism focused upon his earlier work, upon the poems collected from 1909 to 1935, that Eliot was writing his *Quartets* and his plays; and I think it was because he knew, with that horrified humility of his, that such an industry was world-wide, because he was conscious of the fact that he had become a schoolmaster to the modern mind, that he produced the characteristic voice of his later—and greatest—poems, the "key signature" masterfully orchestrated in so many forms over so many years: the note of reserve, of disillusion, of diffidence, of disabused lucidity which demands of us a particularly chastened attention. "Our lives," as he said in those years, "are mostly a constant evasion of ourselves, and an evasion of the visible and sensible world." In the *Quartets* and in the plays there is an ultimate modesty or reticence in the voice which is the unmistakable appanage of wisdom. For Eliot, the surrender of personality was always an important means of achieving and retaining identity.

And in the poems on this record, though they belong to the "scandalous" phase of Eliot's work, what I have called the *chastening* of our attention is already a primary poetic act. For chastity means more than abstinence or asexuality. It is a positive not a negative thing, and when I refer to a chastity of attention, or a chastity of language, as I do with regard to *The Waste Land* or *The Hollow Men*, I intend a recognition of power, not a withdrawal from power. And by that recognition, Eliot became, as he became an older man, a newer writer.

Here, in many of these poems, we have the work of a young man who made one of the two great choices a poet can make: to live on nothing, or to live on a great deal. To live surrounded by the nightmare cloud of our history, or to live, however bleakly, where the air is clear. For American poetry today, it would seem that the first choice is the one we would make. I believe it is really the easier choice—at least Eliot has shown us that it is the less courageous choice if one has not already chosen to live on a great deal. To learn, as I think Eliot learned, all there is to be known about what we have been, what our history, our dreams, our myths, our psychic structures are like, what they do when they confront each other in the one mind, the one body—when it is the poet's mind, the poet's body, that is living on a great deal. Then—and only then—is it possible to make the choice of living on nothing. In his ultimate poetry Eliot made that choice as well, the choice of humility, of ascesis. But here we have him at his richest, his gayest even (in the one Macavity poem), and content—no, not content, but *consenting* to live with—and on—a great deal.

It is worth emphasizing, too, that we may have him, for the first time, without the fuss and foolishness of my own generation's scholia, just as my own generation had cover an enormous fact which has been, for years, obscured: that a man wrote these poems, not an ecumenical committee, and that we may read them, hear them and respond to them as we would to other poems written and read to us by their poet.

This record, then, is a welcome to the third phase of Eliot's career, and it is an incomparable advantage for those interested in poetry to listen to it, on the rim of what Henry James called our "incomparable modernity." We have been educated by T. S. Eliot long enough. It is time we read him and listened to him.

RICHARD HOWARD

Richard Howard, poet, author and translator, recently completed a study of the art of poetry in the United States since 1950 entitled ALONE WITH AMERICA. He has written three volumes of poetry. QUANTITIES, THE DAMAGES and UNTITLED SUBJECTS, which won the Pulitzer Prize for Poetry in 1970.

T. S. Eliot's readings of Whispers of Immortality: the Mystery Cat courtesy of Radio Station WFMT, Chicago.

On the cover and liner: Photograph of T. S. Eliot by Angus McBean design/Brooks-EL Copyright © 1971 Caedmon Records, Inc. Library of Congress Number 75-751386
WARNING: It is expressly forbidden to copy or reproduce this recording or any portion thereof in any manner or form whether for profit, non-profit, institutional, or educational use. Permission for broadcast, telecast or public performance use must be obtained in advance in writing. Caedmon Records, Inc. 505 Eighth Avenue, New York, N. Y. 10018
Made and printed in U.S.A.

Caedmon TC 1326   The Waste Land / and Other Poems read by T. S. Eliot

Caedmon TC 1326   The Waste Land / and Other Poems read by T. S. Eliot

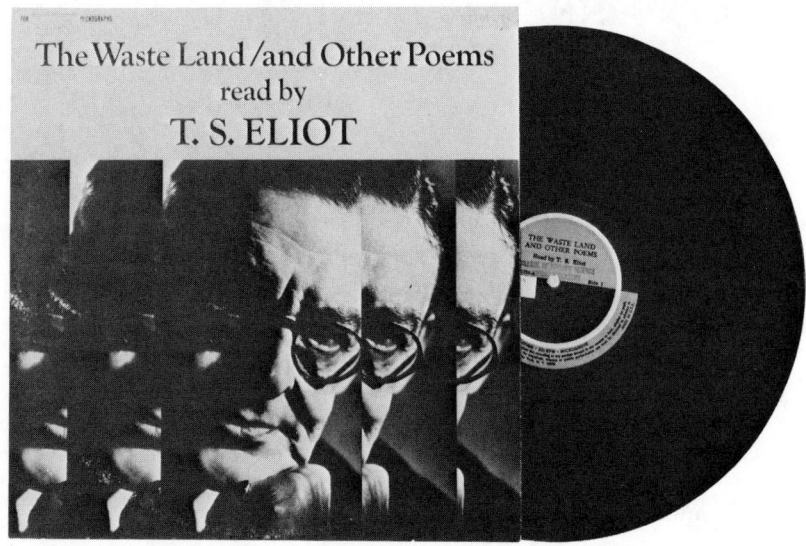

(b)

"THERE'S SOMETHING ABOUT A STORY"

was made possible by

an LSCA grant from

THE STATE LIBRARY OF OHIO
(a)

> ## "THERE'S SOMETHING ABOUT A STORY"
> *Produced and distributed for* The Dayton and Montgomery County Public Library by
> ### CONNECTICUT FILMS, INC.
> Westport, Connecticut
>
> PRINT NO. **262**   TV RIGHTS RESERVED
> ACC. 1363

(b)

FIGURE 3-4   (a) Title frame of a motion picture; (b) label on container.

> There's something about a story [motion picture]. — Westport, Conn. : Produced and distributed by Connecticut Films, [197–?] 1 film reel (27 min.) : sd., col. ; 16 mm.
>
> Produced for the Dayton and Montgomery County Public Library. Made possible by an LSCA grant from the State Library of Ohio. Summary: Uses the comments of storytellers and sequences from storytelling situations to show the value of storytelling with children six through twelve years of age. Discusses where to find stories and how to prepare and present them.
>
> I. Dayton and Montgomery County Public Library.

FIGURE 3-5 Title frames of a filmstrip.

School library quarters planned to meet the needs of an expanding educational program [filmstrip] / produced by Virginia McJenkin ; photographed by Kathleen Moon. — Chicago : American Library Association, c1952.
1 filmstrip (98 fr.) : col. ; 35 mm.

Prepared at the request of the Joint N.E.A.-A.L.A. Committee.
Summary: Shows pictures of large and small school libraries which were planned to meet the needs of expanding educational programs. Demonstrates that careful planning can lead to efficient, adequate, and attractive library quarters in spite of financial limitations.

I. McJenkin, Virginia. II. Moon, Kathleen. III. Joint N.E.A.-A.L.A. Committee.

USING THE CARD CATALOG

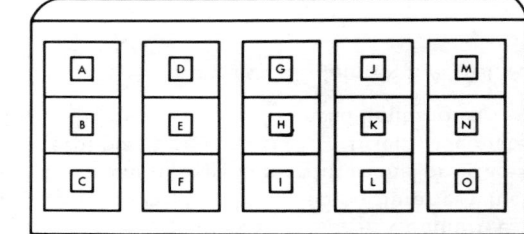

USING

THE

CARD

CATALOG

HAMMOND
INCORPORATED
MAPLEWOOD, NEW JERSEY 07040

1 – Introduction

FIGURE 3-6 *Left*, cover of a teacher's manual; *right*, cover transparency.

Using the card catalog [transparency]. — Maplewood, N.J. :
Hammond, c1969.
16 transparencies : col. ; 24 × 20 cm. + 1 teacher's manual.

(a)

FIGURE 3-7   *Above:* (a) Label on sound cassette; *page 38:* (b) title frames of filmstrip.

New chances [filmstrip] : a report / prepared for the United States Office of Education by the Leadership in Library Education Institute, Florida State University. — Washington (1201 16th St., N.W., Washington, D.C., 20036) : Association for Educational Communications & Technology, c1975.
1 filmstrip (80 fr.) : col. ; 35 mm. + 1 sound cassette (10 min. : 1⅞ ips, mono.)

Sound accompaniment compatible for manual and automatic operation.
Credits: Producer, Howard Hitchens; writer and photographer, Kenn Goldblatt; sound, Neal Hall.
Summary: Discusses the changes that educational media programs are currently undergoing and emphasizes the importance of state departments of education providing aid for local education agencies in this time of transition.

I. United States. Office of Education. II. Leadership in Library Education Institute.

(*Continued on page 38*)

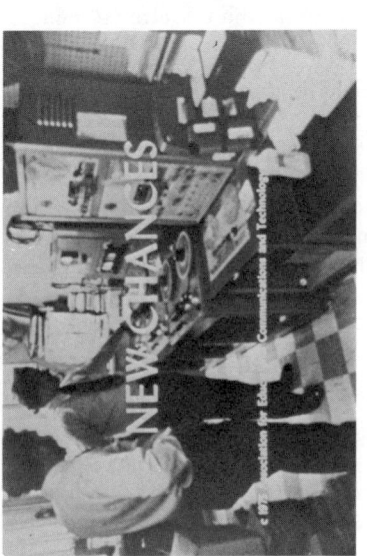

(b)

FIGURE 3-7 *Continued.*

START

Microfilmed by
Department of Photoduplication
The University of Chicago Library
Swift Hall
Chicago 37, Illinois

FURTHER REPRODUCTION OF, OR QUOTATION FROM, THIS MATERIAL MAY NOT BE MADE WITHOUT PERMISSION FROM THE AUTHOR AND DEPARTMENT GRANTING THE DEGREE.

Thesis No. T22110

THE UNIVERSITY OF CHICAGO

J. C. M. HANSON AND HIS CONTRIBUTION
TO TWENTIETH-CENTURY CATALOGING

A DISSERTATION SUBMITTED TO
THE FACULTY OF THE GRADUATE LIBRARY SCHOOL
IN CANDIDACY FOR THE DEGREE OF

DOCTOR OF PHILOSOPHY

BY

EDITH SCOTT

CHICAGO, ILLINOIS
SEPTEMBER, 1970

FIGURE 3-8   Title frames of a microfilm.

Scott, Edith, 1918–
    J.C.M. Hanson and his contribution to twentieth-century cataloging [microform] / by Edith Scott. — Chicago : Department of Photoduplication, University of Chicago Library, 1970.
    1 microfilm reel : negative ; 35 mm.

    Thesis (Ph.D.) — University of Chicago, 1970.
    At head of title: The University of Chicago.
    Bibliography: p. 669–695.

    I. Title.

FIGURE 3-9   Title page and verso of a book.

Bailey, Frederick Randolph, 1871–1923.
Bailey's Text-book of histology [text]. — 13th ed. / revised by
Philip E. Smith and Wilfred M. Copenhaver, with the assistance of
Dorothy D. Johnson. — Baltimore : Williams & Wilkins, 1953.
xviii, 775 p. : ill. (some col.) ; 24 cm.

Includes index.

I. Smith, Philip E. (Philip Edward), 1884–   II. Copenhaver,
Wilfred M. (Wilfred Monroe), 1898–   III. Johnson, Dorothy D.
(Dorothy Dole) IV. Title. V. Title: Text-book of histology.

40

Theories for Teaching

Lindley J. Stiles, editor

by

JOE PARK, SONJA STONE, AND WILLIAM BARRON
B. CLAUDE MATHIS AND WILLIAM MCGAGHIE
HUGH G. PETRIE
PAUL BOHANNAN, WILLIAM POWERS,
AND MARK SCHOEPFLE
DAVID C. EPPERSON
DOLORES E. CROSS AND EMILYE FIELDS
GUSTAVE J. RATH AND TOM MCAULIFFE

A Publication of the Center for the Teaching Professions, Northwestern University, in cooperation with the W. K. Kellogg Foundation

DODD, MEAD & COMPANY *New York* *1974*

(a)

COPYRIGHT © 1974 BY DODD, MEAD & COMPANY, INC.
ALL RIGHTS RESERVED
NO PART OF THIS BOOK MAY BE REPRODUCED IN ANY FORM WITHOUT PERMISSION IN WRITING FROM THE PUBLISHER
ISBN: 0396-06905-3
LIBRARY OF CONGRESS CATALOG CARD NUMBER: 73-15030
PRINTED IN THE UNITED STATES OF AMERICA
DESIGNED BY JEFFREY M. BARRIE

(b)

FIGURE 3-10 (a) Title pages (two facing pages) of a book. (b) Verso.

Theories for teaching [text] : a publication of the Center for the Teaching Professions, Northwestern University, in cooperation with the W.K. Kellogg Foundation / by Joe Park . . . [et al.]. ; Lindley J. Stiles, editor. — New York : Dodd, Mead, 1974.
x, 177 p. : ill. ; 21 cm.

Includes bibliographical references.
ISBN 0-396-06905-3

I. Park, Joe. II. Stiles, Lindley J., ed. III. Center for the Teaching Professions. IV. W.K. Kellogg Foundation.

SCIENCE IN THE COLLEGE CURRICULUM

*A Report of a Conference
Sponsored by Oakland University
and Supported by a Grant from the
National Science Foundation,
May 24-26, 1962*

ROBERT HOOPES

ROCHESTER, MICHIGAN
1963
(a)

Copyright © 1963, Oakland University

Rochester, Michigan
(b)

FIGURE 3-11   (a) Title page of a book. (b) Verso.

> Conference on Education in Science for the Undergraduate Non-
> science Concentrator (1962 : Oakland University)
> Science in the college curriculum [text] : a report of a conference
> sponsored by Oakland University and supported by a grant from the
> National Science Foundation, May 24–26, 1962 / [edited by] Robert
> Hoopes. — Rochester, Mich. : [s.n.], 1963.
>   x, 211 p. ; 22 cm.
>
>   I. Hoopes, Robert, 1920–   ed.   II. Oakland University.   III.
> Title.
>
>   [Name of conference appears in the preface]

THE
CAMBRIDGE HISTORY
OF POLAND

FROM AUGUSTUS II TO PILSUDSKI
(1697–1935)

EDITED BY
W. F. REDDAWAY
J. H. PENSON
O. HALECKI
R. DYBOSKI

CAMBRIDGE
AT THE UNIVERSITY PRESS
1951

PUBLISHED BY
THE SYNDICS OF THE CAMBRIDGE UNIVERSITY PRESS
London Office: Bentley House, N.W.1
American Branch: New York
Agents for Canada, India, and Pakistan: Macmillan

First Edition 1941
Reprinted 1951

Printed in Great Britain at the University Press, Cambridge
(Brooke Crutchley, University Printer)

FIGURE 3-12   Title page and verso of a book.

The Cambridge history of Poland from Augustus II to Pilsudski
(1697–1935) [text] / edited by W.F. Reddaway . . . [et al.]. — 1st ed.
— Cambridge, [Cambridgeshire] : University Press, 1941.
xvi, 630 p. : maps ; 24 cm.

Includes index.
Library's copy lacks maps facing pages 176 and 460.

I. Reddaway, W. F. (William Fiddian), 1872–1949, ed.

LUDWIG WITTGENSTEIN

PHILOSOPHICAL
GRAMMAR

PART I
The Proposition, and its Sense

PART II
On Logic and Mathematics

Edited by
RUSH RHEES

Translated by
ANTHONY KENNY

UNIVERSITY OF CALIFORNIA PRESS
Berkeley and Los Angeles 1974

FIGURE 3-13   Title page of a book.

Wittgenstein, Ludwig, 1889–1951.
　Philosophical grammar [text] / Ludwig Wittgenstein ; edited by
Rush Rhees ; translated by Anthony Kenny. — Berkeley : University
of California Press, 1974.
　495 p. : ill. ; 23 cm.

　Includes bibliographic references.
　Contents: pt. 1. The proposition, and its sense — pt. 2. On logic
and mathematics.
　ISBN 0-520-02664-0

　I. Rhees, Rush, ed.   II. Title.

DEWEY

Decimal Classification

and

Relative Index

Devised by

MELVIL DEWEY

Edition 19

Edited under the direction of
BENJAMIN A. CUSTER

Volume 1
Introduction
Tables

FOREST PRESS
A Division of
Lake Placid Education Foundation

ALBANY, N.Y. 12206 U.S.A.
1979

FIGURE 3-14   Title page from the first volume of a three-volume work.

Dewey, Melvil, 1851–1931.
   Dewey decimal classification and relative index [text] / devised
by Melvil Dewey. — Ed. 19 / edited under the direction of Benjamin
A. Custer. — Albany, N. Y. : Forest Press, 1979.
   3 v. ; 25 cm.

   First published anonymously in 1876 under title: A classification
and subject index. 2nd ed. published under title: Decimal classifica-
tion and relative index.
   Contents: v. 1. Introduction. Tables — v. 2. Schedules — v. 3.
Relative index.
   ISBN 0-910608-23-7

   I. Custer, Benjamin A. (Benjamin Allen), 1912–   ed.   II.
Title.

UNIVERSITY OF BOMBAY PUBLICATIONS
Economics Series No. 1
GENERAL EDITOR :   C. N. VAKIL

Oxford University Press, Amen House, London E.C.4
EDINBURGH GLASGOW NEW YORK TORONTO MELBOURNE
WELLINGTON BOMBAY CALCUTTA MADRAS CAPE TOWN
Geoffrey Cumberlege, Publisher to the University

IMPERFECT COMPETITION

IN

INTERNATIONAL TRADE

BY

First published 1947

S. B. RANGNEKAR, M. A., Ph. D.
Sometime Lecturer in Economics, University of Bombay

Edited by
J. J. ANJARIA
Reader in Economics, University of Bombay

GEOFFREY CUMBERLEGE
OXFORD UNIVERSITY PRESS

Printed by Neville N. R. Mistry at Vakil & Sons Ltd., Ballard Estate, Bombay,
and published by Geoffrey Cumberlege, Oxford University Press, Bombay.

FIGURE 3-15   Title page and verso of a book.

Rangnekar, S.B.
  Imperfect competition in international trade [text] / by S.B.
Rangnekar ; edited by J.J. Anjaria. — Bombay : Geoffrey Cumber-
lege, Oxford University Press, 1947.
  xvi, 187 p. : ill. ; 23 cm. — (University of Bombay publications.
Economics series ; no. 1)

  Originally presented as the author's thesis (doctoral—Bombay)
  Bibliography: p. [185]–187.
  Includes indexes.

  I. Anjaria, J.J., ed.   II. Title.   III. Series.

ISSN 0024-2527

L ibrary

R esources &

T echnical

S ervices

SUMMER
1979

Vol. 23
No. 3

AMERICAN LIBRARY ASSOCIATION

RESOURCES AND TECHNICAL SERVICES DIVISION

FIGURE 3-16   Cover of a journal.

Library resources & technical services [text] / American Library
Association, Resources and Technical Services Division. — Vol. 1,
no. 1 (winter 1957)–   . — Fulton, Mo. : [s.n.], 1957–
v. ; 24 cm.

Quarterly.
Merger of: Serials slants; and, the Journal of cataloging and
classification.
Imprint varies.
Description based on: Vol. 23, no. 3 (summer 1979).
ISSN 0024-2527 = Library resources & technical services.

I. American Library Association. Resources and Technical
Services Division.

The cataloging records shown in Figures 3-1 to 3-16 are of the second level of description. For illustrations of the first level of description of the same items, see Appendix C. In the examples, the main entry heading (if other than the title) appears at the head of the description and the added entries follow the description and are numbered by Roman numerals. This is the format found most frequently in eye-readable cataloging records.

The examples reflect a number of optional rules. For Library of Congress policy concerning the adoption of options, see Appendix A of this book.

ORGANIZATION OF THE DESCRIPTION

The bibliographic description is divided into the following units, called *areas*, and presented in the order given:

Title and statement of responsibility
Edition
Material (or type of publication) specific details
Publication, distribution, etc.
Physical description
Series
Note(s)
Standard number and terms of availability

Each of these areas is further divided into a number of elements which vary according to the type of publication or medium (see Table 3-1). These areas will be discussed in detail later.

PUNCTUATION

One of the unique features of the ISBD is a set of prescribed punctuation. The prescribed punctuation mark precedes each element in the description and signifies the nature of that element. The prescribed punctuation marks are used as a device of recognition for both machine and human manipulation of bibliographic records.

Specific and detailed rules with regard to prescribed punctuation are given in each chapter in AACR 2. Following is a summary of the use of each mark of prescribed punctuation.

Brackets

See *Parentheses; Square brackets.*

Colon

A colon precedes

1. Each unit of other title information
2. The name of a publisher, distributor, printer, manufacturer, etc.
3. Other physical details (e.g., illustrations)
4. Terms of availability

A colon and a space separate introductory wording from the main content of a note.

Comma

A comma

1. Separates units within a statement, e.g., phrases within a title, names of authors within a statement of responsibility
2. Precedes each subsequent edition statement
3. Precedes the date of publication, distribution, printing, manufacture, etc.
4. Precedes the ISSN of a series or subseries in the series area

Dash

A full stop, space, dash, space (. —) precedes each area in the description, unless the area begins a new paragraph.

Diagonal Slash

A diagonal slash precedes the first statement of responsibility.

Ellipses

See *Mark of omission*.

Equals Sign

An equals sign precedes

1. A parallel title
2. An alternative numbering in the numeric or chronological designation area of a serial publication
3. A key-title in the standard number and terms of availability area

Full Stop

1. A full stop, space, dash, space (. —) precedes each area or repetition of an area. It is omitted if the area begins a new paragraph.
2. A full stop ends the last area in a paragraph.
3. A full stop is used as an abbreviation mark (e.g., 2nd ed.; 24 cm.). When the abbreviation mark occurs at the end of an area, the full stop which is part of the prescribed punctuation is omitted (i.e., 2nd ed. — instead of 2nd ed. . —).
4. A full stop precedes the title of a supplement or section.
5. A full stop precedes the title of a subseries.

Hyphen

A hyphen follows the numeric or alphabetic designation, or both, and the date of the first issue of a serial publication.

Mark of Omission

A mark of omission (. . .) is used

1. To indicate an abridged title proper or other title information
2. To indicate omission from the statement of responsibility
3. To replace the date or numbering that varies from issue to issue in the title proper of a serial publication

Minus Sign

A minus sign is used to indicate the Southern Hemisphere when giving the declination of the center of a celestial chart.

Parentheses

Parentheses are used

1. To enclose the details of printing or manufacture (place : name, date)
2. To enclose the full address of a publisher, distributor, etc. (if given) after the name of the place
3. To enclose physical details of accompanying material
4. To enclose each series statement
5. To enclose a qualification to the standard number or terms of availability

6. To enclose the continuous pagination of a multivolume monograph after the number of volumes
7. To enclose the statement of coordinates and equinox in the mathematical data area for cartographic materials
8. To enclose the number of logical records after the designation for a data file; the number of statements and the name of the programming language after the designation for a program file; the number of logical records or statements in each file after the designation for a multipart file; or the name, number, etc., of the machine after the designation for an object program
9. To enclose the number of frames of a microfiche or a filmstrip and the speed of a film or recording
10. To enclose a date following a designation that is numeric, alphabetic, or both, for a serial publication

Period

See *Full stop*.

Plus Sign

A plus sign

1. Precedes a statement of accompanying material
2. Is used to indicate the Northern Hemisphere when giving the declination of the center of a celestial chart

Question Mark

A question mark is used to indicate a conjectural interpolation.

Semicolon

A semicolon precedes

1. Each subsequent statement of responsibility
2. A second or subsequently named place of publication, distribution, etc.
3. Dimensions (e.g., size) in the physical description area
4. Subsequent statements of responsibility relating to a series or subseries
5. The numbering within a series or subseries
6. The projection statement for cartographic materials
7. A new sequence of numbering, etc., in the numeric, alphabetic, chronological, or other designation area for a serial publication

Slash

See *Diagonal slash.*

Space

A space precedes and follows each mark of prescribed punctuation, except the comma, full stop, hyphen, and opening and closing parentheses and square brackets. The comma, full stop, hyphen, closing parenthesis, and square bracket are not preceded by a space; the hyphen, opening parenthesis, and square bracket are not followed by a space.

Square Brackets

Square brackets are used

1. To enclose information taken from outside the prescribed source or sources
2. To enclose the general material designation
3. To enclose a supplied statement of function of a publisher, distributor, etc.

When adjacent elements within one area are to be enclosed in square brackets, they are enclosed in one set of square brackets unless one of the elements is a general material designation, which is always enclosed in its own set of brackets. When adjacent elements are in different areas, each element is enclosed in a set of square brackets.

LEVELS OF DESCRIPTION

Cutter's Levels

Recognizing the different needs of libraries of different sizes and purposes, Cutter proposed in his *Rules for a Dictionary Catalog*[2] the idea of three different levels of cataloging: short, medium, and full. The first edition of the *Anglo-American Cataloging Rules* (1967), as well as the preceding ALA codes, was designed primarily to respond to the needs of general research libraries, with occasional alternative provisions for other types of libraries. On the whole, the level of bibliographic description (i.e., the number and degree of bibliographic details) was suitable for the catalog of a large general research library, a level not required by many libraries.

[2]Charles Ammi Cutter. *Rules for a Dictionary Catalog.* 4th ed. Washington, D.C.: Government Printing Office, 1904. P. 11.

Levels of AACR 2

In the second edition of the *Anglo-American Cataloguing Rules*, there is a return to Cutter's idea of three levels of bibliographic description.

First level (1.0D1)

This level was designed for minor items and for entries in catalogs with a policy of minimum description. The bibliographic elements to be included are set forth in the following schematic illustration:

> Title proper / first statement of responsibility, if different from main entry heading in form or number or if there is no main entry heading. — Edition statement. — Material (or type of publication) specific details. — First publisher, etc., date of publication, etc. — Extent of item. — Note(s). — Standard number.

Second level (1.0D2)

This level was designed for the standard range of items found in the library and for entries in catalogs with a policy of standard description. The following elements are included:

> Title proper [general material designation] = parallel title : other title information / first statement of responsibility ; each subsequent statement of responsibility. — Edition statement / first statement of responsibility relating to the edition. — Material (or type of publication) specific details. — First place of publication, etc. : first publisher, etc., date of publication, etc. — Extent of item : other physical details ; dimensions. — (Title proper of series / statement of responsibility relating to series, ISSN of series ; numbering within the series. Title of subseries, ISSN of subseries ; numbering within subseries). — Note(s). — Standard number.

Third level (1.0D3)

This level represents full description and is recommended for items which, in the context of the catalog, are considered to be important and rare. All elements set forth in the rules which are applicable to the item being described are included.

It is suggested[3] that a library either choose a level of description for all

---

[3]"AACR 2: Background and Summary." *Library of Congress Information Bulletin*, **47**:643, October 20, 1978.

items cataloged for that library or draw up guidelines for the use of all three levels in the same catalog depending on the type of item being described. Since the level of description is essentially a policy matter, it is recommended that in a machine system, each record carry an indication of the level at which the item has been described.

Examples

The following examples show the first and second levels of description for the same item.

First level

Opportunities for education in urban and regional affairs at Canadian universities and community colleges / Policy Planning Division, Central Mortgage and Housing Corporation. — 4th ed., 1973-74. — Central Mortgage and Housing Corporation [1973?]. — xvii, 465 p. — English and/or French.

Second level

Opportunities for education in urban and regional affairs at Canadian universities and community colleges [text] = Programmes de cours en affaires urbaines et regionales offerts par les universités et collèges communautaires canadiens / Policy Planning Division, Central Mortgage and Housing Corporation. — 4th ed., 1973-74 / edited by Ollie Crain. — Ottawa : Central Mortgage and Housing Corporation [1973?]. — xvii, 465 p. ; 28 cm. — English and/or French.

Exercise A

Supply the missing punctuation marks in the following descriptions:

Teaching the basic medical sciences, human biology   text   report of a Macy conference edited by John Z. Bowers and Elizabeth F. Purcell New York   Josiah Macy, Jr., Foundation   Distributed by Independent Publishers Group 1974   vii, 154 p.   23 cm.

Who could forget?   filmstrip   New York's lower east side revisited   Board of Jewish Education New York   The Board 1977   1 filmstrip   76 fr.   sd.   col.   35 mm.   1 teacher's guide

Techniques of decision making   motion picture
United States Office of Education   Washington
The Office   Distributed by National Audiovisual
Center   1977   1 film reel   28 min.   sd.
col.   16 mm.   1 workbook   You in public
service

AREAS OF DESCRIPTION

AACR 2 provides detailed rules with regard to each area of description. The general rules are presented in Chapter 1 and rules for specific types of materials are given in Chapters 2–12. Numerous examples are included to illustrate the rules. The major elements in bibliographic description are discussed below, with examples. Neither the discussion nor the examples are intended to be exhaustive. The reader is advised to consult the text of AACR 2 for details and further examples.

In presenting data in the bibliographic description, information taken from the chief source of information is preferred. If the information required is unavailable or insufficient from the chief source, other sources are used. In Chapters 2–12, which deal with specific types of materials, other sources of information for each area are enumerated. Information taken from outside the prescribed source or sources is enclosed in brackets.

Title and Statement of Responsibility Area (Mnemonic Rule: *.1)

This area contains the following elements: (1) title proper, (2) general material designation; (3) parallel titles; (4) other title information; (5) statement of responsibility. Each of these is discussed in turn below.

1. Title proper (rule * .1B)

The title proper, which includes any alternative titles, is transcribed from the chief source of information exactly as to wording, order, and spelling, though not necessarily as to punctuation and capitalization. It is usually readily identifiable in book-form materials. For nonbook materials, the title proper is often lacking and one must be supplied.

Solar architecture
The Frost report on Britain
Anglo-American cataloguing rules
Carmen (fragments of acts 1 and 2)

> Michael Morcombe's Birds of Australia
> [Letters]
> [Design of a dormitory]
> [Sea shells]
> [Map of the Counties of Sussex and Hants with the Isle of Wight]

The rules for capitalization are presented in Appendix A in AACR 2. The first word of the title proper is always capitalized. Other words are capitalized according to the rules for the language involved. For the English language, proper names and adjectives in the title are capitalized. The word following an initial article is capitalized only if the main entry of the work is under the title as shown in the following example (see Chapter 4 for a discussion of the choice of entry):

> A Basic bibliography on marketing research

Long titles may be abridged:

> Genealogy of the Linney family in England, Virginia,
> Maryland . . . and possibly other states

2. General material designation (rule * .1C)

This is an *optional addition*. The general material designation indicates the broad class of material to which the item being described belongs, for example, map, filmstrip, microform, machine-readable data file, music, sound recording, etc. For printed or book-form material, the term *text* is used as the general material designation. Most libraries probably will choose to use the general material designation for nonbook materials, but not for book-form materials.

For certain forms of materials, British and North American cataloging agencies use different terms as the general material designation. List 1 in Table 3-3 is designed for British use, and list 2 for North American use.

Examples

> Library of Congress subject headings [text]
> Library of Congress subject headings [microform]
> Being safe [filmstrip]
> A Man's reach should exceed his grasp [videorecording]
> The Bronx is burning [motion picture]
> Clean hands [slide]
> Buddy Johnson at the Savoy Ballroom, 1945-1946 [sound re-
> cording]
> Hondius-Kaerius wall map of Europe [map]
> Globe of the moon [globe]
> Monopoly [game]

TABLE 3-3   British and North American Terminology

List 1: British	List 2*: North American
Cartographic material	Map Globe
Graphic	Art original Chart Filmstrip Flash card Picture Slide Technical drawing Transparency
Machine-readable data file	Machine-readable data file
Manuscript	Manuscript
Microform	Microform
Motion picture	Motion picture
Multimedia	Kit
Music	Music
Object	Diorama Game Microscope slide Model Realia
Sound Recording	Sound recording
Text	Text
Videorecording	Videorecording

*The following rules apply to list 2: (1) use *map* for cartographic charts, not *chart;* (2) for material treated in Chapter 8, use *picture* for any item not subsumed under one of the other terms in list 2; (3) use *technical drawing* for items fitting the definition of this term in the Glossary, page 345; for architectural renderings, however, use *art original* or *picture*, not *technical drawing;* (4) use *kit* for any item containing more than one type of material if the relative predominance of components is not easily determinable and for the single-medium packages sometimes called *lab kits.*

NOTE: Consult Appendix A of this book for Library of Congress policy concerning this option.

SOURCE: *AACR 2*, p. 20.

3. Parallel titles (rule *.1D)

A parallel title is the title proper in *another* language or script. It should not be confused with an alternative title or other title information, which is not equivalent in meaning to the title proper.

Forestry [text] = Forêt

Casgliad Llyfrau Cymraeg [text] = Welsh books collection

4. Other title information (rule *.1E)

Other title information includes any title other than the title proper, the parallel title, and variations on the title proper such as spine titles, sleeve titles, etc. Subtitles, avant-titres, and phrases appearing in conjunction with the title proper, parallel titles, or other titles, indicative of the character, contents, etc., of the item or the motives for, or occasion of, its production or publication, all fall into this category.

> Cost analysis of library functions [text] : a total systems approach

> Management training [text] : report of Conference of Industrialists and Symposium on Nationalized Industries, held at the Indian Institute of Science, Bangalore, on 24th and 25th April 1954

> Coordination, concept or reality? [text] : a study of libraries in a university system

> The Captain of a huckleberry party [motion picture] : Henry Thoreau

> Hidden alcoholics [motion picture] : why is Mommy sick?

> Growing up at the table [filmstrip] : teaching feeding skills to the mentally retarded child at home

> Water quality data [text] = Données sur la qualité des eaux : Saskatchewan, 1961–1975

> Labour costs in Canada [text] : manufacturing = Coûts de la main-d'oeuvre au Canada : industries manufacturières

5. Statement of responsibility (rule *.1F)

The statement of responsibility names the persons responsible for the intellectual or artistic content of the item being described, the corporate bodies from which the content emanates, or the persons or corporate bodies responsible for the performance of the content. The persons named include writers, editors, compilers, adapters, translators, revisers, illustrators, reporters, composers, artists, photographers, cartographers, collectors, narrators, performers, producers, directors, and investigators.

> The dream scenes of Invisible man [text] / by L.M. Grow

> Window in the sea [text] / [Jacques Cousteau]

Connecticut union list of serials [text] / compiled and edited by Donald H. Axman

Victorian houses of L.A. [slide] / Virgil Mirano

Laurel and Hardy compendium [motion picture] / MGM

Algerian panorama [text] : a select bibliographical survey, 1965–1966 / African Bibliographic Center

Smokey Bear [motion picture] / National Association of State Foresters, United States Forest Service, and the Advertising Council

The Frost report on Britain [sound recording] / written by David Frost and John Cleese

The American woman in colonial and revolutionary times, 1565–1800 [text] : a syllabus with bibliography / Eugenie Andruss Leonard, Sophie Hutchinson Drinker, Miriam Young Holden

When the statement of responsibility in the source of information contains names of more than three persons or corporate bodies, only the first named is included in the statement of responsibility in the cataloging record.

A Basic bibliography on marketing research [text] / compiled by Robert Ferber . . . [et al.]

When there are two or more statements of responsibility, each naming one or more persons or corporate bodies performing different functions, they are separated by a space-semicolon-space.

A bibliography of Scottish poets from Stevenson to 1974 [text] / compiled with an introduction by Duncan Glen ; with a preface by Hugh MacDiarmid

Korean studies guide [text] / compiled for the Institute of East Asiatic Studies, University of California, by B.H. Hazard, Jr. . . . [et al.] ; edited by Richard Marcus

The poor mouth [text] : a bad story about the hard life / by Flann O'Brien ; translated by Patrick C. Power ; illustrated by Ralph Steadman

Spelling [text] : practical ideas for creative teachers / originally compiled by Leone Harlan ; prepared under the direction of Hollie Bethel ; coordinated by Thomas Nenneman ; reviewed by Hugh A. Harlan, Jerry L. Rutherford, Sharon K. Meyer

Titles and abbreviations of titles of nobility, address, honor, (except British titles of nobility or honor: Sir, Dame, Lord, and Lady) and distinction, initials of societies, qualifications, etc., are generally omitted from the statement of responsibility. Exceptions are made when such a title is necessary grammatically for identification of the person and when the name consists of a given name or a surname only.

> The cat in the hat [text] / by Dr. Seuss

> The cruise of the "Janet Nichol" among the South Sea Islands [text] : a diary / by Mrs. Robert Louis Stevenson

> Stories of Charlemagne and the twelve peers of France from the old romances [text] / by A.J. Church (On title-page: by Prof. A.J. Church, M.A.)

> Human races [text] / by Stanley M. Garn (On title-page: by Stanley M. Garn, Ph.D.)

Edition Area (Rule *.2)

This area contains three elements— (1) edition statement; (2) statements of responsibility relating to the edition; (3) subsequent edition statement—each of which is discussed below.

1. Edition statement (rule *.2B)

An edition statement found on an item, including one for the first edition, is transcribed. Standard abbreviations and numerals (in place of words) are used (see Appendixes B and C of AACR 2).

> 1st ed.
> 5th rev. ed.
> Prelim. ed.
> Research ed.

2. Statements of responsibility relating to the edition (rule *.2C)

A statement of responsibility relating to one or more editions, but not to all editions, is given after the edition statement instead of after the title.

> 4th ed. / edited by Diane Henderson

> Facsim. ed. / with a note by S.J. Butlin

> Anglo-American cataloguing rules [text] / prepared by the American Library Association . . . [et al.]. — 2nd ed. / edited by Michael Gorman and Paul W. Winkler

3. Subsequent edition statement (rule *.2D)

A statement, designating the item as a reissue containing changes from a particular edition, is given after the edition statement and its statements of responsibility.

> 3rd ed., 1974 revision
> 2nd ed., enl. and up to date

This subsequent edition statement may be followed by its own statement(s) of responsibility, if there is any (rule *.2E).

Material (or Type of Publication) Specific Details Area (Rule *.3)

This area is applicable only to (1) cartographic materials and (2) serials.

1. Cartographic materials (rule 3.3)

Called *mathematical data area*, this area contains the statement of scale, the statement of projection, and the statement of coordinates and equinox (optional).

> The world [map] / James M. Darley. — Scale 1:39,283,200
>
> Globe of the moon [globe]. — Scale ca. 1:22,243,000
>
> United States [map] / U.S. Coast and Geodetic Survey. — Scale 1:3,000,000 ; Lambert conformal conic proj.

2. Serials (rule 12.3)

For serial publications, this area, called *numeric and/or alphabetic, chronological, or other designation area*, contains the numeric or alphabetic designation, or both, and the chronological designation relating to the first and last issue (if the serial is completed).

> The American digest of foreign orthopaedic literature [text]. — 1970-
>
> Journal of physical oceanography [text]. — Vol. 1, no. 1 (Jan. 1971)-
>
> Studies on the British pottery industry [text] . — No. 1-
>
> Potomac Basin reporter [text]. — Vol. 27, no. 7 (July 1971)-
>
> Annual report [text] / Canadian Council on Social Development. — 51st (1970/71)-
>
> AAVSO report [text]. — No. 28 (Dec. 1970)-

Studies in public communication [text]. — No. 1 (summer 1957)-no. 4 (autumn 1962). —

Regmi research series [text]. — Year 1 (Nov. 1, 1969)-

Philosophical papers [text]. — 1st (1969)-   ser. —

Studies in philosophical linguistics [text]. — Ser. 1-

Publication, Distribution, etc., Area (Rule *.4)

This area records information about the place, name, and date of all types of activities relating to publishing, distributing, issuing, and manufacturing of the item being described.

If the item being described displays two or more places of publication, distribution, etc., or names of publishers, distributors, etc., the first-named place of publication, distribution, etc., and the corresponding publisher, distributor, etc., are recorded. However, if the first-named place is in a foreign country and a place in the country of the cataloging agency is named in a secondary position, with or without a corresponding publisher, etc., the latter is recorded also.

The elements in this area are recorded in the following order: (1) place of publication; (2) name of publisher; (3) date of publication; (4) place of manufacture, name of manufacturer, date of manufacture.

1. Place of publication, distribution, etc. (rule *.4C)

The place of publication, etc., is recorded in the form and the grammatical case in which it appears. The name of the country, state, province, etc. (abbreviated according to Appendix B of AACR 2), is added to the name of the place if it is considered necessary for identification, or if it is considered necessary to distinguish the place from others of the same name.

Chicago
Rome
Georgetown, Calif.
Roma
Moscow, Idaho
Metuchen, N.J.
København
Christchurch, N.Z.

If the place is not known, the abbreviation S.l. (sine loco) is given.

This element is not applicable to the description of manuscripts or of naturally occurring objects.

2. Name of publisher, distributor, etc. (rule *.4D)

The name of the place is followed by the name of the publisher, distributor, etc.

> Chicago : American Marketing Association

> Toronto ; Buffalo : Published for the Faculty of Library Science by the University of Toronto

> Amsterdam : Theatrum Orbis Terrarum ; Norwood, N.J. : W.J. Johnson

> New York : Josiah Macy, Jr., Foundation : Distributed by Independent Publishers Group

> Atlanta : National Medical Audiovisual Center ; Washington : Distributed by National Audiovisual Center

If the name of the publisher, distributor, etc., has appeared in the title and statement of responsibility area, a shortened form is used here.

> Italian history and literature [text] / Harvard University Library. — Cambridge, Mass. : The Library : Distributed by the Harvard University Press.

> Bibliographie [text] : statistique bayesienne = Bibliography : Bayesian statistics / Alfred Houle. — [S.l.] : A. Houle

For a sound recording, if both the name of the publishing company and the name of a subdivision of that company or a trade name or brand name are displayed on the item, the latter is recorded.

For a motion picture or videorecording, this element contains the name of the publisher, distributor, releasing agency, etc., and a production agency or producer not named in the statements of responsibility.

For a machine-readable data file, this element contains the name of the publisher, distributor, etc., and any agency responsible for the production or dissemination of the file.

If the name of the publisher, distributor, etc., is not known, the abbreviation for sine nomine (s.n.) is given.

> Hartford : [s.n.], 1974

3. Date of publication, distribution, etc. (rule *.4F)

The date of publication, distribution, etc., of the edition named in the edition area is recorded in western-style arabic numerals. If there is no edition statement, the date of the first edition is recorded. If the date transcribed from the item is known to be incorrect, the correct date is added in square brackets.

New York : McGraw-Hill Films, 1976

[Rome?] : American Institute of Musicology, 1975

Chicago : [s.n.], 1964 [i.e. 1946]

It is optional to add the latest date of copyright following the date of publication, distribution, etc., if it is different.

If the dates of publication, etc., are not known, the copyright date or, lacking such, the date of manufacture is given in its place.

New York : Macmillan, c1979

Chicago : American Library Association, 1970 printing

If none of the dates discussed above can be assigned to the item being described, an approximate date of publication is given.

Ottawa : Central Mortgage and Housing Corporation, [1973?]

Luzern : Gilhofer & Ranschburg BmbH, [197-]

If a multipart item contains more than one date, the earliest and the latest dates are recorded.

New York : Academic Press, 1969-1973

If the multipart item is not yet complete, the earliest date followed by a hyphen is given.

Paris : Les Belles Lettres, 1968-

For a manuscript, the date is given in this area unless it is already included in the title.

For an art original, unpublished photograph, or other unpublished graphic item (rule 8.4F2), the date of creation is recorded.

For a naturally occurring object (unless it has been mounted for viewing or packaged for presentation), no date is recorded. For artefacts not intended primarily for communication, the date of manufacture is recorded.

4. Place of manufacture, name of manufacturer, date of manufacture (rule *.4G)

If the name of the publisher is unknown, the place and name of the printer or manufacturer are recorded if they are found on the item, its container or case, or accompanying printed material.

[S.l.] : [s.n.], 1954 (Bangalore : Bangalore Press)

[S.l.] : [s.n.], 1930 (Oxford : John Johnson, Printer to the University)

The date of manufacture is included here if it has not been used in place of an unknown date of publication, distribution, etc.

Physical Description Area (rule *.5)

This area presents the physical characteristics of the item being cataloged. It contains the following basic elements: (1) extent of item; (2) other physical details; (3) dimensions; (4) accompanying material. The terms with which each type of material is described vary greatly. These are enumerated below.

1. Extent of item (including specific material designation) (rule *.5B)

The number of physical units and parts are recorded in arabic numerals followed by the specific material designation (abbreviated according to Appendix B, AACR 2).

The specific material designations used for different types of material are listed below. In the description, each of these terms is preceded by the number of units (e.g., 436 p.; 3 film cassettes, etc.). For a multipart item that is not yet complete, the specific material designation alone preceded by three spaces is given.

Books, pamphlets, and printed sheets
v. (*for volume or volumes*)
p. (*for page or pages*)
leaf
column
broadside
sheet
portfolio

Cartographic materials
aerial chart
aerial remote sensing image
anamorphic map
atlas
bird's-eye view or map view
block diagram
celestial chart
celestial globe
chart

globe (*for globes other than celestial globes*)
hydrographic chart
imaginative map
map
map profile
map section
orthophoto
photo mosaic (controlled)
photo mosaic (uncontrolled)
photomap
plan
relief model
remote-sensing image
space remote-sensing image
terrestrial remote-sensing image
topographic drawing
topographic print

Manuscripts
leaf
p.
item (*for a collection of manuscripts*)
box (*for a collection of manuscripts*)
ft. (*if the collection occupies more than 1 linear foot of shelf space*)

Music
score
condensed score
miniature score
piano (violin, etc.) conductor part
vocal score
piano score
chorus score
part

Sound recordings
sound cartridge
sound cassette
sound disc
sound tape reel
sound track film reel (cassette, etc.)
piano (organ) roll, etc.

Motion pictures and videorecordings
film cartridge
film cassette
film loop
film reel

videocartridge
videocassette
videodisc
videoreel

Graphic materials
art original
art print
art reproduction
chart
filmslip
filmstrip
flash card
flip chart
photograph
picture
postcard
poster
radiograph
slide
stereograph
study print
technical drawing
transparency
wall chart

Machine-readable data files
data file ([*no.*] logical records)
program file ([*no.*] statements, [*name of programming language*])
object program ([*name, number, etc., of the machine*])

Three-dimensional artefacts and realia
diorama
exhibit
game
microscope slide
mock-up
model
[*the specific name of the item or the names of the parts of the item*]

Microforms
aperture card
microfiche
microfilm cartridge (cassette, reel)
microopaque

Serials
[*the appropriate specific material designation selected from the terms listed above*]

2. Other physical details (rule *.5C)

Other physical details are added for the following types of materials:

Books, pamphlets, and printed sheets (rule 2.5C)
illustrative matter (use *ill.* for general illustrative matter and specify one or more of the following if considered important: charts, coats of arms, facsimiles, forms, genealogical tables, maps, music, plans, portraits, samples)

Cartographic materials (rule 3.5C)
number of maps in an atlas
colour
material
mounting

Manuscripts (rule 4.5C)
name of material (if not paper) on which a single manuscript is written
illustrative matter

Music (rule 5.5C)
illustrations

Sound recordings (rule 6.5C)
type of recording (sound track films)
playing speed
groove characteristic (discs)
track configuration (sound track films)
number of tracks (tape cartridges, cassettes, and reels)
number of sound channels
recording and reproduction characteristics (tapes)

Motion pictures and videorecordings (rule 7.5C)
aspect ratio and special projection characteristics (motion pictures)
sound characteristics
colour
projection speed (motion pictures)
playing speed (videodiscs)

Graphic materials (rule 8.5C)
medium (chalk, oil, pastel, etc.) and the base (board, canvas, fabric, etc.) (*for art originals*)
process in general terms (engraving, lithograph, etc.) or specific terms (copper engraving, chromolithograph, etc.) (*for art prints*)
method of reproduction (photogravure, collotype, etc.) (*for art reproductions*)
sound (if integral) (*for filmstrips and filmslips*)
double sides (*for flip charts*)

transparency or negative print (*for photographs*)
sound (if integral) (name of the system) (*for slides*)
method of reproduction (blueprint, photocopy, etc.) (*for technical drawings*)
colour (col., sepia, b&w, etc.) (*for art prints, art reproductions, filmstrips and filmslips, flash cards, flip charts, photographs, pictures, postcards, posters, slides, stereographs, study prints, transparencies, and wall charts*)

Machine-readable data files (rule 9.5C)
(*other physical details of the file are given in the note area*)

Three-dimensional artefacts and realia (rule 10.5C)
material
colour

Microforms (rule 11.5C)
negative
illustrations
colour

Serials
(*physical details appropriate to the item being described as outlined above*)

3. Dimensions (rule *.5D)

Books, pamphlets, and printed sheets (rule 2.5D)
size (the height of the volume or volumes in centimeters, to the next whole centimeter up)

Cartographic materials (rule 3.5D)
height × width in centimeters, to the next whole centimeter up)
   (*for two-dimensional cartographic items, relief models*)
height of the volume or volumes (*for atlases*)
diameter (*for globes*)

Manuscripts (rule 4.5D)
height
height × width (if width is less than half the height or greater than the height)

Music (rule 5.5D)
same as for books, pamphlets, etc.

Sound recordings (rule 6.5D)
diameter of the disc in inches (*for sound discs*)
gage (width) in millimeters (*for sound track films*)
dimensions of the cartridge and width of the tape (if other than the standard measurement) in inches (*for sound cartridges and sound cassettes*)

diameter of the reel in inches and width of the tape (if other than standard) in fractions of an inch *(for sound tape reels)*

Motion pictures and videorecordings (rule 7.5D)
gage (width) in millimeters and (if 8 mm) whether single, standard, super, or Maurer *(for motion pictures)*
gage (width) in inches *(for videotapes)*
diameter in inches *(for videodiscs)*

Graphic materials (rule 8.5D)
height and width in centimeters *(for all graphic materials except film-strips, filmslips, and stereographs)*
gage (width) in millimeters *(for filmstrips and filmslips)*

Machine-readable data files
not applicable

Three-dimensional artefacts and realia (rule 10.5D)
dimensions of the object in centimeters
name and dimensions of container (if any)

Microforms (rule 11.5D)
diameter of reel (if other than three inches) in inches and the width of the film in millimeters *(for microfilms)*
height × width in centimeters *(for other microforms)*

Serials (rule 12.5 D)
dimensions appropriate to the format of the item being described

4. Accompanying material (rule *.5E)

There are four ways of describing accompanying material:

1. record the details in a separate entry
2. record the details in a multilevel description (i.e., as an analytic)
3. record the details in a note
4. record the name of the material at the end of the physical description

Examples of physical description are given below:

> *Books*
> ca. 250 p. ; 21 cm.
> 29 p. : chiefly ill. ; 31 cm.
> xvi, 336 p., [20] leaves of plates : ill. ; 21 cm.
> 129 p. : facsims. ; 21 cm.
> [16] p. : facsims. ; 27 cm.
>   v. : ill. ; 25 cm.
> xiii, 165 p., [1] leaf of plates : 8 ill. ; 19 cm.

2 v. ; 28 cm.
560 leaves ; 28 cm.
102, 77 leaves ; 23 × 31 cm.

Cartographic materials
1 map on 8 sheets
1 map in 8 sections ; 131 × 161 cm., sections each 71 × 45 cm.
1 globe : col. ; 33 cm. in diam.
2 maps : col. ; 52 × 57 cm. and 51 × 63 cm.

Microforms
16 microfiches; 11 × 15 cm.

Music
1 miniature score (34 p.) ; 19 cm.
1 score (5 p.) + 1 part ; 31 cm.

Sound recordings
2 sound discs (90 min.) : 33^1/$_3$ rpm, mono ; 12 in.

Motion pictures
1 film reel (30 min.) : sd., col. ; 16 mm. + 1 study guide.
1 film cartridge (12 min.) : sd., col. ; super 8 mm.
2 film reels (60 min.) : sd., col. ; 16 mm. + 1 study guide.
1 videocassette (27 min.) : sd., col. ; ^{3}/$_4$ in.

Graphic materials
12 postcards : col. ; 11 × 15 cm.
1 filmstrip (160 fr.) ; 35 mm. + 1 study guide
117 slides : col. + 1 instructor's guide

In the description of different types of materials, the greatest variations occur in the physical description area. For more details and further examples, consult the Anglo-American Cataloguing Rules.

Note: Multimedia items (rule *.10)
If an item consisting of two or more components belonging to two or more distinct material types has been described in terms of the predominant component in the preceding areas, the physical description is also presented in terms of the predominant component with details of the subsidiary component given as accompanying material (cf. rule 1.10).

1 filmstrip (127 fr.) : col. ; 35 mm + 1 sound cassette

An item that has no predominant component is described as a kit if it has a collective title. The term [kit] is used as the general material designation and the physical description may be presented by one of the following methods:

1. Physical descriptions of all components are presented in the same statement.

> 45 flash cards, 50 worksheets, 12 duplicating masters, teacher's guide ; in container ; 16 × 24 × 18 cm.

2. Physical description of each component is presented separately.

> 1 filmstrip (74 fr.) : col ; 35 mm.
> 1 sound disc (17 min.) : 33⅓ rpm, mono ; 12 in.

3. A general statement, if the item consists of a large number of heterogeneous components, is used.

> various pieces *or* 16 various pieces

Series Area (Rule *.6)

This area contains the following elements. In recording these elements, the corresponding rules in the title and statement of responsibility area are followed.

1. Title proper of series (rule *.6B)
2. Parallel titles of series (rule *.6C)
3. Other title information of series (rule *.6D)
4. Statements of responsibility relating to series (rule *.6E)
5. ISSN (International Standard Serial Number) of series (rule *.6F)
6. Numbering within series (rule *.6G)
7. Subseries (rule *.6H)
8. More than one series statement (rule *.6J)

This area is not applicable to the description of manuscript texts. In describing a microform, the series to which the original belongs is recorded in a note.

> (The ocean world of Jacques Cousteau)
>
> (Australian historical reprints)
>
> (Action reading kits)
>
> (Single concept drug films : a series)
>
> (Recorders and strings series ; no. 44)
>
> (One man's China ; 4)
>
> (Conflicts between parents and children ; set 1)
>
> (The John Coffin memorial lecture ; 1973)

(Studies in logic and the foundations of mathematics ; v. 73)

(Bibliography series / American Marketing Association ; no. 2)

(Special bibliographic series / African Bibliographic Center ; v. 5, no. 2)

(Occasional paper / University of Birmingham, Centre for Urban and Regional Studies ; no. 24)

If the item belongs to a subseries which is named in the item along with the main series, both series are recorded within the same set of parentheses.

(Publications of the American Folklore Society. Memoir series ; v. 60)

(Encyclopedia of the organ. Series 1, Composers ; v. 7–8)

If the item belongs to two or more series, the series statements are enclosed in separate parentheses. The more specific series, if it can be determined, is listed first.

(Jacobean drama studies ; 37) (Salzburg studies in English literature)

(Clinical electrocardiography ; pt. 1) (MEDCOM famous teachings in modern medicine)

Note Area (Rule *.7)

Useful descriptive information which cannot be presented in the other areas is presented in notes. Some notes supplement or clarify information given in the preceding areas. Others provide additional bibliographic information about the item. The notes may be based on information taken from any suitable source. In notes containing data relating to those in the preceding areas, prescribed punctuation is used, except that a full stop is used in place of a full stop-space-dash-space. Quotations from the item or other sources used as notes are enclosed in quotation marks.

The kinds of notes used are listed with examples below in the order in which they are to appear on the cataloging record.

1. Nature, scope, or artistic form of the item

   Comedy sketches

2. Language of the item and/or translation or adaptation

Translation of: Der Zauberberg / Thomas Mann

Spanish version of the filmstrip entitled: Mexico City

English and / or French

Introductory matter in English, French, and Spanish.

3. Source of title proper

   Title from heading area

4. Variations in title

   Title on jacket: Catalog of out-of-print books

   Title on container: Report on Britain

5. Parallel title and other title information

6. Statements of responsibility

   Based on the author's paper of the same title in the book entitled: Advances in American medicine: essays at the Bicentennial

   Program notes by B. Serota on container

7. Edition and history

   Continues: The Fifties

   Continued by: The Sixties

   Photoreprint of edition published: London : R. Willis, 1622

   Sequel to: Introduction to social psychology

8. Material specific details (used with types of materials listed in Table 3-4)

   Examples of Material Specific Details

   Scale 1:39,283,200 or 620 miles to the inch at the equator

   On cover sheet: Paducah, Ky.

   Plainsong notation

   Original in British Museum, London

   PL/I

   Report year ends Sept. 30

   Vols. for 1971–   called also época 2-

9. Publication, distribution, etc.

Table 3-4 Material Specific Details

Type of Material	Notes Regarding
Cartographic materials	Mathematical and other cartographic data
Manuscripts	Place of writing
Music	Notation
Graphic materials	Characteristics of original of art reproduction, poster, postcard, etc.
Machine-readable data files	Program version, level, or both
Serials	Numbering and chronological designation

First released in Canada

Recorded in London, 1968–1970

10. Physical description

Sound accompaniment compatible for manual and automatic operation

Reverse side of disc contains same program without signals

11. Accompanying materials and supplements

With instructor's manual, student's manual, tests, and miscellaneous teaching materials

Supplements accompany some issues

12. Series

Originally issued in the series: The Century social science series

13. Dissertations

Thesis (Diploma in Librarianship)—University of the Witwatersrand

14. Audience

For primary grades

15. Reference to published descriptions (used with manuscripts)

Described in: Papers / Henry Knox

16. Other formats available

Also issued as filmstrip

17. Summary

Summary: The story of the attempts to rescue a young actress from a giant ape that has taken her as a bride

18. Contents

Includes index

Bibliography: p. 356–368

Contents: v.1. Classification schedule. Classified listing by call number. Chronological listing—v. 2. Author and title listing.

Contents: 1. Think safe, act safe—2. Cars, bikes, and people—3. Delicious or deadly?—4. Watch where you go—5. Fun or fearful?—6. Helpful or harmful?

19. Numbers borne by the item (other than those presented in the Standard number and terms of availability area)

Serial number on program booklet: SLS 890

20. Copy being described and library's holdings

Library copy lacks maps facing pages 176 and 460

21. "With" notes

With: Concerto, piano, G major / M. Ravel

Standard Number and Terms of Availability Area (Rule *.8)

This area contains the following elements: (1) standard number; (2) key title; (3) terms of availability.

1. Standard number (rule *.8B)

The number recorded is the International Standard Book Number (ISBN), International Standard Serial Number (ISSN), or any other internationally accepted standard number.

This element does not apply to the description of manuscripts.

2. Key title (rule *.8C)

This element applies to a serial publication only.

3. Terms of availability (rule .8D)

This element is optional.

> *Examples*
>
> ISBN 0-914178-050-9 : $7.95
>
> ISBN 3-921719-01-3 : DM 29.80
>
> ISSN 0190-4663 = Chronicle career index annual

SUPPLEMENTARY ITEMS

A supplement, which is an item that complements or adds to an existing publication, can be treated in one of two ways: (1) as a separate item; (2) as a dependent item.

As a Separate Item

A separate cataloging record is created for the supplement. The supplement is linked to the main item by means of an added entry for the latter and a note explaining the relationship between the two.

As a Dependent Item

The supplement is recorded in the description of the main item as accompanying material or in a note.

ANALYTICS

An analytic entry is a bibliographic record that describes a part or parts of a larger item. The part or parts being described may be a monograph within a monographic series or a part of a volume.

Analytics of Monographic Series and Multipart Monographs

An individual part of a monographic series or of a multipart monograph can be described in one of three ways: (1) in a separate record; (2) in a contents note; (3) with analytical added entries.

In a separate record (rule 13.2)

If the part being described has a distinctive title, a complete record describing the part is created with details of the series or comprehensive item given in the series area.

In a contents note (rule 13.3)

The title or name and title of the part is cited in a contents note in the record of the comprehensive entry for the larger work.

With analytical added entries (rule 13.4)

An added entry (consisting of the part's main entry heading plus uniform title) is made to the comprehensive entry for the larger work. In this case, the part should be displayed either in the title and statement of responsibility area or in the note area.

"In" Analytics (Rule 13.5)

In this method, the part being analyzed is presented in the description, and the citation of the larger item is given in a note beginning with the word *In*.

The record contains the following elements which are applicable to the item being described:

> Title and statement of responsibility area. — Edition area. — Numeric or other designation. — Publication, distribution, etc., area. — Extent and specific material designation of the part : other physical details ; dimensions. — Notes.

> *In* [Main entry. Uniform title]. Title proper. — Edition statement. — Numeric or other designation of a serial, or publication details of a monographic item.

Example

Developing a national foreign newspaper microfilming program [text] / John Y. Cole. — p. 5–17 ; 24 cm.

In Library resources & technical services. — Vol. 18, no. 1 (Winter 1974)

Exercise B

Prepare a bibliographic description for each of the following:

1. *The Poet's Poet and Other Essays* (see reproduction of title page, Figure 3–17).
2. *The Contradictions of Leadership* (see reproduction of title page and verso, Figure 3–18).
3. *Remodeling the Elementary School Library.* (A filmstrip — see reproductions of title frames, Figure 3–19. Other physical details : the filmstrip contains 65 colored frames, silent, width of film is 35 millimeters.)
4. *American Libraries* (official bulletin of the American Library Association).
5. *Joy to the World.* (A sound recording — see reproduction of labels, Figure 3–20.)
6. *How to Live with Your Parents and Survive.* [A slide-tape presentation — see reproduction of title frame and cover of teacher's guide with labels from cassette tape, Figure 3–21. Other physical details: the set contains eighty 2 by 2 color slides with plastic mounts in a carousel cartridge, accompanied by a sound disc (12 inches, 33$^1/_3$ revolutions per minute) , a cassette (1⅞ inches per second, 14 minutes) and a teacher's guide including script and sources.]

Note: Figures 3-17 to 3-21 are on the following pages, 80–84.

THE POET'S POET

AND

Other Essays

WILLIAM A. QUAYLE

SECOND EDITION

CINCINNATI: CURTS & JENNINGS
NEW YORK: EATON & MAINS
1897.

FIGURE 3-17   Exercise B, 1. On verso: Copyright, 1897, by Curts & Jennings.

The Contradictions
of Leadership

A Selection of Speeches by

James F. Oates, Jr.

Introduction by Blake T. Newton, Jr.

With an interpretative essay

by Robert K. Merton

Edited by Burton C. Billings

Appleton-Century-Crofts
Educational Division
Meredith Corporation
NEW YORK

FIGURE 3-18 Exercise B, 2.

Remodeling the Elementary School Library

AMERICAN LIBRARY ASSOCIATION, 1961

1

COMMITTEE ON PLANNING SCHOOL LIBRARY QUARTERS,

BUILDINGS AND EQUIPMENT SECTION,
LIBRARY ADMINISTRATION DIVISION,
AMERICAN LIBRARY ASSOCIATION

Copyright 1961 By American Library Association

2

Produced by
THE BOARD OF EDUCATION OF BALTIMORE COUNTY,
TOWSON 4, MARYLAND

3

Prepared Cooperatively by the
Department of Library Services,
Engineering, ∘
and Audio-Visual Aids

4

FIGURE 3-19 Exercise B, 3.

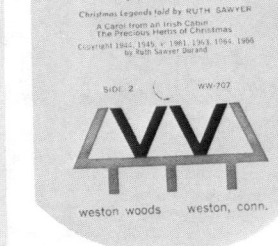

FIGURE 3-20   Exercise B, 5.
On the back of slipcase:

Side 1
   The Two Lambs: A Legend from Ancient Arabia
   This is the Christmas: A Legend from Serbia

Side 2
   A Carol from an Irish Cabin
   The Precious Herbs of Christmas: An Irish Fairytale

WW-707   weston woods   weston, conn.

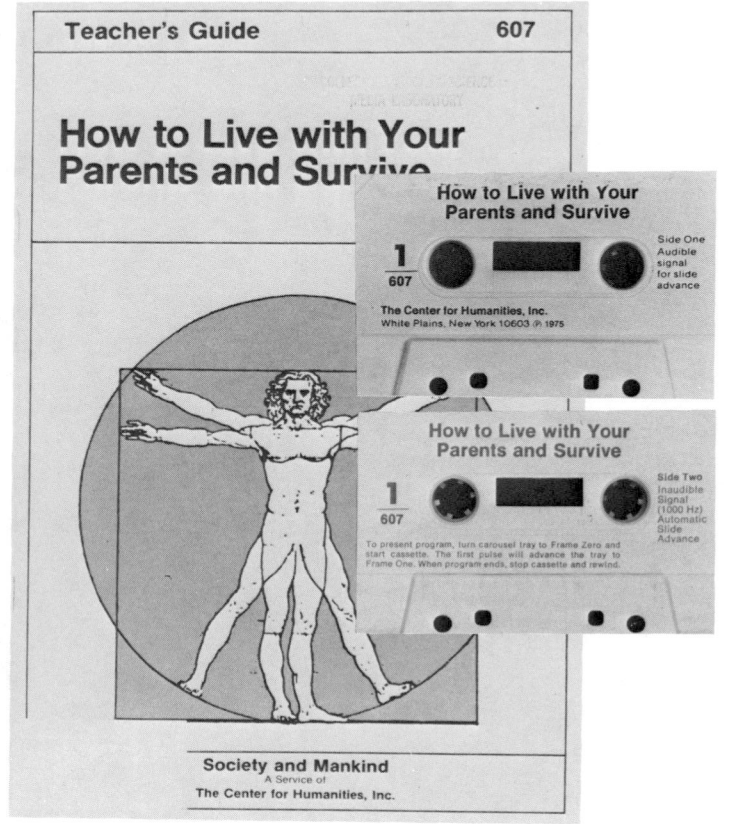

FIGURE 3-21 Exercise B, 6.

CHAPTER 4
Choice of Access Points

Each bibliographic record is given one or more *access points* through which the record can be retrieved. For a cataloging record, an access point is presented in the form of a heading added to the description. Each heading applied to a record then results in a catalog entry. The basis for the access point may be the subject content of the work. In this case, it is called a subject entry and the heading used is called a subject heading (to be discussed in Part Three). Or the basis for the access point may be a bibliographic identifier, such as the author or the title of the work. This kind of access point is determined by descriptive cataloging rules. The four types of bibliographic entry found in a catalog are:

1. Names of persons who perform certain functions:
   a. Authors
   b. Editors and compilers
   c. Translators
   d. Illustrators
   e. Other related persons (e.g., the addressee of a collection of letters; a person honored by a Festschrift)
2. Names of corporate bodies related to the item being described in a function other than solely as distributor or manufacturer
3. Titles
4. Series

Sometimes the heading is in the form of a name-title combination.

CONCEPTS

Main Entry

Among the entries or access points assigned to a catalog record, one is designated as the *main* entry. The other access points are called *added* entries. The record that bears the main entry represents a complete catalog record of the item and is presented in the form by which the item is to be uniformly identified and cited.

In recent years, the concept of main entry has been challenged. It is questioned whether, in a multiple-entry file, the main entry has any real significance.[1] Some feel that since the user can retrieve the catalog record through any of the entries, they have equal value.

Nonetheless, in AACR 2, the concept of main entry is still maintained as being valid at least under the following circumstances:[2]

1. In making a single entry listing
2. In making a single citation for a work (as required for entries for related works and for some subject entries)
3. In assigning uniform titles and in promoting the standardization of bibliographic citation

Chapter 21 of AACR 2 is devoted to the choice of access points and the designation of the main entry.

Authorship

The rules for entry in AACR 2 are largely based on the Paris Principles. The key statement regarding choice of main entry in this document is that the functions of the catalog "are most effectively discharged by an entry for each book under a heading derived from the author's name or from the title."[3] The author's name is, therefore, the primary choice as the main entry. The author as main entry represents a long cataloging tradition. A brief examination of the concept of authorship may be helpful in the understanding of this tradition.

Definition of *author*

In order to grasp the rules for the choice of entry, an understanding of the meaning of the term *author* is essential. Because the rules for the choice of entry are centered on the concept of authorship, a clear, unambiguous definition contributes to the effective application of the rules. Ironically, such a definition is difficult to arrive at. The difficulty is attested to by the attempts at defining the term *author* through the evolution of the cataloging codes.[4]

---

[1] For a thorough examination of this issue, see M. Nabil Hamdy. *The Concept of Main Entry as Represented in the Anglo-American Cataloging Rules: A Critical Appraisal with Some Suggestions: Author Main Entry vs. Title Main Entry.* Littleton, Colo.: Libraries Unlimited, 1973.

[2] *Anglo-American Cataloguing Rules.* 2d ed. Chicago: American Library Association, 1978. P. 2.

[3] International Conference on Cataloguing Principles, Paris, 1961. *Report of International Conference on Cataloguing Principles.* A. H. Chaplin and Dorothy Anderson, eds. London: Organizing Committee of ICCP, 1963, p. 92.

[4] Paul S. Dunkin. *Cataloging USA.* Chicago: American Library Association, 1969. Pp. 24–26.

Cutter:

Author, in the narrower sense, is the person who writes a book; in a wider sense it may be applied to him who is the cause of the book's existence by putting together the writings of several authors (usually called *the editor*, more properly to be called *the collector*). Bodies of men (societies, cities, legislative bodies, countries) are to be considered the authors of their memoirs, transactions, journals, debates, reports, etc. (p. 14)

ALA 1908:

1. The writer of a book, as distinguished from translator, editor, etc. 2. In a broader sense, the maker of the book or the person or body immediately responsible for its existence. Thus, a person who collects and puts together the writings of several authors (compiler or editor) may be said to be the author of a collection. Corporate bodies may be considered the authors of publications issued in their name or by their authority. (p. xiii)

ALA 1941:

Same as ALA 1908 except that "corporate bodies" is replaced by "a corporate body."

ALA 1949:

1. The writer of a work, as distinguished from the translator, editor, etc. By extension, an artist, composer, photographer, cartographer, etc. 2. In the broader sense, the maker of the work or the person or body immediately responsible for its existence. Thus, a person who collects and puts together the writings of several authors (compiler or editor) may be said to be the author of a collection. A corporate body may be considered the author of publications issued in its name or by its authority. (p. 230)

AACR 1967:

The person or corporate body chiefly responsible for the creation of the intellectual or artistic content of a work, e.g., the writer of a book, the compiler of a bibliography, the composer of a musical work, the artist who paints a picture, the photographer who takes a photograph. (p. 343)

AACR 2:

A personal author is the person chiefly responsible for the creation of the intellectual or artistic content of a work. (p. 284)

Personal authorship

The concept of authorship in cataloging is parallel to the tradition of scholarly practice in the western world. Although the title has been traditionally the main element of bibliographic identification in the orient, particularly in ancient times, the western tradition, probably derived from the classical Greco-Roman tradition, has emphasized the author as the chief element of identification of works.[5] Classical works have generally been identified by their authors—Homer, Plato, Herodotus, etc.

On the other hand, the concept of authorship was not stressed in the Germanic tradition. Many of the Germanic sagas, Anglo-Saxon poems, and early epics and tales, for example, are anonymous, constituting the bulk of what is known as "anonymous classics." The concept of authorship continued to be vague and diffusive in the Middle Ages. However, since the Renaissance, the practice of identifying works by their authors, representing perhaps a revival of the Greco-Roman tradition, has prevailed in western scholarship. This concept of authorship was no doubt strengthened by the invention of printing, which affirmed the authors' rights in literary property. Even in the orient, modern works are now mostly identified by their authors, perhaps as a result of the influence of western practice.

The practice of assigning main entry under the author in library catalogs can be considered a conformity to the scholarly tradition.

Corporate authorship

Until the middle of the nineteenth century, the concept of authorship was confined mainly to personal authors. Corporate authorship (i.e., attributing authorship of a work to a corporate body) as an element of bibliographic identification is a relatively new concept. Early bibliographies and catalogs did not provide for entries under corporate bodies, nor did Germanic cataloging practice before the Paris Principles . In the Anglo-American cataloging tradition, the recognition of corporate authorship began in the nineteenth century. The rules for the British Museum Catalogue became the first major cataloging code to prescribe corporate author entries.[6]

As an entry element, corporate authors have always presented problems. Lubetzky's attack on the corporate complex resulted in a thorough examination of the problem before the Paris Conference. Although the Paris Principles include specific guidelines relating to corporate authorship and corporate main entry, criticisms and discussions following the publication of the AACR (1967) and other cataloging codes based on the Paris Principles have demonstrated that the rules for works of corporate authorship are open to diverse

---

[5]Ibid. Pp. 23–24.

[6]Åke I. Koel. "Can the Problems of Corporate Authorship Be Solved?" *Library Resources and Technical Services*, **18**:349, Fall, 1974.

interpretations and are therefore unsatisfactory. This state of confusion prompted Eva Verona's recent study on corporate headings in catalogs, national bibliographies, and cataloging codes of many countries. Her study reveals the chaotic state of corporate authorship: "Among the great number of cataloguing codes recognizing corporate authorship, it is scarcely possible to find even two which interpret the concept in the same way." [7] One major problem is the lack of even a general agreement among different codes as to the definition of corporate authorship. Efforts are now being made toward international consensus on the definition and treatment of corporate authorship.

In AACR 2, a shift in the concept of corporate authorship has occurred. There is a redefinition of the role of corporate bodies in that the term "corporate authorship" is no longer used. Instead, the rules are phrased in terms of works "emanating from one or more corporate bodies," i.e., works issued by, caused to be issued by, or originating with, one or more corporate bodies. [8] Although the rules still provide for entering certain works under a corporate body, the number of instances in which corporate bodies are assigned as main entries has been greatly reduced. (See later discussion for details of such instances.) This shift in the concept of corporate authorship brings AACR 2 closer than its predecessor to the Paris Principles which also avoid the use of the term *corporate authorship*.

CHOICE OF MAIN ENTRY

For works written by one person, the choice of main entry presents little problem. However, when more than one person is responsible for the existence of the work, particularly if these persons perform different functions, the choice becomes a complicated one. Throughout the evolution of the definition of the term *author*, an attempt has been made to exclude certain contributors to the existence of the work, such as translators, textual editors, illustrators, and publishers. On the other hand, corporate bodies are included, and until 1975, compilers and editorial directors of works were also given the status of author. In 1975, Rules 4 and 5 in AACR (1967) which contained such provisions were revised to exclude compilers and editorial directors in the choice of main entry. This principle is continued in AACR 2.

[7] Eva Verona. *Corporate Headings: Their Use in Library Catalogues and National Bibliographies: A Comparative and Critical Study.* London: IFLA Committee on Cataloguing, 1975. Pp. 8–9.
[8] AACR 2. P. 285.

Types of Main Entry

The main entry of a work is always a personal name entry, corporate name entry, or title entry. Most of the book-form materials have main entry under personal authors. Government publications are generally entered under corporate bodies. Serial publications and nonbook materials usually have title main entries.

Conditions of Authorship

The choice of main entry is based on the condition of authorship of each work. The rules for the choice of entry in AACR 2 are organized according to these conditions of authorship:

> Works for which a single person or corporate body is responsible
> Works of unknown or uncertain authorship or by unnamed groups
> Works of shared responsibility (i.e., collaboration between two or more persons or corporate bodies performing the same kind of activity in the creation of the content of an item)
> Collections and works produced under editorial direction
> Works of mixed responsibility (i.e., collaboration between two or more persons or corporate bodies performing different kinds of activities, e.g., adapting or illustrating a work written by another person)

Rules for Choice of Entry

Following is a summary of the rules for the choice of entry grouped by types of main entry.

Entry under personal author

1. Single personal authorship
For works of single personal authorship (the term author includes writers of books, composers of music, compilers of bibliographies, cartographers, artists, photographers, and, in certain cases, performers of sound recordings, films, and videorecordings), entry is under the author (rule 21.4A):

> Islands in the stream [text] / Ernest Hemingway (*main entry under the heading for Hemingway*)
>
> Job evaluation [transparency] / Herbert H. Oestreich (*main entry under the heading for Oestreich*)

Carmen [sound recording] / Georges Bizet (*main entry under the heading for Bizet*)

Connecticut union list of serials [text] / compiled and edited by Donald H. Axman (*main entry under the heading for Axman*)

2. Shared responsibility

For works of shared responsibility, entry is under (a) principal author if indicated (rule 21.6B):

Chronological bibliography of English language fiction in the Library of Congress through 1950 [text] / compiled by R. Glenn Wright, assisted by Barbara E. Rosenbaum (*main entry under the heading for Wright; added entry under the heading for Rosenbaum*)

Japanese religion and philosophy [text] / Donald Holzman, with Motoyama Yukihiko . . . [et al.] (*main entry under the heading for Holzman*)

or (b) author named first if responsibility is shared between two or three persons and no principal author is indicated (rule 21.6Cl):

Our lady of rhyme [text] / Thomas Wood Stevens & Alden Charles Nobel (*main entry under the heading for Stevens; added entry under the heading for Noble*)

The American woman in colonial and Revolutionary times, 1565–1800 [text] / Eugenie Andrus Leonard, Sophie Hutchinson Drinker, Miriam Young Holden (*main entry under the heading for Leonard; added entry under the headings for Drinker and Holden*)

Taliesin West [slide] / Julius Shulman & Jeffrey Cook (*main entry under the heading for Shulman; added entry under the heading for Cook*)

3. Mixed responsibility

For works of mixed responsibility, entry is under (a) adapter for a paraphrase, rewriting, adaptation for children, or version in a different literary form (e.g., novelization, dramatization) (rule 21.10):

Il pozzo e il pendolo [text] / Bruno Bettinelli (*an opera based on Edgar Allan Poe's The pit and the pendulum*) (*main entry under the heading for Bettinelli; added entry (name-title) under the heading for Poe*)

(b) writer of the text for a work that consists of a text for which an artist has provided illustrations (rule 21.11A):

> Gavilla de fabulas sin amor [text] / Camilo Jose Cela ; illus. de
> Picasso (*main entry under the heading for Cela; added entry under the
> heading for Picasso*)

(c) artist for separately published illustrations (rule 21.11B):

> Blake's Grave [text] : a prophetic book, being William Blake's
> illustrations for Robert Blair's The grave (*main entry under the
> heading for Blake; added entry (name-title) under the heading for Blair*)

(d) original author of an edition that has been revised, enlarged,
updated, abridged, condensed, etc., by another person if the original
author is still considered to be responsible for the work (rule 21.12A):

> Commonsense cataloging [text] / Esther J. Piercy. — 2nd ed.
> / revised by Marian Sanner (*main entry under the heading for
> Piercy; added entry under the heading for Sanner*)

(e) reviser of an edition if the original author is no longer considered to
be responsible for the work (rule 21.12B):

> Cataloguing [text] : a guidebook / by Eric J. Hunter (*A
> revision and rearrangement of Patrick Quigg's Theory of cataloguing*)
> (*main entry under the heading for Hunter; added entry (name-title)
> under the heading for Quigg*)

(f) commentator of a work consisting of a text and a commentary by a
different person, if the latter is emphasized (rule 21.13B):

> Camus [text] / Jean Claude Brisville (*Contains also selections from
> Camus's works*) (*main entry under the heading for Brisville; added entry
> under the heading for Camus*)

(g) author of the text of a work consisting of a text and a commentary
by a different person, if the text is emphasized (rule 21.13C):

> A casebook on Gerontion [text] / T.S. Eliot ; edited by E. San
> Juan, Jr. (*Includes the text and a number of critical articles on
> Gerontion*) (*main entry under the heading for Eliot; added entry under
> the heading for San Juan*)

(h) original author of a translation (rule 21.14A):

> Îles à la dérive [text] / Ernest Hemingway ; traduit de
> l'anglais par Jean-René Major (*main entry under the heading for
> Hemingway*)

(i) biographer-critic of a work by a writer accompanied by (or
interwoven with) biographical or critical material by another person, if
the latter is emphasized (rule 21.15A):

Henry Wadsworth Longfellow [text] : a sketch of his life /
by Charles Eliot Norton, together with Longfellow's chief
autobiographical poems (*main entry under the heading for Norton;
added entry under the heading for Longfellow*)

(j) writer of a work accompanied by, or interwoven with, biographical
or critical material by another person who is presented as editor,
compiler, etc. (rule 21.15B):

The life and letters of Frederic Shields [text] / edited by
Ernestine Mills (*main entry under the heading for Shields; added
entry under the heading for Mills*)

Entry under corporate body

Main entry under a corporate body[9] is determined by the same
principles governing the choice of a personal author as the main entry
with the restriction that the work being cataloged must fall into one or
more of the following categories (rule 21.1B2):

1. Works of an administrative nature dealing with the corporate
body itself or its internal policies, procedures, and/or operations, its
finances, its officers and/or staff, or its resources (e.g., catalogues,
inventories, membership directories)

Union list of serials held in the University libraries [text] /
University of Queensland Library (*main entry under the heading
for the library*)

Annual report of the Director [text] / University of
Michigan, University Library (*main entry under the heading for
the library*)

2. Some legal and governmental works of the following types:
laws (see 21.31); decrees of the chief executive that have the force of
law (see 21.31); administrative regulations (see 21.32); treaties, etc.
(see 21.35); court decisions (see 21.36); legislative hearings.

Regulations relating to the administration of the
[Minnesota] Office of Liquor Control Commission (*main
entry under the heading for the office*)

The constitution of the State of Hawaii (*main entry under the
heading for Hawaii with uniform title for the constitution*)

---

[9]A corporate body is defined as "an organization or group of persons that is
identified by a particular name and that acts, or may act, as an entity." AACR 2. P. 565.

3. Works that record the collective thought of the body (e.g., reports of commissions, committees, etc.; official statements of position on external policies)

> Report and recommendations [text] / Governor's Commission on Compensation of Unclassified Personnel, St. Paul, Minnesota (*main entry under the heading for the commission*)

> Manifesto of the Central Committee of the Communist Party of India on the New Constitution (*main entry under the heading for the committee*)

4. Works that report the collective activity of a conference (proceedings, collected papers, etc.), of an expedition (results of exploration, investigation, etc.), or of an event (an exhibition, fair, festival, etc.) falling within the definition of a corporate body (see 21.1B1), provided that the conference, expedition, or event is prominently named in the item being cataloged

> A point of view [text] : proceedings of the first American Conference on Teachers' Centers in Mathematics Education (*main entry under the heading for the conference*)

> West coast 74, Black image [text] : 1974 invitational exhibition / Crocker Art Gallery Association and E.B. Crocker Art Gallery (*main entry under the heading for the association; added entry under the heading for the gallery*)

5. Sound recordings, films, and videorecordings resulting from the collective activity of a performing group as a whole where the responsibility of the group goes beyond that of mere performance, execution, etc. (For corporate bodies that function solely as performers on sound recordings, see 21.23.)

> The early Beatles [sound recording] / sung and played by the Beatles (*main entry under the heading for the Beatles*)

Official communications from heads of state, heads of government, heads of international bodies, popes, patriarchs, bishops, etc., are entered under their corporate headings (rule 21.4D1).

> Humanae vitae (*Pope Paul VI's encyclical*) (*main entry under the corporate heading for Pope Paul VI*)

> Urbanaid [text] / proposed by Mayor John V. Lindsay, City of New York (*main entry under the corporate heading for the mayor*)

Entry under title

By way of elimination, works that do not fall into the categories of works which require main entry under a person or a corporate body are entered under the title. In other words, a work is entered under the title when:

1. The personal authorship is unknown, diffuse (i.e., authorship being shared among four or more persons without indication of principal responsibility), or cannot be determined, and the work does not emanate from a corporate body

> The song of Roland [text] / translated by W.S. Merwin (*an anonymous classic*) (*main entry under the uniform title for the song; added entry under the heading for Merwin*)
>
> The Atlantic monthly [text] (*main entry under title*)
>
> Mary Cassatt, an American impressionist [filmstrip] (*main entry under title*)
>
> A Basic bibliography of marketing research [text] / compiled by Robert Ferber . . . [et al.] (*main entry under title*)

2. It is a collection or a work produced under editorial direction

> The Modern poets [text] : an American-British anthology / edited by John Malcolm Brinnin and Bill Read (*main entry under the title; added entries under the headings for Brinnin and Read*)
>
> Literature in America [text] / general editor, Robert C. Albrecht (*main entry under title; added entry under the heading for Albrecht*)

3. It emanates from a corporate body but does not fall into one or more of the categories listed and is not of personal authorship

> Journal of physical oceanography [text] / American Meteorological Society (*main entry under title; added entry under the heading for the society*)
>
> Boilers and their operation—types of naval boilers [motion picture] / United States Navy Department (*main entry under title; added entry under the heading for the department*)

4. It is accepted as sacred scripture by a religious group

> The Old Testament (*main entry under the uniform title for the Bible*)
>
> Upanishads du yoga (*main entry under the uniform title for the Upanishads*)

Changes in Title Proper (Rule 21.2)

Monographs in one physical part

If the title proper of a monograph in one physical part changes between one edition and another, make a separate main entry for each edition.

Monographs in more than one physical part

If the title proper of a monograph in more than one physical part changes between parts, use the predominant title proper as the title of the whole monograph. If none of the titles predominates, use the title proper of the first part.

Serials

If the title proper of a serial changes, make a separate main entry for each title.

> The Journal of the reading specialist [text]. — Vol. 1 (1961)-
> v. 11, no. 1 (Oct. 1971) (*Continued by: Reading world*)

> Reading world [text]. — Vol. 11, no. 2 (Dec. 1971)-
> (*Continues: The Journal of the reading specialist*)

Changes of Persons or Bodies Responsible for a Work (Rule 21.3)

Monographs

In the case of a change in responsibility between the parts of a multipart monograph, main entry is made under the person or corporate body that has predominant responsibility. If none is predominant, main entry is made under the heading appropriate to the first part. In the latter case, if more than three persons or corporate bodies are responsible for the completed work, change to entry under title.

Serials

A new entry is made for a serial even if the title proper remains the same and the numbering continues (1) if the name of the person or corporate body under which a serial is entered changes, or (2) if the main entry for a serial is under a personal or corporate heading and the person or corporate body responsible for the serial changes.

ADDED ENTRIES (RULES 21.29–21.30)

In addition to the main entry heading, added entries are assigned to bibliographic records in order to provide additional access points. Added entries appear in the form of personal name headings, corporate headings, titles, series, and name-title headings.

Added Entries under Personal Names

These are made for the following:

1. Collaborators (up to three). If there are four or more collaborators, added entry is made for the first named.
2. Writers.
3. Editors and compilers (rarely made for a serial publication).
4. Translators (made in certain cases only).
5. Illustrators (made in certain cases only).
6. Other related persons. These are persons related to the work in a way other than being responsible for the creation of the content of the work, e.g., the addressee of a collection of letters, a person honored by a Festschrift.

Added Entries under Corporate Names

An added entry is made under a corporate body that is prominently named in the work unless it functions solely as distributor or manufacturer. If four or more corporate bodies are involved in a particular work, an added entry is made under the first named.

Added Entries under Title

An added entry is made under the title proper if it has not been used as the main entry, unless the title added entry duplicates the main entry heading or a subject heading (in an undivided dictionary catalog). An added entry is also made for any other title (cover title, caption title, running title, etc.) which differs significantly from the title proper.

Added Entries under Series

An added entry is made under the heading for a series to which the item belongs except in the following cases:

1. If the items in the series are related to one another only by common physical characteristics, or

2. If the items in the series have been numbered primarily for stock control or to benefit from lower postage rates, or
3. If all items in the series are entered under the heading for one person.

Analytical Added Entries

This is an added entry made for a work contained within the work being cataloged. The heading for the added entry is determined by the way the work contained would be entered, except that a name-title heading is used in cases requiring entry under a person or a corporate body.

Tracing

In library catalogs in the card or book form, the added entries are recorded in a paragraph called *tracing* which appears on the main entry record. Each added entry is preceded by a roman numeral in the tracing. Subject entries are preceded by arabic numerals.

Exercise

1. Determine the main and added entries for the items in Exercise B, Chapter 3.
2. Determine the main and added entries for the following:
   Library of Congress Subject Headings
   Sears List of Subject Headings

CHAPTER 5

Headings and Uniform Titles

FORMS OF HEADINGS

After the main entry and added entries for a work have been determined, the next step is to decide in what form these entries are to be presented in the catalog. Chapters 22–25 of AACR 2 are devoted to the forms of headings to be used in catalog entries.

Principle of Uniform Heading

One of the functions of the catalog, as stated in the Paris Principles, is to ascertain which works by a particular author are in the library [cf. Paris Principles, 2.2(*a*)]. This is achieved by entering all works by a particular author under a *uniform heading*, regardless of how many names or how many forms of a name an author has used. This principle of uniform heading is observed with very few exceptions in the case of personal name headings. However, in the case of headings for corporate bodies, the principle is somewhat modified as will be discussed later.

This principle also applies to title entries. When a work has appeared under various titles, one is chosen as the uniform title (see the discussion on pages 113–115).

Name Authority File

In order to ensure that all works written by a particular author are entered under the same heading in the catalog and to save the time and effort of having to establish the heading each time a work by the same author is cataloged, libraries generally maintain a *name authority file*. A name authority record is made when an author's heading is established for the first time. This record generally contains the following information:

1. The heading to be used in catalog entries
2. The sources upon which decisions were based in establishing the heading
3. Tracing for cross-references to this heading

Until a change of the heading is necessitated by changes in the author's name or upon additional information, this established heading is to be used in cataloging records whenever the author's heading is required as a catalog entry, including main entries, added entries, and subject entries.

Frequently, a person changes his or her name or uses a different form of a name, and the rules require that the new name or form be used in catalog entries. In such cases, the name authority record should be updated and all previously prepared catalog entries under the person's heading should be recataloged. This is an important part of catalog maintenance.

Examples of name authority records are shown in Figure 5-1.

In recent years, the Library of Congress and many large research libraries have converted their name authority files into machine-readable form. It is hoped that in this way, name authority control will be more effective and less time consuming than in the past.

HEADINGS FOR PERSONS

The determination of a personal name heading is normally based on information obtained from the chief sources of information in works by that person issued in his or her language. If the author has written other works than the one being cataloged, it is important to take into consideration the information contained in the other works. If the library does not have all the works or most of the works by the author, reference sources, particularly bibliographical and biographical sources, will have to be consulted. For persons who work in a nonverbal context (e.g., painters, performers) or are not known primarily as authors, the headings are determined from reference sources issued in their languages.

In determining the uniform heading for a person, there are three basic aspects: (1) choice of name; (2) choice of form; and (3) choice of entry element.

Choice of Name (Rule 22.2)

A large number of people have had more than one name in their lifetime. In many cases, an author uses a name which is different from his or her real name or uses more than one name in his or her writings. If the catalog is to show what works by a particular author are in the library, all his or her works must be listed under the same name. Therefore, the first question that must be answered is, which name should be used?

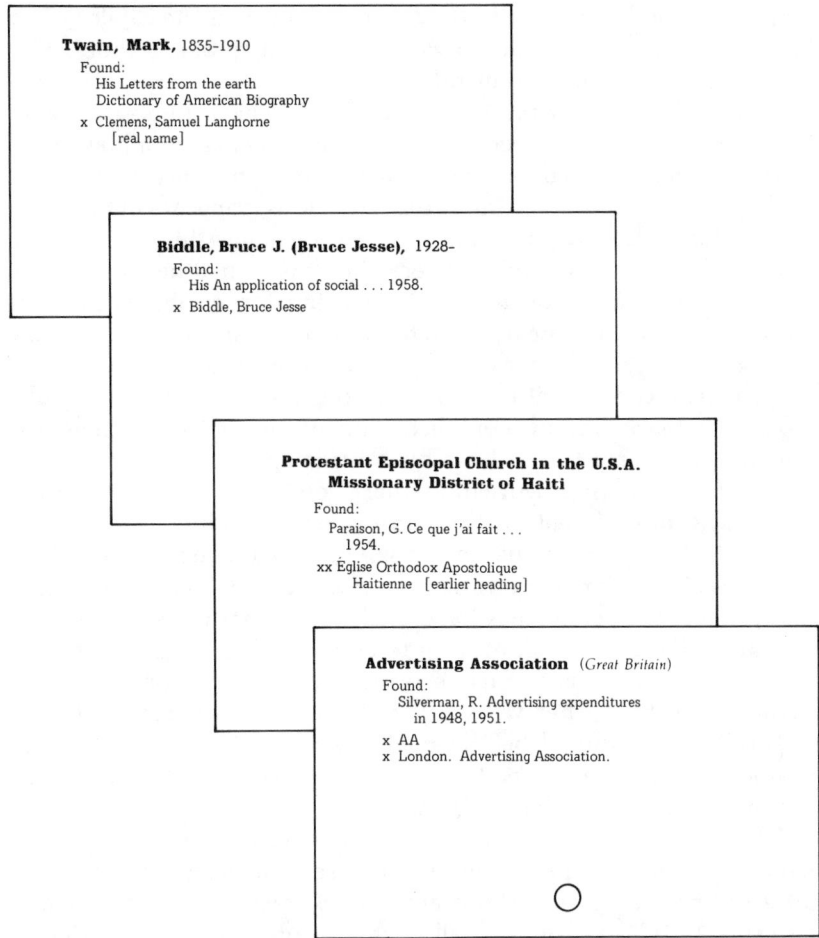

Twain, Mark, 1835-1910
Found:
    His Letters from the earth
    Dictionary of American Biography
x Clemens, Samuel Langhorne
    [real name]

Biddle, Bruce J. (Bruce Jesse), 1928-
Found:
    His An application of social . . . 1958.
x Biddle, Bruce Jesse

Protestant Episcopal Church in the U.S.A.
Missionary District of Haiti
Found:
    Paraison, G. Ce que j'ai fait . . .
        1954.
xx Eglise Orthodox Apostolique
    Haitienne [earlier heading]

Advertising Association (*Great Britain*)
Found:
    Silverman, R. Advertising expenditures
        in 1948, 1951.
x AA
x London. Advertising Association.

FIGURE 5-1 Name authority records.

Before this question can be answered, another, more basic question must be examined. Is a person who writes necessarily only one author? If a person writes under two names for different purposes, could he or she not be considered two authors? A scientist who uses his or her real name in scientific works may choose to use a pseudonym in writing science fiction. It is not unreasonable to treat these works as by two different authors. In this case, this person's works may be listed under two different names in the catalog. The basic question is then, can a person be more than one author?

In analyzing this problem, Dunkin points out two basic approaches. He calls the first the rigid approach. The person's real name is chosen as the heading, regardless of what other names or how many names the person has used. The second is called the relaxed approach. In this case, the heading is the author's name as it appears in the work being cataloged. If an author has used several names, his or her works would then be listed under several headings. In other words, "A uniform heading is not a uniform heading for an individual person. . . . Instead, it is the uniform heading for an author. But a person may be as many authors as he (or she or it) wishes."[1]

The ALA codes until 1967 followed the first approach. As a result, works by Mark Twain were listed under the heading "Clemens, Samuel Langhorne" and those by Novalis appeared in the catalog under "Hardenberg, Friedrich, Freiherr von."

AACR 1967, based on the Paris Principles, adhered to neither approach strictly. It may be viewed as a modified rigid approach. Each person is allowed only one personal name heading, regardless of how many names the person may have used in his or her works. However, this name heading does not have to be the person's real name. The criterion for the choice of name rests on the author's preference as evidenced in his or her works. The Paris Principles state that "the *uniform* heading should be the name by which the author is most frequently identified in editions of his works, in the fullest form commonly appearing there." [§8.2]

AACR 2 follows the same principle of choosing the predominant name as the heading. However, in the case of an author having used different pseudonyms without any one of them being predominant (see rule 22.2C3–4), the rules allow the use of the name appearing in each item as the heading for that item. In other words, a person may have more than one heading in such cases. This reflects the relaxed approach mentioned by Dunkin and represents a relaxation of the principle of uniform heading.

Choice of Form of Name (Rule 22.3)

After a name has been chosen from among two or more names for the same person, the next step is to determine which form of a name (if it appears in more than one form) is to be used in the heading. Question of form of name involves the following aspects: (1) fullness, (2) language, and (3) spelling.

[1]Dunkin. Op. cit. P. 29.

1. Fullness

A person's name may vary in fullness, in terms of the number of elements involved or in terms of abbreviations or initials used. Again, the basis for choice is the predominant form, e.g., **Friedrich von Schiller** instead of **Johann Christoph Friedrich von Schiller** and **D.H. Lawrence** instead of **David Herbert Lawrence.**

2. Language

A person's name may appear in different language forms, particularly in the case of famous authors and internationally known persons, e.g., **Domingo de Guzman** or **Saint Dominic; Quintus Horatius Flaccus** or **Horace; Karl V, Carlos I,** or **Charles V.** There is no simple, clear-cut criterion. The basis for choice varies according to the languages involved, the types of names (given names or names containing surnames), and the periods involved. In general, there is a strong preference for well-established English forms and Latin and Greek forms over vernacular forms.

3. Spelling

The same name may be spelled in more than one way, and a decision must be made regarding which spelling should be used in the heading. The basis for choice is official orthography or predominant spelling.

Choice of Entry Element

After it has been determined which form of a name is to be used in a heading, the next step is to decide which element in the name, if the name contains more than one element, is to be used as the entry word. The names of the majority of people living in modern times are entered under the surname. Certain surnames, such as compound surnames and surnames with separately written prefixes, contain more than one word. In such cases, one of the words in the surname is chosen as the entry word.

Some people, particularly people of earlier times and royalty, do not have surnames or do not use them. Headings for these people are in the form of the given name. Again, if the given name contains more than one word, the entry element must be determined.

The general principle for choice of entry element of a personal name is the person's preference (if known) or the way the name would normally be listed in authoritative alphabetic lists in his or her language or country.

1. Entry under surname (rule 22.5)

A name containing a surname is entered under that surname, e.g., **Shakespeare, William.** If the surname consists of several elements, one of them is chosen as the entry element, as follows.

Compound surnames
A surname consisting of two or more proper names is entered according to the preferred or established form (if known), e.g., **Lloyd George, David.** Otherwise, entry is under the first element except names of married women. The name of a married woman, which consists of a maiden name and husband's surname, is entered under the husband's surname (except names in Czech, French, Hungarian, Italian, or Spanish). For example, **Lindbergh, Anne Morrow.**

Surnames with separately written prefixes
Many surnames include an article or preposition or combination of the two. These names are entered according to the usage of the person's language or country of residence. Because usage varies among different languages and countries, separate rules are provided based on languages or language groups. For American and British names, the entry element is the prefix, e.g., **Van Der Slik, Jack R.**

2. Entry under title of nobility (rule 22.6)

For persons who use their titles rather than their personal surnames in their works or are listed under their titles in reference sources, the entry element is the proper name in the title of nobility. The elements in the name are arranged in the following order:

> Proper name in the title, personal name in direct order, the term of rank in the vernacular.

Shaftesbury, Anthony Ashley Cooper, Earl of

3. Entry under given name, etc. (rule 22.8)

A name that consists of a given name or given names only is entered under the part of name as listed in reference sources, e.g., **Thomas Aquinas; Thomas,** *of Sutton.*

4. Entry of roman names (rule 22.9)

The name of a Roman living before A.D. 476 is entered according to the practice in reference sources, e.g., **Cicero, Marcus Tullius.**

5. Entry under initials, letters, or numerals (rule 22.10)

A name consisting of initials, or separate letters, or numerals, or consisting primarily of initials, is entered under the first initial, letter, or numeral, e.g., **H.D.; A.E.; 110908.**

6. Entry under phrase (rule 22.11)

A name consisting of a phrase or other appellation that does not include a real name is entered under the first element.

Additions to Names

The following elements are added to the headings for persons.

1. Titles of nobility and terms of honour and address, etc. (rule 22.12)

The title of nobility or the term of honour and address is added after the name if the title (not used as the entry element) or term appears commonly in association with the name in the person's works or reference sources, e.g.,

> **Scott,** *Sir* **Walter**[2]
> **Disraeli, Benjamin,** *Earl of Beaconsfield*

2. Saints (rule 22.13)

The word *Saint* is added after the name of a Christian saint (excluding popes, emperors, empresses, kings, or queens).

> **Francis,** *of Assisi, Saint*
> **Gregory I,** *Pope*
> (instead of Gregory, Saint, Pope)

3. Spirits (rule 22.14)

The word *(Spirit)* is added to a heading established for a spirit communication.

> **Parker, Theodore** *(Spirit)*

---

[2]Note that rule 22.12B requires the placement of the term before the forename, but the Library of Congress practice places it after the forename, i.e., **Scott, Walter,** *Sir.*

4. Additions to names entered under surname only (rule 22.15)

The addition is in the form of a word or phrase associated with the name in works by the person or in reference sources.

> **Seuss,** *Dr.*

5. Full names (rule 22.16)

If part or all of a name is represented in the heading by initials, the spelled out form (if known) is added in parentheses.

> **Eliot, T.S. (Thomas Stearns)**
> **Luce, R. Duncan (Robert Duncan)**
> **Shelley, Bruce L. (Bruce Leon)**
> **H.D. (Hilda Doolittle)**

6. Additions to names entered under given name, etc. (rule 22.17)

(a) *Royalty.* A phrase consisting of the title and the name of the state or people governed is added.

> **Baudouin I,** *King of the Belgians*
> **Goshirakawa,** *Emperor of Japan*
> **Rainier III,** *Prince of Monaco*

(b) *Popes.* The word *Pope* is added.

> **John Paul II,** *Pope*

(c) *Bishops, etc.* The title or a phrase consisting of the title and the name of a place is added.

> **Cyprian,** *Saint, Bishop of Carthage*

Distinguishing Persons with the Same Name

As a corollary to the principle of uniform heading, it follows that a particular heading should represent one person only. When two or more persons have the same name, additional elements are added to distinguish between them. The most common element used for this purpose is the person's dates (birth, death, etc.) (see rule 22.18). Optionally, the dates may be added to all personal names even when there is no need to distinguish between headings.

> **Shakespeare, William,** 1564-1616
> **Eliot, T.S. (Thomas Stearns),** 1888-1965
> **Mumford, Lewis,** 1895-
> **Pann, Anton,** *ca.* 1797-1854

If the dates are not available or fail to distinguish between two or more identical names, another element is used for this purpose. The element may be a suitable brief term (for headings in the form of given names only, see rule 22.19A), a term of address, title of position or office, initials of an academic degree, initials denoting membership in an organization, etc. (see rule 22.19B), e.g.,

Blair, William, *Inspector of schools*

GEOGRAPHIC NAMES IN HEADINGS

Because geographic names are used in headings for various purposes—to distinguish between corporate bodies with the same name, as additions to other corporate names, and as headings for governments, a separate chapter in AACR 2, Chapter 23, is devoted to the forms in which geographic names are to be presented in headings.

Language (Rule 23.2)

The basic principle is to use the English form of the name of a place if there is one in general use. Otherwise, the vernacular form is used.

English form
Germany
(not Deutschland)
Naples
(not Napoli)
Munich
(not München)

Vernacular form
São Paulo
Puerto Rico
Rio de Janeiro

Additions to Place Names (Rule 23.4)

When there are two or more places bearing the same name, the name of a larger place (abbreviated according to Appendix B in AACR 2) is added to each name in order to distinguish between them.[3] Normally, the name of the country is added with certain exceptions noted below.

---

[3]The Library of Congress adopts the option of adding the name of the larger geographic entity to certain types of place names even when there is no need to distinguish between places.

Naples (*Italy*)
Rio de Janeiro (*Brazil*)
Friedberg (*Bavaria, Germany*)
Friedberg (*Hesse, Germany*)

Exceptions

A place in a state, province, or territory in Australia, Canada, or the United States	Add the name of the state, province, or territory
A county, region, or islands area in the British Isles	Add *England, Ireland, Northern Ireland, Scotland, or Wales*
A place in England, Wales, or the Republic of Ireland	Add the name of the county in which it is located
A place in a constituent state of Malaysia, the U.S.S.R., or Yugoslavia	Add the name of the state

Examples
Lexington (*Mass.*)
Tyrone (*Northern Ireland*)
Boston (*Lincolnshire*)
Kiev (*Ukraine*)

HEADINGS FOR CORPORATE BODIES

Definition

A corporate body is defined as "an organization or group of persons that is identified by a particular name and that acts, or may act, as an entity."[4] By this definition, corporate bodies include associations, institutions, business firms, radio and television stations, nonprofit enterprises, governments, government agencies, religious bodies, local churches, conferences, expeditions, projects and programs, exhibitions, fairs, festivals, etc.

The three aspects involved in the determination of a personal name heading—(1) choice of name, (2) choice of form, and (3) choice of entry element—also pertain to corporate headings. These are discussed below.

[4]AACR 2. P. 565.

Choice of Name (Rule 24.1)

Corporate bodies frequently undergo name changes. When a corporate body has been identified by more than one name, a decision must be made as to how the corporate body will be represented in the heading. In dealing with corporate bodies which have undergone changes of name, the principle of uniform heading is suspended. While each person is normally represented by one heading only, a corporate body with a changed name is treated as a separate entity and represented by a different heading. In other words, each time a corporate body undergoes a name change, a new heading is established to be used in cataloging works issued by the body under that name. As a result, the former names as well as the current one may be used as headings in the same catalog. This principle is called successive entry. The publications issued by the corporate body are entered under the name used at the time of publication, with *see also* or explanatory references connecting the successive entries.

> **Association of College and Research Libraries**
> For works by this body, see also the earlier heading:
> **Association of College and Reference Libraries**
>
> **Association of College and Reference Libraries**
> For works by this body, see also the later heading:
> **Association of College and Research Libraries**

Choice of Form

As in the case of personal names, a corporate name may exist in different forms. Here, the principle of uniform heading generally applies, in that one of the variant forms is chosen to be used in the heading, with references from the other forms.

Fullness of name (rules 24.2–24.3)

If the name has appeared in various degrees of fullness, the criteria for choice (in the order of preference) are: the form found in the chief sources of information, the predominant form, or a distinctive brief form (including an initialism or an acronym).

> **American Library Association**
> **Henry E. Huntington Library and Art Gallery**
> **Unesco**

Language (rule 24.3)

While the basic principle is to choose the form in the official language, the rules reflect a strong preference for the form in the English language. This is particularly evident in the cases of ancient and international bodies, religious orders and societies, and governments.

> **United Nations**
> **International Federation of Municipal Engineers**

Spelling (rule 24.2C)

If the form of the name varies in spelling, the following criteria (in the order of preference) are used: the form resulting from an official change in orthography, the predominant spelling, or the spelling found in the first item cataloged.

Modifications (rules 24.4–24.11)

In certain cases, modifications are made to the form chosen.

Additions
The following elements are sometimes added to the corporate name:

1. A general (or generic) designation is added if the name alone does not convey the idea of a corporate body, e.g., **Queen Elizabeth** (*Ship*), or if the following additions fail to distinguish between two or more bodies having the same name.
2. The name of the place in which the corporate body is located is added in order to distinguish two or more bodies having the same name, e.g., **Trinity College** (*Hartford, Conn.*), **Trinity College** (*Burlington, Vt.*).
3. The name of an institution (with which the corporate body is commonly associated) instead of the local place name is added to distinguish two or more bodies having the same name.
4. The year of founding or the inclusive years of existence are added if the local place names fail to distinguish two or more bodies with the same name.

Omissions
Elements generally omitted from the heading are (1) initial articles, (2) citations of honors, and (3) terms indicating incorporation.

Other modifications
Names of certain types of corporate bodies, including governments; conferences; exhibitions, fairs, festivals, etc.; chapters, branches, etc.; local churches; and radio and television stations require specific modifications (rules 24.6–24.11).

Choice of Entry Element

When a corporate body is entered under its own name, the entry element is generally the initial word in the name with a few exceptions such as initial articles, ordinal numbers, and terms denoting royal privileges. Previous cataloging codes often required the use of the name of the place in which the corporate body was located as the entry element, e.g.,

Pennsylvania. University.

This practice has been discontinued in the Anglo-American Cataloguing Rules. Most names are now entered directly, e.g.,

University of Pennsylvania.

The principle of entering a corporate body directly under its name applies to most corporate bodies except certain subordinate or related bodies and government bodies and officials.

Subordinate and related bodies (rules 24.12–24.13)

In the case of a subordinate or affiliated body, the entry element is a more complex problem. A subordinate body may be entered under its own name or entered as a subheading under the name of a higher body, depending on various factors discussed below.

In general, a subordinate body or a related body is entered directly under its own name, with the exception of five types of subordinate and related bodies (see rule 24.13). These are subordinate bodies which are normally identified in close association with the names of their higher bodies or parent bodies, or whose names contain a word implying subordination (e.g., division, department, committee, commission, etc.), e.g.,

University of Illinois. *Library.*
American Petroleum Institute. *Division of Refining.*

Direct or indirect subheading (rule 24.14)

Often, a corporate body is subordinate to another body which is subordinate to yet another higher body. In some cases, there may be several levels in the hierarchy. The general rule is to enter a subordinate body, after it has been decided that it should be treated as a subheading, under the lowest element in the hierarchy that is entered under its own name. In other words, all intervening elements are omitted, unless the omission results, or is likely to result, in a conflict, i.e., two or more bodies with the same heading. Then, the name of the lowest element in the hierarchy that will distinguish between the bodies is interposed. A heading is *direct* when an intervening element has been omitted. An *indirect* heading includes intervening elements. For example,

> *Direct subheading*
> **American Library Association.** *Descriptive Cataloging Committee*
> *Hierarchy:* American Library Association
> > Resources and Technical Services Division
> > Cataloging and Classification Section
> > Descriptive Cataloging Committee

> *Indirect subheading*
> **American Library Association.** *Resources and Technical Services Division. Education Committee.*
> *Hierarchy:* American Library Association
> > Resources and Technical Services Division
> > Education Committee

Conferences, congresses, meetings, etc. (rule 24.7)

By definition, conferences, congresses, meetings, etc., are a type of corporate body. Headings for these are established in the form of

> **Name of conference** *(number if any : date : place or institution).*

> **Conference of Coordinators of Regional Medical Programs** *(1968 : Arlington, Va.)*

> **Symposium on Anatomy of Tropical Seed Plants** *(1st : 1966 : Muslim University)*

Governments and government bodies (rules 24.3E, 24.6, 24.17–24.26)

Because of certain special characteristics of governments and government bodies, separate rules concerning the entry element of their names are provided.

The heading for a government is normally the conventional name, i.e., the geographic name of the area over which the government exercises jurisdiction, unless the official name is in common use. For example,

> **United States**
> (*not* United States of America)

> **Kentucky**
> (*not* Commonwealth of Kentucky)

> **Greater London Council**

A body created or controlled by a government is normally entered under its own name, with the exception of ten types (rule 24.18) of government bodies which are entered as subheadings under the headings for the governments. The government agencies that are entered subordinately are those with names implying administrative subordination and those serving an executive, legislative, or judicial function. The subordinate body is entered as a direct or indirect subheading (rule 24.19) based on similar principles for other corporate bodies.

> **National Science Foundation** *(U.S.)*
> **University of North Dakota**
> **Library of Congress**
> **United States.** *Internal Revenue Service*
> **Pennsylvania.** *Bureau of Criminal Justice Statistics*

Government officials (rule 24.20)

Certain government officials (heads of state, heads of governments and of international intergovernmental bodies, governors of dependent or occupied territories) have corporate headings in the form of

> Heading for government. Title of the office

e.g., **California.** *Governor*

For heads of state, a separate heading is established for each incumbent in the form of

> Heading for government. Title of the office
> (inclusive years of the reign or incumbency : name of
> person in brief form)

e.g., **United States.** *President (1961-1963 : Kennedy)*
> **France.** *Sovereign (1814-1824 : Louis XVIII)*

As a result of this provision, each head of state has a corporate heading in addition to his or her personal heading. The corporate heading is used as the main entry for official communications with an added entry under the personal heading. The personal heading is used as the main entry for other works (see rule 21.4D1). Works by popes, patriarchs, bishops, etc., are treated similarly.

> **Catholic Church.** *Pope (1978-   : John Paul II)*

UNIFORM TITLES

A uniform title is "the particular title by which a work that has appeared under varying titles is to be identified for cataloguing purposes."[5] The uniform title brings together under one heading the various manifestations (e.g., editions, translations) of a work regardless of how many different titles it has appeared under. This device is particularly useful when the main entry of the work is under title. Without the use of a uniform title, the various manifestations of a work bearing different titles may be scattered throughout the catalog. It is also useful for famous authors, such as Shakespeare, whose works have been published by many publishers in different countries under various titles.

The rules for uniform titles are not used for a manifestation of a work that is a revision or updating in the same language of the original work. Revised and updated editions with different titles are treated as separate works with a note on the entry for the revision or updating as a connecting device.

Chapter 25 of AACR 2 provides rules for uniform titles. Special rules are given for the use of uniform titles in cataloging special types of materials such as manuscripts, legal materials, sacred scriptures, liturgical works, and music. However, to what extent the rules are applied in cataloging is a policy matter to be decided by individual cataloging agencies. The decision is normally based on the extent of the collection and on the nature and purpose of the collection (e.g., whether it is a research library).

Anonymous Classics Written before 1501

Almost all libraries apply the rules of uniform titles to the cataloging of anonymous classics written before 1501. The rules pertaining to anonymous classics are summarized and discussed below.

Format

The uniform title is given as the heading on the catalog entry, occupying the position normally taken by the author heading.

Choice of uniform title (rule 25.4)

The criteria in the order of preference for choosing the title to be used as the uniform title are:

1. Title by which the work is identified in modern reference sources
2. Title most frequently found in modern editions
3. Title most frequently found in early editions
4. Title most frequently found in manuscript copies

[5]AACR 2. P. 572.

Language

The title in the original language is used except for a work originally written in classical Greek or in a language not in the roman script, when a well-established English title is preferred.

Following is a list of uniform titles frequently found in library catalogs:

Arabian nights
Aucassin et Nicolette
Avicenna
Beowulf
Book of the dead
Chanson de Roland
Everyman
Gawain and the Green Knight
Gudrun
Havelok the Dane
King Horn
Mabinogion
Mother Goose
Nibelungenlied
Pearl (*Middle English poem*)
Robin Hood
Tristan

Special Rules for the Bible (Rules 25.17–25.18A)

Sacred scriptures are entered under uniform titles. Because of the numerous manifestations, certain elements are added in the form of subheadings to the uniform title. These are set forth in special rules.

The general formula for a heading for the Bible is given below. Omit elements that are not applicable in a particular case.

Bible. [*O.T.* or *N.T.*]. [individual book or group of books]. [language]. [version]. [year].
e.g., **Bible.** *N.T. Luke. English. New English. 1965.*

For selections and miscellaneous extracts from the Bible, the elements are arranged in the following manner:

Bible. [language]. [version]. *Selections.* [date].
e.g., **Bible.** *English. Authorized. Selections. 1972.*

Bible. [*O.T.* or *N.T.*]. [individual book or group of books]. [language]. [version]. *Selections.* [date].
e.g., **Bible.** *N.T. Revelation. English. Phillips. Selections. 1970.*

CHAPTER 6

References

To provide access to names or forms of names not used as headings and to connect related headings in the catalog, references, also called cross-references, are provided. Chapter 26 of AACR 2 contains rules for making references. Because references are directly associated with the choice of names and forms used in headings, Chapter 26 complements Chapters 22–25. There are four kinds of references:

1. See reference. A *see reference* directs the user from a name or title not used as a heading to the one chosen as a name heading or uniform title.
2. See also reference. A *see also reference* connects related headings.
3. Name-title reference. This is a *see* or *see also* reference in the form of *name* and *title*. This form is used when the reference is made from a title entered under a personal or corporate heading.
4. Explanatory references. This is a *see* or *see also* reference containing an explanatory note giving more detailed guidance to the user.

Before a reference is made, it is generally recommended that at least one entry appear under the heading referred to. It is general practice to record (or trace) the terms from which references have been made on the name authority record for the heading referred to. The symbol *x* on the name authority record means a *see* reference has been made from the term following, and the symbol *xx* means a *see also* reference has been made.

The most common kinds of references made to each type of heading are summarized below.

PERSONAL NAME HEADINGS

See **References**

See references are made from the following:

1. Names not used as headings: pseudonyms, phrases used in lieu of names, real names, secular names, names in religion, earlier names, and later names.
2. Forms of the name not used as the heading: full names, initials, different language form, different spelling, and different romanization.

3. Different entry elements: different elements of a compound name, prefix, part of surname following a prefix, first given name of person without surname, epithet or byname, person as saint, family name of saint or ruler, inverted form of initials, direct form.

See also **References**

See also references are made between different headings for the same person when the person's works have been entered under more than one heading (cf. rule 26.2D1).

Examples of personal name references are shown in Figure 6-1.

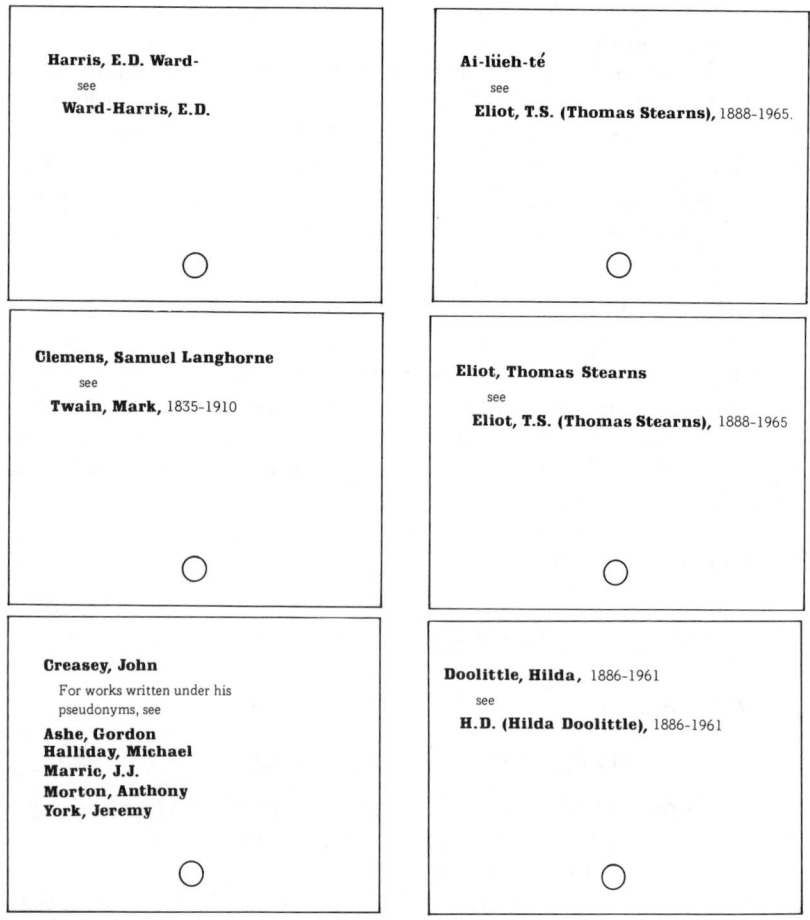

FIGURE 6-1   Personal name references.

NAMES OF CORPORATE BODIES AND GEOGRAPHIC NAMES

1. *See* references are made from variant names, different forms of a name, and initials.
2. *See also* references are made between independently entered but related corporate headings.
3. Typically, explanatory references are made between earlier headings and the later heading of a corporate body.

Examples of corporate name references are shown in Figure 6-2.

UNIFORM TITLES

1. *See* references are made from the different titles and variants of the uniform title to the uniform title.
2. *See also* references are made to connect uniform titles of related works.

Examples of uniform titles are shown in Figure 6-3.

Exercise

1. Prepare name authority records for the headings used as main or added entries in the exercise on page 98.
2. Prepare name authority records for the following persons:

   Michelangelo Buonarroti
   Pearl S. Buck
   Mrs. John F. Kennedy
   Queen Elizabeth I

3. Prepare name authority records for the following corporate bodies:

   The First International Conference on Educational Measurement (held in 1967 in Berlin)
   Queen Elizabeth I (corporate heading)
   The Federal Bureau of Investigation

Topics for Discussion

1. The Anglo-American Cataloguing Rules specify the bibliographic elements to be included in a cataloging record. From the user's point of view, evaluate the relative importance of each of these elements:

Arab Republic of Egypt

see

Egypt

Église Orthodox Apostolique Haitienne

For works by this body see also
the later heading:

**Protestant Episcopal Church in the
U.S.A. Missionary District
of Haiti**

London. Advertising Association

see

Advertising Association (*London, Eng.*)

Hershey Chocolate Company

The Hershey Chocolate Company was established in 1803. On
Oct. 24, 1927, the name was changed to Hershey Chocolate Corporation and on Jan. 30, 1968, to Hershey Foods Corporation.
Works by this body are found under the name used at the time of
publication.

AA

see

Advertising Association (*Great Britain*)

Hershey Chocolate Corporation

The Hershey Chocolate Company was established in 1803. On
Oct. 24, 1927, the name was changed to Hershey Chocolate Corporation and on Jan. 30, 1968, to Hershey Foods Corporation.
Works by this body are found under the name used at the time of
publication.

**Protestant Episcopal Church in the
U.S.A. Missionary District
of Haiti**

For works by this body see also
the earlier heading:

Église Orthodox Apostolique Haitienne

Hershey Foods Corporation

The Hershey Chocolate Company was established in 1803. On
Oct. 24, 1927, the name was changed to Hershey Chocolate Corporation and on Jan. 30, 1968, to Hershey Foods Corporation.
Works by this body are found under the name used at the time of
publication.

FIGURE 6-2   Corporate name references.

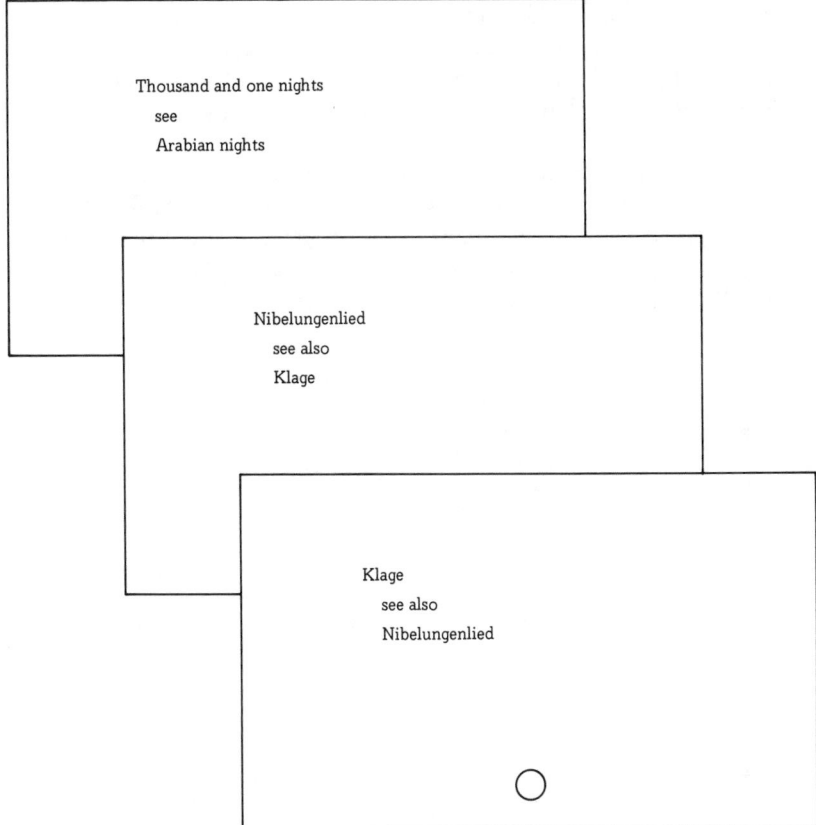

FIGURE 6-3   References for uniform titles.

title, statement of responsibility, edition statement, publisher, physical description, series statement, notes, ISBN, etc. As a user, have you made use of each of these elements at least on one occasion?

2. Discuss the concept of main entry in terms of different types of bibliographic records, e.g., catalogs, bibliographies, single- or multiple-entry listings.

3. In the definitions of "author" given in various codes, the descriptive phrase changed from "the *cause* of the book's existence" to "the person or body *immediately* responsible for its existence" to "the person or corporate body *chiefly* responsible for the creation of the intellectual or artistic content of a work." Compare these phrases and discuss their implications in the rules for choice of access points.

4. While in the Anglo-American tradition, corporate authorship has

been accepted, the Germanic tradition has only recently accepted the concept of corporate authorship. Discuss the concept of authorship in terms of the two types of authors: persons and corporate bodies. In what ways are they similar? In what ways different?

5. In establishing a heading for a personal author, two basic approaches were discussed (see page 102). Consider the advantages and disadvantages of each approach and consider how each approach would function in different types of libraries: academic, special, public, school, or research and nonresearch libraries.

PART THREE

Subject Cataloging

BASIC TOOLS

Austin, Derek. *PRECIS: A Manual of Concept Analysis and Subject Indexing.* London: Council of the British National Bibliography, 1974.

Library of Congress, Subject Cataloging Division. *Library of Congress Subject Headings.* 9th ed. Washington, D.C.: Library of Congress, 1980. (With quarterly supplements accumulated annually. Also available in microform with the entire list cumulated quarterly.)

Sears List of Subject Headings. 11th ed. Barbara M. Westby, ed. New York: The H. W. Wilson Company, 1977.

BACKGROUND READING

Angell, Richard S. "Library of Congress Subject Headings—Review and Forecast." In Hans (Hanan) Wellisch and Thomas D. Wilson, eds., *Subject Retrieval in the Seventies.* Westport, Conn.: Greenwood, 1972. Pp. 143–163.

Austin, Derek, and Jeremy A. Digger. "PRECIS: The Preserved Context Index System." *Library Resources and Technical Services,* **21**:13–30, Winter 1977.

Chan, Lois Mai. *Library of Congress Subject Headings: Principles and Application.* Littleton, Colo.: Libraries Unlimited, 1978. Pp. 13–44, 146–155.

Dunkin, Paul S. "What Is It About? Subject Entry." *Cataloging USA.* Chicago: American Library Association, 1969. Pp. 65–95.

Foskett, A. C. "PRECIS." *The Subject Approach to Information.* 3d ed. Hamden, Conn.: Linnet Books; London: Clive Bingley, 1977. Pp. 224–244.

Needham, C. D. *Organizing Knowledge in Libraries: An Introduction to Information Retrieval.* 2d rev. ed. London: André Deutsch, 1971. Pp. 91–108, 177–198.

"Principles of the Sears List of Subject Headings." In Barbara M. Westby, ed., *Sears List of Subject Headings.* 11th ed. New York: The H.W. Wilson Company, 1977. Pp. xi–xxxiv.

FURTHER READING

Austin, Derek. "The Development of PRECIS, and Introduction to Its Syntax." In Hans H. Wellisch, ed., *The PRECIS Index System: Principles, Applications, and Prospects, Proceedings of the International PRECIS Workshop.* Sponsored by the College of Library and Information Services of the University of Maryland, October 15–17, 1976. New York: The H. W. Wilson Company, 1977. Pp. 3–28.

Austin, Derek. "The Semantics of PRECIS: Vocabulary Control and RIN System." In Hans H. Wellisch, ed., *The PRECIS Index System: Principles, Applications, and Prospects, Proceedings of the International PRECIS Workshop.* Sponsored by the College of Library and Information Services of the University of Maryland, October 15–17, 1976. New York: The H. W. Wilson Company, 1977. Pp. 29–53.

Cutter, Charles Ammi. *Rules for a Dictionary Catalog.* 4th ed. Washington, D.C.: Government Printing Office, 1904. (First published under the title *Rules for a Printed Dictionary Catalogue* in 1876.)

Daily, Jay E. "Subject Headings and the Theory of Classification." *American Documentation,* 7:269–274, October 1957.

Frarey, Carlyle J. "Subject Headings." *The State of the Library Art.* Vol. 1, part 2. New Brunswick, N. J.: Graduate School of Library Science, Rutgers State University, 1960.

Haykin, David Judson. *Subject Headings: A Practical Guide.* Washington, D.C.: Government Printing Office, 1951.

Lancaster, F. W. *Vocabulary Control for Information Retrieval.* Washington, D.C.: Information Resources Press, 1972.

Metcalfe, John. *Information Retrieval, British and American, 1876–1976.* Metuchen, N.J.: Scarecrow, 1976.

Pettee, Julia. *Subject Headings: The History and Theory of the Alphabetical Subject Approach to Books.* New York: The H. W. Wilson Company, 1947.

Shera, Jesse H., and Margaret Egan. *The Classified Catalog: Basic Principles and Practices.* Chicago: American Library Association, 1956.

CHAPTER 7
General Principles

INTRODUCTION

In addition to author and title entries, the catalog provides a topical approach through entries which represent the subject content of the works. These subject entries provide access to library materials of which only the subject is known. They also show what the library has on a given subject. In this sense, the subject entries serve the dual function of location and collocation.

The early library catalogs were primarily finding-lists providing author or catchword entries for each item and a symbol indicating its location in the collection. The catchword entry played an important role in the evolution of subject headings. The catchword was usually the leading word in the title, or the word most indicative of its content. In cases where the leading word in the title failed to express the subject content of the book, the proper word representing the subject was introduced as an added entry. This practice represented a step from the catchword entry to the true subject entry. Thus, by the middle of the nineteenth century, librarians had begun to be aware of the significance of the subject approach as well as the author approach to library material.[1]

ARRANGEMENT OF SUBJECT ENTRIES

Subject entries in a catalog may be arranged in various ways.

Classed or Classified Catalog

This is probably the earliest form of subject arrangement. The entries are organized systematically and logically according to their subject relationships, usually based on a particular classification scheme. The order of progression in a classed catalog is from the general to the specific. Using such a catalog usually requires an accompanying alphabetical subject index similar to the relative index to the Dewey Decimal Classification.

[1]Julia Pettee. *Subject Headings: The History and Theory of the Alphabetical Subject Approach to Books.* New York: The H. W. Wilson Company, 1947. P. 151.

This form of subject catalog as a public tool has been replaced by the dictionary or alphabetical catalog in American libraries. However, as a working tool, it still exists in the form of the shelflist which is arranged according to the classification system used by the library. The main difference between the shelflist and a classed catalog is that the shelflist contains only one entry for each document filed by the class number assigned to the document. The classed catalog, on the other hand, includes added entries for those documents which deal with more than one subject and can therefore be classed in more than one number or listed under more than one heading.

Alphabetico-Classed Catalog

This is a hybrid of the classified arrangement and the alphabetical arrangement. The entries for coordinate subjects are arranged alphabetically. Each subject is then subdivided hierarchically by the next order of comprehensiveness (i.e., the lower level in the hierarchical structure) and each subdivision may be further subdivided by a still lower order, as in the classified catalog. The difference between the classed catalog and the alphabetico-classed catalog lies in the arrangement of the coordinate subjects on each level of the hierarchy. In the alphabetico-classed catalog, the coordinate divisions are arranged alphabetically, rather than systematically.

Alphabetical Subject Catalog

In this type of catalog, the subject entries, in the form of the specific names of the subjects represented, are arranged in alphabetical order without regard to their subject relationships or hierarchical status. Subject collocation is sacrificed for quick and direct access. This form of catalog was a later development than the classed and the alphabetico-classed catalogs. It was introduced in the latter part of the nineteenth century and quickly and almost completely replaced the other forms in the libraries in the United States. Because it is the predominant form of subject catalog, the alphabetical subject catalog will be discussed in detail below.

In the catalogs in many libraries, the alphabetical subject entries are interfiled with the author and title entries to form a single alphabetical sequence. A catalog with this kind of arrangement is called a *dictionary catalog*. The term *divided catalog* refers to a catalog in which entries are divided to form more than one alphabetical sequence. There are several ways by which the entries may be divided, for example, with subject entries in one alphabetical sequence and author and title entries in another or with name entries in one alphabetical sequence and subject and title entries in another.

THE DICTIONARY CATALOG

The rules for subject headings in a dictionary catalog were set forth by Charles Ammi Cutter in his *Rules for a Dictionary Catalog*.[2] These are the first, and to date virtually the latest, rules concerning the formation of subject headings for a dictionary catalog. Later writers have attempted to clarify and amplify Cutter's rules, but very little, in terms of fundamental principles, has been added to Cutter's rules which still form the basis for subject cataloging in American libraries.

Before there was a standard list for subject headings, it was necessary for catalogers in individual libraries to form their own headings. As a result, books on the same subject did not always appear under the same subject heading from library to library. With the increase in interlibrary operations and the introduction of centralized cataloging through the distribution of Library of Congress printed cards, the advantages of having a standard list became apparent. Such a list would ensure consistency within the same library catalog as well as among catalogs of different libraries, and thereby facilitate interlibrary cooperation and library use for those readers who went from library to library.

In 1895, the first standard list for subject headings appeared. The *List of Subject Headings for Use in Dictionary Catalogs,* produced by an American Library Association committee of which Cutter was a prominent member, was based on Cutter's principles. It went through three editions (1895, 1898, 1911). In 1910–1914, when the Library of Congress began publishing its list entitled *Subject Headings Used in the Dictionary Catalogues of the Library of Congress,* it was found unnecessary to continue the ALA list.

Since the Library of Congress began distributing printed cards at the beginning of the twentieth century, the Library's practice has become de facto standard for cataloging in the United States. Its subject headings list has served as the standard tool for subject cataloging for libraries that use LC's cataloging services.

The principles of alphabetical subject entries are the basis for the LC list, which represents a record of headings used in the LC catalogs. The list is revised periodically and has gone through nine editions (1910–1914, 1919, 1928, 1943, 1948, 1957, 1966, 1975, 1980). In the eighth edition, the title was changed to *Library of Congress Subject Headings* (LCSH). Between editions, additions and changes are published in quarterly supplements cumulated annually. Beginning with the eighth edition, the list is also issued in microform which is reissued quarterly

---

[2]Charles Ammi Cutter. *Rules for a Dictionary Catalog.* 4th ed. Washington, D.C.: Government Printing Office, 1904. (First published in 1876.)

and incorporates the additions and changes. This virtually results in a new cumulative edition every three months.

The *Library of Congress Subject Headings* list reflects the practice of a large research collection and is not always suited for a medium-sized or small collection. The publication of the *List of Subject Headings for Small Libraries* compiled by Minnie Earl Sears in 1923 complemented the Library of Congress list. It was renamed *Sears List of Subject Headings* and has gone through eleven editions. The latest edition appeared in 1977. Together, the Library of Congress list and the Sears list have become the standard lists for subject headings in American libraries. The principles of alphabetical subject cataloging first propounded by Cutter are the basis for both lists. However, the Sears list is not an abridgment of the LC list; they vary in many respects.

Objectives of Subject Entries

Regarding the subject approach provided by the catalog, Cutter states two objectives: (1) to enable a person to find a book of which the subject is known, and (2) to show what the library has on a given subject.[3] As with the author and title entries in the catalog, the first objective of subject entries represents a function of locating individual items, and the second a function of collocating library materials which deal with the same subject. On the basis of these functions, Cutter set forth the basic principles of subject entry.

Basic Principles

The user and usage

For Cutter, the most important consideration in the cataloging of library materials is the best interest of the user.[4] He calls this principle "the convenience of the public." He feels that the catalogers should be concerned with "the public's habitual way of looking at things," that these habits should not be ignored, even if they demand a sacrifice of logic and simplicity. On this principle, the public's usage becomes an important factor in determining the terms and the forms of subject headings.

The major difficulty in this approach is how to define the *user* and *usage*. There is no such thing as a "typical library user." Users come into the library with different backgrounds and different purposes. There has not been any objective way of determining how the users approach

---

3Cutter. Op. cit. P. 12.
4Ibid. P. 6.

the catalog and for what purposes. As a result, subject headings have been formed on the basis of what the catalogers presume to be the needs and habits of users.

Uniform heading

In order to show what the library has on a given subject, the catalog must bring under one heading all the material dealing principally or exclusively with that particular subject. This is similar to the principle of uniform heading with regard to personal authors. If a subject has more than one name, one must be chosen as the heading with *see* references from the others. In general, it is hoped that the term chosen is unambiguous and the most familiar to the users of the catalog. If there are variant spellings of the same term, e.g., "marihuana" and "marijuana," only one is used as the heading.

Therefore, in the catalog, each subject is represented by one heading. Conversely, the same term should not be used for more than one subject. If the same term must be used in more than one sense, as is often the case when different disciplines or fields of knowledge are involved, some qualification or clarification must be added so that it will be clear to the user which meaning is intended.

The principle of uniform heading also applies in the case of different forms and different entry elements of the same heading, particularly in the case of headings containing more than one term. If **Air quality** has been chosen as the heading to represent the subject, other forms such as *Air—Quality* or *Quality of air* are not to be used. Instead, there will be *see* references from these forms. If **Agricultural chemistry** is the form chosen, then *Chemistry, Agricultural* is not used. If American history is listed under **United States—History,** it is not listed under *History—United States* as well. However, in a few cases, exceptions are made to this rule and duplicate entries are made for certain headings. For example, both **United States—Foreign relations—Japan** and **Japan—Foreign relations—United States** are used, although they are two forms of the same heading.

The main reason for the principle of uniform heading is economy. It reduces considerably the number of subject entries in the catalog. This is an important consideration, particularly in the case of a card or book catalog in which each additional heading assigned to a work represents a separate entry.

In recent years, there has been a gradual relaxation of the principle of uniform heading. The Library of Congress practice now allows many more duplicate entries than previously. In some cases, when updating terminology, both the previous, obsolete term and the new, up-to-date term are retained in the catalog. This is often done when there is a large file of entries under the old heading. The old and the new forms of the heading are then linked by *see also* references. The reason for this practice, called *split files*, is to minimize extensive recataloging. For example, the heading **Insurance, Social** was changed to **Social security**. However, the materials already cataloged under the old heading were left unchanged, so that library materials on the same subject were entered under two different headings. The *see also* references help the users to be aware of such a practice.

Terminology

Since subject headings are verbal representations of the subject content, language (or vocabulary) control becomes a major concern. Two problems, in particular, are of great importance: synonymous terms and changing usage.

Because of the principle of uniform heading which requires each subject to be represented by one heading, a choice is often necessary when the subject can be represented by more than one name or expressed in different terms. Ascorbic acid is also known as vitamin C. An underground railroad is more frequently called a *subway*, and in Britain is known as *the tube*. In representing these subjects in the catalog, it then becomes necessary to choose for each subject one term among several possibilities. In general, the guiding principle is common usage when it can be determined that one of the terms is in wider or more common use than the others. However, in many cases, when common usage is not distinct enough or allows more than one choice, then the choice becomes necessarily arbitrary. As a safeguard, *see* references are made from the synonymous terms.

In the matter of choosing between a popular term and a scientific one, the former is preferred in a general library serving a clientele from various subject fields. This policy is usually followed by standard lists of subject headings designed for general collections.

The problem of changing usage presents many practical difficulties. A term may have been chosen on the basis of common usage at the time the heading was established. However, because the English language is in a constant state of flux, the term chosen often becomes obsolete later on. For example, **Moving-pictures** is used in the Library of Congress list instead of the more current term *motion pictures.*

Obsolete spelling is another aspect of the problem of changing usage. For example, the heading **Aeroplanes** remained in the Library of Congress list until 1974, when it was changed to **Airplanes**. The problem becomes much more complicated when social attitudes are involved and the issue becomes an emotional one. For instance, headings containing the words **Negro** or **Negroes,** acceptable terms when the headings were established, have become objectionable and were finally changed to **Black(s)** and **Afro-American(s)**.[5]

Another problem is with newly established subjects, where well-established names are not yet in use. For example, when the computer first appeared, the heading chosen for it was **Electronic calculating machines;** this was later changed to **Computers.**

The theoretical and ideal way to solve these problems is to update the headings when the usage has changed or when a well-established name for the new subject becomes available. However, in practice it is not always economically feasible because of the cost involved in changing the existing entries in the catalog. The practice of split files mentioned above is one solution, even though it results in scattering library materials on the same subject.

Specific and direct entry

The principle of specific entry governs both the formation and application of subject headings in an alphabetical subject, or dictionary, catalog. In the formation of subject headings, the heading should be as specific as the topic it is intended to cover. Conversely, the heading should not be broader than the topic. In the application of subject headings in cataloging, the principle of specific entry requires that a work be entered under the *most specific* heading which represents its subject content. Ideally, the heading should be coextensive with (no broader or narrower than) the subject content of the work.

The rule for specific entry is set forth by Cutter in his *Rules for a Dictionary Catalog*:[6]

> Enter a work under its subject headings, not under the heading of a class which includes that subject. . . . Put Lady Cust's book on 'The Cat' under *Cat*, not under *Zoölogy* or *Mammals*, or *Domestic animals*; and put Garnier's 'Le fer' under *Iron*, not under *Metals* or *Metallurgy*.

Cutter claims that this rule is the main distinction between the dictionary catalog and the alphabetico-classed catalog. In an alphabetico-classed catalog, the subject **cats** would appear under a heading such as:

Zoology—Vertebrates—Mammals—Domestic animals—Cats

Actually, there is no difference in terms of specificity between this heading and the heading **Cats** used in an alphabetical subject catalog. The difference lies in the access point. In the alphabetico-classed catalog, the heading contains a series, or chain, of hierarchical terms beginning with, and therefore listed under, the broadest term and

---

[5]"Subject Heading 'Negroes'." *Cataloging Service*, **115**:25, Fall 1975.
[6]Cutter. Op. cit. P. 66.

leading to the most specific; while in the alphabetical subject catalog, the subject is listed directly under its own name. In other words, the major characteristic of the alphabetical subject catalog is that its entries are both *specific* and *direct*.

Cross references

Three types of cross references are used in the subject headings structure: the *see* reference, the *see also* reference, and the *general* reference.

See reference
Because the principle of uniform heading requires that only one name for each subject be used as the heading in the catalog, *see* references are provided which lead the user from synonymous terms to the heading that has been chosen, or from different forms of a heading to the one used (e.g., from a direct phrase to an inverted phrase heading), to make sure that users who happen to consult the catalog under different names of the subject or different forms of the name will be able to locate material on the subject. These references guide users *from* terms that are not used as entries *to* those that are.

See also reference
This type of reference serves two functions: it connects related headings and refers the user from the general to the specific headings. Unlike the *see* reference, a *see also* reference relates headings that are all used as entries in the catalog. The headings involved may overlap in meaning, but may never be synonymous. By connecting related headings, the *see also* reference calls the user's attention to material related to his or her interest. By referring from the general to the specific, the *see also* reference provides the dictionary catalog with some of the advantages of the classed catalog, in that the user is guided to specific branches or aspects of a subject.

General reference
A specific *see* or a *see also* reference directs the user from the term being consulted to another individual heading. A *general* reference, on the other hand, directs the user to a group or category of headings instead of individual members of the group or category. It is sometimes called a *blanket reference*. The advantage of using general references is economy of space. They obviate the need of making long lists of specific references.

METHODS OF SUBJECT ANALYSIS

Subject analysis of a particular work or document involves basically three steps.

Step 1

The first step is to examine the work and determine its subject content. While the most reliable and certain way is to read or examine the work in detail, it is not always economical to do so. Catalogers usually have to adopt alternative methods.

The title of the work often gives an indication of the subject content, e g., *An Introduction to Chemistry, Principles of Librarianship,* and *How to Determine Author & Title Entries According to AACR.* Nevertheless, it is not safe to analyze the content of a work by its title alone, because many titles are misleading. For example, *Tourist Attraction* is the title of a novel rather than a travel book. The cataloger should always make further investigation to confirm the subject. When the title is vague or ambiguous, there is no choice but to look beyond the title for the subject content of the work. A title such as *Do It Later* does not tell very much about the content, which may range from teenage marriage to the American space program.

Other features in the work provide excellent guides to the subject matter. These are abstract, table of contents, chapter headings, preface, introduction, book jacket, slipcase, or other accompanying descriptive material (particularly in the case of nonbook materials).

When these elements fail to provide a clear picture of what the work is about, external sources, such as bibliographies, catalogs, review media, and other reference sources, may prove to be helpful. Occasionally, subject specialists may have to be consulted, particularly when the subject matter is unfamiliar to the cataloger.

Step 2

After the subject of the work is understood by the cataloger, the next step is to identify the main subject or subjects or principal concepts, including different aspects of the subject such as author's point of view, time, and place. Frequently, a work may deal with several subjects separately. In many cases, a work treats two or more subjects in relation to each other. The interrelationships of subjects in a work are called *phase relations.* Some examples of phase relations follow:

> *Influence phase.* The influence of one thing, one concept, or one person on another is a very common approach in scholarly works.

Bias phase. Some works on a particular subject have a *bias* toward, or aim at, a specific group of readers or audience; for example, *Fundamentals of Physical Chemistry for Premedical Students.*

Tool phase or *application phase.* This relationship is common particularly among scientific and technical works; for example, *Chemical Calculations: An Introduction to the Use of Mathematics in Chemistry.*

Comparison phase. This relationship is common in literary and social science studies.

Step 3

The third step is to represent the subject and concept according to a particular system or scheme. The first two steps are the same in all subject analysis operations. The third step varies according to the ways of representing the subjects, i.e., by means of subject headings, indexing terms, or classification numbers.

HOW TO ASSIGN SUBJECT HEADINGS

After the subject content of the work being cataloged is determined and the principal concepts are identified, the subject headings list can be consulted. In many cases, the cataloger must adapt his or her own wording or phrasing of the subject to the terminology of the list. From the list, a subject heading is chosen which will best express the subject content of the work. In general, choose the most specific heading provided by the list to cover the content of the work.

Number of Headings Assigned

The ideal situation is one in which one heading will suffice to express the subject of the work being cataloged. However, in many cases the subject content of a particular work may not be totally expressed by a single heading, and more than one heading may be required for a particular work. While there is no theoretical or physical limit to the number of headings which may be assigned to a particular work, in practice a limit is often placed on the cataloger because of economy of entries. Again, the cataloger's magic number—three—is often used as a general guideline. A beginner in subject cataloging is advised to consider twice before assigning more than three headings to a work. More than three headings for a work may be an indication that the cataloger is not quite certain of the subject of the work; or that the cataloger has chosen headings which are too specific and that a broader heading may be more appropriate.

General versus Specific Headings

One general guideline for assigning subject headings is: do not assign both a *general* and a *specific* heading to the same body of material when the general heading encompasses the specific one. In other words, for a work about cats, assign the heading **Cats** alone instead of **Cats** *and* **Domestic animals, Animals,** or **Zoology.** Use the most specific heading which expresses the subject of the work.

In some cases, a specific heading may be assigned to a portion of the work, while a more general heading is assigned to the entire work. For example, if a large portion of a book on mathematics in general is devoted to algebra, both the general heading **Mathematics** and the specific heading **Algebra** may be assigned. The latter is essentially an analytical subject entry. This is often used when a portion, or portions, of a work has local interest and the cataloger wishes to bring it to the attention of the user.

Multitopical Works

For a multitopical work, more than one heading is usually required. For a work dealing with two or three distinctive subjects or concepts separately, assign two or three separate headings, unless the two or three subjects constitute the totality of a general subject. In the latter case, assign the heading for the general subject. For example, for a book about Chinese and Japanese literature, assign two separate headings. But for a book about Greek and Latin literature, assign the heading for classical literature. When a work deals with four or more subjects, all of which form parts of a larger subject, assign the heading for the larger subject, e.g., use the heading **South America—Description and travel** for a book about traveling in Argentina, Brazil, Chile, and Ecuador. If the subjects do not belong to a particular broad subject, assign separate headings when no more than four topics are treated in the work. If there are more than four topics involved, assign either several very general headings or a form heading only, e.g., **French essays.**

Multielement Works

For a multielement work—i.e., a work which treats a single central topic considered from different aspects or containing various elements (such as form, place, and time)—assign a heading which brings out these aspects or elements, if one is available. If such a heading is not available, a new heading may be established or several headings may be used to bring out the aspects and elements as appropriate. Whether all the concepts, aspects, and elements identified in the subject of a work should be represented in the catalog depends on the type of users for whom the catalog is intended. The main criterion is the potential value or usefulness of the headings for the users.

Standard Lists of Subject Headings

For subject cataloging, most libraries rely on standard lists of subject headings. In the United States, the most commonly used lists are the *Library of Congress Subject Headings, Subject Headings for Children's Literature,* and the *Sears List of Subject Headings.* Lists of subject headings have also been developed for special fields. The best known among these is *Medical Subject Headings.*

Outside of the United States, the newly developed PRECIS (Preserved Context Index System) is being used for subject indexing of books in the *British National Bibliography.* It has been adopted by a number of libraries and bibliographies in Great Britain, Europe, and Canada. Although it has not been adopted for use in the United States, the system is gaining attention.

Chapters 8, 9, and 10 discuss these standard lists and systems in detail.

CHAPTER 8

Library of Congress Subject Headings

INTRODUCTION

Library of Congress Subject Headings (*LCSH*), available in both print and microform, is a list of subject headings developed and used by the Library of Congress on its cataloging records. It is also used as a standard list by most of the large general libraries and some of the *now 12th* smaller libraries and special libraries. The list, now in the ninth edition (1980), was begun by the Library of Congress at the end of the nineteenth century and first published in 1909. The main list is supplemented by *Supplement to LC Subject Headings* issued quarterly and cumulated annually and sometimes biennially. There is also a micro-fiche edition of the list which cumulates the main list and the supplement every three months.

 Library of Congress Subject Headings is essentially a subject authority list. There is no code for subject cataloging comparable to AACR 2 for descriptive cataloging. David Judson Haykin's *Subject Headings: A Practical Guide* (1951) contains a discussion of the guiding principles of the Library of Congress subject headings system and a description of the Library's practice with regard to subject cataloging. However, the work has not been revised since 1951 and has become somewhat dated.

MAIN HEADINGS

Format

Main headings to be used on cataloging entries are printed in boldface type, e.g., **Art, Book jackets, Cowboys, Illustration of books,** etc. Those printed in lightface roman are not to be used as subject entries. They are synonymous terms or variant forms of regular headings and are followed by *see* references to the terms that are used as headings, e.g.,

> Fine arts
> See Art
>   Arts

Farming
See Agriculture

Book illustration
See Illustration of books

On a catalog card, the subject heading appears in red or in capital letters in order that it will not be confused with title entries consisting of the same term.

Forms

On the basis of their syntactical structure, the main headings may be divided into the following categories: (1) single-noun headings; (2) adjectival headings; (3) conjunctive-phrase headings; (4) prepositional-phrase headings.

1. Single noun headings

The simplest form of main heading consists of a noun or substantive, e.g., **Cabbage; Cats; Economics; Poetry; Locomotion; Cataloging; Aged; Poor.** When a noun represents more than one subject or concept, a modifier is added in parentheses to limit the heading to one subject or concept, e.g., **Chlorosis (Plants); Cold (Disease); Corruption (in politics).**

2. Adjectival headings

When a subject or concept cannot be properly expressed by a single noun, a phrase is used. The most common type of phrase headings consists of a noun or noun phrase with an adjectival modifier. The adjectival modifier can be in one of several forms: a common adjective, a proper adjective, a geographic name, a noun modifier, or a proper or common noun in the possessive case, e.g., **Agricultural credit; Juvenile automobile drivers; Abelian varieties; English literature; California Railroad Strike, 1894; Library science; Cowper's glands; Carpenter's square;** etc.

Inverted adjectival headings. In many cases, the adjectival phrase is inverted in order to bring the noun into a prominent position as the entry element, e.g., **Geography, Historical; Maps, Statistical;** and **Motor bus drivers, Physically handicapped.**

3. Conjunctive-phrase headings *(Compound)*

This type of heading consists of two or more nouns, noun phrases, or both, with or without modifiers, connected by the word *and* or ending with *etc.* This form serves three purposes: (a) to express a relationship between two things or concepts, e.g., **Literature and science; Church and social problems,** etc.; (b) to connect subjects or topics, sometimes opposite, which are often treated together in works, e.g., **Emigration and immigration, Open and closed shelves, Debtor and creditor, Skis and skiing,** and **Children's encyclopedias and dictionaries;**[1] and (c) to specify the meaning and scope of a noun by adding a second noun which serves to explain the first, more general noun, e.g., **Forces and couples, Bolts and nuts,** etc.[2]

4. Prepositional-phrase headings *(phrase heading)*

Another type of phrase heading consists of nouns, noun phrases, or both, with or without modifiers, connected by a preposition, e.g., **Breach of contract; Children in motion pictures; Federal aid to youth services.** These phrase headings usually serve the following purposes:

(1) to limit a concept, or make it more specific, when this cannot be done by using a single noun, e.g., **Costume in art; Electric discharges through gases.** In each case, the prepositional phrase (**in art** or **through gases**) renders the main concept (**Costume** or **Electric discharges**) more specific.

(2) to express a relationship between two objects or concepts, e.g., **Children as artists; Mites as carriers of disease.**

(3) to represent a concept commonly expressed by a phrase only, e.g., **Figures of speech; Fathers of the church.**[3]

(4) to express the role played by one subject in another, e.g., **Television in education; Love in literature;** etc.

(5) to bring out an aspect of a subject or concept, e.g., **Mysteries of the Rosary; Cataloging of art; Stability of airplanes.**

For reasons similar to those given for adjectival headings, phrase headings are sometimes inverted to bring the main concept forward. In general, a phrase heading is inverted when the first element in effect qualifies the second and the second element also appears in the catalog as an independent heading, e.g., **Knowledge, Sociology of.**

Some headings in LCSH combine the various forms and can be rather long and involved, for example, **Opening of the eyes of one blind at Bethsaida (Miracle); Harp and percussion with string orchestra.**

---

[1] The Library of Congress recently decided not to use this form in newly established headings. Now each element is to be represented by a separate heading, or, when the coordinate elements overlap to a large extent, one of the elements is chosen as the heading with a *see* reference from each of the other elements.

[2] David Judson Haykin. *Subject Headings: A Practical Guide.* Washington, D.C.: Government Printing Office, 1951, P. 24.

[3] Ibid. P. 22.

Scope Notes

Scope notes follow immediately the headings with which they are used. They are provided for the purpose of specifying the range of subject matter to which a heading is applied in the LC catalogs and draw necessary distinctions between related headings or state which of several meanings of a term is the one to which its use in the LC catalogs is limited, e.g.,

Assessment.
Here are entered works on tax assessment. Works on the technique of property valuation for other than taxation purposes are entered under specific headings with subdivision Valuation, *e.g.*, Real property—Valuation.

Charities.
Here are entered works on privately supported welfare activities. Works on tax-supported activities are entered under Public welfare. Treatises on the methods employed in welfare work, public or private, are entered under Social service.

Irreligion.
Here are entered works dealing with a condition of complete absence of religion.

CROSS REFERENCES

Cross references are provided in the catalog as a device to connect headings. The *see* references direct the users from terms that are not used as headings to those that are. The *see also* references have two functions: to direct the users from general to specific headings and to connect headings which are related in a way other than hierarchically. The symbol *sa* means that a *see also* reference is to be made from the heading above it to the term or terms following the symbol. For example, an entry in LCSH would be:

Squirrels
   sa Abert squirrel
      Fox squirrel
      Gray squirrel

The reference would be as shown in Figure 8-1. In a card catalog the headings on cross reference cards, like the subject headings on catalog entries, appear either in red or in capital letters to differentiate them from title entries consisting of the same words.

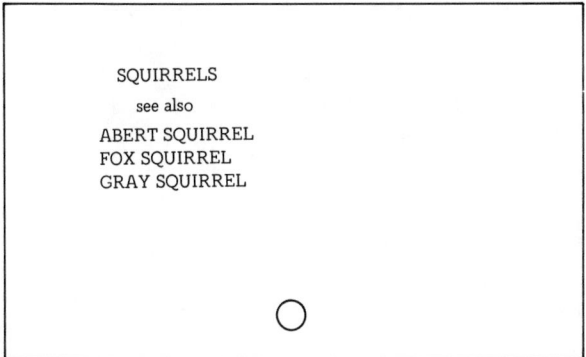

FIGURE 8-1   *See also* reference.

The symbol *x* indicates that a *see* reference is to be made from each of the terms following it to the heading listed above it. For example, an entry in LCSH would be:

Squirrels
   x Tree squirrels

The reference would be as shown in Figure 8-2.

The symbol *xx* means that a *see also* reference is to be made *from* each of the terms following the symbol *to* the heading listed above it. For example, an entry in LCSH would be:

Squirrels
   xx Rodentia

The reference would be as shown in Figure 8-3.

FIGURE 8-2   *See* reference.

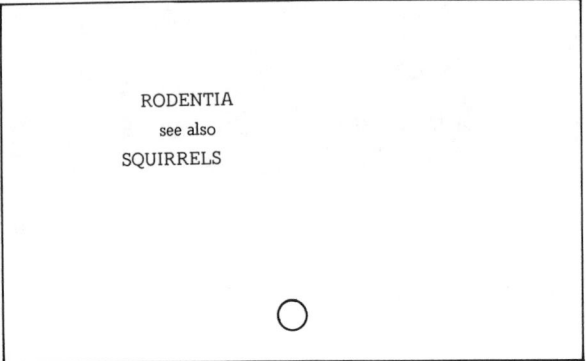

FIGURE 8-3 *See also* reference.

In explanation, the cross references mean that "Tree squirrels" is a synonymous term not used as a heading to the subject heading **Squirrels,** that **Abert squirrel, Fox squirrel,** and **Gray squirrel**—all valid headings—represent more specific kinds of the subject **Squirrels,** and that, on the other hand, the heading **Rodentia** is treated as a broader term than **Squirrels.** Since *see also* references are made from the general to the specific, and *not* vice versa, there are no references from **Squirrels** to **Rodentia,** or from **Abert squirrel,** etc., to **Squirrels.**

See also references between terms related in a sense other than hierarchical are made in both directions, e.g.,

> **God**
> *sa* Theism
> *xx* Theism

Instructions for making a cross reference are provided under both terms involved, e.g.,

> **Squirrels**   [same as] Tree squirrels
> *x* Tree Squirrels   =   *See* Squirrels
>
> **Squirrels**   **Rodentia**
> *xx* Rodentia   =   *sa* Squirrels

In addition to the *see* and *see also* references, there are also general or blanket references which refer from one heading to a group of headings or to subdivisions used under other headings, e.g.,

> **Courts of last resort**
> *sa* Appellate courts
> *names of individual supreme courts, e.g.,*
> United States. Supreme Court

Cranberries
—Diseases and pests
sa names of pests, e.g., Cranberry root-worm

Atlases
sa subdivision Atlases *under subjects, e.g.,* Anatomy,
Human—Atlases; Obstetrics—Atlases; Worms,
Intestinal and parasitic—Atlases; and *subdivision* Maps
under names of countries, cities, etc., e.g., Germany—Maps;
New York (N.Y.)—Maps

SUBDIVISIONS

Main headings may be subdivided by one or more of four kinds of
subdivisions: form, topical, period, and geographic. Some of the form
and topical subdivisions are of general application and are known as
free-floating subdivisions. Although, in appearance, a heading with
subdivisions resembles an entry in an alphabetico-classed catalog, the
subdivisions used with main headings in LCSH, with few exceptions,
represent a form or aspect of the main subject, instead of a subordinate
class of the main subject.

In LCSH, under a main heading, period subdivisions (arranged
chronologically) appear first, followed by form and topical subdivisions (arranged alphabetically), and then by geographic subdivisions (also arranged alphabetically).

In many cases, a main heading may be subdivided by several
subdivisions, thus resulting in a string of elements, e.g., **United
States—History—Civil War, 1861-1865—Juvenile participants—
Juvenile literature**

Form Subdivisions

Form subdivision has been defined as an extension of a subject heading
based on the form or arrangement of the subject matter in the work.
While the main heading normally expresses what the work is about,
the form subdivision represents what it is, i.e., what form the
treatment of the subject takes.[4] A group of works may deal with the
same subject but are represented in different forms, e.g.,

> **Engineering—Addresses, essays, lectures**
> **—Bibliography**
> **—Dictionaries**

[4]Ibid. P. 27.

—**Examinations, questions, etc.**
—**Indexes**
—**Manuscripts**
—**Periodicals**
—**Yearbooks**

Certain subdivisions which have traditionally been regarded as form subdivisions actually represent a particular approach to the subject rather than the bibliographic form of the work, e.g.,

Engineering—Congresses
—**History**
—**Juvenile literature**
—**Study and teaching**

Topical Subdivisions

A subject, or topical, subdivision which constitutes a species or a kind of the subject represented by the main heading, e.g., Biology—Botany, is characteristic of the alphabetico-classed catalog and is against the principle of specific entry. In general, LCSH avoids this type of subject subdivision, although there are a small number of exceptions, e.g., **Wages—Minimum wage.**

On the other hand, many headings with topical subdivisions resemble alphabetico-classed headings in their outward form only. For example, in the heading **Social psychology—Research** or **Agriculture— Accounting,** the subdivisions are not constituent parts or kinds of the subjects represented by the main headings. In other words, the resultant headings do not represent the genus-species or class-inclusion relationships. The heading **Agriculture—Accounting** means accounting as applied to agricultural purposes and does not mean accounting as a division of the subject agriculture. This type of topical subdivision is used extensively in LCSH, e.g.,

Advertising—Libraries
Libraries—Automation

Free-Floating Form and Topical Subdivisions

In order to ensure consistency and better control of subject headings, the subdivisions and main headings are not combined randomly or at will by each cataloger at the Library of Congress. With the exceptions discussed below, each new combination of a subdivision with a main heading must be approved by an editorial committee of the Subject Cataloging Division before its use becomes authorized.

An exception to the rule stated above is a group of common subdivisions called *free-floating subdivisions*. The term refers to those commonly-used form or topical subject subdivisions which subject catalogers at the Library of Congress are authorized to use at will, where applicable and appropriate, under a particular subject or author heading for the first time without establishing the new usage editorially. Consequently, these subdivisions will appear on LC entries without the usage appearing in the printed list.

The introduction to the eighth edition of *Library of Congress Subject Headings* includes a section entitled "Most Commonly Used Subdivisions."[5] All the subdivisions listed in this section, with the exceptions noted below, are free-floating, subject to the limitations stated in the explanatory notes under each subdivision.

The following subdivisions are *not* free-floating:

- **—Art collections**
- **—Biography** (under names of disciplines)
- **—Coin collections**
- **—Ethnological collections**
- **—Interviews** (under names of disciplines)
- **—Law and legislation**
- **—Library**
- **—Photograph collections**
- **—Private collections**

Free-floating subdivisions under geographical headings

The introduction to the eighth edition of LCSH includes a section entitled "Subdivisions Under Place Names" which lists free-floating subdivisions used under two categories of headings: (1) regions, countries, states, etc., (2) cities.

Headings serving as patterns for sets of subdivisions

Certain form or topical subdivisions are common in a particular subject field or applicable to headings in a particular category. Instead of repeating them under each subject or heading within the category, they are listed under a chosen heading in the category. This chosen heading then serves as a pattern or model heading of subdivisions for headings in that category. In other words, subdivisions listed under a heading that serves as a pattern may be transferred and used with another heading in the same category even though the combination

[5]This section was inadvertently omitted from the ninth edition of LCSH.

does not appear in LCSH. For example, under **English language,** the model heading for languages, the subdivision —**Pronoun** is listed. Therefore, the combination **Chinese language—Pronoun** may be used, even though it is not printed in the list as such. In effect, the form and topical subdivisions under a model heading are free-floating among the headings in that category.

Table 8-1 is a list of model headings in LCSH.

TABLE 8-1   Model Headings in LCSH

(a) Free-floating subdivisions under personal names

Categories	Model Headings
Founders of religion	Jesus Christ
Philosophers	Thomas Aquinas, Saint
Statesmen, politicians	Lincoln, Abraham (preferred)
	Napoleon
	Washington, George
Musicians	Wagner, Richard
Literary authors	Shakespeare, William

*(b) Free-floating subdivisions controlled by model headings**

Subject Field	Category	Model Headings
Philosophy and religion	Monastic and religious orders	Jesuits
	Religions	Buddhism
	Christian denominations	Catholic Church; Baptists
	Sacred works (including parts)	Bible
	Special theological topics	Salvation
The Arts	Groups of authors	Authors, English; Poets, English; Dramatists, English; etc.
	Philology	English philology
	Languages	English language
	Literatures (including particular genres)	English literature; English poetry; Short stories, English; English periodicals; etc.
	Newspapers of particular countries, e.g., Canadian newspapers	Newspapers

TABLE 8-1 (Continued)

(b) Free-floating subdivisions controlled by model headings (Continued)

Subject Field	Category	Model Headings
History and geography	Legislative bodies (including individual chambers)	United States. Congress
	Military services (including armies, navies, marines, etc.)	United States. Army; United States. Navy; United States— Armed Forces
	Wars	World War, 1939-1945; United States— History—Civil War, 1861-1865
	Indians (including specific tribes)	Indians of North America
Education	Types of institutions	Universities and colleges
	Universities	Harvard University
Social sciences	Industries	Retail trade: Construction industry†
Science and technology	Land vehicles	Automobiles
	Materials	Concrete; Metals
	Chemicals	Copper
	Organs and regions of the body	Heart; Foot
	Diseases	Cancer; Tuberculosis
	Plants and crops	Corn
	Animals	Fishes
	Livestock	Cattle

*Consult the ninth edition of *Library of Congress Subject Headings* and its supplements for complete lists of subdivisions under the model headings.
†Preferred model.

Period Subdivisions

Period, or chronological, or time subdivisions are used with headings for the history of a place or subject. Certain subject areas—such as history, politics, and government of individual countries; music; art; and national literatures—lend themselves particularly to historical or chronological treatment. Period subdivisions are also used in other subject areas, such as science and technology, although to a lesser extent.

Period subdivisions are listed individually under the appropriate headings in *Library of Congress Subject Headings*. They are not free-floating, with the exception of the following:

—History—16th century
—History—17th century
—History—18th century
—History—19th century
—History—20th century

These subdivisions may be used under topical headings to which the free-floating subdivision —**History** can be assigned appropriately. However, they are not used with headings which begin with the name of a region, country, etc., for example, "America—History—19th century," because period subdivisions under names of places are enumerated in the list.

Period subdivisions in LCSH appear in various forms. Examples are given below.

The name of a monarch, an historical period or an event followed by dates:

Great Britain—History—Modern period, 1845-
English literature—Middle English, 1100-1500
United States—History—Civil War, 1861-1865
France—History—Louis XIII, 1610-1643

The preposition "to" followed by a date:

Great Britain—History—To 1485

Dates alone:

English language—Grammar—1500-1800
English language—Grammar—1950-
Great Britain—Description and travel—1801-1900
Greece, Modern—History—1453-1821

The name of the century:

English fiction—19th century
United States—History—20th century

An inverted "noun, adjective" heading:

Sculpture, Ancient
Sculpture, Baroque
Sculpture, Medieval
Sculpture, Renaissance
Sculpture, Rococo
Sculpture, Romanesque

The modifiers in these headings in fact denote both period and subject characteristics. They are generally not considered to be true period subdivisions and therefore are interfiled alphabetically with other subdivisions that have no period connotation.

The phrase "early works to" followed by a date:

Mathematics—Early works to 1800.

Period subdivision of this type refers to the date of publication of the work and is usually used with headings in science and technology.

Frequently, both a broad period subdivision and period subdivisions covering events or lesser epochs falling within the broad period are listed under the same main heading. However, they are not usually used together for the same work; the heading closest to the period treated is the one chosen.

> **Great Britain—History—Norman period, 1066-1154**
> **—History—Medieval period, 1066-1485**
> **—History—1066-1687**
> **—History—Angevin period, 1154-1216**
> **—History—Plantagenets, 1154-1399**
> **—History—13th century**
> **—History—14th century**
> **—History—Wars of the Roses, 1455-1485**

The heading **Great Britain—History—Norman period, 1066-1154** is assigned to a work such as *The Reign of William Rufus and the Accession of Henry the First*, while the heading **Great Britain—History—1066-1687** is used with a work covering the history of England from 1200 to 1640.

Exercise A

Assign Library of Congress subject headings to the following topics:

1. The rhythm and intonation of spoken English.
2. Mining and metallurgy: a technical study.
3. Speech and hearing disorders in children.
4. The Bible doctrine of salvation.
5. The management of savings banks.
6. An English-Swedish, Swedish-English dictionary.
7. Anglo-Saxon magic and medicine.
8. Young people and parents: the generation gap.
9. A historical study of the doctrine of the Trinity.
10. ABC: a child's first book.
11. Anglo-American cataloging rules.
12. Twenty-three days with the Viet Cong: a personal narrative concerning the Vietnamese war.

13. Cavalry uniforms of Britain in color.
14. The principal voyages and discoveries of the English nation to 1600.
15. Public attitudes toward life insurance.

Geographic Subdivisions

Many headings for subjects which lend themselves to geographical treatment are subdivided by the name of a country or other political entity, a region, or a geographic feature. These headings are indicated by the designation (*Indirect*) immediately after the heading.

Previously, the designation (*Direct*) meant that in geographic subdivision by the name of a local place, the name of the local place follows the heading or another subdivision immediately without the interposition of the name of a larger geographic entity (e.g., **Education, Elementary—Lexington, Mass.**). The designation (*Indirect*) required that the name of a larger geographic entity be interposed (e.g., **Music—Austria—Vienna**). This distinction has been removed and headings which may be subdivided geographically are now coded (*Indirect*).

Instruction

Instruction for geographic subdivision follows:[6]

1. When a heading is designated (*Indirect*), subdivide locally by interposing the name of the country between the topical heading and the name of any entity falling wholly within that country's territorial limits, including subordinate political jurisdictions (e.g., provinces, counties, cities), historic kingdoms, geographic features and regions, and islands, as shown:

> **Agriculture—France—Rhône Valley**
> **Music—Switzerland—Zurich**

2. When subdividing locally, always use the latest name of any entity whose name has changed during the course of its existence, regardless of the form of the name used in the work cataloged, e.g.:

> Title: The Banks of Leopoldville, Belgian Congo.
> 1950.
> 1. **Banks and banking—Zaire—Kinshasa.**[7]

---

[6]The instruction given here appeared in *Cataloging Service*, **120**: 10–11, Winter 1977. It replaces the instruction given in the introduction to the 8th edition of LCSH.
[7]Provide a cross reference from Leopoldville, Belgian Congo, to **Kinshasa, Zaire.**

3. Subdivide locally only in accordance with the present territorial sovereignties of existing nations, regardless of the past territorial divisions described in the work cataloged. For a region or jurisdiction which existed in the past under various sovereignties, always interpose the name of the country now in possession, as long as the region or jurisdiction is located wholly within that country, e.g.:

> Title: The Present Status of Education in
> Alsace. 1910.
> 1. **Education—France—Alsace.**

4. Exceptions.

a. Assign directly first order political subdivisions of the following countries:

Country	*Divisions*
Canada	Provinces
Great Britain	Constituent countries
Soviet Union	Republics
United States	States

Subdivide these entities further, if required, by names of counties, cities, or other subordinate units, e.g.:

Music—Quebec (Province)—Quebec
Sports—England—London metropolitan area
Nursing—Ukraine—Kiev (Province)
Education—California—San Joaquin Valley

b. Assign directly the name of any jurisdiction or region which does not lie wholly within a single existing country or first order political subdivision of the four countries of (a.) above. Such jurisdictions or regions may include: the names of the four countries of (a.) above; historic kingdoms, empires, etc.; geographic features and regions, such as continents and other major regions, bodies of water, mountain ranges, etc., for example, **Europe; Siberia; Great Lakes; Mexico, Gulf of; Rocky Mountains; Nile Valley.**

c. Assign directly names of islands or groups of islands which are situated some distance from land masses, even if they do not represent autonomous political rules, e.g., **Geology—Bermuda Islands.**

Assign indirectly islands which lie close to a large land mass (usually within the territorial limits of a country) and are politically a subdivision of the country, etc., for example, **Agriculture—Italy—Sicily.**

Assign indirectly an individual island within an island group situated some distance from a land mass, even if the group is not an independent nation, e.g., **Water supply—Canary Islands—Teneriffe.**

d. Assign directly the names of the following cities: Berlin, Jerusalem, New York, and Washington, D.C.

5. When subdividing locally, if the geographic qualifier of the subordinate entity is identical to the name of the country or the name of the first-order political subdivision of the countries in 4a. above, omit the geographical qualifier to avoid redundancy, e.g.:

> **Sill River** (*Austria*)

but

> **Stream measurements—Austria—Sill River**

> **Amazonas** (*Brazil : State*)

but

> **Transportation—Brazil—Amazonas** (*State*)

Do not delete the qualifier when the qualifier and the country subdivision are not identical, e.g.:

> **Stone age—Yugoslavia—Porodin** (*Macedonia*)

Order of precedence of local subdivisions

When the geographic subdivision and other subdivision(s) are applied to the same heading, the order of subdivisions varies as follows:

1. When the designation (*Indirect*) in LCSH follows the main heading but not the topical, period, or form subdivision, the geographic subdivision is interposed between the main heading and the other subdivision, e.g.,

> **Farm buildings—Kentucky—Fayette County—Fires and fire prevention**

> **Geology—Russia—Ural Mountains—Addresses, essays, lectures**

> **Art—Italy—Naples—Galleries and museums**

2. When the designation (*Indirect*) in LCSH follows the topical, period, or form subdivision, the geographic subdivision follows the other subdivision, e.g.,

> **Farm buildings—Contracts and specification—Kentucky—Fayette County**
> **Art—Study and teaching—Italy—Naples**
> **Art, Modern—20th century—Italy**

CATEGORIES OF HEADINGS OMITTED

Many headings used in the LC catalogs do not appear in LCSH, particularly headings which represent proper names. It is not feasible to include all the names of persons, corporate bodies, or places which can possibly become subjects of books. Therefore, only a few proper names are included in LCSH as examples. A list of the principal categories of headings omitted appears in the introduction to LCSH.

In forming individual headings that fall within these categories, there are certain general guidelines or patterns which one may follow.

Personal Names

In order to group together in the catalog works written by and about the same person, the same form of personal heading used as main or added entry is used as subject entry. In other words, personal headings serving as subject entries are established according to the *Anglo-American Cataloguing Rules.*

The personal headings may be subdivided by following the model headings discussed on pages 145–146.

Subdivisions found under the model headings may be used with any personal heading falling within that category, e.g.,

> **Kant, Immanuel, 1724-1804—Ontology**
> **Milton, John, 1608-1674—Political and social views**
> **Carter, Jimmy, 1924-   —Inauguration**

Family names are often used as subject headings. Examples are given under the headings **Genealogy** and **Family histories,** e.g.,

> **Lincoln family**
> **Bakewell family**
> **Kennedy family**

Names of gods, goddesses, and legendary characters are also used as subject headings, e.g.,

> **Robin Hood**
> **Arthur, King**
> **Baal (Deity)**

Until recently, names of gods and goddesses of classical mythology were established in the Latin form only. Current practice is to establish the names of Roman or Greek gods as required by the work being cataloged. In other words, the Greek and Roman names of the same god or goddess may exist simultaneously with *see also* references connecting them, e.g.,

> Aphrodite
> Venus (Goddess)
>
> Jupiter
> Zeus

Corporate Names

Names of corporate bodies are used as subject headings for works that describe their origin and development and analyze and discuss their organization and function. The form of the corporate heading should conform to that used as main or added entry in the catalog. The most common types of corporate bodies are associations and firms, governments and their agencies, institutions, committees and commissions, e.g.,

> American Library Association
> Akademiia Nauk SSSR. Institut Vostokovedeniia
> United States. Food and Drug Administration
> Germany. Luftwaffe
> Johns Hopkins University
> Joint Commission on Rural Reconstruction in China (U.S.
>   and China)

The more common types of corporate bodies can be subdivided according to the models listed below:

> Catholic Church (as model for Christian denominations)
> United States. Congress (for legislative bodies)
> United States. Army (for armies)
> United States. Navy (for navies)
> Harvard University (for higher educational institutions)

Geographic Names

Names of places and geographic features serve both as main headings and as subdivisions. For a given place, the form of the geographic name should be the same when used in either position. Geographic headings that serve also as main or added entries in descriptive cataloging are established according to the Anglo-American Cataloguing Rules. In addition, names of natural geographic features which are not used as main or added entries are required as subject headings. In general, the Library of Congress conforms to the names established by the Board on Geographic Names.

Geographic qualifiers

The term *geographic qualifier* refers to the addition of a larger geographic entity (normally the name of the country) to a place name.[7] The rules governing geographic names in descriptive cataloging are applicable to those used in subject cataloging.

The name of a natural feature generally does not require a geographic qualifier unless it is wholly contained within one jurisdiction, e.g.,

> **Ohio Valley**
> **Amazon River**
> **San Juan River** (*Nicaragua*)

Political and other qualifiers

When the same name is used for different jurisdictions in the same country or state, a political or ecclesiastical qualifier (in parentheses) follows the name, e.g.,

> **New York** (*Archdiocese*)
> **New York** (*Colony*)
> **New York** (*State*)

Generic qualifiers

The names of many natural features contain a generic term, e.g., **Mississippi River; Black Sea.** If the name does not contain such a term and it is needed to distinguish between headings with the same name, a generic qualifier is added in parentheses, e.g.,

> **Golden Gate** (*Strait*)

Entry element

When a geographic name consists of more than one word, it is entered in the direct order, with the following exceptions:

1. For names of natural geographic features consisting of a specific and a generic term, the inverted form is used when the generic term precedes the specific term, e.g.,

---

[7]If the place is in Canada, Great Britain, Malaysia, the Soviet Union, the United States, or Yugoslavia, the name of the appropriate first-order political subdivision (i.e., state, province, constituent country, etc.) is used as the geographic qualifier, e.g., **Athens** (*Ga.*); **Tyasmin River** (*Ukraine*).

Smoky Mountains
Ohio River

but

Michigan, Lake
Mexico, Gulf of
Kennedy, Cape

2. When the geographic heading consists of a geographic name preceded by a directional adjective which is not an integral part of the proper name, the inverted form is often used, e.g.,

Asia, Southeastern
California, Southern
Tennessee, East

but

South America
South Dakota
East Anglia

Exercise B

1. Apply the following place names as subdivisions to the main headings **Markets** and **Music:**

Athens, Georgia
Athens, Greece
Bavaria, Germany
Brittany, France
Cambridge, England
Cambridge, Massachusetts
Munich, Bavaria, Germany
Nashville, Tennessee
New York City
New York State
Ottawa, Ontario
Rio de Janeiro, Brazil (the city)
Rio de Janeiro, Brazil (the state)
Tennessee
The Mississippi Valley

2. Assign Library of Congress subject headings to the following topics or titles:

a. New Zealand historic buildings.

b. Joint farming in India: an experiment in cooperation.
c. Norman illumination of manuscripts at Mont St. Michel, 966–1100.
d. Street maps of northern Virginia.
e. The genesis of the Alleger family of Ulster County, New York.
f. Life in a Japanese Zen Buddhist monastery.
g. The federal income tax reform act of 1969.
h. American social welfare institutions.
i. The Princes of Wales.
j. Wootton: the anatomy of an Oxfordshire village, 1945–1968.
k. The German community in Cincinnati.
l. Freedom of the press in Yugoslavia.
m. Battle of Wake Island, fought in 1941.
n. The animated cartoon film in Belgium.
o. College curriculum in the United States.
p. A pictorial guide to San Francisco.
q. Cornerstone for nursing education: a history of the Division of Nursing Education of Teachers College, Columbia University.
r. Social services to children in New York City: a general survey.
s. The search for King Arthur.
t. Catalogue of Great Britain railway letter stamps, 1957–1970.

SUBJECT HEADINGS FOR LITERARY WORKS
Works about Literature in General

Assign appropriate headings regarding the approach, type, or form of literature treated in the work, e.g.,

> **Literature—Study and teaching**
> **Literature—History and criticism**
> **Criticism**
> (for a work about literary criticism, e.g., Sutton, *Plato to Alexander Pope: Backgrounds of Modern Criticism;* not used with a work of criticism)
> **Drama—20th century—History and criticism**
> **Poetry, Modern—20th century—Congresses**
> **American poetry—Bibliography**

For works discussing the relationship between literature and other subjects, use headings such as **Literature and history; Literature and science; Art and literature; Religion and literature;** etc.

For discussions about particular themes in literature use **(subject or theme) in literature** in addition to the appropriate literature heading, e.g.,

> **Politics in literature** (For a study of political themes in
> twentieth-century American fiction, assign this heading
> in addition to **American fiction—20th century—History
> and criticism.**)
> **Art in literature**
> **Catholics in literature**

For discussions about particular individuals as themes or characters in literature, fiction, drama, poetry, etc., assign also the heading [**name of person** in the form of author entry] **in fiction, drama, poetry, etc.,** e.g.,

> **Shakespeare, William, 1564-1616, in fiction, drama, poetry, etc.**

> **Nixon, Richard M. (Richard Milhous) 1913-** in **fiction, drama, poetry, etc.**

The following types of headings are used for collective biographies of literary authors:

> **Authors, American**
> **Novelists**
> **Poets, Russian**

Anthologies and Collections of Literary Works by More than One Author

A literary form heading is assigned in addition to any other appropriate topical headings.

> **Literature, Modern—20th century**
> (for an anthology or collection of twentieth-century
> literature not limited to a language, nationality or form;
> note that the subdivision —**Collected works** or —
> **Collections,** is not used)

> **American drama—20th century**

In this case, the literature heading represents the form rather than the subject content of the work. This is called a *form heading*. Note that the subdivision —**Collections** is no longer used by the Library of Congress. Distinguish between a collection of and a discussion of literature by adding to the latter the subdivision —**History and criticism.**

If the collection is organized around a particular theme, an additional subject heading with an appropriate literary form subdivision is also assigned, e.g.,

An Anthology of Christmas Poetry [U.S.]
   1. **American poetry.**
   2. **Christmas—Poetry.**

Bugle-Echoes: A Collection of Poems of the Civil War
   1. **American poetry—19th century.**
   2. **United States—History—Civil War, 1861-1865—Poetry.**

The Praise of Lincoln: An Anthology of Poems
   1. **American poetry—19th century.**
   2. **Lincoln, Abraham, 1809-1865—Poetry.**

Works Written by Individual Authors

Literary form headings are *not* assigned to individual works. In other words, do not assign the heading **American fiction—20th century** to Hemingway's *Farewell to Arms* or the heading **English poetry—19th century** to Tennyson's *In Memoriam*. In the case of collected works by one author, assign the literary form heading only when the form is highly specific, e.g., **Allegories; Fables; Fairy tales; Radio stories; Amateur theatricals; Carnival plays; Children's plays; College and school drama; Didactic drama; Radio plays.**

If a literary work in the form of a drama or poetry features a specific theme or is based on the life of a real person (except literary authors), a topical heading in the form of the topic or the personal name with the subdivision —**Drama** or —**Poetry** is used, e.g.,

   Becket, by Jean Anouilh
      1. **Thomas à Becket, Saint, Archbishop of Canterbury, 1118?-1170—Drama**

Note that the subdivisions (—**Drama,** —**Poetry**) used are different from the form (**[name] in fiction, drama, poetry, etc.**) used for a *discussion* of (i.e., a work about) the person as a character in literature (see discussion on page 158).

   For a *collection* of novels or stories by an individual author, the form subdivision —**Fiction** is assigned under any identifiable topic, e.g.,

   Automobile racing—Fiction

For an individual novel or story, a topical heading with the subdivision —**Fiction** is assigned only if the work is biographical fiction, historical fiction, or animal stories, e.g.,

   Stone, Irving. *Those Who Love: A Biographical Novel of Abigail and John Adams.*

    1. **Adams, John, 1735-1826—Fiction.**
    2. **Adams, Abigail Smith, 1744-1818—Fiction.**

Mitchell, M. *Gone with the Wind*
    1. **United States—History—Civil War, 1861-1865—**
    Fiction.

In other words, the heading **Slavery in the United States—Fiction** is assigned to a collection of novels or stories, but not to an individual novel such as *Uncle Tom's Cabin*.

For a literary work based on the life of a literary author, the form **[author's name] in fiction, drama, poetry, etc.**, is used, e.g.,

    Courtney, W. L. *Kit Marlowe* (a one-act play)
    1. **Marlowe, Christopher, 1564-1593, in fiction, drama, poetry, etc.**[8]

Works about Individual Authors: Biography and Criticism

Follow the pattern of subdivisions under **Shakespeare** for other literary authors. The heading consists of the name of the author in the same form as used for author entry with or without a subdivision, e.g.,

Pound, Ezra, 1885-1972
Greene, Robert, 1558?-1592—Bibliography
Wordsworth, William, 1770-1850—Political and social views

The subdivision **—Biography** is used only when the work in hand is a true biography of the author.[9] If the work contains both biographical information and criticism of the author's works, assign only his or her name without subdivision. Critical works without biographical information are assigned the personal heading with the subdivision **—Criticism and interpretation** or another more specific subdivision designating criticism, e.g.,

Brontë, Charlotte, 1816-1855—Biography
(for a true biography)
Camus, Albert, 1913-1960
(for a work containing both biographical and critical material)

---

[8]Note that *Marlowe, Christopher, 1564-1593—Drama* is not used as a heading because it may be interpreted to mean a work about Marlowe's drama.

[9]In this case, a second heading representing the class of persons to which the author belongs is also assigned, e.g., **Novelists, English—19th century—Biography.**

Rossetti, Dante Gabriel, 1828-1882—Criticism and
interpretation
(for a work such as *The Dark Glass: Visions and Technique in
the Poetry of Dante Gabriel Rossetti*)

Works about Individual Works

For a work which contains criticisms or commentaries on another
work, a subject heading is assigned in the form of the uniform heading
for the work commented on. If the work commented on is of known
authorship, a [**name. title**] subject entry is used, e.g.,

Brontë, Emily, 1818-1848. Wuthering Heights
(for a work such as *The Inner Structure of Wuthering Heights* by
Elisabeth Th. M. van de Laar)

Note that for a foreign work, the uniform heading consists of the
author's name and the title in the original language regardless of the
language in which the criticism is written, e.g.,

Camus, Albert, 1913-1960. L'Étranger
Mann, Thomas, 1875-1955. Der Zauberberg
(for a work such as R. D. Miller's *The Two Faces of Hermes: A
Study of Thomas Mann's Novel, "The Magic Mountain"*)

For a work entered under its title, the subject entry consists of the
title alone, e.g.,

Atlantic monthly

For an anonymous classic or a sacred work, the subject entry is in
the form of the uniform title used as the main entry, e.g.,

Arabian nights
Beowulf
Chanson de Roland

SUBJECT HEADINGS FOR BIOGRAPHY
Collective Biography

When a work consists of four or more life histories, it is generally
considered a collective biography. The heading **Biography** is assigned
to a collective biography not limited to a place or a specific class of
persons, e.g., *International Who's Who.*

When the persons belong to a specific period, a period subdivision
is added, e.g.,

Biography—20th century

When the persons are from a particular place, the subject heading consists of the name of the place with the subdivision —**Biography,** e.g.,

United States—Biography

When the persons belong to a particular ethnic group or a particular profession or subject field, the appropriate term for the members of that group with the subdivision —**Biography** is used as the subject heading, e.g.,

Jews—Biography
British in India—Biography
Shipmasters—Biography
Chemists—Biography

The subdivision —**Biography** is also used under names of corporate bodies and historical events, periods, etc., for example,

Catholic Church—Biography
United States—History—Civil War, 1861-1865—Biography

When the required term referring to a special class of persons is not available in LCSH, the subject heading consists of the name of the relevant subject or discipline with the subdivision —**Biography,** e.g.,

Baseball—Biography

If the work contains lists of works of authors active in particular fields as well as biographical information about those authors, use the subdivision —**Bio-bibliography** under subjects, including names of places, literatures, religious orders or sects, or topical headings generally, e.g.,

American Literature—Bio-bibliography
Franciscans—Bio-bibliography

Do not use this subdivision with names of individual persons.

Individual Biography

The subject heading for the biography of an individual consists of the name of the biographee, established in the same form as the author entry. If the biography focuses on a specific aspect of the person's life, an appropriate subdivision is added. The patterns of subdivisions are established under the names of Lincoln, Napoleon, Shakespeare, Thomas Aquinas, Wagner, and Washington. Note that the subdivision

—Biography is not used under names of individual persons except literary authors. *differs from Sears (see p181)*

> **King, Martin Luther**
> **Castro, Fidel, 1927-**   **—Relationship with women**
> **Chaucer, Geoffrey, d. 1400—Biography**

For an autobiography, a subject heading in the same form as the main entry is assigned, particularly if the library has a divided catalog, e.g.,

> *Autobiography of Benvenuto Cellini*
> 1. **Cellini, Benvenuto, 1500-1571.**

In addition to the personal heading, a *biographical* heading in the form of [class of persons]—[place]—[subdivision indicating type of biographical work] is assigned. This practice represents a recent Library of Congress policy and is not reflected in earlier cataloging records. For example,

> *Mr. Clutch: The Jerry West Story*
> 1. **West, Jerry.**
> 2. **Basketball—Biography.**
> *Am I Your President? Starring Richard M. Nixon*
> 1. **Nixon, Richard M. (Richard Milhous) 1913-**
>   **—Portraits, caricatures, etc.**
> 2. **Presidents—United States—Caricatures and cartoons.**

For a partial biography or a biography which includes material about the field in which the biographee was involved, an additional topical heading, or headings, is assigned to bring out the subject, e.g.,

> *Oppenheimer's Personal Efforts to Develop the Bomb*
> 1. **Oppenheimer, J. Robert, 1904-1967.**
> 2. **Atomic bomb—History.**
> 3. **Physicists—United States—Biography.**

To a work about a statesman, ruler, or head of state[10] which contains information on his or her personal life but does not deal to any significant extent with the historical events of his or her reign or administration, assign two headings: (1) the personal name heading, and (2) the biographical heading, e.g.,

> *Shepherd, G., The Last Habsburg*
> 1. **Karl I, Emperor of Austria, 1887-1922.**
> 2. **Austria—Kings and rulers—Biography.**

[10]Cf. *Cataloging Service,* **117**:12, Spring 1976 and **119**:22, Fall 1976.

If the work presents the history of the jurisdiction for the period of his or her reign or administration, but does not contain personal facts concerning his or her life, assign the heading for the history of the period, e.g.,

> Black, J. B. *The Reign of Elizabeth, 1558-1603*
>   1. **Great Britain—History—Elizabeth, 1558-1603.**

If the work deals with both aspects, assign all three headings, e.g.,

> Bryant, A. *King Charles II*
>   1. **Great Britain—History—Charles II, 1660-1685.**
>   2. **Charles II, King of Great Britain, 1630-1685.**
>   3. **Great Britain—Kings and rulers—Biography.**

The corporate heading, e.g., **Great Britain.** *Sovereign (1660-1685 : Charles II)*, which is used in descriptive cataloging as a main or added entry, is not used as a subject heading. Instead, the appropriate heading for the history of the period is used.

Exercise C

Assign subject headings to the following topics:

1. Black arts: an anthology of black writers in the twentieth century.
2. A collection of writings by American black authors.
3. Characterization in Jacobean tragedies: a critical study.
4. A commentary on Beowulf.
5. A commentary on the epistles of Peter and Jude.
6. A collection of seventeenth-century French drama.
7. A history of science fiction in the United States.
8. A study of the theme of friendship in fifteenth-century Chinese literature.
9. A study of the theme of alienation in twentieth-century American fiction.
10. The diaries of Mark Twain.
11. Images of a queen, Mary Stuart, in sixteenth-century literature: a critical study.
12. A study of Shakespeare's great tragedies.
13. *October rain:* a collection of poems, by Ray Smith (twentieth-century American poet).
14. A reader's guide to Walt Whitman.
15. A critical study of Melville's *Moby Dick.*
16. Sources of Shakespeare's plots.
17. Journal of twentieth-century Spanish literature.

18. A biography of Louis XV of France.
19. World Jewish register.
20. Abraham Lincoln as a criminal lawyer.

SUBJECT HEADINGS FOR CHILDREN'S LITERATURE
Library of Congress List

The list of subject headings for children's literature was also developed by the Library of Congress. In 1965, the library initiated the Annotated Card (AC) Program for children's materials, with the purpose of providing more appropriate and in-depth subject cataloging of juvenile titles through more liberal application of subject headings and through the use of headings more appropriate to juvenile users. In some cases, existing Library of Congress subject headings must be reinterpreted or modified in order to achieve these purposes. In other cases, new headings have to be added. As a result, a list of over three hundred headings which represent exceptions to the master Library of Congress list has been compiled and published as *Subject Headings for Children's Literature*. In application, this list must be used in conjunction with the master list. This list was first issued as a separate publication. Beginning with the eighth edition of *Library of Congress Subject Headings*, it has been published both as a part of the master list (p. lxxiii–lxxxi) and as a separate publication and is kept up to date by means of additions published in the front of each issue of *Supplement to LC Subject Headings*.

Subject Cataloging of Children's Materials

There are two ways of treating children's materials in the Library of Congress subject headings system. One is to treat them in the same manner as other materials by assigning headings from the regular list in *Library of Congress Subject Headings*. The level of the material is generally specified by the subdivisions **—Dictionaries, Juvenile; —Juvenile drama; —Juvenile fiction; —Juvenile films; —Juvenile literature** (for nonliterary works); **—Juvenile phonorecords** (not used with musical sound recordings); and **—Juvenile poetry**. This method is usually used when the children's materials are integrated into the general collection of the library.

The second method, used when the materials are in a separate collection for children's use, is to follow the Annotated Card Program of the Library of Congress by assigning subject headings according to *Subject Headings for Children's Literature*. In this case, subject headings (without the subdivisions listed above) are assigned more liberally, particularly to belles-lettres. Many topical headings, which are not generally used with adult literature, are assigned to juvenile fiction and drama.

On the annotated cards for children's materials issued by the Library of Congress, two sets of subject headings are given: the regular headings based on Library of Congress Subject Headings, and headings for children's literature. The juvenile headings, which may or may not differ from the regular headings, are enclosed in brackets on Library of Congress cataloging records.

Title: *Change of Focus*, by Jems L. Summers
[1. **Photography—Fiction**]

Title: *Thalassine*, by V. Corinne Renshaw
[1. **Brittany—Fiction.**
2. **Fantasy**]

Title: *France and the French*, by Harvey Edwards
1. **France—Juvenile literature.**
[1.   **France**]

Title: *I Don't Like Timmy*, by Joan Hanson
[1. **Brothers and sisters—Fiction**]

Title: *Air pollution*, by George Laycock
1. **Air—Pollution—Juvenile literature.**
[1.   **Air—Pollution**]

Title: *At the Pond*, by Franklin Russell
1. **Animals, Legends and stories of.**
[1.   **Animals—Stories**]

Title: *Folk Tales and Legends from Great Britain*
        (Sound recording)
1. **Tales, English—Juvenile phonorecords.**
[1.   **Folklore—Great Britain**]

CHAPTER 9

Sears List of Subject Headings

The first edition of *List of Subject Headings for Small Libraries*, prepared by Minnie Earl Sears, appeared in 1923. The publication of this standard list met the needs of small libraries for which neither the ALA list nor the Library of Congress list was suitable. Since then, the list has gone through eleven editions. Sears was responsible for the first three editions (1923, 1926, 1933). The fourth (1939) and fifth (1944) editions were edited by Isabel Stevenson Munro. Bertha M. Frick was responsible for editing the sixth (1940), seventh (1954), and eighth (1959) editions. Barbara M. Westby assumed the editorship beginning with the ninth (1965) edition. With the sixth edition, the title was changed to *Sears List of Subject Headings*.

The fourth through eighth editions included Dewey Decimal Classification numbers corresponding to the subject headings. This feature was excluded with the ninth and the tenth editions. It was reinstated in the eleventh edition upon the request of the users.

The Sears list is used widely by school libraries and small public libraries in the United States. The Sears and the Library of Congress lists together serve as the two standard lists for subject headings for general libraries in this country.

Recognizing the advantages of uniformity, Minnie Earl Sears decided to follow the general principles which underlie the Library of Congress list in the development of *List of Subject Headings for Small Libraries*, with certain exceptions which were made generally because of the particular needs of the small libraries. Therefore, although the Sears list is not an abridgment of the Library of Congress list, it is very similar in format and structure. In the preparation of each edition of the Sears list, the editor often consulted the Library of Congress list. Recent editions of the Sears list have incorporated many of the headings contained in the Library of Congress *Subject Headings for Children's Literature*. Variations and modifications usually occur in the following areas: terminology and spelling, e.g., **Biochemistry** instead of *Biological chemistry* (cf. *LCSH*); simplification of phrasing, e.g., **City planning** rather than *Cities and towns—planning* (cf. *LCSH*); and less specificity, e.g., combining closely related headings such as Art, French and Art—France into **Art, French** only.

The general principles on which the Library of Congress list is based also apply to the Sears list. These are the principles of an *alphabetical subject catalog:* specific entry, uniform headings, common usage, and syndetic devices.[1] (Cross references to connect related headings)

FORMAT

Headings and their subdivisions used as subject entries in a catalog are printed in boldface type. Those printed in lightface roman are not to be used as subject entries. They are synonymous terms or variant forms of regular headings and are followed by *see* references to the terms that are used as headings, e.g.,

>Conundrums. See **Riddles**

>Microwave cookery. See **Cookery, Microwave**

>Agricultural pests—Biological control. See **Pests—Biological control**

On the subject entry in a card catalog or printed catalog, the subject heading appears in red or in capital letters so that it can be readily distinguished from a title entry containing the same term.

FORMS OF HEADINGS

Single Noun Headings

Most of the broad fields of knowledge and concrete objects are represented by headings consisting of a single noun, e.g., **Chemistry; Education; Law; Books; Rocks; Water;** etc. When a noun has more than one meaning, a qualifier is added in parentheses to limit the heading to one subject or concept, e.g., **Bridge (Game); Masks (Sculpture).** The choice of the singular or the plural form depends on the term involved. In general, abstract concepts are represented by the singular noun, e.g., **Credit,** while concrete objects are represented by the plural, e.g., **Books.** In some cases, both the singular and the plural forms of a noun are used as headings. In such cases, they carry different meanings, e.g., **Short story** (the technique) and **Short stories** (the works); **Symphony** (as a musical form) and **Symphonies** (musical scores).

[1]For a discussion of these principles, see Chapter 7.

Compound Headings

This form of heading consists of two nouns or noun phrases connected by the word *and*. They are used for the following purposes:

1. To connect topics or concepts which are usually treated together in books, e.g., **Skis and skiing; Clans and clan system; Cliff dwellers and cliff dwellings**
2. To connect opposite subjects that are usually treated together in books, e.g., **Open and closed shop**
3. To express a relationship between two concepts or things, e.g., **Church and education; Medicine and religion.**

Adjective-with-Noun Headings

When a subject or concept cannot be properly expressed by a single noun, a phrase is used. The most common type of phrase heading consists of a noun or noun phrase with one or more adjectival modifiers, e.g., **English language; Space flight; Ground effect machines; College students; Clergymen's wives;** etc. In many cases, the heading is inverted in order to bring the noun forward as the entry element, e.g., **Chemistry, Physical and theoretical; Trusts, Industrial.**

Phrase Headings

Some concepts are expressed by nouns or noun phrases connected by prepositions which express their relationships, e.g., **Cookery for the sick; Electricity in agriculture; Religion in the public schools;** and **Detergent pollution of rivers, lakes, etc.**

CROSS REFERENCES

To guide the users who consult the catalog under terms other than those used as subject headings or to call their attention to materials related to the topics being consulted, cross references are provided in the catalog. While a subject heading may appear many times in the catalog, a reference is made only once regardless of how many times the heading has been used. Cross references appear in three forms for different purposes: specific *see* references, specific *see also* references, and general references.

Specific *See* References

These refer the user from terms that are not used as headings to those that are. In the Sears list, instruction for making *see* references is given after the heading. The symbol x means that *see* references are to be made *from* the terms that follow *to* the heading immediately above it, e.g.,

<table>
<tr><td>**Adolescence**</td><td>**Art, Modern**</td></tr>
<tr><td>x Teen age</td><td>x Modern art</td></tr>
</table>

The references are shown in Figure 9-1.

Note that in the Sears list, reverse instructions appear under the terms Teen age and Modern art:

> Teen age. *See* **Adolescence**
> Modern art. *See* **Art, Modern**

In general, *see* references are made from synonymous or near-synonymous terms and inverted forms which are not used as subject headings. Occasionally, a *see* reference is made from a more specific term which is not used as a heading to the more general term which is used (see Figure 9-2).

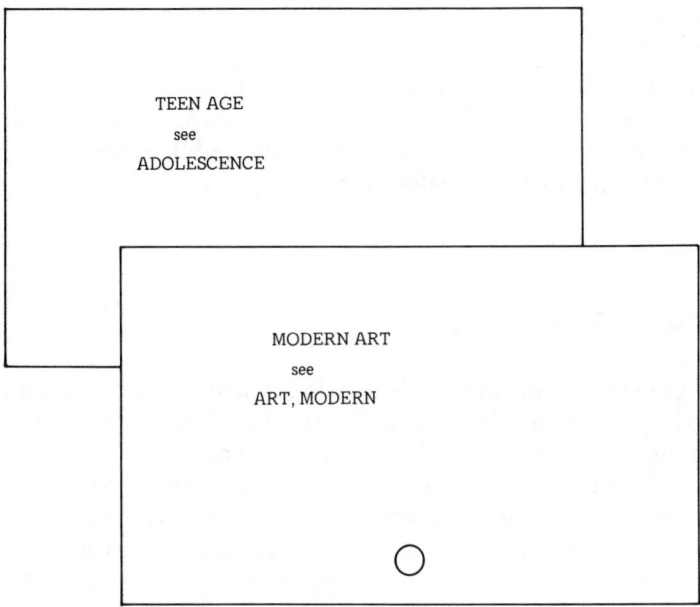

FIGURE 9-1   Specific *see* references.

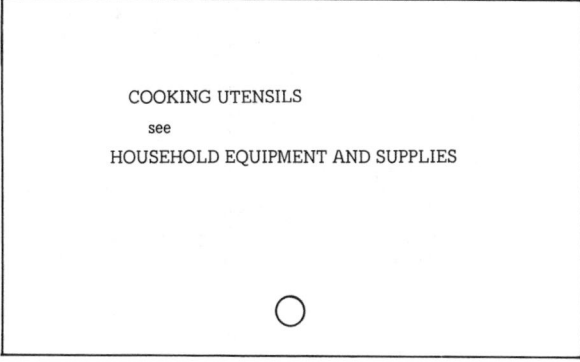

COOKING UTENSILS
see
HOUSEHOLD EQUIPMENT AND SUPPLIES

FIGURE 9-2   *See* reference made from a more specific to a more general term.

Specific *See also* References

A *see also* reference connects a heading to another related heading or headings. Before making the reference, the cataloger should ascertain whether the library has material listed under both headings. The *see also* references are made for two purposes: (1) to refer from a general subject to more specific parts of it, and (2) to refer from a subject to a related subject of more or less equal specificity.

See also references are indicated by the symbol *xx* (meaning *see also from*) in the Sears list. A reverse instruction indicated by the phrase *see also* appears under the other heading involved., e.g.,

Bees	**Honey**
See also **Honey**	—*See also* **Bees**
xx **Honey; Insects**	xx **Bees** (see also from)

The references are shown in Figure 9-3.

Bees and **Honey** are related subjects. Therefore, *see also* references are made both ways. On the other hand, because **Insects** is a general term which encompasses **Bees,** a *see also* reference is made from **Insects** to **Bees,** while no reference is made from **Bees** to **Insects.**

General References

A general reference, in either the *see* or the *see also* form, covers an entire category or class of headings rather than individual headings. This device is used in order to save space in both the subject headings list and the library catalog. A general explanation or direction is given instead of enumerating many individual headings, e.g.,

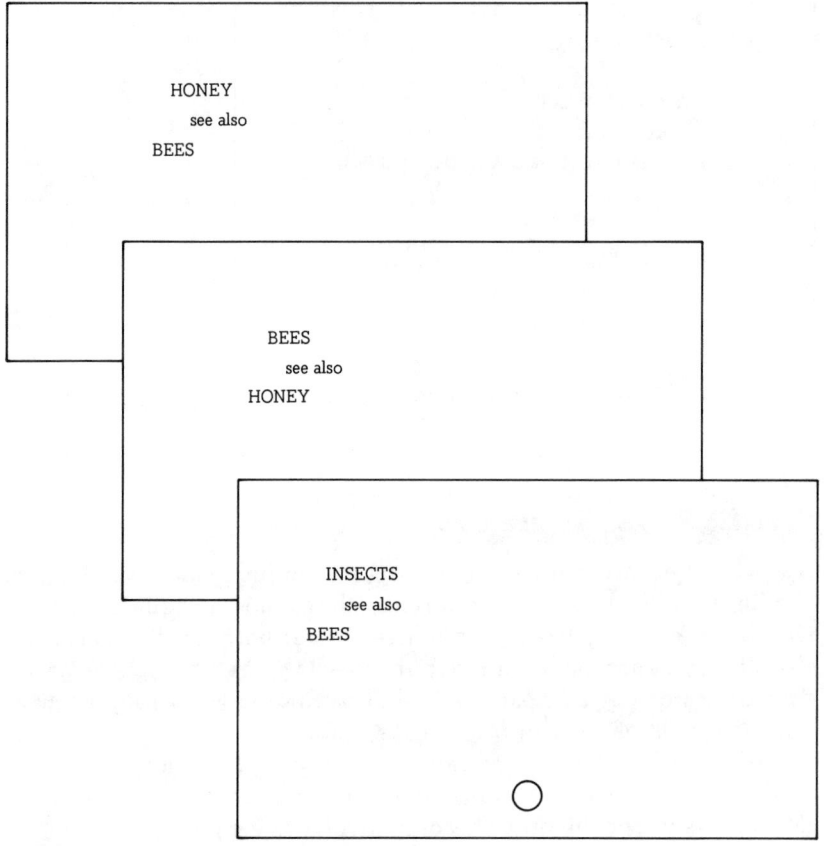

FIGURE 9-3   Specific *see also* references.

Dogs
  See also classes of dogs, e.g., **Guide dogs;** etc.; also names of
  specific breeds, e.g., **Collies;** etc.

Rivers
  See also **Dams; Floods;** . . . also names of rivers

Rocket planes
  See also names of rocket planes, e.g., **X-15 (Rocket
  aircraft);** etc.

Army. *See* **Armies; Military art and science;** and names of
  countries with the subhead Army, e.g., **U.S. Army;** etc.

Following is an example of different types of cross references required
for a particular heading.

Automobiles
See also **Buses; Sports cars; Trucks;** also names of specific makes and models of automobiles, e.g., **Ford automobile;** etc.

x   Cars (Automobiles); Locomotion; Motor cars

xx **Transportation; Transportation, Highway; Vehicles**

The references are shown in Figure 9-4.

SUBDIVISIONS

In the Sears list, many general subjects are subdivided to indicate their special aspects or to provide a subarrangement for a large number of works on the same subject. There are several types of subdivisions: subject or topical; form; period or chronological; place, local, or geographic.

Subject or Topical Subdivisions

A subject or topical subdivision added to a main heading brings out a special aspect or characteristic of the general subject, e.g.,

> **English language—Business English**
> **English language—Dialects**
> **English language—Etymology**
> **Education—Curricula**
> **Education—Finance**

Form Subdivisions

A form subdivision expresses the physical or bibliographic form of the work being cataloged, e.g.,

> **Chemistry—Dictionaries**
> **Library science—Bibliography**
> **Railroads—Maps**
> **Space sciences—Periodicals**

Some of the so-called *form subdivisions* actually represent the author's point of view or approach to the subject, e.g.,

> **Economics—History**
> **Science—Philosophy**
> **Gold—Law and legislation**
> **Library science—Study and teaching**

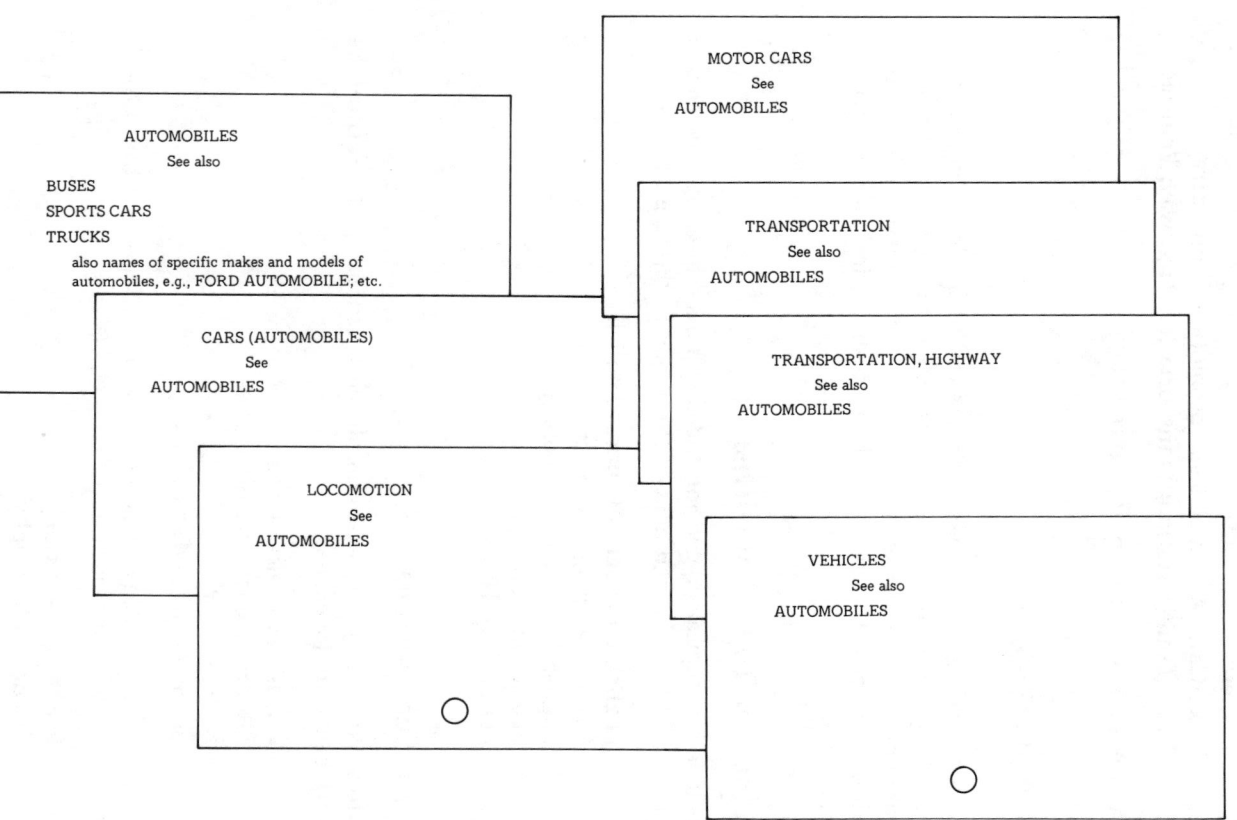

FIGURE 9-4 Different cross references required for a particular heading.

The form subdivisions are comparable to the standard subdivisions in the Dewey Decimal Classification. Because many of the form subdivisions and some of the topical subdivisions are so common that they are applicable to many subjects, they are not enumerated under each subject to which they may be added as subdivisions. Instead, the common subdivisions are listed together in the introduction (pages xl–xli) to the Sears list (eleventh edition). These subdivisions may be used under subject headings where applicable. Therefore, the following combinations may be made by the cataloger even though they are not actually so listed:

> **Physicians—Directories**
> **Music—Bibliography**
> **Television—Law and legislation**
> **Chemistry—Terminology**

In addition to the list of common subdivisions mentioned above, instructions for use of these subdivisions are also provided in the list under the appropriate terms, e.g.,

> **Bibliography**
> *also* names of persons, places and subjects with the subdivision *Bibliography,* e.g., **Shakespeare, William— Bibliography; U.S.—Bibliography; Agriculture— Bibliography;** etc.

> Terminology. *See* **Names;** and subjects with the subdivision *Terminology,* e.g., **Botany—Terminology,** etc.

The following headings serve as the key patterns for subdivisions. The subdivisions listed under these headings may be used whenever appropriate with other headings in the same categories. For example, the subdivisions listed under **World War, 1939-1945** may be used with the heading for another war.

Category	*Key heading*
Country	**United States**
State	**Ohio**
City	**Chicago**
Language	**English language**
Literature	**English literature**
Author	**Shakespeare, William**
President	**Presidents—U.S.**
War	**World War, 1939-1945**

Exercise A

Assign subject headings from the Sears list:

1. *Reading Habits of Adolescents*
2. *Advertising by Mail*
3. *Encyclopedia of Science and Technology*
4. *Library Journal*
5. *Handbook of Chemistry and Physics*
6. *History of the First World War*
7. *Journal of Plant Pathology*
8. *A List of Scientific Journals*
9. *Time* (magazine)
10. *A Russian-English Dictionary of Medical Terms*
11. *A Bibliography of Library and Information Science*
12. *Opportunities in Textile Careers*
13. *The Amateur Photographer's Handbook*
14. *Sears List of Subject Headings*

Period or Chronological Subdivisions

National history lends itself to chronological treatment. In the Sears list, chronological or period subdivisions are provided under the history of the United States and other countries that are likely to be included in large volume in American libraries. The period subdivisions appear as sub-subdivisions under the subdivision—**History.**

> U.S.—History —Colonial period, 1600-1775
> —King William's War, 1689-1697
> —Revolution, 1775-1783
> —Civil War, 1861-1865
>
> Japan—History—To 1868
> —1868-1945
> —Allied occupation, 1945-1952
> —1952-

Place, Local, or Geographic Subdivisions

Many works deal with a subject with regard to a specific locality. For many subjects which lend themselves to such a treatment, geographic subdivisions are provided. The instruction for geographic subdivision is given in the form of a parenthetical statement following the main heading. For example, a heading such as

> **Flowers** (May subdiv. geog.)

indicates that the following headings, though not listed, can be used as subject entries:

> **Flowers—U.S.**
> **Flowers—Hawaii**
> **Flowers—Honolulu**

Some geographic subdivisions appear in the adjectival form, e.g.,

> **Folk art** (May subdiv. geog. adjective form, e.g.,
> **Folk art, Swedish;** etc.)

Exercise B

Assign subject headings from the Sears list:

1. *Museums in New York City*
2. *Popular Music in U.S.A.*
3. *History of Flemish Painting*
4. *Canadian Foreign Policy, 1945–1954*
5. *The Eisenhower Years: A Historical Assessment*
6. *Political Parties in Australia*
7. *Directory of Hospitals in Athens, Georgia*
8. *The Reign of Elizabeth, 1558–1603*
9. *A Pictorial Guide to San Francisco*
10. *Famous American Military Leaders of World War II*
11. *Norwegian Folk Tales: A Collection*
12. *Getting To Know Iran and Iraq*
13. *The Land and People of Switzerland*

CLASSES OF HEADINGS OMITTED

Personal names, corporate names, and other proper names are potential subject headings because many works are written about individual persons, institutions, individual places, events, etc. It is not possible to list all names which may become subjects of works. There are many headings that serve as subject entries in the catalog but are not listed in the Sears list. For these, the cataloger must provide the specific names as headings when needed. They include certain common names as well.

Proper Names

1. Names of persons. The form of a personal heading and its cross references is established according to the Anglo-American Cataloguing

Rules in order that works written by and about the same person will be grouped together in the catalog. The name authority record established for a person as an author will serve to determine the form of both author and subject entries for the person. If a person whose name is required as a subject heading has not appeared as an author in the catalog, a name authority record should be established according to the same procedure as in descriptive cataloging. Examples of names of persons as subject headings are:

> **Boone, Daniel**
> **Einstein, Albert**

By way of exception, a few personal headings are included in the list. For example, **Jesus Christ** is included because of unique subdivisions; **Shakespeare, William** is included to show subdivisions which may be used under names of other voluminous authors; and **Napoleon I, Emperor of the French—Drama** is included because it is used as an example under the heading **Drama**.

   2. Names of families. The heading consists of the family name followed by the word **family,** e.g., **Kennedy family, Brontë family,** etc.

   3. Names of places.
      a. Political units:
         (1) Countries (e.g., **India, Belgium,** etc.). A number of countries are included to show their unique period subdivisions. **United States** serves as a pattern heading. The subdivisions (except period subdivisions which are not transferable) under **United States** may be used with names of other countries, e.g.,
         India—Geography
         Belgium—Population
         (2) States (e.g., **Colorado, Wyoming,** etc.). **Ohio,** as a key state, is listed with subdivisions which can be used under names of other states.
         (3) Provinces, etc. (e.g., **England; Ontario; British Columbia;** etc.).
         (4) Counties (e.g., **Cook County, Ill.**).
         (5) Cities (e.g., **San Francisco; Athens, Ga.; Dijon, France,** etc.). Add the name of the country or the state (if in the United States) to the name of a city when there are other cities by the same name or when the name is not a familiar one to the users. For subdivisions, **Chicago** is the key city.
      b. Groups of states or countries (e.g., **Gulf States; Baltic States**)
      c. Geographic features:

(1) Mountain ranges and individual mountains (e.g., **Smoky Mountains; Mont Blanc,** etc.)

(2) Island groups and individual islands (e.g., **Virgin Islands; Jamaica;** etc.)

(3) River valleys and individual rivers (e.g., **Ohio Valley; Mississippi River;** etc.)

(4) Regions, oceans, lakes, etc. (**Indian Ocean; Kentucky Lake;** etc.)

4. Names of nationalities (e.g., **Belgians; Germans;** etc.)

5. Names of national languages and literatures (e.g., **Turkish language; Austrian literature;** etc.). **English language** and **English literature** are the key headings.

6. Names of battles (e.g., **Waterloo, Battle of, 1815**)

7. Names of treaties (e.g., **Portsmouth, Treaty of, 1905**)

8. Names of Indian tribes (e.g., **Navaho Indians; Oneida Indians;** etc.)

Corporate Names

Works about individual corporate bodies are assigned headings in the form of their names established according to the Anglo-American Cataloguing Rules and that are compatible with headings used as main and added entries.

1. Names of societies, clubs, etc. (e.g., **American Chemical Society; American Library Association;** etc.)

2. Names of institutions: colleges, libraries, hospitals, etc. (e.g., **Smith College; Florida State University; New York Public Library; Massachusetts General Hospital;** etc.)

3. Names of government bodies (**U.S. Navy; California. Legislature;** etc.)

4. Names of buildings, parks, ships, etc. (e.g., **Empire State Building; Yellowstone National Park; Christina (Ship);** etc.)

Common Names

In addition to the proper names mentioned above, there are a large number of generic names, mostly in scientific fields, which may be used as subject headings even though they are not listed. In each category, the more common species are named in the list.

1. Names of
   a. Animals (e.g., **Rhinoceroses; Kangaroos;** etc.)
   b. Birds (e.g., **Swallows**)
   c. Fishes (e.g., **Perch; Trout;** etc.)

d. Flowers (e.g., **Carnations**)
e. Games (e.g., **Badminton; Backgammon;** etc.)
f. Nuts (e.g., **Chestnut**). Use the singular form because the same heading is used for the tree.
g. Tools (e.g., **Hammers**)
h. Trees (e.g., **Pine; Maple; Peach;** etc.). Use the singular form.
i. Vegetables (e.g., **Carrots; Spinach;** etc.)
2. Names of diseases (e.g., **Measles**)
3. Names of organs and other parts of the body (e.g., **Kidney; Legs;** etc.)
4. Names of chemicals (e.g., **Glycine; Potassium chloride;** etc.)
5. Names of minerals (e.g., **Chlorite; Topaz;** etc.)

In the Sears list, instructions for providing the headings mentioned above are included under the broad terms, e.g.,

> **Trees** (May subdiv. geog.)
> Names of trees are not included in this list but are to be added as needed in the singular form, e.g., **Oak;** etc.

> **Tools**
> *See also* **Agricultural machinery;** . . . also names of specific tools, e.g., **Saws;** etc.

Exercise C

Assign subject headings from the Sears list:

1. *Swedish Word Origins*
2. *Poems for Thanksgiving* (by various authors)
3. *Russian Grammar*
4. *The Peace Corps in Action*
5. *Chemicals of Life: Enzymes, Vitamins, Hormones*
6. *A History of the American Medical Association*
7. *NATO and Europe*
8. *The German Community in Cincinnati*
9. *Wonders of the Himalayas*
10. *Eastern Europe: Czechoslovakia, Hungary, Poland*
11. *The Department of Defense: A History*
12. *Sparrows of Asia*

SUBJECT HEADINGS
FOR SPECIAL TYPES OF MATERIALS

Certain types of library materials require special treatment; of these, the most common are biography and literature.

Subject Headings for Biography

Individual biography

For a biography of one, two, or three individuals, the subject heading is comprised of the name or names of the individual or individuals. The form of the heading should agree with the author entry for the same person. A biography of Robert F. Kennedy, for example, is assigned the heading

Kennedy, Robert F., 1925-1968—Biography.

differs from LC (see p. 163)

The dates may or may not be included, depending on the practice of the library. A biography of two or three of the Kennedy brothers will be assigned headings under the name of each.

Frequently, when the biography of a person also contains material about the field in which the person is concerned, a second subject heading representing the subject field is added. For example, if the biography of President John F. Kennedy contains a substantial amount of material on his administration, a second heading **United States— History—1961-1974** is assigned in addition to the personal heading.

For persons about whom there is a large amount of material, subdivisions are used for subarranging numerous titles with the same subject heading. The list includes two personal headings, **Jesus Christ** and **Shakespeare, William,** with subdivisions, which serve as patterns for other personal headings when there is a large amount of material. In small libraries, for most individual biographies, the personal name alone without any subdivision is sufficient as the heading.

For autobiographical writings such as autobiographies, journals, memoirs, and letters, a subject heading identical to the author entry is often assigned. This is necessary, especially when the catalog is divided so that subject headings appear in a separate file. If the library has a dictionary catalog in which the author and subject headings are interfiled, the personal subject heading for an autobiographical work may be unnecessary.

Collective biography

For a biography of more than three persons, a subject heading covering the entire group is assigned, instead of individual personal headings. Various kinds of collective biographies are discussed below:

General biography

If the collective biography is not limited to any geographic area or subject field or a particular class of people, the general form heading **Biography** is assigned, for example, Van Loon's *Lives*. For a book about biography, the heading **Biography (as a literary form)** is used. For biographical reference works that are arranged in the dictionary form, e.g., *Webster's Biographical Dictionary* or *International Who's Who*, the heading **Biography—Dictionaries** is used.

Local biography
When the collective biography contains lives of people from a particular geographic area or a specific ethnic group, e.g., *Who's Who in Australia*, and *Canadian Who's Who*, the subject heading is in the form of the geographic or ethnic name with the subdivision **—Biography** or **—Biography—Dictionaries:**

> **Australia—Biography—Dictionaries**
> **Canada—Biography—Dictionaries**
> **Blacks—Biography**

Classes of persons
When the collective biography contains lives of persons of a particular subject field or a class, the subject heading is assigned in the form of the term representing the members of the field or the class, e.g., **Chemists; Explorers; Philosophers; Seamen;** etc. In some cases, the heading may be divided geographically, using the adjective form, e.g., **Actors and actresses, American; Composers, German; Statesmen, British;** etc.

When there is no appropriate term to represent a member of a field or when the name of the class or group refers to the subject in general rather than to individuals, the heading assigned is in the form of the name of the field with the subdivision **—Biography:**

> **Baseball—Biography**
> **France—History—Revolution, 1789-1799—Biography**
> **Women—Biography**

The headings used with collective biographies are not assigned to individual biographies. For example, the heading **Composers** or **Composers, German** is not used with a biography of Beethoven. However, a reference should be made from the collective heading to the individual headings, e g.,

> **Composers.** *See also* names of individual composers.

Subject Headings for Literature

There are two distinctive categories of works in the field of literature: (1) works *about* literature, and (2) literary works or specimens. These receive different treatment in subject cataloging.

Works about literature

These works, in which literature *is* the subject, are treated like other works with subject headings representing the content and the scope of the works, e.g.,

> **Literature** (with or without subdivisions depending on the scope)
> **American literature** (use **English literature** as the pattern for subdivisions)
> **Drama**
> **German drama—History and criticism**
> **Essay**
> **French essays—History and criticism**

Many of the more general literature headings are subdivided for special aspects. These may be used when appropriate. In addition, the general subdivisions listed in the introduction to *Sears* (pp. xl–xli) may also be used. Note that the subdivision —**History and criticism,** instead of —**History,** is used with literature headings.

The headings discussed above do not apply to works about individual authors or about works written by them. A work about an individual author or about his or her works is assigned a heading in the form of the author's name, e.g., **Dickens, Charles.** Shakespeare is included as a key heading for subdivisions used with voluminous authors.

Literary works or specimens of literature

In these works, literature is the *form* rather than the *subject*. There are two categories of literary works: collections of works of more than one author, and single or collected works by individual authors.

Collections of works of more than one author
A literary form heading, e.g., **Essays; American drama—Collections;** etc., is assigned to collections of works of more than one author. To differentiate a subject heading from a form heading containing the same term, the singular form is used as the subject heading (for a work *about* the literary form) and the plural form, when there is one, is used as the form heading (for the specimens). When there is no acceptable plural form of a noun, the subdivision —**Collections** is added:

Subject Heading	Form heading for collections
Essay	**Essays**
Short story	**Short stories**
Literature	**Literature—Collections**

Spanish literature	Spanish literature—Collections
Poetry	Poetry—Collections
German poetry	German poetry—Collections

Works by individual authors

For individual titles, no literary form heading is assigned. In other words, do not assign **English drama** to a play written by Shakespeare, or **American fiction** to Hemingway's novel *The Old Man and the Sea*.

For collected works by an individual author, no literary form heading is assigned if the works are in one of the major forms such as drama, fiction, and poetry. However, for collected works in a minor form such as parodies, satire, and short stories by an individual author, headings similar to those used with collections by more than one author are assigned. For example, E. A. Poe's *Selected Tales* is assigned the heading **Short stories, American**. Minor literary forms are not listed under the national adjectives. However, the introduction to *Sears* (p. xxiv) indicates that the national adjective may be added after the name of the form if national treatment is needed.

Literary forms used as subdivisions

Subject entries are often assigned to novels, poems, and plays based on lives of individuals or historical events. Add the subdivisions —**Fiction, —Poetry**, or —**Drama** to the subject heading, to distinguish these works from factual accounts on the subjects, e.g.,

> **U.S.—History—Civil War, 1861-1865—Fiction** (for a work such as *Gone with the Wind* by Mitchell)
>
> **Lincoln, Abraham, 1809-1865—Drama** (for a work such as *Abe Lincoln in Illinois* by Sherwood)

Exercise D

Assign subject headings from the Sears list:

1. *Lives of Famous French Dramatists*
2. *American Men and Women of Science*
3. *French Short Stories: A Collection*
4. *Stories of Maupassant*
5. *Commentaries on the New Testament*
6. *Life of Pablo Picasso*
7. *Modern American Secret Agents*
8. *Famous New Yorkers*
9. *Life of Daniel Boone*

10. *The Agony and the Ecstasy* (an American novel based on the life of Michelangelo)
11. *Best Sports Stories*
12. *A Day in the Life of President Johnson* (Lyndon B.)
13. *The Combat Nurses of World War II*
14. *Book of Poetry for Children*
15. *A Man for All Seasons* (an English drama based on the life of Sir Thomas More)
16. *A Study of Mark Twain's Novels*

CHAPTER 10
PRECIS

PRECIS (Preserved Context Index System) is the indexing system developed and used by the British National Bibliography for producing entries in the subject index in the weekly and cumulative issues of the bibliography which lists new British books. As a system primarily (though not exclusively) applied to the subject analysis of books, its function is similar to that of the subject headings system used in the United States.

In 1968, the British National Bibliography (BNB) became involved in the UK/MARC (machine-readable cataloguing) Project. A new indexing system capable of providing coextensive subject indexing for each document in the MARC database and amenable to computer manipulation was needed. A project, under the direction of Derek Austin, was undertaken to develop such a system. After initial experiments and trials, a prototype version of a new indexing system called PRECIS was adopted by BNB from January 1971 to the end of 1973. In the meantime, further research was conducted. In January, 1974, a new and improved version of PRECIS became operational, which is the system now being used by BNB and a number of other bibliographies, indexes, and library catalogs, mostly in the British Commonwealth countries.

Recent developments and research on the system include a translingual project, studying the applicability of PRECIS in languages other than English and the feasibility of automatic language switching by means of a multilingual thesaurus designed for computer manipulation.

PRECIS[1] is essentially a system for producing alphabetical subject

---

[1] This discussion is based on the following documents:

Derek Austin. "The Development of PRECIS, and Introduction to Its Syntax" and "The Semantics of PRECIS: Vocabulary Control and the RIN System." In Hans H. Wellisch, ed., *The PRECIS Index System: Principles, Applications, and Prospects, Proceedings of the International PRECIS Workshop.* Sponsored by the College of Library and Information Services of the University of Maryland, October 15–17, 1976. New York: The H. W. Wilson Company, 1977. Pp. 3–28, 29–53.

Derek Austin. *PRECIS: A Manual of Concept Analysis and Subject Indexing.* London: Council of the British National Bibliography, 1974.

Derek Austin and Jeremy A. Digger. "PRECIS: The Preserved Context Index System." *Library Resources and Technical Services,* 21:13–30, Winter 1977.

Material from a PRECIS Training Course conducted by Derek Austin and Jutta Sørensen in 1978.

indexes in a page format (including paper, microform, or display on a computer terminal). It is generally (though not invariably) used with computer assistance. The labor involved in index production is divided between the human indexer and the computer. The indexer undertakes the intellectual tasks which require human judgments, i.e., determining the subject content of the document, producing an input string, establishing indexing terms with references, and issuing instructions for the computer. The computer, on the other hand, follows these instructions and carries out the mechanical chore of implementing the human decisions, producing the correct entries and references.

PRECIS is generally presented as a two-stage index, i.e., a subject index in which each entry is followed by one or more addresses (e.g., Dewey decimal class numbers in the case of the British National Bibliography) which indicate the positions of the relevant bibliographic entries in another file.

PRINCIPLES AND CHARACTERISTICS

In developing PRECIS, Austin applied modern theory of classification as well as linguistic principles. Many of the theories and ideas developed in the 1960s by the Classification Research Group in Britain in search of a general classification scheme were adopted in the development of PRECIS by Austin, who has been an active member of the group.

Underlying PRECIS is the theory of facet analysis and synthesis. The subject of a document is broken down into individual concepts, which are then recombined into a meaningful and logical string that summarizes the content of the document. This string functions as the source from which index entries are generated.

When PRECIS began, it was based on modern classification theory, but it has moved gradually toward a linguistic analysis approach. Breaking down a subject into its component parts is based on classification theory. Reordering the parts into a meaningful string, on the other hand, draws upon linguistic principles. The relationships shown in the thesaurus, to be discussed later, are based on classification principles.

One basic principle of PRECIS is that each entry should represent the complete theme or topic of a document in summary form. This is called the principle of "coextensivity."

The basic criteria for useful index entries have been outlined as follows:

1. An entry can be made under any term likely to be sought in a string.

2. Each entry should be intelligible, and it should state the subject unambiguously.
3. Entries should be consistent in structure, so that they collocate with those produced from other strings on similar themes.[2]

These criteria led to the development of the principle of "context dependency." This principle requires that the individual concepts in an entry should be organized in a one-to-one relationship in context-dependent order. In other words, each term in the entry is related to the one immediately preceding and the one immediately following it. Each term sets the next term into its obvious context.

This can be illustrated by an example of a string summarizing the content of a document on "the training of skilled personnel in textile industries in France":

FRANCE—TEXTILE INDUSTRIES—SKILLED
PERSONNEL—TRAINING

The four concepts which together summarize the total content of the document are arranged in a context-dependent order. The concept "France" establishes the environment in which the concept of "textile industries" is considered; the concept "textile industries" identifies the contextual whole of which "skilled personnel" forms a part; while the act of "Training" is performed on the entity "skilled personnel." Once the concepts are arranged in this order, each is placed in closest proximity to the concept or concepts most closely related to it. These two notions—context dependency and one-to-one relations—are basic to this indexing system.

In the subject index, the string is displayed in multiple configurations, each beginning with a significant term in the string, thus providing multiple access points to the subject.

INDEX ENTRIES

In order to preserve the one-to-one relationships in context-dependent order, each PRECIS entry is presented in a two-line and three-position format:

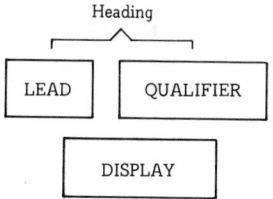

[2]Derek Austin and Jeremy A. Digger. Op. cit. P. 17.

Following is an example of a PRECIS input string with the entries generated from it.

Input string (the blank boxes indicate that no entry has yet been generated):

```
┌──────────┐  ┌──────────────────────┐
│          │  │                      │
└──────────┘  └──────────────────────┘
   ┌──────────────────────────────────┐
   │ France. Textile industries. Skilled │
   │ personnel. Training                  │
   └──────────────────────────────────┘
```

Entries

> **France**
>> Textile industries. Skilled personnel. Training
>
> **Textile industries.** France
>> Skilled personnel. Training
>
> **Skilled personnel.** Textile industries. France
>> Training
>
> **Training.** Skilled personnel. Textile industries. France

A separate entry is generated with each significant term in the lead position. The lead which contains the entry element, printed in boldface type, must be occupied. The qualifier may contain any number of terms, which are of successively wider context to the right of the line. The terms in the display are of progressively narrower context to the right of the line.

The device of bringing each significant term to the lead position while maintaining the context-dependent order is called *shunting*. The two-line/three-position format and the established procedure of shunting ensure that each concept is placed immediately next to those most closely related to it, whatever position this particular concept may occupy in a particular entry. In the second entry in the example above, the concept "textile industries," when it is moved to the lead position, remains next to both "France" and "skilled personnel."

The example above shows the standard format. In certain cases, slightly different formats are used in order to maintain context dependency.

The format discussed above is used for entries of individual documents. The references in PRECIS appear in formats similar to those used in other indexing systems. Examples:

> **Industries**
>> *See also*
>> **Textile industries**
>
> **Employees** *See* **Personnel**

Staff *See* **Personnel**

Manpower
   See also
      Personnel
Education
   See also
      Training

TWO-PART STRUCTURE: SYNTAX AND SEMANTICS

In PRECIS, two categories of relationships between terms used in indexing are recognized and handled by different procedures: syntactic relationships and semantic relationships.

Syntactic relationships refer to *a posteriori* relationships which are document-dependent. In other words, the terms are not originally related, but the relationship has been established within the context of a particular document. For example, a work about hospital management establishes a relationship between the concepts "hospitals" and "management" which possess no inherent relationship outside of the context of a document. Such relationships are generally handled by the string assigned to each document.

Semantic relationships, on the other hand, refer to *a priori* relationships which are invariable and independent of the treatment of the concepts in any particular document. The two main types of semantic relationships are hierarchy and synonymy. In PRECIS, semantic relationships are handled in a thesaurus.

Figure 10-1 illustrates the two categories of relationships between indexing terms.

The *syntax* and the *semantics* are handled by two separate procedures in PRECIS. These are discussed below.

Syntax

This procedure deals with the analysis of individual documents and the assignment of input strings. The first step, as in subject cataloging and classification, is to identify the subject content of the document. The next step is to isolate the individual concepts in the subject and identify the relationships between them. In order to maintain the one-to-one relationships in context-dependent order and to achieve consistency in indexing practice, a schema of "role operators" (Figure 10-2) has been developed to serve as the indexer's "grammar." Each term in a string is coded with a role operator which expresses, in a

Subject: The management of hospitals in West Germany

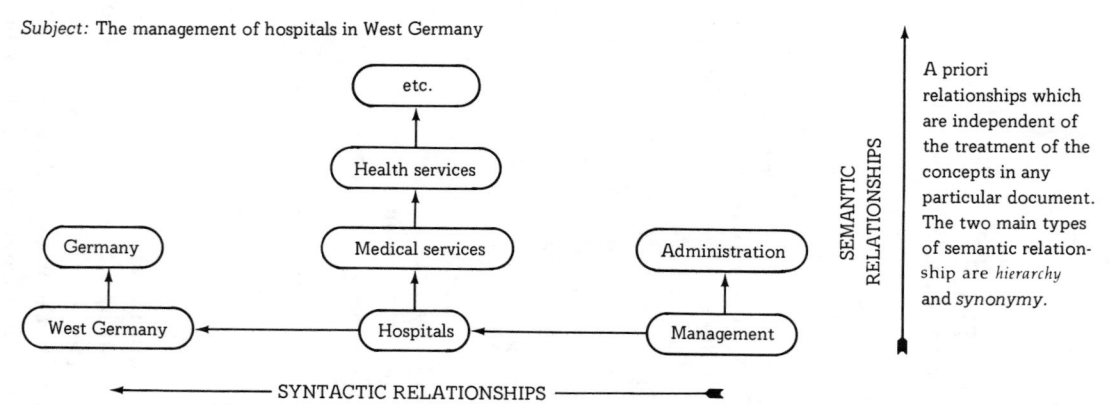

Relationships between concepts which are a posteriori; i.e., they are document-specific.

FIGURE 10-1 Syntactic and semantic relationships.

Main-line operators

Environment of observed system	0	Location
Observed system (Core operators)	1	Key system: *object of transitive action; agent of intransitive action*
	2	Action/Effect
	3	Agent of transitive action; Aspects; Factors

A ————————————————————————

Data relating to observer	4	Viewpoint-as-form
Selected instance	5	Sample population/Study region
Presentation of data	6	Target/Form

Interposed operators

Dependent elements	p	Part/Property
	q	Member of quasi-generic group
	r	Aggregate
Concept interlinks	s	Role definer
	t	Author attributed association
Coordinate concepts	g	Coordinate concept

B ————————————————————————

Differencing operators	01	Non-lead direct difference
(prefixed by $)	21	Lead direct difference
	j	Salient difference
	02	Non-lead indirect difference
	22	Lead indirect difference
	n	Non-lead parenthetical difference
	o	Lead parenthetical difference
	d	Date as a difference

Connectives

(Components of linking phrases; prefixed by $)	v	Downward reading component
	w	Upward reading component

C ————————————————————————

Theme interlinks	x	First element in coordinate theme
	y	Subsequent element in coordinate theme
	z	Element of common theme

FIGURE 10-2 Role operators.

machine-readable form, its role in the subject and its position in the string. The role operators also have built-in computer instructions with regard to format of the index entry, typography of each term, and its associated punctuation.

A string assigned to a document may contain any number of terms. Each string must begin with a main line operator in the range from 0 to 2 and must contain at least one term coded either (1) or (2). Examples:

Subject
Cars

String

(1) cars✓ (the check ✓ indicates a lead term under which an entry is made)

Entry
Cars

Subject
Marketing of cars

String

(1) cars✓

(2) marketing✓

Entries
Cars
   Marketing
Marketing. Cars

Subject
Car production in Germany

String

(0) Germany✓

(1) cars✓

(2) production

Entries
Germany
   Cars. Production
Cars. Germany
   Production

There is a direct connection between the main line operators, 0, 1, 2, and 3, and certain grammatical structures in everyday speech. The operator 0 corresponds to the locative case in grammar. The operators 1, 2, and 3 are used with terms which generally correspond to the object, verb (in the case of a transitive verb), and subject of a sentence. In the case of an intransitive verb, the operators 1 and 2 are used with terms which function as the subject and verb of a sentence. The role operators are devices for constructing the input strings and serve as instructions to the computer. They do not appear in the index entries.

Examples of use of other operators:

Subject
Birth control (a Roman Catholic viewpoint)

String

(2) birth control

(4) Roman Catholic viewpoints

Subject
Bibliography on U.S. trade unions

String

(0) United States

(1) trade unions

(6) bibliographies

Subject
A comparison between Christianity and Judaism

String

(1) Christianity
(*t*) compared with
(1) Judaism

Dependent elements

Dependent elements of a term coded (0) through (6), (*s*), (*t*), or (*g*) are coded with the role operators (*p*), (*q*), and (*r*). These follow immediately the term on which they are dependent. Examples:

(1) aircraft
(*p*) noise

(2) advertising
(*p*) costs

(1) pests
(*q*) birds

(1) schools
(*p*) curriculum subjects
(*q*) geography

(1) eleṗhants
(r) herḋs

(1) skilled personnel
(r) tradė unions

(1) fiṡh
(2) phẏsiology
(5) study examples
(q) macḳerel
(5) study regions
(q) Souṫh China sea

Compound terms

Many concepts are represented by compound terms. In most cases, it is
desirable to bring each of the elements into the lead. A device called
differencing is used to identify each component of a compound term. In
general, the word (or words) coded as a *difference* is a modifier. If it
modifies the noun or substantive (the *focus* of the term), it is called a
direct difference and coded with a $01 if it is not to appear as a lead, or with
a $21 if it is used as a lead. If the word modifies another word (or
words) coded as a *difference* itself, it is called an *indirect difference* and coded
with a $02 if nonlead and a $22 if lead.[3]
    Examples:

(1) paintings $21 portrait $21 oil

Both "oil" and "portrait" are *direct differences* as they both directly qualify
the noun "paintings."

(1) bridges $21 concrete $22 reinforced

"Concrete" is a *direct difference* in the sense that it specifies a kind of
bridge in *direct* terms of its material. "Reinforced," on the other hand,
does not refer directly to the focus (these are not "reinforced bridges")
but qualifies instead the material "concrete." It is, therefore, an *indirect
difference*.

[3] The second digit ranges from 2 to 9 depending on the level of the difference, i.e.,
how far removed the *difference* is from the *focus*, e.g., (1) boats $21 plastic $22 reinforced
$23 fiber.

Connectives and substitutes

In many cases, in order to preserve natural word order, the devices of connectives and substitutes are used. The role operator $v indicates a downward-reading connective, and $w an upward-reading connective, e.g.,

String

(1) electronic͟ equipment
(2) design $w of
(*s*) applications $v of $w in
(3) computer͟ systems

Entries
Electronic equipment
   Design. Applications of computer systems
Computer systems
   Applications in design of electronic equipment

String

(1) mild͟ steel
(2) production $w of
(2) quality͟ control

Entries
Mild steel
   Production. Quality control
Quality control. Production of mild steel

In some cases, when the use of connectives does not achieve the desired results, a substitute must be used, e.g.,

Subject
Forecasting increases in costs of spray painting of car doors

String

(1) cars͟

(*p*) doors͟

(2) painting͟ $21 spray
(sub 34↑) (2) spray painting of car doors

(*p*) costs͟ $w of

---

[4]Refers to the number of terms to be substituted. The ↑ means that the terms *above* are to be substituted.

(2) increases $w in

(2) for̂ecasting ⱽ

Entries
Cars
   Doors. Spray painting. Costs. Increases. Forecasting
Doors. Cars
   Spray painting. Costs. Increases. Forecasting
Painting. Doors. Cars
   Spray painting. Costs. Increases. Forecasting
Spray painting. Doors. Cars
   Costs. Increases. Forecasting
Costs.[5] Spray painting of car doors
   Increases. Forecasting
Forecasting.[5] Increases in costs of spray painting of car doors

The substitution restores natural language in the qualifier. Furthermore, it eliminates ambiguities in some cases. Without substitution, the last two entries in the example above would have been:

   Costs. Spray painting. Doors. Cars
      Increases. Forecasting
   Forecasting. Increases. Costs. Spray painting. Doors. Cars

In the last entry, in particular, an ambiguity exists with regard to the relationship between the terms *Forecasting* and *Increases*. The substitution removes this ambiguity.

The following example illustrates substitution by means of adjectival phrases:

Subject
Financial assistance for medical research in the United States

String

(0) Unitêd States ⱽ

(2) medîcine ⱽ

(*p*) research

(sub 2[6]↑) (2) medical research

(2) finan̂cial assistance ⱽ

Entries
United States
   Medicine. Research. Financial assistance

---

[5]Entries containing the substitute.
[6]Refers to the number of terms to be substituted. The ↑ means that the terms *above* are to be substituted.

Medicine. United States
  Research. Financial assistance
Financial assistance. Medical research. United States

Example of a complicated string and the entries generated from it:

Subject
Teaching English to immigrant children in London's
primary schools

String
(0) Lo͜ndon
(1) pr͜imary schools
(p) st͜udents
(q) i͜mmigrants
(3) curriculum subjects
(q) En͜glish language
(sub 4↑) (p) English language to immigrants
(2) te͜aching

Entries
London
  Primary schools. Students: Immigrants. Curriculum
    subjects: English language. Teaching
Primary schools. London
  Students: Immigrants. Curriculum subjects: English
    language. Teaching
Students. Primary schools. London
  Immigrants. Curriculum subjects: English language.
    Teaching
Immigrants. Students. Primary schools. London
  Curriculum subjects: English language. Teaching
English language. Curriculum subjects. Immigrants.
    Students. Primary schools. London.
  Teaching
Teaching. English language to immigrants. Primary
    schools. London

Note that in order to establish the proper context, to remove
ambiguities between terms, or both, additional terms may be required
in the string, such as "students" and "curriculum subjects" in the
example above.

The subject indicator number (SIN)

The subject indicator number is one of the elements in an indexing record that uniquely locates the address in a computerized file at which all the indexing data will be stored (including the PRECIS string, the Dewey classification number, the Library of Congress classification number, and the Library of Congress subject heading or headings). In indexing a particular document, if the indexer discovers that the PRECIS string required is already in the SIN file, he or she can simply quote the SIN on the cataloging record for the document being indexed and no further subject indexing will be necessary. The SIN file is an important time-saving device, particularly as the body of already indexed material grows.

Semantics

The vocabulary used in PRECIS has been described as open-ended, in that each new term encountered in the literature can be admitted to the vocabulary.

In order to achieve vocabulary control, all terms which have been used as lead terms in indexing are entered in a machine-held thesaurus. In addition, nonpreferred synonymous terms and other related terms are also included in the thesaurus because these also function as users' access points. Relationships between each term and other terms are indicated.

There are three basic thesaural relationships: equivalence, hierarchical, and associative.

1. Equivalence relationship—code ($m):
   a. *Synonyms*
      Birds/Aves
   b. *Quasisynonyms*
      Hardness/Softness
2. Hierarchical relationship—code ($o):
   a. *Generic relationship*
      Rodents
        Mice
        Rats
   b. *Hierarchical whole-part relationship*
      (1) *Geographical regions*
         United States
           California
             Los Angeles
             San Francisco

(2) *Systems and organs of the body*
  Circulatory system
    Cardiovascular system
      Vascular system
        Arteries
        Veins
(3) *Areas of discourse*
  Science
    Biology
      Botany
      Zoology
3. Associative relationship—code ($n):

This relationship exists between terms which are not synonyms nor hierarchically related, but are nevertheless mentally associated. One of the terms is entailed by the other, and frequently plays a part in its explanation or definition:

Birds/Ornithology
Teeth/Dentistry

References link the related terms. *See* references are made from terms which are not used in index entries to preferred or target terms which are used consistently to represent that concept. *See also* references are made between terms either of which could appear as a lead in an index entry. The codes ($m, $o, and $n) expressing thesaural relationships have built-in machine instructions for generating appropriate references for a particular index. For hierarchically related terms, *see also* references are made from the broader term to the narrower, but not reciprocally.

The references are generated from a computerized file which consists of independent but interrelated addresses. Each address holds a unique reference indicator number (RIN), the term (either a referred-from or referred-to term) assigned to that address, and possibly one or more reference-generating codes, each followed by the RIN of a referred-from term. For each record of this kind, a record in the card form is made and kept in an alphabetical file which serves as the indexer's main authority file of terms. Examples from this card file representing a network of terms are shown in Figure 10-3.

The codes have built-in machine instruction for generating all references indicated. However, if all the terms in a network of a particular index (Figure 10-4) have not been used as leads, there is a bypass routine for avoiding blind references, i.e., references to terms under which there is no entry in that index. This bypass is illustrated in Figure 10-5.

Figure 10-6 shows an extract from the PRECIS Index.

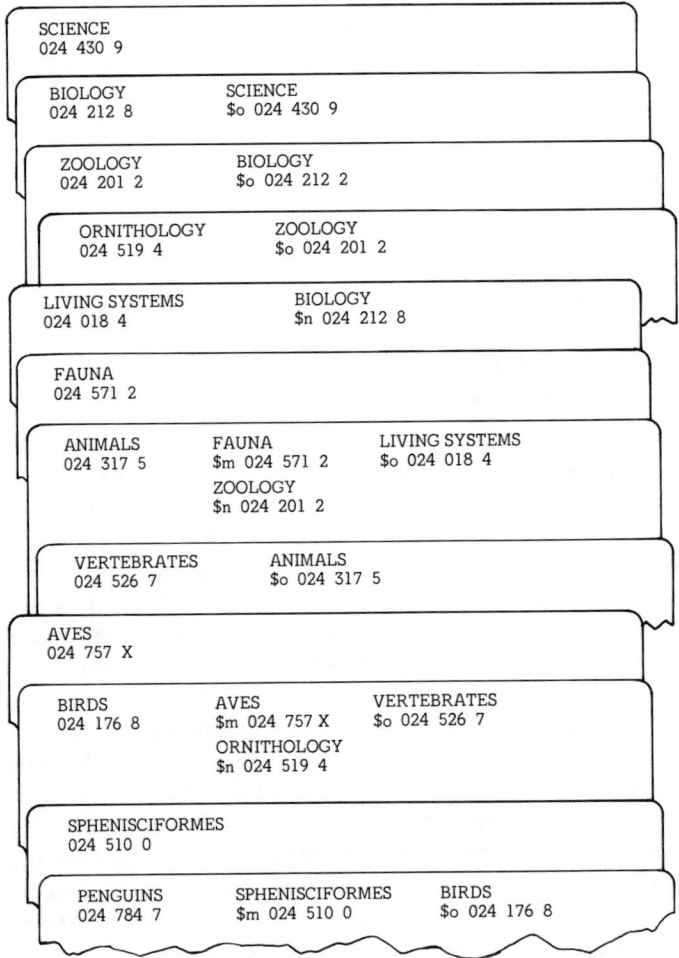

FIGURE 10-3 PRECIS thesaurus: records filed for input. (*Source:* "PRECIS Training Course, 1978: Handouts," 1978.)

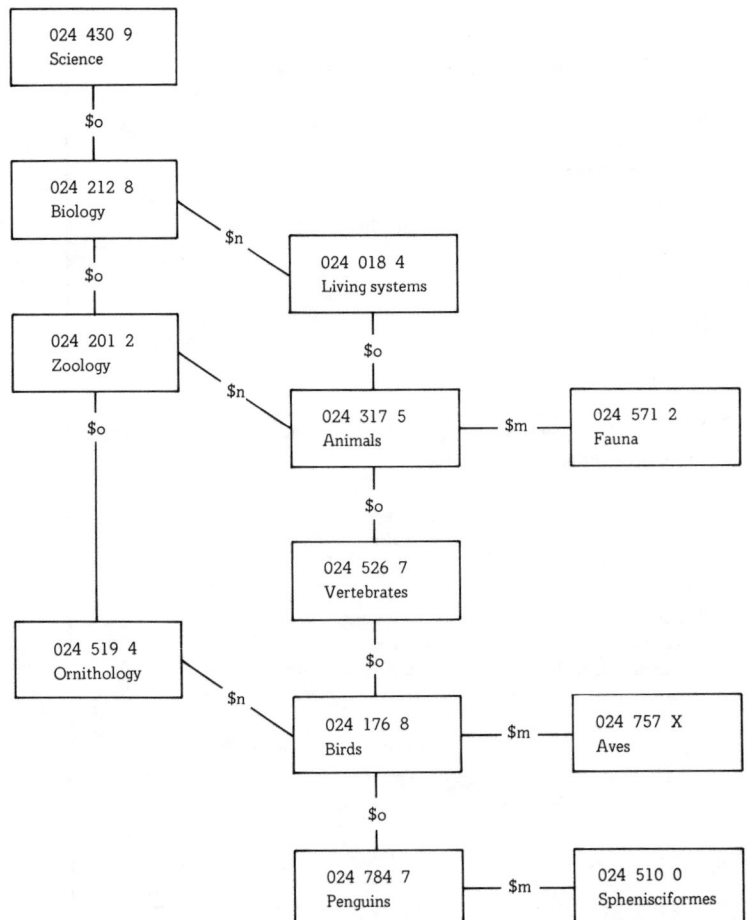

FIGURE 10-4   Network of terms linked by thesaural relationships.

(1) ONE-STEP REFERENCES PRODUCED BY $m & $n

Biology
  See also
    Living systems

Zoology
  See also
    Animals

Ornithology
  See also
    Birds

Fauna *See* Animals

Aves *See* Birds

Sphenisciformes *See* Penguins

(2) BY-PASS REFERENCES PRODUCED BY $o WHEN ONLY ENTRY UNDER 'PENGUINS' PRESENT IN INDEX

Science
  See also
    Ornithology

Zoology
  See also
    Ornithology

Biology
  See also
    Ornithology

Animals
  See also
    Penguins

Living systems
  See also
    Penguins

Vertebrates
  See also
    Penguins

Birds
  See also
    Penguins

FIGURE 10-5 The bypass routine.

EMO system. Anaesthesia. Medicine	617'.962
Employees *See* **Personnel**	
Employers. Engineering industries. Great Britian	
Recognition of white-collar trade unions	
—*Reports, surveys*	331.88'11'6200942
Engineering equipment	
Metric sizes—*Standards*	620'.0021'2
Engineering industries	
See also	
Construction industries	
Electronic engineering industries	
Engineering industries. Great Britain	
Manpower planning. Effects of technological	
development—*Inquiry reports*	331.1'1
White-collar workers. Trade unions. Recognition	
by employers—*Reports, surveys*	331.88'11'6200942
Engines	
See also	
Heat engines	
Tidemills	
Windmills;	
Engines	
—*Juvenile literature*	621.4
Engines. Railways *See* **Locomotives**	
England	
See also	
Names of individual counties	
England	
Areas of outstanding beauty. Description & travel	914.2'04'85
Beaufort, Henry Somerset, *Duke of, 1629-1700*	
—*Biographies*	942.06'092'4
Chilterns. Description & travel	914.25
Cotswold. Social life, *1600-1914*	914.24'1
Etc.	

FIGURE 10-6 Extract from PRECIS Index (*British National Bibliography*).

TOPICS FOR DISCUSSION

1. Discuss the advantages and disadvantages of an alphabetical subject, or dictionary, as opposed to an alphabetico-classed, catalog.
2. *See also* references are made from the general to the specific but not vice versa. Discuss the rationale for this principle.
3. Since some phrase headings in LCSH are inverted and others appear in the direct form, discuss the problem in maintaining consistency in form. Examine the following groups of LC headings and determine whether there are any consistent patterns:

Church music	Bessel's functions
Music, African	Functions, Abelian
African languages	Abelian groups
Languages, Universal	Groups, Continuous

English drama	Epic poetry, English
English poetry	Folk-drama, English
English fiction	Short stories, English

    (Compare parallel headings in other languages)

Discuss the implications of these variant forms for the users and the adequacy of the device used to connect the variant forms.

4. The phrases *Stability of ships*, *Ships' stability*, and *Ships—Stability* all express the same concept. So do *Chemical research* and *Chemistry—Research*. Because of the principle of uniform heading, only one form is used in LCSH with *see* references from the others. Examine similar groups of headings in LCSH to see whether there is any consistent pattern for determining which type of phrase is to be used as the heading.
5. By interpolating the name of a larger geographic area between the subject heading and the local subdivision, the indirect form is a violation of the principle of specific entry. The reason given for this form is that "indirect subdivision assumes that the interest and significance of certain subjects are inseparable from the larger area—the country or state—or that the study of subordinate geographic areas is best considered as contributing to the study of the larger area."[7] Examine headings in LCSH to see whether materials on a particular subject treated from the point of view of subordinate geographic areas (e.g., states, counties, or cities) are grouped together with those treated from larger areas (e.g., continents, countries, states) which encompass the local area.
6. Compare and contrast LCSH and PRECIS in terms of format of entry and the reference structure.

[7]David Judson Haykin. *Subject Headings: A Practical Guide*. Washington, D.C.: U.S. Government Printing Office, 1951.

PART FOUR

Classification

BASIC TOOLS

Cutter, C. A. *C. A. Cutter's Three-Figure Author Table. (Swanson-Swift revision.* 1969) Chicopee, Mass.: H. R. Huntting Company, 1969[?].

Cutter, C. A. *C. A. Cutter's Two-Figure Author Table. (Swanson-Swift revision.* 1969) Chicopee, Mass.: H. R. Huntting Company, 1969[?]

Cutter, C. A. *Cutter-Sanborn Three-Figure Author Table. (Swanson-Swift revision.* 1969) Chicopee, Mass.: H. R. Huntting Company, 1969[?].

Dewey, Melvil. *Abridged Dewey Decimal Classification and Relative Index.* Ed. 11. Edited under the direction of Benjamin A. Custer. Albany, N.Y.: Forest Press, Division of Lake Placid Education Foundation, 1979.

Dewey, Melvil. *Dewey Decimal Classification and Relative Index.* Ed. 19. 3 vols. Edited under the direction of Benjamin A. Custer. Albany, N.Y.: Forest Press, Division of Lake Placid Education Foundation, 1979.

Library of Congress Classification Schedules: A Cumulation of Additions and Changes. Detroit: Gale Research Company, 1974–.

Library of Congress. Subject Cataloging Division. *Classification.* 34 vols. Washington, D.C.: Library of Congress. 1901–.

Library of Congress. Subject Cataloging Division. *LC Classification—Additions and Changes.* Washington, D.C.: Library of Congress. List 1–   Mar./May 1928–.

BACKGROUND READING

Chan, Lois Mai. *Immroth's Guide to the Library of Congress Classification.* 3d ed. Littleton, Colo.: Libraries Unlimited, 1980.

Custer, Benjamin A. "Editor's Introduction." *Dewey Decimal Classification and Relative Index.* Ed. 19. Albany, N.Y.: Forest Press, Division of Lake Placid Education Foundation, 1979. Vol. 1, pp. xxi–lxxv.

Custer, Benjamin A. "Editor's Introduction." *Abridged Dewey Decimal Classification and Relative Index.* Ed. 11. Albany, N.Y.: Forest Press, Division of Lake Placid Education Foundation, 1971. Pp. 7–37 [if the abridged edition is used].

Dunkin, Paul S. "Where Does It Go? Call Numbers." *Cataloging U.S.A.* Chicago: American Library Association, 1969. Pp. 96–137.

Langridge, Derek. *Approach to Classification for Students of Librarianship.* Hamden, Conn.: Linnet Books; London: Clive Bingley, 1973.

Maltby, Arthur. *Sayers' Manual of Classification for Librarians.* 5th ed. London: Andre Deutsch, 1975. Pp. 143–158, 174–189.

FURTHER READING

Allerton Park Institute. *Major Classification Systems: The Dewey Centennial.* Papers presented at the Allerton Park Institute. Sponsored by Forest Press, Inc., University of Illinois Graduate School of Library Science, and University of Illinois Office of Continuing Education and Public Service, held November 9–12, 1975, Allerton Park, Monticello, Illinois. Urbana-Champaign: University of Illinois Graduate School of Library Science, 1976.

Comaromi, John Phillip. *The Eighteen Editions of the Dewey Decimal Classification.* Albany, N.Y.: Forest Press Division, Lake Placid Education Foundation, 1976.

Encyclopedia of Library and Information Science. Allen Kent and Harold Lancour, eds. William Z. Nasri, asst. ed. New York: Marcel Dekker, Inc., 1968–. (Articles on Bliss Bibliographic Classification, Expansive Classification, Colon Classification, etc.)

Foskett, A. C. *The Subject Approach to Information.* 3d ed. Hamden, Conn.: Linnet Books; London: Clive Bingley, 1977. Pp. 127–223.

Maltby, Arthur, ed. *Classification in the 1970s: A Second Look.* Rev. ed. London: Clive Bingley, 1976.

Mills, J. *A Modern Outline of Library Classification.* London: Chapman & Hall, Ltd. 1967. Pp. 1–73, 89–102.

Painter, Ann F., ed. "Classification: Theory and Practice." *Drexel Library Quarterly,* vol. 10, no. 4. Philadelphia: Drexel University, 1974.

Palmer, Bernard I. *Itself an Education: Six Lectures on Classification.* 2d ed. London: Library Association, 1971.

Ranganathan, S.R. *Prolegomena to Library Classification.* 3d ed. Assisted by M. S. Gopinath. London: Asia Publishing House, 1967.

The Use of the Library of Congress Classification. Proceedings of the Institute on the Use of the Library of Congress Classification. Richard H. Schimmelpfeng and C. D. Cook, eds. Sponsored by the American Library Association, Resources and Technical Services Division, Cataloging and Classification Section, New York City, July 7–9, 1966. Chicago: American Library Association, 1968.

CHAPTER 11

General Principles of Classification

DEFINITION

Classification, broadly defined, is the act of organizing the universe of knowledge into some systematic order. It has been considered the most fundamental activity of the human mind. The act of classification consists of the dichotomous process of distinguishing things or objects which possess a certain property or characteristic from those that lack it and of grouping things or objects which have the property or characteristic in common into a class.

The act of classification applied to libraries and information centers has been defined as

> The systematic arrangement by subject of books and other material on shelves or of catalogue and index entries in the manner which is most useful to those who read or who seek a definite piece of information.[1]

In other words, library classification serves a dual function: (1) as a shelving device, which is considered to be the primary purpose of classification, particularly in the United States, and (2) as a means of organizing bibliographic entries in printed catalogs, bibliographies, and indexes in a systematic order. For example, the British National Bibliography and the Wilson Standard Catalogs for libraries are organized according to the Dewey Decimal Classification.

As a shelving device, library classification has two objectives: (1) to help the user identify and locate a work through a call number, and (2) to group all works of a kind together. In order to fulfill the first objective, any method of numbering or marking would be sufficient so long as there is a correspondence between the number or mark on the document and that on the cataloging entry. The second objective, on the other hand, represents a collocating function and requires the grouping of like materials together, on the basis of certain characteristics. The characteristics for division may vary, according to the purpose of the collection. For example, library materials may be

---

[1] Arthur Maltby. *Sayers' Manual of Classification for Librarians.* 5th ed. London: Andre Deutsch, 1975. P. 15.

grouped by author, physical form, size, date of publication, or subject. In modern library classification systems, subject is the predominant characteristic for grouping.

Classification refers both to the arrangement in some logical order of the field of knowledge and to the art of arranging books or other objects in conformity with such a scheme. In other words, it means both the creation of a classification scheme and its application. However, the people who are involved in these two processes are given different names. The inventor or creator of a classification scheme or a person who is engaged in the theory of classification is called a classificationist, while the person who applies such a scheme is referred to as a classifier.

BASIC CONCEPTS

The traditional ideas of library classification were borrowed from the logical or philosophical principles of classification. Classification begins with the universe of knowledge as a whole and divides it into successive stages of classes and subclasses, with a certain characteristic as the basis for each stage. On the whole, the progression is from the general to the specific, forming a hierarchical structure or an "inverted tree," each class being a *species* of the one on the preceding stage and a *genus* to the one below it. The elements within each stage, usually mutually exclusive categories, form a coordinate relationship to one another and are collocated according to the affinity of their relationships.

The Dewey Decimal Classification and the Library of Congress Classification, the most widely used library classification systems today, both originated from the latter part of the nineteenth century and adhere generally to these taxonomic and hierarchical principles.

The characteristics of, or bases for, division vary from subject to subject. For example, architecture can be classified according to schools and styles, periods, or types of buildings. Literature can be divided by language, form, or period. Each characteristic is called a *facet*. Figure 11-1 illustrates the division of literature in the Dewey Decimal Classification based on the three facets named above.

The coordinate elements on each level or stage of division form an *array*, e.g., American literature, English literature, German literature, etc. The term *chain* refers to a string of subjects, each of which represents a different level in the classification, e.g.,

> Literature—English literature—English poetry—Elizabethan poetry.

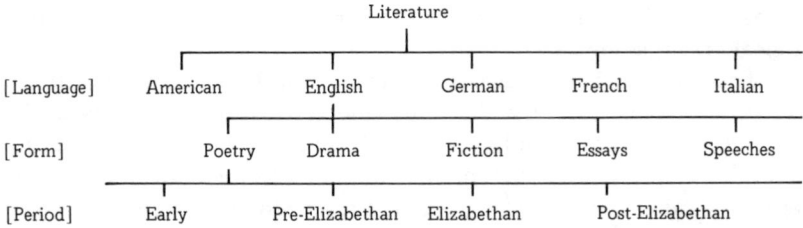

FIGURE 11-1   Division of literature in the Dewey Decimal Classification.

There is not always a built-in or natural order of the characteristics or facets in each class. For example, literature may be divided first by language and then by form. Or, it may also be divided first by form and then by language. In order to maintain consistency, each classification system will determine the order of the facets to be used. This is called *citation order.*

Traditional library classification schemes tend to enumerate all subjects and their subdivisions and provide ready-made symbols for them. This is referred to as an *enumerative* classification. Among the existing library classification schemes, the Library of Congress Classification is considered to be the most enumerative.

Modern classification theory, on the other hand, places emphasis on *facet analysis* and *synthesis*—the analysis and breaking up of a subject into its component parts and reassembling these parts as required by the document to be represented. Instead of enumerating all subjects in a hierarchical structure, modern theory argues that a classification scheme should identify the basic components of subjects by listing under each discipline or main class basic concepts or elements isolated according to certain characteristics or *facets*. In addition, recurring divisions, such as form, geographical, and chronological divisions, are listed separately for application to all classes. In applying such a scheme, the act of classification essentially consists of *synthesis,* or the identification and fitting together of the component elements which make up the subject of the document being classified. The components are fitted together according to a predetermined order, called a *citation formula,* prescribed for that particular class. A system based on these principles is called a *faceted* or *analytico-synthetic classification.* An example is the Colon Classification (see discussion in Chapter 14).

NOTATION

Each classification scheme adopts a system of symbols as class marks which represent the classes and divisions. The purpose of using such a device, called *notation,* is to designate briefly the subjects and sometimes their relationships as well and to provide a sequential order for a logical arrangement.

The notation is usually in the form of numbers or letters or both. A *pure notation* is one in which only one type of symbol is used. An example is the notation of the Dewey Decimal Classification consisting of arabic numerals. A system that employs more than one type of symbol is called a *mixed notation*, e.g., the notation used by the Library of Congress Classification which combines letters and arabic numerals.

A *hierarchical notation* is one that reflects the structural order or hierarchy of the classification and an *expressive notation* is one that expresses the relationships among the subjects. The notation used with the Dewey Decimal Classification is hierarchical and that of the Universal Decimal Classification is both hierarchical and expressive. The notation of the Library of Congress Classification is neither.

Another feature of a notation is called *mnemonics,* or aids to memory. The term means that when a certain topic recurs in the scheme it is represented by the same symbol. For example, in the Dewey Decimal Classification, poetry is represented by the number 1, hence, 811 (American poetry), 821 (English poetry), 831 (German poetry), and so on.

HOW TO CLASSIFY

Assigning subject headings and classifying begin with the same intellectual process of determining the subject content and identifying the principal concepts in the work being represented. This process has been described in Chapter 7 (pages 133–134). While in subject cataloging the content of a work is represented by verbal terms, a symbol, called *notation,* is used in classification. If classification is used mainly as a shelving or location device, as is usually the case in American libraries, only one classification number is chosen for each work; in subject cataloging, on the other hand, any number of subject headings may be assigned to a work.

Choosing a Number: General Guidelines

If the work is on a clearly defined subject, classifying it is a relatively simple operation. One needs simply to choose the appropriate number from the scheme being used. However, a work may deal with more than one subject, or more than one aspect of a subject. The different subjects may be treated together as parts of a broader subject. They may have been brought together by the author because they are affinitive subjects, yet considered separately. Or, they may have been treated in terms of their relationship to each other. In recent years, there has been an increasing number of interdisciplinary works.

The faceted classification schemes such as the Universal Decimal Classification or Colon Classification provide for the combination of class numbers in order to bring out every subject or aspect treated in the work. However, in classifying a multisubject work according to a traditional scheme, such as the Dewey Decimal Classification or Library of Congress Classification, a choice often has to be made between two or more numbers, each representing part of the subjects or aspects treated in the work.

The use of each classification system involves certain unique procedures. The specific procedures for the use of the Dewey Decimal Classification and the Library of Congress Classification will be discussed in Chapters 12 and 13. The following is a discussion of some of the general principles and guidelines that apply to the classification of library material in general.

1. Consider usefulness

When a work can be classed in more than one number in a scheme, consider where it will be most useful to the readers.

2. Subject is usually prior to form

Class by subject, then by form, except in literature, where subject is secondary to form.

3. Use the most specific number

Class the work in the most specific number that will contain it. There may not be an exact number for every subject encountered. When there is no specific number for the work, place it in the next most specific category above it, depending on which scheme is used. For example, classify a history of Chicago in the number for the city, if available, instead of with the history of a larger geographic unit, such as the county, the state, or the United States. If the system does not provide a specific number for Chicago, place it in the number for Cook County or, lacking such, in the number for the history of Illinois.

4. Do not classify from the index alone

The index or indexes that accompany each classification scheme provide help in locating class numbers. However, the chosen number should always be checked in the schedules to make sure that the subject has been placed properly in the overall structure and that the instructions in the schedules restricting or elaborating the use of the number have been observed. In using classification systems based on division by discipline, such as the Dewey Decimal Classification and the Library of Congress Classification, always check the number in the schedules to be sure that the subject has been placed in the appropriate discipline.

Choosing a Number: Multitopical Works

There is no hard and fast rule for the choice of a number for a multitopical work. The following is a summary and discussion of certain guidelines based on the works of classificationists.[2]

1. Determine dominant subject or phase relations

Dominant subject
Classify under the dominant subject, if one can be determined. If the subjects are treated separately, a ready indication of preponderance may be the amount of space devoted to each subject. The author's intention or purpose may be another guide.

Phase relations
More complicated is a work in which the different subjects are viewed in relationship to each other. In such a case, an analysis of the relationship may help to determine the emphasis of the work. The interrelationships of subjects treated in a work are sometimes called *phase relations* and have been discussed in the chapter dealing with subject cataloging. Some examples of phase relations are discussed below.

Influence Phase In classifying a work about the influence of one thing or author on another, the general guideline is to place it under the subject or author being influenced.

Bias Phase Classify a work on a particular subject written with a "bias" toward, or aiming at, a specific group of readers, for example,

---

[2]Benjamin A. Custer. "Editor's Introduction." *Dewey Decimal Classification and Relative Index*, Ed. 19. Albany, N.Y.: Forest Press, Division of Lake Placid Education Foundation, 1979. Vol. 1, Pp. lvii–lix.; Paul S. Dunkin. *Cataloging U.S.A.* Chicago: American Library Association, 1969. Pp. 116–122; William Stetson Merrill. *Code for Classifiers.* 2d ed. Chicago: American Library Association, 1939. Pp. 3–7; W. C. Berwick Sayers. *A Manual of Classification for Librarians and Bibliographers.* 3d rev. ed. London: Andre Deutsch, 1955. Pp. 234–242.

Fundamentals of Physical Chemistry for Premedical Students, under the subject (physical chemistry), not the element to which it is "biased" (premedical or medical sciences).

Tool Phase, or Application Phase Classify a work such as *Chemical Calculations: an Introduction to the Use of Mathematics in Chemistry* under the subject (chemistry) instead of the tool (mathematics).

Comparison Phase Class with the subject emphasized or the first subject.

2. Class under first subject

If the dominant subject cannot be ascertained—e.g., in works treating two or more subjects separately or in comparison without any indication of preponderance—class under the first subject. In the Dewey Decimal Classification, *first* means the one coming first in the schedules. For example, a work dealing equally with Judaism (296) and Islam (297) would be placed in 296. Lacking such specific instruction, *first* may mean the subject treated first in the work.

3. Class under broader subject

A work dealing with two or three subjects which are subdivisions of a broader subject and together constitute the major portion of the broader subject is classed with the broader subject, e.g., choosing the number for classical languages for a work about Greek and Latin. Likewise, a work dealing with more than three subjects, all of which are divisions of a broader subject, is classed in the number which covers them all, e.g., using the number for chemistry for a work about analytical, physical, inorganic, and organic chemistry.

Note

It should be stressed that these are only *general* guidelines. If a work on the influence of one subject or one author on another clearly places emphasis on the subject or author exerting the influence, it should be classed with that subject or author. Similarly, if a work on a subject written for a specific group of readers is of little value to other readers, it should be classed in the number reflecting the intended readers.

CHAPTER 12

Dewey Decimal Classification

HISTORY

The Beginning

The publication in 1876 of a pamphlet entitled *A Classification and Subject Index for Cataloguing and Arranging the Books and Pamphlets of a Library* marked the beginning of the Dewey Decimal Classification (DDC) system, which was soon adopted by many libraries in the United States and later by libraries around the world. Today, in its nineteenth edition, *20th 1989* the Dewey Decimal Classification has become the most widely-used library classification system. A recent survey reveals that over 85 percent of all types of libraries in the United States and Canada use this system.[1] It is also widely used in other countries, particularly in the United Kingdom. The scheme has been translated into many languages.

Melvil Dewey (1851–1931), the founder of the system which was named after him, was assistant librarian at Amherst College when he developed the scheme. In the preface to the 1876 edition, Dewey states that the system was developed early in 1873 as a result of several months' study of some hundreds of books and pamphlets and of over fifty personal visits to various American libraries. Thus, DDC was conceived as a classification of knowledge for the purpose of organizing a library.

The 1876 edition, consisting of merely forty-four pages and published anonymously, contains a brief preface outlining Dewey's principles, the schedules for ten main classes subdivided decimally to form a total of 1,000 categories numbered 000–999, and an alphabetical subject index.

The division of the main classes was based on an earlier classification system (1870) devised by W. T. Harris, who, in turn, based his scheme on an inverted order of Francis Bacon's classification of

---

[1]John P. Comaromi, Mary Ellen Michael, and Janet Bloom. *A Survey of the Use of the Dewey Decimal Classification in the United States and Canada.* Albany, N.Y.: Forest Press Division, Lake Placid Education Foundation, 1975. P. 12.

TABLE 12-1   Classification Systems of Bacon, Harris, and Dewey

Bacon		Harris	Dewey
[Original]	[Inverted]	*Science*	
History (Memory)	Philosophy	Philosophy Religion Social and political science Natural sciences and useful arts	General works Philosophy Religion Sociology Philology Science Useful arts
		Art	
Poesy (Imagination)	Poesy	Fine arts Poetry Pure fiction Literary miscellany	Fine arts Literature
		History	
Philosophy (Reason)	History	Geography and Travel Civil history Biography	History Biography Geography and Travel
		Appendix	
		Miscellany	

knowledge.[2] Bacon divides knowledge into three basic categories—history, poesy, and philosophy—corresponding to the three basic faculties of the human mind—memory, imagination, and reason. The classifications of Bacon, Harris, and Dewey are compared in Table 12-1.

In his new classification scheme, Dewey introduced two new features: relative location and relative index. Prior to Dewey, books in libraries were numbered according to their locations on the shelves. In other words, each book had a fixed location. The Dewey system, on the other hand, numbers books in terms of their relationship to one another without regard to the shelves or rooms where they are placed. Relative location allows indefinite intercalation; books can be moved about in the library without altering the call numbers. In the relative

[2] Arthur Maltby. *Sayers' Manual of Classification for Librarians.* 5th ed. London: Andre Deutsch, 1975. P. 121. John Phillip Comaroni, on the other hand, argues that Hegel provided the philosophic underpinnings of Harris's and Dewey's classification systems (cf. his *The Eighteen Editions of the Dewey Decimal Classification.* Albany, N.Y.: Forest Press Division, Lake Placid Education Foundation, 1976. P. 29).

index, Dewey brings together under one term the locations in the scheme of a subject which, in many cases, falls in several fields of study.

Early Editions

The second edition of DDC, a considerable expansion from the 1876 edition, appeared in 1885. A number of relocations—i.e., shifting of subjects from certain numbers to other numbers—were made. This edition set the notational pattern for all subsequent editions. It was also in this edition that Dewey laid down his famous injunction of the "integrity of numbers." Being a pragmatist and a realist, Dewey was fully aware that a system which changed substantially from edition to edition would not be acceptable to librarians, because changes, particularly relocations, necessitate reclassification. Therefore, in the preface to the second edition, Dewey declared that the numbers may be considered "settled" and henceforth there would be expansions when necessary, but few relocations. This policy of "integrity of numbers," or stability of numbers, has served as a restraining and stabilizing factor in the subsequent revisions of DDC, particularly in the early editions, in which relocations were kept to a minimum, although many expansions were made. Nonetheless, in order to cope with new developments in knowledge, certain changes could not be avoided.

Dewey himself supervised the revision through the thirteenth edition of DDC until his death in 1931. His interest in simplified spelling was reflected in the schedules, e.g., Filosofy and Geografy.

Fifteenth Edition

The fourteenth edition maintained basically the same editorial policy as the earlier editions, with ever-expanding details but with little change in the basic structure. The expansion had not always been balanced. There were many underdeveloped areas. With the fifteenth edition, it was decided that a new approach was necessary and several innovations were introduced. In order to give the work an even structure, details were cut back in many areas until all the subjects reflected equal degrees of subdivision. Some 31,000 entries in the fourteenth edition were reduced to 4,700 in the fifteenth edition. It was also recognized that the scheme had not kept up with the new developments in knowledge, particularly in science and technology, probably because of adherence to the policy of "integrity of numbers" in the earlier editions. It was decided to relocate a large number of subjects in the fifteenth edition. At the same time, the index was also pruned drastically. Simplified spelling used in the earlier editions was discontinued.

After the publication of the fifteenth edition in 1951, it soon became clear that the changes proved to be too much for practicing librarians, most of whom refused to accept the new edition and continued to use the fourteenth. Criticism of the fifteenth edition was fierce and vehement. Many critics even pronounced the system dead.

Sixteenth Edition and Later Editions

The sixteenth edition, under the editorship of Benjamin A. Custer, appeared in 1958, setting the pattern of the seven-year revision cycle. It was decided to return to the former policy of detailed enumeration while incorporating some of the innovative features of the fifteenth edition, such as standard spelling, current terminology, and a pleasing typographical presentation.

The seventeenth through nineteenth editions, also under the editorship of Custer, continued to develop along similar lines. Attempts were made to keep pace with knowledge while observing the policy of "integrity of numbers" within reasonable bounds.

Abridged Dewey Decimal Classification

To provide a short form of the Dewey Decimal Classification more suitable to the needs of small and slowly growing libraries, an abridged edition of the scheme was issued in 1894. The abridgment was about two-fifths the size of the full edition. At present, the abridged version is in its eleventh edition, which was published shortly after the nineteenth full edition. The abridged edition is used by most of the school libraries and many small public libraries in this country. It is also widely used in other countries. In Great Britain, for example, many school libraries are users of the abridged DDC.

In the beginning, the abridged edition was revised when the need arose. Later, it was considered desirable to follow each full edition with an abridged edition. The present eleventh abridged edition accompanied the full nineteenth edition. Through the ninth abridged edition, the numbers on the whole represented true abridgment of those in the full edition. In the tenth abridged edition, there came a basic change. Some numbers represented adaptation rather than abridgment of those in the full edition. In other words, many subjects were represented by numbers that were different rather than merely shorter than those found in the full edition. In this sense, it was at times an adaptation and at times an abridgment. Upon the request of users, the eleventh abridged edition returned to being a true abridgment of the full edition.

The abridged edition has been designed specifically for the elementary and secondary school, small public libraries with a collection that is not expected to grow beyond 20,000 titles, and other collections of a general nature.

REVISION

Current Procedures for Revision

The editor of DDC oversees and is responsible for the revision of the scheme. The editorial office is a part of the Processing Department of the Library of Congress. Forest Press, the publisher of DDC, has a contractual arrangement with the Library of Congress for the editorial work. Between these two organizations is a group called the Decimal Classification Editorial Policy Committee, composed of practicing librarians and library educators, which advises both the editor and the Forest Press concerning matters related to the revision of DDC. The Committee examines the proposed revisions and makes appropriate recommendations to Forest Press. The editor of DDC is also the chief of the Decimal Classification Division of the Library of Congress, which is responsible for assigning DDC numbers to LC cataloging records. The joint appointment ensures consistency and a great degree of coordination between the revision and the application of the system.

Presently, DDC is being revised at approximately seven-year intervals. During each seven-year period, all the schedules and tables are reexamined and revisions are made as required.

Forms of Revision

Revisions usually take the following forms.

Expansion

This method is used to introduce new subjects as well as to provide more minute and specific subdivisions under existing subjects. The numerical notational system of DDC is such that new subjects can only be introduced as subdivisions under existing subjects. This is a reasonable approach since new subjects seldom emerge totally independent of existing knowledge but usually appear as an offspring or outgrowth of an existing field of knowledge. For existing knowledge, as library material proliferates, more minute subdivisions of existing topics are also required.

Reduction

Occasionally, existing subdivisions that are rarely used are discontinued and the subtopics are classed with the more general topic. In general, reductions are far outnumbered by expansions.

Relocation

In each edition, a number of existing topics are removed to different locations (i.e., numbers) in the scheme. Relocation is generally necessitated by one of the following reasons:

1. To rectify an improper placement by moving the topic to where it really belongs. For example, in the eighteenth edition of DDC, Yiddish language and literature, formerly in 492.49 and 892.49 (as subdivisions of Hebraic languages and literature) were relocated in 437.947 and 839.09 (as branches of Germanic languages and literature).
2. To eliminate dual provisions when two or more numbers represent the same meaning or overlap to a large extent. For example, Securities exchanges (formerly in 332.61) and Exchange of securities on organized exchanges (formerly in 332.642) have been combined as one subject, Exchange of securities, and placed in the number 332.642 in the eighteenth edition.
3. To make room for new subjects when there is no available number. For example, in the eighteenth edition of DDC, Antarctica was moved from the areas notation -99 to -989 in order that -99 may be used for Extraterrestrial worlds. In general, a number vacated as a result of relocation is not reused until a later edition. However, in this case, the urgency to accommodate the Extraterrestrial worlds outweighed this policy of "starvation."
4. As a result of realignment of fields of knowledge. A new subject, which had been introduced as a subdivision under an existing subject, may turn out to belong more properly in a different field of knowledge. For example, Astronautics, which was originally placed in 629.1388 (as a subdivision under Aeronautics) was moved to 629.4 (as one of the "other branches" of engineering).

Phoenix schedules

This is the most drastic form of revision. With this method, an entire schedule, such as 510 in the eighteenth edition of DDC and 324 in the nineteenth edition of DDC, is reconstructed without regard to previous divisions. The policy of integrity of numbers is suspended and the editor is not hampered by the notational constriction in rearranging existing subjects and in inserting new subjects. As a result, massive relocations occur within that schedule. In recent editions, the following schedules have been given the "phoenix" treatment:

> 546 (Inorganic chemistry) and 547 (Organic chemistry) in edition 16

> 130 (Pseudopsychology, parapsychology, occultism) and 150 (psychology) in edition 17

> 340 (Law) and 510 (Mathematics) in edition 18

Edition 19 includes the following phoenix schedules:

> 301–307 (Sociology), 324 (The political process), and -41 and -42 (Areas notations for Great Britain)

BASIC PRINCIPLES

Classification by Discipline

To say that classification groups together materials on the same subject is an oversimplification. In fact, both the Dewey Decimal Classification and the Library of Congress Classification, the major systems in use in this country, are classification by discipline. The division of main classes and subclasses is based on academic discipline, or field of study, rather than subject. As a result, the same subject may be classed in more than one place in the scheme. For example, the subject "family," depending on the author's approach, may be classed in ethics, religion, sociology, social customs, family planning, home economics, or genealogy.

In the Dewey Decimal Classification, knowledge was divided into nine basic classes: Philosophy, Theology, Sociology (later Social sciences), Philology, Natural science, Useful arts, Fine arts, Literature, and History (see Table 12-2). These were recognized as academic disciplines in Dewey's time. Some of them are not considered disciplines today, but rather areas of study, each of which includes several academic disciplines. Based on the curriculum of a modern university, one would group such fields as Philosophy, Languages, Fine Arts, and Literature as disciplines under the area, Humanities, which parallels other areas of study such as Social sciences and Physical sciences, each of which also consists of various disciplines. In DDC, Philosophy, Languages, Literature, etc., have been established

TABLE 12-2   Outline of Dewey Decimal Classification

000	**Generalities**	**500**	**Pure sciences**
010	Bibliography	510	Mathematics
020	Library and information sciences	520	Astronomy and allied sciences
030	General encyclopedic works	530	Physics
040		540	Chemistry and allied sciences
050	General serial publications	550	Sciences of earth and other worlds
060	General organizations and museology	560	Paleontology
070	Journalism, publishing, newspapers	570	Life sciences
080	General collections	580	Botanical sciences
090	Manuscripts and book rarities	590	Zoological sciences
100	**Philosophy and related disciplines**	**600**	**Technology (applied sciences)**
110	Metaphysics	610	Medical sciences
120	Epistemology, causation, humankind	620	Engineering and allied operations
130	Paranormal phenomena and arts	630	Agriculture and related technologies
140	Specific philosophical viewpoints	640	Home economics and family living
150	Psychology	650	Management and auxiliary services
160	Logic	660	Chemical and related technologies
170	Ethics (Moral philosophy)	670	Manufactures
180	Ancient, medieval, oriental	680	Manufacture for specific uses
190	Modern western philosophy	690	Buildings
200	**Religion**	**700**	**The arts**
210	Natural religion	710	Civic and landscape art
220	Bible	720	Architecture
230	Christian theology	730	Plastic arts Sculpture
240	Christian moral and devotional	740	Drawing, decorative and minor arts
250	Local church and religious orders	750	Painting and paintings
260	Social and ecclesiastical theology	760	Graphic arts Prints
270	History and geography of church	770	Photography and photographs
280	Christian denominations and sects	780	Music
290	Other and comparative religions	790	Recreational and performing arts
300	**Social sciences**	**800**	**Literature (belles-lettres)**
310	Statistics	810	American literature in English
320	Political science	820	English and Anglo-Saxon literatures
330	Economics	830	Literatures of Germanic languages
340	Law	840	Literatures of Romance languages
350	Public administration	850	Italian, Romanian, Rhaeto-Romanic
360	Social problems and services	860	Spanish and Portuguese literatures
370	Education	870	Italic literatures Latin
380	Commerce (Trade)	880	Hellenic literatures Greek
390	Customs, etiquette, folklore	890	Literatures of other languages
400	**Language**	**900**	**General geography and history**
410	Linguistics	910	General geography Travel
420	English and Anglo-Saxon languages	920	General biography and genealogy
430	Germanic languages German	930	General history of ancient world
440	Romance languages French	940	General history of Europe
450	Italian, Romanian, Rhaeto-Romanic	950	General history of Asia
460	Spanish and Portuguese languages	960	General history of Africa
470	Italic languages Latin	970	General history of North America
480	Hellenic Classical Greek	980	General history of South America
490	Other languages	990	General history of other areas

SOURCE: Melvil Dewey. *Dewey Decimal Classification and Relative Index.* Ed. 19. Edited under the direction of Benjamin A. Custer. Albany, N.Y.: Forest Press, Division of Lake Placid Education Foundation, 1979. Vol. 1, p. 472.

as coordinate subjects with Social sciences, Pure sciences, and Applied sciences. The fact that six of the nine main classes in DDC belong to the area of Humanities reflects the state of learning in the nineteenth century. Dewey gave each of these equal classification value as that of Social sciences, Pure sciences, and Applied sciences. Advancement of knowledge in all fields since Dewey's time has not been uniform in terms of either quantity or velocity. This phenomenon has resulted in the unevenness in the scheme as it stands today. Classes such as Philosophy and Religion have remained fairly stable throughout the successive editions; while others, such as Sociology (later developed into Social sciences) and Useful arts (later called Technology/Applied sciences) have undergone tremendous development and expansion.

Hierarchical Structure

Added to the nine main subject classes is a generalia class, making a total of ten classes. Each main class is divided into subclasses which are further subdivided into various levels as required. Each level, divided on a base of ten because of the notational system (to be discussed later), is subordinate to the level above it, thus forming a hierarchical structure, progressing from the general to the specific (Figure 12-1).

In general, arrangement is first by discipline, then by subject, with various levels of subject subdivisions, then by geographic and period specification, then by form of presentation. Exceptions to this pattern are found in the Literature (800) and the Generalia (000) classes. In the Literature class, arrangement of belles-lettres is first by the discipline (literature), then by original language, then by literary form, then by period of composition. In the Generalia class, certain categories of materials, including general encyclopedias (030), periodicals (050), newspapers (071–079), collections (080), and general publications of general organizations (061–068), are arranged first by form, then by

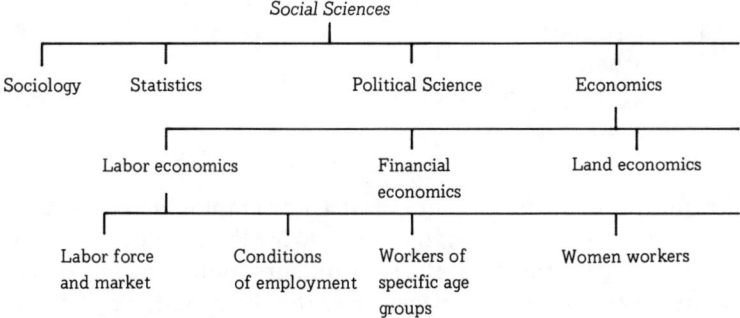

FIGURE 12-1   Hierarchical structure going from general to specific.

language or place as provided by the schedules. Since these general materials do not deal with any specific subject and therefore do not belong to any specific discipline, there is no subject specification. The 800 class and these portions of the 000 class are sometimes called *form* classes.

NOTATION

Symbols

Dewey adopted a pure notation based on arabic numerals. Each topic in the scheme is represented by a number expressed in arabic numerals only, e.g., 346.7304695. This notational system has the advantage of being universally recognized and of transcending any language barriers.

A base of ten, which is the primary characteristic of the arabic numeral system, has also become the major characteristic of the Dewey Decimal Classification. The universe of knowledge is divided on the base of ten:

    0 Generalities
    1 Philosophy and related disciplines
    2 Religion
    3 The Social sciences
    4 Language
    5 Pure sciences
    6 Technology (applied sciences)
    7 The Arts
    8 Literature (belles-lettres)
    9 General geography and history and their auxiliaries

For further division of the main classes, the decimal principle is employed:

    5 Pure sciences
    51 Mathematics
    52 Astronomy and allied sciences
    53 Physics
    etc.

In application, a three-digit number is used by employing zeros to fill out the base number to three digits, e.g., 500 for Pure sciences, 510 for Mathematics, 700 for the Arts, etc. For numbers containing more than three digits, a decimal point is placed after the third digit, e.g., 512.56, 745.92251.

Hierarchical Structure

Another major characteristic of the notation is its hierarchical structure. Dewey decided that the notation should express the hierarchical order of the classification. The notation expresses the relationship between each unit of knowledge and its subordinate elements. Each main class is divided into ten divisions. The second position in the notation represents the division. In this position, $\underline{0}$ is again used for general works on the entire main class, and 1–9 are used for subclasses. Thus, 500 is used for general works on Pure sciences, and 510–590 for the division of sciences, e.g., 510, Mathematics.

Each division, in turn, is divided into ten sections, represented by the number in the third position of the notation, e.g.,

510	Mathematics
511	Generalities
512	Algebra
513	Arithmetic
514	Topology
540	Chemistry and allied sciences
541	Physical and theoretical chemistry
542	Chemical laboratories, apparatus, equipment
543	Analytical chemistry

The system allows further subdivision into various degrees of specificity by means of a continued decimal notation. The decimal point is always placed after the third digit, followed by as many digits as required by the subject matter. The notation never ends with a zero after the decimal point, since a terminal zero after a decimal point has no arithmetical value.

The following example illustrates the hierarchical structure present in both the notation and the classificatory categories:

500	Pure sciences
510	Mathematics
516	Geometry
516.3	Analytic geometries
516.37	Metric differential geometries
516.372	Euclidean

As the classification progresses from the general to the specific, each level of division is indicated by the addition of one new digit. There are a few exceptions to the hierarchical structure, e.g., 574 (Biology), 580 (Botanical sciences), and 590 (Zoological sciences). On the whole, the hierarchical classificatory structure is reflected in the hierarchical notation.

Mnemonics

In assigning numbers to subjects, Dewey frequently used consistent numbers for recurring subjects. For example, Italy is represented by the notation 5, which recurs in numbers related to that country: 945, history of Italy; 914.5, description of Italy; 450, Italian language; 554.5, Geology of Italy; 195, Italian philosophy; and 075, a newspaper in the Italian language. In literature, the number 1 represents poetry, therefore, 811, American poetry; 821, English poetry; 851, Italian poetry, etc. This device helps the readers to memorize or recognize the class numbers more readily. Furthermore, it has enabled the system to develop from an enumerative system to a more analytico-synthetic scheme.

In the earlier editions, the mnemonic device was used most prominently in the following areas: form divisions, geographical divisions, languages, and literature. As the analytico-synthetic nature of the system increased, the mnemonic device has become a standard practice.

DDC began as a basically enumerative system, in that the individual subjects are enumerated in the scheme. In the second edition, the table for form divisions was introduced and certain numbers in the scheme were to be divided like certain other numbers, particularly regarding geographic subdivision. Thus, a limited amount of synthesis, or number building, existed from the early editions.

In edition 17, an areas table for geographic subdivisions was introduced. Then, in edition 18, five more auxiliary tables were introduced; these enhance greatly the analytico-synthetic nature of the system.

EVALUATION

A great deal has been written about the merits and the demerits of the Dewey Decimal Classification. Following is a brief summary of some of the opinions.

Merits

1. It is a practical system. The fact that it has survived many storms in the past hundred years and is still the most widely used classification scheme in the world today attests to its practical value.

2. Relative location was an innovation introduced by Dewey, even though it is now taken for granted.

3. The relative index brings together different aspects of the same subject scattered in different disciplines.

4. The pure notation of arabic numerals is universally recognizable. People from any cultural or language background can adapt to the system easily.

5. The self-evident numerical sequence facilitates filing and shelving.

6. The hierarchical nature of the notation expresses the relationships between and among the class numbers.

7. The use of the decimal system enables infinite expansion and subdivision.

8. The mnemonic nature of the notation helps the readers to memorize and recognize the class numbers.

9. The periodic revision at regular intervals ensures the currentness of the scheme.

Demerits

1. The Anglo-American bias is obvious particularly in 900, Geography and history, and 800, Literature. A heavy bias toward American protestantism is especially evident in 200, Religion.

2. Related disciplines are often separated, e.g., 300, Social sciences from 900, Geography and history; and 400, Languages, from 800, Literature.

3. The proper placements of certain subjects have also been questioned; for example, Library science in general works (000s), Psychology as a subdivision under Philosophy (100s), and Sports and Amusements in the Fine arts (700s).

4. In 800, literary works by the same author are scattered according to literary form when most scholars would prefer to have them grouped together.

5. The base of ten limits the hospitality of the notational system by restricting to nine divisions the capacity for accommodating subjects on the same level of the hierarchy.

6. The different rate of growth in various disciplines has resulted in an uneven structure. Some classes, such as 300, Social sciences; 500, Sciences; and 600, Technology, have become overcrowded.

7. Even though an existing subject can be expanded indefinitely by virtue of the decimal system, no new numbers can be inserted between coordinate numbers—e.g., between 610 and 620—even when required for the accommodation of new subjects. The present method of introducing a new subject is to include it as a subdivision under an existing subject.

8. While the capacity for expansion is infinite, it also results in lengthy numbers for specific and minute subjects. The long numbers have been found inconvenient, particularly when the system is used as a shelving device.

9. Relocations and phoenix schedules, while necessitated by keeping up with knowledge, create practical problems in terms of reclassification for libraries using the scheme.

NOTATIONAL SYNTHESIS: FULL EDITION[3]

Probably because of the influence of modern classification theory, DDC has become less enumerative and increasingly analytico-synthetic in recent editions. Many numbers exist which are not enumerated in the schedules. A considerable degree of synthesis is required in order to obtain the desired specific numbers, particularly with the provisions of the auxiliary tables. Following is a discussion, with illustrations, of notational synthesis, or number building, in DDC.

The main or base number is always taken from the schedules. The additional elements may come from either the schedules or the auxiliary tables, or both. The order of the elements in each case is determined by instructions in the schedules or tables. In building numbers, remove all decimal points. After the process of synthesis is completed, insert a decimal point after the third digit.

Adding a Number or a Part of a Number from the Schedules to a Base Number from Another Part of the Schedules

Adding an entire number to a base number

A bibliography of physics	<u>016.53</u>
1. The index provides a number for subject bibliographies.	<u>016</u>
2. Turning to the schedules, the classifier finds under 016.1–016.9 a note saying "Add 100–900 to base number 016," which means that any number within that range can be added to 016 to obtain a number for the bibliographies of that subject.	
3. Look up the number for Physics.	<u>530</u>
4. Add this number to the base number.	<u>016 530</u>
5. Insert decimal point after the third digit and remove any terminal 0 after decimal point	<u>016.53</u>
Paper industry	<u>338.47 676 2</u>
1. Base number for Secondary industries of	<u>338.47</u>

Handwritten margin notes: "DCC 19", "A, could be classed under disciplin 530.16", "338.4 sec indust economics", "goods + services"

³Instruction in the use of the abridged edition follows on pages 248–257.

specific goods and services, with instruction
to add 001–999.

main entry in schedules

2. Number for Paper and Paper products   ⬭676 2⬭
3. Add (2) to (1).   338 47 676 2
4. Insert decimal point.   338.476762

Adding a fraction of a number or fractions of numbers to a base number

ok A general Russian periodical   057.1
1. Index provides number for all serial   050
   publications.
2. Schedules enumerate subdivisions of 050 by
   languages among which is one for Slavic
   languages, with instruction: "Add to base   057
   number 057, the numbers following 037 in
   037.1–037.9."
3. Determine the appropriate number in the
   sequence.   037.1
4. Add the number following 037 to (2).   057 1
5. Insert decimal point.   057.1

ok A Presbyterian guide to Christian life   248.485
1. Base number for Guides to Christian life
   with instruction: "Add to base number   248.48
   248.48 the numbers following 28 in
   280.2–289.9."
2. Find the number for the Presbyterian
   Church in the sequence.   285
3. Add the number following 28 to (1).   248 485
4. Insert decimal point.   248.485

? Photographs of scientific subjects   779.95
1. Base number for photographs with   779
   instruction: "Add to base number 779 the
   numbers following 704.94 in
   704.942–704.949."
2. Find the most appropriate number in the   704.949
   sequence: Iconography of other specific
   subjects, with instruction: "Add 001–999
   to base number 704.949."
*?→*3. Find the number for Science.   500
4. Add (3) to (2).   704 949500
5. Add the number following 704.94 to (1).   779 9500
6. Insert decimal point and remove terminal 0s. 779.95

you other from the 10 main classes?

Exercise A

Assign Decimal Classification Numbers to the following subjects:

1. India under the British rule.
2. Discipline of students in the public schools.
3. Television commercials.
4. A thesaurus of water resources terms.
5. Planning public library buildings.
6. A bibliography on diagnostic x-ray techniques.
7. Inbreeding in relation to human eugenics.
8. Commentaries on the Gospel of John.
9. Colligative properties of electrolytic solutions.
10. Unemployment in library services.
11. Embryology of vertebrates.
12. Curriculum design in schools.

Adding a Notation or Notations from the Auxiliary Tables to a Base Number

In the nineteenth edition of DDC, there are seven auxiliary tables:

Table 1: standard subdivisions
Table 2: areas
Table 3: subdivisions of individual literatures
Table 4: subdivisions of individual languages
Table 5: racial, ethnic, national groups
Table 6: languages
Table 7: persons

Notations from all tables, except those in Tables 3 and 4, are applicable throughout the entire schedules. Notations from Table 1 may be used wherever applicable. Notations from Tables 2, 5, 6, and 7 are used only when instructed.[4] Tables 3 and 4 apply only to certain schedules: Table 3 is used with 810–890 and Table 4 is used with 420–490. They are used only when specifically instructed.

All notations from the auxiliary tables are preceded by a dash, indicating that these are not complete class numbers, but must be used in conjunction with numbers from the schedules. In some cases, the notations from one table may be added to those of another table or other tables, and the combination is then used with the appropriate number from the schedules.

[4]However, notations from Tables 2, 5, and 7 may be added, according to instructions, to -09, -89, and -88, respectively, in Table 1, and the results are then used as standard subdivisions, i.e., may be used whenever appropriate.

Table 1: Standard subdivisions

After a specific number has been chosen for a work, the classifier should then consider whether further specification concerning the bibliographic form or the author's approach is desirable, i.e., whether any of the standard subdivisions is applicable. Table 1 lists nine categories of standard subdivisions which are further subdivided into more detailed specifications. All notations for standard subdivisions begin with a 0, e.g., -01, -07154.

Notations from auxiliary tables are never used alone, or as main numbers. With the exception of -04, the classifier does not need any specific instruction in the schedules in order to add the notations for standard subdivisions. Appropriateness and applicability are the general guide. For example, for a journal of inorganic chemistry, the standard subdivision -05 (for serial publications) is added to the base number 546 to form the number 546.05. The standard subdivision -04 is reserved for special topics which have general application throughout the regular subdivisions of certain specific subjects. Therefore, it varies from subject to subject and is to be used only when the special topics are spelled out in the schedules.

Although standard subdivisions may be applied wherever they are appropriate, there are certain restrictions on their use. In addition to individual restrictions appearing in the schedules relating to specific numbers (e.g., do not use 362.09; class in 362.9), certain general restrictions are set forth in the editor's introduction to DDC:

1. Unless there are instructions in the schedules permitting their use, the classifier should be cautious about adding a standard subdivision to the number chosen for a work that deals with a subject more specific than the content of the number, i.e., when the subject represented in the work does not have its own specific number. For example, a history of classification systems is classed in 025.4309, but a history of the Russian Library-Bibliographical Classification, which does not have its own number, is classed in 025.43, instead of 025.4309.

2. "The classifier should not add standard subdivisions when they are redundant." Therefore, for a history of the United States, do not add -09 to 973, which already means history. Likewise, it is redundant to add -03 to 423, which already means a dictionary of the English language.

3. "The editors recommend that the classifier not add one standard subdivision to another standard subdivision unless there are specific instructions to do so." When more than one standard subdivision is applicable to a work, choose one. In choosing a standard subdivision, observe the table of precedence

found at the beginning of Table 1, e.g., 020.7 for *Journal of Education for Librarianship* rather than 020.5 or 020.705. On the other hand, in some cases, the schedules permit the use of more than one standard subdivision, e.g., 610.7305 for a journal of nursing, although both -073 and -05 appear to be standard subdivisions.[5]

Before adding a standard subdivision to a base number, the classifier should remove all the zeros which are used as fillers in the base number. Therefore, standard subdivision -03 added to the base number 100 results in 103, not 100.03. A journal of library science is classed in 020.5, not 020.05.

However, there are exceptions to the single-zero rule. In many cases, notations beginning with -0, -00, or even -000 have been assigned meanings other than those for standard subdivisions. In these cases, the classifier is instructed to use more than one zero for standard subdivisions, e.g.,

> 320 Political science
> .01 Philosophy and theory
> .02–.08 other standard subdivisions
> Hence, 320.05 for a journal of political science.

> 352 Local government
> Use 352.0001–352.0008 for standard subdivisions
> Hence, 352.00025 for a directory of local governments

> 350 Public administration
> Use 350.0001–350.0009 for standard subdivisions
> Hence, 350.0009 for a history of public administration

Table 2: Areas

Areas notation specifies the geographic subdivision of a subject and may be used with numbers throughout the schedules as instructed. It is used in the following ways.

Used directly when so noted with numbers from schedules

Geology of Finland	554.897
1. Geology of Europe, with instruction to add areas notation -41 to -49 to base number 55.	554
2. Areas notation for Finland.	-4 897
3. Add (2) to (1) and insert decimal point.	554.897

5-073 is an irregular standard subdivision.

o¹ᵘ Social welfare in New York City   362.97471
1. Social welfare: geographical treatment   362.91–.99
   with instruction:"Add 'Areas' notation
   1–9 from Table 2 to base number
   362.9."
2. Areas notation for New York City.   -7471
3. Add (2) to base number in (1) and insert
   decimal point.   362.94741

o¹ᵘ Emigration from Italy to New York City   325.245097471
1. Base number for emigration from spe-
   cific continents, countries, localities.   325.2
2. Areas notation for Italy.   -45
3. As instructed under 325.23–.29,   325.245
   add (2) to (1).
4. As further instructed, add 09 to (3).   325.24509
5. And to the result add areas notation
   for place entered (i.e., –7471)   325.245097471

o¹ᵘ Foreign relations between Japan and
Great Britain   327.41052
1. Base number for foreign relations
   between specific nations as listed
   under 327.3–327.9.   327
2. Areas notation for Japan.   -52
3. Areas notation for Great Britain.   -41
4. As instructed, add areas notation for
   one nation to the base number, add 0
   and to the result add area notation for
   the other nation. The order of the
   areas notation is determined by the
   emphasis of the work. If Japan is
   emphasized.   327.52041
5. If Great Britain is emphasized.   327.41052
6. If the emphasis is equal, give priority
   to the one coming first in the sequence
   of areas notations.   327.41052

Used through the interposition of standard subdivisions notation -09 from Table 1
In Table 1, under -093 to -099, there is an instruction to add areas
notation 3–9 from Table 2 to base number -09, e.g., -0973, for
historical and geographical treatment of subject with regard to U.S.
Since -09 is a standard subdivision and can be added to any number
from the schedules as desired, virtually every number in the DDC
system can be subdivided geographically. However, when direct

geographic subdivision is provided as illustrated on pages 234–235, it takes precedence over the use of -09 and its subdivisions.

Commercial policy of the United States	382.30973
1. Number for Commercial policy, with no provision for geographic subdivision.	382.3
2. Standard subdivision for United States.	-0973
3. Add (2) to (1) and insert decimal point.	382.30973
Paper industry in England	338.4767620942
1. Number for Paper industry as constructed under Paper industry on p. 230.	338.476762
2. Standard subdivision for England.	-0942
3. Resulting number.	338.4767620942

Used when so noted with numbers from other tables

American Chemical Society	540.6073
1. Number for Chemistry	540
2. Standard subdivision for national organizations	-0 60
3. Add areas notation to (2).	-0 6073
4. Add (3) to (1).	540.6073

American Physical Society	530.06073

Similar to the example above, except that the number 530 requires two 0s for standard subdivisions.

Library science students in the United States	020.73
1. Number for library science.	020
2. Standard subdivision for students.	-0 73
3. Standard subdivision for the United States.	-0973
4. Since the classifier has been advised not to add one standard subdivision to another one, (2) is chosen according to the order of precedence for standard subdivisions. Add (2) to (1) after the terminal 0 has been removed.	020.73

Used with another number from Table 2

Areas notation -3 to -9 may be used with areas notation -1 for a combination of geographic features with localities.[6] Instruction for adding is given under areas notation -1 in Table 2.

Fresh water fishes in the lakes of Kentucky	597.092916920769
1. Fresh water fishes, with instruction to add areas notation -1 to -9.	596.0929
2. Areas notation for lakes.	-1692
3. Areas notation for Kentucky.	-769
4. As instructed under areas notation -1, add 0 to (2) and then add (3).	-16920769
5. Add (4) to (1).	597.092916920769
North Dakota century school code	344.7840702632
1. Social law	344
2. Social law of North Dakota, by adding areas notation to base number.	344.784
3. School law.	344.07
4. As instructed, add the numbers following 344 in 344.001–344.099 to (2).	344.78407
5. Special form division for collected laws as listed under 342–347.	-02632
6. Add (5) to (4).	344.7840702632

Exercise B

1. Assign Decimal classification numbers to the subjects listed in Table 12-3.

2. Assign Decimal classification numbers to the following subjects:
    a. Planning for the education of the handicapped child in Ohio.
    b. Brooklyn Public Library.
    c. The Library of Congress.
    d. History of classical languages.
    e. A dictionary of modern music and musicians.
    f. Popular music in the United States.
    g. *American Libraries* (official journal of the American Library Association).
    h. A teacher's handbook of social studies.

[6]Note that this is an optional provision.

TABLE 12-3 Exercise B, 1

	United States	Tennessee	Belgium	Scotland	Iran	Egypt
Areas Table Notation						
History of						
Geography of						
Atlas of						
Gazetteer of						
Libraries in						
Tourist guide to						
Newspapers of						
Folk songs of						
Economic conditions in						
Political Conditions in Late Nineteenth Century						
Painters from						
Geology of						

i. The government of American cities.
j. *Journal of Physical Oceanography.*
k. Foreign relations between Russia and Japan.
l. The civil rights movement in the United States.
m. Social conditions in Japan after World War II.
n. *Masterpieces of Painting in the Metropolitan Museum of Art: An Exhibition Catalog.*
o. Life and health insurance laws (United States).
p. Illinois rules and regulations for fire prevention and safety, as amended 1968.
q. Arizona library laws (a compilation).

Table 3: Subdivisions of individual literatures

Notations from Table 3 are used when applicable with the base numbers for individual literatures identified by * under 810–890 in the schedules. Synthesis of notation for literature represents the most complex procedures in the DDC system. The application of Table 3 is discussed in "Classification of Literature," pages 241–246.

Table 4: Subdivisions of individual languages

Notations from Table 4 are used with base numbers for individual languages identified by * under 420–490 in the schedules.

Intonation of the German language	431.6
1. Base number for German language.	43
2. Subdivision for intonation from Table 4.	-1 6
3. Add (2) to (1) and insert decimal point.	431.6
An English-Spanish dictionary	463.21
1. For a bilingual dictionary. Determine first which language to be used as the base number. As the instruction under -32 to -39 in Table 4 indicates, it will be more useful to class this dictionary with the Spanish language. Base number for Spanish.	46
2. Subdivisions for bilingual dictionaries.	-32–39
3. Add Languages notation (-21 for English) from Table 6 to base number -3. *discontinued in DCC 20*	-3 21

4. Add (3) to (1) and insert decimal
point.   463.<u>21</u>

A German-French dictionary   443.<u>31</u>

1. "If classification with either
language is equally useful, class
with the language coming later in
the sequence." In this case, French.   <u>44</u>

2. Add Languages notation (-31) to
subdivision for dictionaries (-3).   -<u>3 31</u>

Descontinued in DC 020

3. Add (2) to (1) and insert decimal
point.   443.<u>31</u>

Table 5: Racial, ethnic, national groups

Notations from Table 5 are used with those numbers from the
schedules and other tables to which the classifier is instructed to add
Racial, Ethnic, National Groups notation.

Social structure among the Hindis   305.<u>89143</u>

1. Base number for Social structure of
specific racial, ethnic, national
groups with instruction to add   305.<u>8</u>
notation from Table 5

2. Notation for Hindis from Table 5   -<u>9143</u>

Decorative arts of Chinese   745.<u>089951</u>

1. Base number for Decorative and
minor arts   <u>745</u>

2. Standard subdivision for treatment
among specific racial, ethnic,
national groups with instruction
to add notation from Table 5   -<u>089</u>

3. Notation for Chinese from Table 5   -<u>951</u>

Table 6: Languages

Notations from Table 6 represent the language aspect, or facet,
of a subject and are used with base numbers from the schedules.
They are added as instructed, a procedure similar to that employed
with Tables 2 and 5.

A French Bible   220.5<u>41</u>
A Swahili Bible   220.5<u>96392</u>

The Old Testament in French   221.5<u>41</u>

The Old Testament in Swahili	221.5<u>96392</u>
The Book of Job in French	223.105<u>41</u>
The Book of Job in Swahili	223.105<u>96392</u>
A general Japanese periodical	059.<u>9</u> <u>56</u>

Table 7: Persons

The procedure for using notations from Table 7 is similar to that employed for Tables 2, 5, and 6.

Children as artists	704.<u>054</u>
Paintings by preschool children	75<u>0</u>.<u>880543</u>

Exercise C

Assign Decimal classification numbers to the following subjects or titles:

1. Swahili grammar.
2. A bibliography of anonymous works in German.
3. A Chinese-English, English-Chinese dictionary.
4. Islamic painting.
5. *Osiris: The Egyptian Religion of Resurrection.*
6. *Analyzing Children's Art.*
7. *Babylonian and Assyrian Religion.*
8. *The Art Stealers.*
9. *Patrons and Patriotism: The Encouragement of the Fine Arts in the United States.*
10. *Studies in Italian-American Social History.*
11. *La Raza: The Mexican-Americans.*
12. *Syrian Christians in Muslim Society.*
13. *They Sought a Country: Mennonite Colonization in Mexico.*
14. *Our Crowd: The Great Jewish Families of New York.*
15. *Das Neue Testament Deutsch* (a German version of the New Testament).

Classification of Literature

In the classification of literature, the subject or topical aspect is secondary to language, literary form, and period, which are the main facets of literature.

Citation order

With a few exceptions, the citation order is:

1. Main class literature is represented by the base number <u>8</u>.
2. Language is the second element in the number, e.g., 8<u>2</u>- for English literature, 89<u>5</u>.<u>1</u>- for Chinese literature, 8<u>0</u>- for literature not limited to a language.
3. Literary form is the third element. Mnemonics are employed, e.g., -<u>1</u> for poetry, -<u>2</u> for drama, etc. Hence, 82<u>1</u> (English poetry), 895.1<u>2</u> (Chinese drama), 82<u>0</u> for English literature not limited to a particular form.
4. Period, if applicable, follows literary form, e.g., 811.<u>1</u> (colonial American poetry).
5. Standard subdivisions with rather elaborate sub-subdivisions for feature and theme are displayed under -<u>08</u> (collections) and -<u>09</u> (history and criticism).

Examples

Classification of literature, particularly literature of specific languages, by DDC represents the most complex process of number building. Two tables, Table 3 and Table 3-A, are used with the 800 class. Because of the complexity, the editor has provided detailed step-by-step instructions with regard to number building in the 800 class. The instructions are printed both in the schedules and at the beginning of Table 3. These should be carefully studied. The following examples show the many possible combinations of facets in the classification of literature. The examples are divided by various types of literary works and works about literature: (1) collections of literature by more than one author, (2) works about literature, (3) works written by individual authors, (4) works about individual authors, and (5) works about individual works.

1. Collections of literature by more than one author

An anthology of world literature	<u>808</u>.<u>8</u>
A Collection of nineteenth-century literature (Facet: Period)	<u>808</u>.<u>80034</u>
1. Base number for a collection of literature	<u>808</u>.<u>800</u>
2. Standard subdivision for nineteenth century from Table 1	-090<u>34</u>
A collection of Christmas literature (Facet: Feature/theme)	<u>808</u>.<u>8033</u>

A collection of nineteenth-century poetry (Facets: Form, period)	808.81034
1. Base number for a collection of poetry	808.810
2. Period notation from Table 1	-09034

A collection of Christmas poetry (Facets: Period plus Feature/theme)	808.81933
1. Base number for a collection of poetry displaying specific features	808.819
2. Add the number following 808.80 in 808.8033 (holidays)	33

An anthology of Spanish literature (Facet: Language)	860.8
1. Base number for Spanish literature	86
2. Subdivision for collections from Table 3	-0 8

A collection of eighteenth-century Spanish literature (Facets: Language plus Period)	860.8004
1. Base number for Spanish literature	86
2. Notation for collections from specific periods from Tables 3 and 3-A	-0 800
3. Notation from the period table for Spanish literature	4

A collection of Spanish poetry (Facets: Language plus Form)	861.008
1. Base number for Spanish literature	86
2. Notation from Table 3 for a collection of poetry	-1 008

A collection of eighteenth-century Spanish drama (Facets: Language plus Form plus Period)	862.408
1. Base number for Spanish literature	86
2. Notation for drama from Table 3	2
3. Notation from period table for Spanish literature	4
4. To the result add the numbers following -10 in -1001 to -1009 for a collection	-1008

A collection of American Christmas poetry (Facets: Language plus Form plus Feature/theme)	811.008033
1. Base number for American literature	81
2. Collections of poetry featuring holidays (Tables 3 and 3-A)	-1 008033

A collection of nineteenth-century American Christmas poetry (Facets: Language plus Form plus Period plus Feature/theme)	811.408033
1. Base number for American literature	81
2. Poetry (Table 3)	1
3. Nineteenth century (period table for American literature)	4
4. To the result add the numbers following -10 in -1001 to -1009	-1008033

2. Works about literature

Using examples similar to those listed above, one may synthesize the following numbers for works about literature:

A history of world literature	809
A study of nineteenth-century literature	809.034
A study of Christmas literature	809.9333
A study of nineteenth-century poetry	809.1034
A study of Christmas poetry	809.1933
A history of Spanish literature	860.9
A study of eighteenth-century Spanish literature	860.9004
A study of Spanish poetry	861.009
A study of eighteenth-century Spanish drama	862.409
A study of American Christmas poetry	811.00933
A study of nineteenth-century American Christmas poetry	811.40933

3. Works written by individual authors

DDC classes literature by form. Works by individual authors are therefore classed in different numbers according to their literary forms.

The notation for works written by individual authors contains the following facets: Literature (8), language, form, and period, e.g.,

The Adventures of Huckleberry Finn by Mark Twain	813.4
The Celebrated Jumping Frog of Calaveras County by Mark Twain	817.4
Essays by G. K. Chesterton	824.912
The Heart of Midlothian by Sir Walter Scott	823.7
The Lady of the Lake by Sir Walter Scott	821.7

Selected and collected works by individual authors are classed according to literary forms in the same numbers as individual works without the use of -08, e.g.,

Short Stories by Sir Walter Scott	823.7
Selected Tales by Edgar Allen Poe	813.3

When the collected works are in different forms, the problem is then which number to use. In general, the number for the predominant form is chosen, e.g.,

The Writings of Mark Twain	817.4
	or 813.4
Selected Prose and Poetry by Ralph Waldo Emerson	814.3

When no predominant form can be determined, or when the collection includes works in a variety of forms, the number -8 for Miscellaneous writings is used, e.g.,

Selected Prose, Poetry, and Eureka by Edgar Allen Poe	818.309
The Wisdom of Sir Walter: Criticisms and Opinions Collected from the Waverley Novels and Lockhart's Life of Sir Walter Scott	828.709
Selections from Voltaire	848.509
The Works of Mark Twain	818.409

In DDC, literary authors do not receive individual unique class numbers as in LCC. Authors writing in the same form and the same period share the same number. For example, all late nineteenth century American novelists are assigned the number 813.4. The only exception to this rule is Shakespeare as a dramatist, to whom the unique number 822.33 has been assigned.

In many libraries, fiction in English is not classified in the 800 numbers. Instead, it is assigned the letter F and subarranged alphabetically by author.

4. Works about individual authors
Works about an individual author are classed in the same number as assigned to the author's works, as instructed in Table 3 (cf. note under -11–19), e.g.,

Ezra Pound: A Collection of Critical Essays, edited by Walter Sutton	811.52
A Study of the Sonnets of Shakespeare	821.3
Aldous Huxley: A Study	823.912
An Essay on the Genius and Writings of Pope	821.5

In literature, it is difficult to separate biography and criticism of an author. Usually, they are both classed in the 800s, e.g.,

The Letters of Sir Walter Scott	828.709
Romain Rolland and a World at War	848.91209

Note that the standard subdivision -0924 for individual biography is not used.

5. Works about individual works
Individual works and works about them are classed in the same numbers, as instructed in Table 3. The subdivision -09 is not used, e.g.,

A Critical Study of Thackeray's *Vanity Fair*	823.8
A Study of Marlowe's *Doctor Faustus*	822.3

Exercise D

Assign Decimal classification numbers:

1. A collection of German literature for and by Jews.
2. Characterization in Jacobean tragedies: a critical study.
3. A collection of devotional poetry from colonial America.

4. A collection of seventeenth century French drama.
5. A history of science fiction in the United States.
6. A study of the theme of friendship in fifteenth-century Chinese literature.
7. Abraham Lincoln in American literature: a critical study.
8. A study of the theme of alienation in twentieth-century American fiction.
9. The diaries of Mark Twain.
10. A history of Irish Gaelic poetry in the early period.
11. A study of the theme of death in twentieth-century American poetry.
12. A study of the characters in seventeenth-century French drama.
13. A study of Shakespeare's tragedies by Clifford Leech.
14. Collected poems of Byron.
15. The art of writing short stories.
16. An anthology of American short stories.
17. Literary history of the United States: twentieth century.

Segmentation

As the examples given above indicate, DDC class numbers can be rather long and unwieldy. The examples show the maximum specificity permitted by the system. In practice, some of these long numbers are found to be undesirable, particularly in smaller collections. Since the notational structure is hierarchical, it allows various degrees of specificity by reducing the length of the numbers. However, it is not desirable to cut the numbers arbitrarily. In each case, there are certain points at which the number can be shortened logically. It also ensures consistency by cutting the numbers at these logical points. To help librarians determine the appropriate places to cut a DDC number, these points are indicated on Library of Congress cataloging copy by means of prime marks, e.g., 559'.4238, 621.36'7, 338.7'62'515, or 344'.784'0702632. This practice is called *segmentation*. It is particularly useful in handling numbers such as 344'.73'012813317950262.

DDC numbers on Library of Congress cataloging copy and in the *British National Bibliography* are presented in one to three segments. A number which is printed in one segment, e.g., 629.2, should not be shortened. When a number appears in two segments, it is recommended that the small libraries consider using only the first segment. When a number is printed in three segments, the first segment is recommended for use in small libraries, the first two segments by medium-sized libraries, and the entire number by large libraries. In the case of a very long number, one or more synthetic elements from the last segment may be omitted, e.g., 344.7301281 or 344.7301281331-795, based on the example given above.

NOTATIONAL SYNTHESIS: ABRIDGED EDITION

In many cases, the classifier will find that the abridged edition supplies a number representing a much broader subject than the content of the work being classified, because it is a characteristic of the abridged edition to provide a broad classification without minute details.

Since this is a partially analytico-synthetic scheme, a certain degree of notational synthesis, or number building, is required even in using the abridged edition, particularly with the provisions of the auxiliary tables.

The main or base number is always taken from the schedules. The additional elements may come from either the schedules or the auxiliary tables, or both. The order of the elements in each case is determined by instructions in the schedules or tables. In building numbers, remove all decimal points. After the process of synthesis is completed, insert a decimal point after the third digit.

Adding a Number or a Part of a Number from the Schedules to a Base Number from Another Part of the Schedules

Adding an entire number to a base number

Bibliography of Adult Education	016.374
1. The index provides the number of a subject bibliography.	016
2. Turning to the schedules, the classifier finds under 016.1–016.9 the note: "Add 100–900 to base number 016," which means any number in classes 100–900 can be added to 016 to obtain a number for the bibliographies of that subject.	
3. Look up the number for Adult education.	374
4. Add (3) to (1) and insert decimal point after the third digit.	016.374

Adding a fraction of a number to a base number

An Interpretation of the Old Testament	221.6
1. Number for the Old Testament	221
2. Under 221.1–221.9, there is a note saying "Add to base number 221 the numbers following 220 in	

220.1–220.9." Find the number in
that range which means an inter-
pretation.   220.<u>6</u>
3. Add to (1) the number following
220 and insert decimal point.   <u>221.6</u>

Exercise E

Assign Dewey classification numbers (abridged edition) to the following subjects:

1. Magnetism of the earth.
2. Guidance and counseling in schools.
3. Cataloging and classification of books in libraries.
4. *Séance: A Book of Spiritual Communications.*
5. A bibliography of bacteriology.
6. Landscaping for homes.
7. Acquisition of audiovisual materials in libraries.
8. The causes of the Civil War.
9. A bibliography of local transportation.
10. The kinesiology of weight lifting.
11. Designing dormitories.
12. *Kentuckiana: A Bibliography of Books about Kentucky.*
13. A concordance of the New Testament.
14. A critique of Marx's *Das Kapital.*
15. Smallpox vaccination.
16. Newspapers in Russia.
17. Position of women in the Old Testament.
18. Paintings from the United States.
19. An atlas of the moon.
20. Public library administration.
21. Greek mythology.
22. *How to Prepare for College Entrance Examinations.*

Adding a Notation or Notations
from the Auxiliary Tables to a Base Number

In the abridged edition, there are four auxiliary tables:

Table 1: standard subdivisions
Table 2: areas
Table 3: subdivisions of individual literatures
Table 4: subdivisions of individual languages

Notations from Table 1 are applicable throughout the schedules wherever appropriate. Those from Table 2 also apply to all classes but can be used only when instructed. Table 3 applies only to the numbers 810–890 and is used only when specifically instructed. Table 4 applies to the numbers 420–490 and is also used with specific instructions.

All notations from the auxiliary tables are preceded by a dash, indicating that these are not complete class numbers but must be used in conjunction with numbers from the schedules. In some cases, a notation from one table may be added to one from another table, and the combination is then used with the appropriate number from the schedules.

Table 1: Standard subdivisions

After a specific number has been chosen for a work, the classifier should then consider whether further specification concerning the bibliographic form or the author's approach is desirable, i.e., whether any of the standard subdivisions is applicable. Table 1 lists nine categories of standard subdivisions, which are further subdivided into more detailed specifications. All notations for standard subdivisions begin with a 0, e.g., -01 and -075.

Notations from auxiliary tables are never used alone or as main numbers. With the exception of -04, the classifier does not need any specific instruction in the schedules in order to add the notations for standard subdivisions. Appropriateness and applicability are the general guide. For a journal of inorganic chemistry, the standard subdivision -05 (for serial publications) is added to the base number 546 to form the number 546.05. The standard subdivision -04 is reserved for special topics which have general application throughout the regular subdivisions of certain specific subjects, e.g., 604, and its subdivisions. Therefore, it varies from subject to subject and is to be used only when the special topics are spelled out in the schedules.

Although standard subdivisions may be applied wherever they are appropriate, there are certain restrictions on their use. In addition to restrictions appearing in the schedules relating to specific numbers (e.g., do not use 362.09; class in 361), certain general restrictions are set forth in the editor's introduction to DDC:

1. The classifier should not add standard subdivisions when they are redundant. Therefore, for a history of the United States, do not add -09 to 973, which already means history. Likewise, it is redundant to add -03 to 423, which already means a dictionary of the English language.
2. The classifier should not add one standard subdivision to another standard subdivision unless there are specific instructions to do so. When more than one standard subdivision is

applicable to a work, choose one according to the table of precedence, which is found at the head of Table 1, e.g., choosing -068 over -05.

When a standard subdivision (e.g., 5<u>07</u>) or a span of standard subdivisions (e.g., 73<u>0</u>.<u>3</u>–73<u>0</u>.<u>7</u>) is specifically named in the schedules, it is understood that the subsubdivision to these standard subdivisions may be used (e.g., 5<u>07</u>.<u>4</u> for science museums, or 73<u>0</u>.<u>75</u> for collections of sculpture) unless there are contrary instructions in the schedules.

In adding a standard subdivision to a base number, the classifier should first remove all the zeros which are used as fillers in the base number. Therefore, standard subdivision -<u>03</u> added to the base number <u>100</u> results in <u>103</u>, not 100.03. A journal of library science is classed in <u>020</u>.<u>5</u>, not 020.05.

However, there are exceptions to the single-zero rule. In many cases, notations beginning with 0 have been assigned meanings other than those for standard subdivisions. In these cases, the classifier is instructed to use more than one zero for standard subdivisions, e.g.,

> 300   Social sciences
> Use 300.1–300.9 for standard subdivisions
> Hence, 300.3 for an encyclopedia of social sciences
>
> 523   Descriptive astronomy
> Use .001–.009 for standard subdivisions
> Hence, 523.005 for a journal of descriptive astronomy

Table 2: Areas

Areas notation specifies the historical or geographic treatment of a subject and may be used with numbers throughout the schedules as instructed. It is used in the following ways:

Used directly when so noted with numbers from the schedules

Geology of Romania	<u>554</u>.<u>98</u>
1. Base number for regional geology.	<u>55</u>
2. Areas notation for Romania from Table 2.	-<u>4</u> <u>98</u>
3. Add (2) to (1) and insert decimal point.	<u>554</u>.<u>98</u>
The U.S. Congress	<u>328</u>.<u>73</u>
1. Base number for legislative branch of specific jurisdictions.	<u>328</u>
2. Areas notation for U.S. from Table 2.	-<u>73</u>

3. Add (2) to (1) and insert decimal
   point.   328.73

A History of Bulgaria   949.77
1. Base number for general history of
   specific countries. Cf. note under
   930–990.   9
2. Areas notation for Bulgaria from
   Table 2.   -49 77
3. Add (2) to (1) and insert decimal
   point.   949.77

Used through the interposition of standard subdivisions notation -09 from Table 1
In Table 1, under -093 to -099, there is an instruction to add areas notation 3–9 from Table 2 to base number -09, e.g., -0973 for historical and geographical treatment of a subject with regard to the United States. Since -09 is a standard subdivision and therefore can be added to any number from the schedules when appropriate, virtually every number in the DDC system can be subdivided geographically, unless there is specific instruction in the schedules not to use the standard subdivision under the particular number. When direct geographic subdivision as explained above is provided, it takes precedence over the use of -09 and its subdivisions.

Economic Geology of Germany   553.0943
1. Base number for economic geology.   553
2. Standard subdivision for geo-
   graphic treatment for Germany.   -0943
3. Add (2) to (1) and insert decimal
   point.   553.0943

Exercise F

Assign Decimal classification numbers (abridged edition) to the following subjects:

1. How to teach cooking.
2. Life on Mars? A scientist's view.
3. Labor union discrimination against black American textile workers.
4. Rocks from the moon.
5. Flora and fauna of Alaska.
6. Nursing education.
7. A history of Kentucky during the Civil War.
8. Monetary policy of France.
9. Political parties in Australia.

10. An encyclopedia of engineering.
11. A travel guide to Florida.
12. A bibliography of Ohio imprints.
13. A history of Christian churches in Iowa.
14. Journal of political science.
15. Farming in Iowa.
16. A history of New Orleans.
17. Interior decoration in Sweden.
18. Social conditions in the United States.
19. A history of Singapore.
20. A collection of fairy tales.
21. A gardener's handbook on diseases of flowers.
22. Political conditions in the United States.
23. Geology of Iran.

Table 3: Subdivisions of individual literatures

Notations from Table 3 are used when applicable with the base numbers for individual literatures identified by * under 810–890 in the schedules.

Before proceeding with the instruction concerning the use of Table 3, a discussion of the classification of literature in general is in order.

A number for literature usually contains the following elements:

1. Main class *Literature* is represented by the base number 8.
2. *Language* is the second element, e.g., 82- for English literature, 895.1 for Chinese literature, etc. When the work is not limited to any language, the -0- is used to fill the second digit, e.g., 80- for world literature.
3. *Literary form* is the third element. Mnemonics are employed, e.g., -1 for poetry, -2 for drama, etc. Hence, 821 (English poetry), 891.72 (Russian drama), etc. When the work covers more than one form, the -0 is used, e.g., 820, English literature not limited to any particular form.
4. Standard subdivisions when applicable, e.g., 830.5 (a journal of German literature).

Following is a discussion with illustrations of different types of literary works.

Collections of literature by more than one author

An Anthology of World Literature	808.8
An Anthology of World Drama	808.82
1. Base number for a collection from more than one literature.	808.8

2. Determine the number following
   808 in 808.1–808.7 which means
   drama. -<u>2</u>
3. Add (2) to (1). 808.<u>82</u>

An Anthology of English Literature 820.8
1. Base number for English literature. <u>82</u>
2. Notation for collections from
   Table 3. -<u>0</u> <u>8</u>

An Anthology of French Poetry 841.<u>008</u>
1. Base number for French literature. <u>84</u>
2. Notation from Table 3 for a collection
   of poetry by more than one author. -<u>1</u> <u>008</u>

Works about literature

A History of World Literature <u>809</u>

A Study of World Drama 809.<u>2</u>
1. Base number for a critical appraisal
   of more than one literature. <u>809</u>
2. Add the number following 808 in
   808.1–808.7 which means drama,
   i.e., 808.<u>2</u>. 809.<u>2</u>

A History of English Literature 820.<u>9</u>
1. Base number for English literature. <u>82</u>
2. Notation for a history of more than
   one form by more than one author. -<u>0</u> <u>9</u>

A Teacher's Handbook of French Literature 840.<u>7</u>
1. Base number for French literature. <u>84</u>
2. Notation from Table 1 for standard
   subdivision meaning study and
   teaching. -<u>0</u> <u>7</u>
   (Note that -02 for a handbook is
   not added because the number
   already has one standard
   subdivision.)

Works written by individual authors
The Dewey Decimal Classification classes literature by form. Works
by the same author are classed in different numbers according to their
forms. Standard subdivisions are not used with works by individual
authors.

Poems by Henry Wadsworth
Longfellow <u>811</u>

Ivanhoe by Sir Walter Scott	823
Charles Lamb's *Essays*	824

In many libraries, all fiction is grouped together without regard to language and assigned a simple notation F with the author's name or a **Cutter number (see discussion on pages 258–266).**

Selected and collected works by individual authors are classed in the same numbers as individual works, e.g.,

Selected Poems by Edgar Allen Poe	811
Plays by Christopher Marlowe	822

When the collection contains works in various forms, class in the number for the predominant form or the form by which the author is best known, e.g.,

The Writings of Mark Twain	817 or 813
Selected Prose and Poetry by Ralph Waldo Emerson	814

Works about individual authors
Works about individual authors are classed in the same numbers as the works written by them, as instructed under -1, -2, etc., in Table 3. The standard subdivision -09 is not used.

A Study of Longfellow's Poems	811
Commentary on Homer's Iliad	883
A Critical Appraisal of Sir Walter Scott's Novels	823

Table 4: Subdivisions of individual languages

Notations from Table 4 are used with base numbers for individual languages identified by * in 420–490 in the schedules.

A Dictionary of the Russian Language	491.73
1. Base number for Russian	491.7
2. Notation for dictionaries from Table 4.	-3
English Word Origins	422
1. Base number for English.	42
2. Notation for etymology from Table 4	-2

Classification of Biography

Under 920 in the schedules, several methods of classing biography are presented. The preferred treatment is to class both individual and collected biography of persons associated with a specific subject with the subject, using standard subdivisions notation -092 from Table 1, e.g.,

A Biography of Melvil Dewey	020.92
Biographical Directory of Librarians in the United States and Canada	020.92
A Biography of Abraham Lincoln	973.7092
Presidents of the United States	973.092

Note that biographies of heads of states are classed in the numbers for the history of their periods instead of in the number for political science.

Some libraries may find it desirable to use one of the optional methods:

1. Class all individual biography regardless of subject orientation in 92 or B and all collected biography regardless of subject orientation in 92 or 920 without subdivision, e.g.,

A Biography of Melvil Dewey	92 or B
Biographical Directory of Librarians in the United States and Canada	92 or 920
A Biography of Abraham Lincoln	92 or B
Presidents of the United States	92 or 920

2. Class both individual and collected biography of persons associated with a specific subject in 920.1–928, e.g.,

A Biography of Melvil Dewey	920.2
Biographical Directory of Librarians in the United States and Canada	920.2
A Biography of Abraham Lincoln	923
Presidents of the United States	923

3. Class individual biography of men in 920.71 and of women in 920.72.

Exercise G

Assign Decimal classification numbers (abridged edition) to the following subjects:

1. A history of American literature.
2. An encyclopedia of Austrian literature.
3. A biography of President Lyndon Baines Johnson.
4. A biography of Walter Cronkite.
5. A teacher's handbook of Latin literature.
6. A study of twentieth-century drama.
7. An English-Japanese, Japanese-English dictionary.
8. A study of Russian novels.
9. A history of Chinese poetry.
10. The collected works of Henry Fielding.
11. A handbook for sign language teachers.
12. A critical study of the Afro-American as a character in American fiction.
13. Remedial reading for French.
14. A collection of Portuguese essays (by various authors).
15. A study of political themes in twentieth-century British literature.

CALL NUMBERS

To distinguish books on the same subject, an author notation is usually added to the classification number to form a call number. The name probably came from the fact that in the earlier days of closed stacks, a library user "called" for a book by means of its unique number.

There are various kinds of author notation, depending on the size of the collection and the classification system used. With the Dewey Decimal Classification system, several kinds of author notation are employed. The simplest form, used by many small school, public, and church libraries, is the initial of the author's last name, for example:

        512   822.3
        D   M

For slightly larger collections, more letters from the author's last name may be used, hence:

        512   822.3
        Dic   Mar

An extreme of this method is to use the complete surname, e.g.,

512   822.3
Dickenson   Marlowe

However, this device is clumsy and used by very few libraries, in spite of its ability to distinguish between authors' names which begin with the same letters.

Cutter Numbers

Most libraries use a device called Cutter numbers, named after its designer, Charles Ammi Cutter. It was developed originally for use with the Cutter Expansive Classification, but is now widely used with the Dewey Decimal Classification; a simplified form is used with the Library of Congress Classification (to be discussed in Chapter 13).

In this system, the author number is derived by combining the initial letter or letters of the author's last name with numbers from a numerical table which has been designed to ensure an alphabetical arrangement of names, for example, D556 (Dickens), D557 (Dickenson), and D558 (Dickerson). This device provides a shorter author number which is also easier to arrange and to read on the shelves.

There are now three Cutter tables: *Two-Figure Author Table, Three-Figure Author Table,* and the *Cutter-Sanborn Table,* listed in the order of increasing details. The following instruction is based on the *Three-Figure Author Table.*

The Cutter number is formed according to the following procedures:

1. Locate on the Cutter table the first few letters of the author's surname or corporate name which is the main entry of the work. Use only the bold face letters shown in the combination and the arabic numbers next to it, e.g.,

Dewes   514
Dewey   515
Dewil   516

Based on the above figures, the Cutter number for Melvil Dewey is D515.

Certain letters in the alphabet appear more frequently as initial letters of names. In order to keep the Cutter numbers short, two letters are used in the combination for names beginning with vowels and the letter S, and three letters are used for names beginning with the letters Sc, e.g.,

813.54   813.54   813.54   813.54
Ed98   Sch56   Sm64   V896

2. Where there is no Cutter number that fits a name exactly, use

the first of the two numbers closest to the name, e.g., <u>T325</u> for Thackeray, based on:

> <u>T</u>hacher U 325
> <u>T</u>had   326

3. Cutter numbers are treated decimally. Therefore, numbers can be inserted when required by adding extra digits at the end. For example, if <u>Sm52</u> has been assigned to Benjamin Smith and <u>Sm53</u> has been assigned to Charles Smith, and a Cutter number must be provided for Brian Smith, the number Sm525 can then be used. The filing order is Sm52, Sm525, Sm53. The number 5 or 6 is often chosen as the extra digit in order to leave room on both sides for future interpolation.

For the same reason, although the Tables provide many numbers ending in 1, it is advisable to add a digit and not to use a Cutter number ending in 1, because it places a limit on the expansion. For example, use L5115 instead of L511 for David Lee. In general, the use of zero is to be avoided, because it is easily confused with the letter o. Care should be taken to distinguish the number 1 from the letter l.

4. When two authors classified in the same number share the same Cutter number also, assign a different number for the second author by adding a digit, e.g., M315 for Heinrich Mann and M3155 for **Thomas Mann. If Thomas Mann has been assigned the number** M315 before a number for Heinrich Mann is required, the number M3145 then can be used for the latter.

5. Names beginning with Mc, M', and Mac are treated as though they were all spelled Mac. The apostrophe is ignored, i.e., O'Hara being treated as Ohara.

6. When the main entry is under title, the Cutter number is taken from the first word (disregarding initial articles) of the title. *Encyclopaedia Britannica* is assigned En19. Therefore, it is more accurate to state that the Cutter number is derived from the main entry of the work which may or may not be the author of the work.

7. An exception is made for biographies. In order to group all biographies of the same person together, the Cutter number is taken from the name of the biographee instead of the main entry. All biographies of Napoleon are grouped in the Cutter number N162. In many libraries, this practice is extended to include works about corporate bodies, particularly firms and institutions.

Unique Call Numbers

Many libraries adopt the principle of unique call numbers. Each item in the library is assigned a unique number different from any other call number in the collection. In this sense, the call number serves as the true address of the item. As discussed above, when two authors with the same last name wrote on the same subject they are assigned different author or Cutter numbers, e.g., D557 for David Dickenson and D558 or D5575 for Robert Dickenson. When the same author has written more than one book on a particular subject, further devices—work marks, edition marks, and copy and volume numbers— are used to create unique call numbers. These are discussed below.

Work mark

A work mark, (sometimes called a work letter) consisting of the first letter or letters in lower case from the first word (disregarding articles) in the title, is added to the author or Cutter number to distinguish different titles on the same subject by the same author, e.g.,

512 D557i	*Introduction to Algebra* by D. Dickenson
512 D557p	*Principles of Algebra* by D. Dickenson
512 D557pr	*Progress in Algebra* by D. Dickenson
813.4 J233a	*The Ambassadors* by Henry James
813.4 J233am	*The American* by Henry James
813.4 J233ame	*American Novels and Stories of Henry James*
813.4 J233p	*The Portrait of a Lady* by Henry James

In some cases, when books in a series by the same author on the same subject all begin with the same word, it is customary to use the first letter from each key word in the titles, e.g.,

738.2 H324ce	Hayden's *Chats on English China*
738.2 H324co	Hayden's *Chats on Old China*
738.2 H324cr	Hayden's *Chats on Royal Copenhagen Porcelain*

Practices in assigning work marks vary slightly from library to library. There are as yet no definitive rules concerning this aspect of cataloging. The examples presented here should be understood as one of the various methods and should not be taken as the *only* method. Nonetheless, they illustrate the basic function of the call number, which is to provide a unique symbol for each item of library material and to ensure a logical arrangement of works on the same subject and sharing the same class number.

Work marks are particularly important in cases where a large number of books share the same class number, for example, B (Biography) and F (Fiction).

Work marks for biographies and literary works require special consideration.

Biography

In order to group all biographies of the same person together on the shelf, the Cutter number is taken from the name of the biographee instead of the author. All biographies of Washington are cuttered under W277, and the work mark is then taken from the first letter of the author's surname or the main entry. To place all autobiographical writings before biographies written by other people, the work mark a is reserved for this purpose. A biography written by an author whose surname begins with the letter a is then assigned two letters as the work mark, e.g., W277ad (for Adams, etc.). When there is more than one autobiographical work, an arbitrary arabic number is added to the work mark. For example,

W277a	Washington, George. *Autograph Letters and Documents of George Washington Now in Rhode Island Collections.*
W277a1	Washington, George. *Affectionately Yours, George Washington: A Self-Portrait in Letters of Friendship,* edited by T. J. Fleming.
W277a2	Washington, George. *Last Will and Testament of George Washington of Mount Vernon.*
W277ad	Adams, R. G. *Five Radio Addresses on George Washington.*
W277b	Bellamy, F. R. *The Private Life of George Washington.*
W277d	Delaware. Public Archives Commission. *George Washington and Delaware.*
W277h	*Honor to George Washington and Reading about George Washington.*

Literary works[7]

In the Dewey Decimal Classification, critical appraisals and biographies of individual authors are classed in the same numbers assigned to their works. It is then the function of the work mark to distinguish the works written by and those written about an author since they share the same class number and Cutter number. In this area particularly, libraries vary in their practices. For example, some libraries use an additional Cutter number for works about individual authors. There are as yet no standards or rules in this regard. The following is presented here as an example.

Works by Individual Authors   These are assigned work marks taken from the titles, e.g.,

821.5	Pope, Alexander
P8115d	*The Dunciad*
P8115ep	*An Epistle from Mr. Pope to Dr. Arbuthnot*
P8115es	*An Essay on Criticism*
P8115ess or P8115esm	*An Essay on Man*
P8115r	*The Rape of the Lock*

Biography and Criticism of Individual Authors   Critical appraisals and biographies of an individual author, since they share the same class number and Cutter number with the author's works, require special work marks if the library does not wish to interfile these two categories of works. The most common device is to insert the letter *z* between the Cutter number and the work mark, e.g.,

P8115zc	Clark, D. B. *Alexander Pope.*
P8115zr	Russell, J. P. *Alexander Pope: Tradition and Identity.*

By the use of the letter *z*, works about Pope will be filed after works written by him. The letter *z* in this case is followed by the regular work mark taken from the author's surname. In this way, the letter *z* alone is reserved for any title by the author with the first word beginning with the letter *z*, e.g.,

---

[7]In many libraries, the practice outlined in this section also applies to philosophers and artists when works written by and about them are classed in the same numbers.

833.912	
M317z	Thomas Mann. *Der Zauberberg.*
M317zl	Herbert Lehnert. *Thomas-Mann-Forschung.*

In some libraries, serial publications devoted to the study of an individual author are assigned the work mark zz so that these publications will be filed after other critical works about the author, e.g., M317zz for *Blätter der Thomas Mann Gesellschaft.*

In some libraries, instead of using the letter z as a work mark for works about an author, a second Cutter number based on the main entry of the work is used, e.g.,

821.5	
P8115	Clark, D. B.
C547	*Alexander Pope*

821.5	
P8115	Russell, J. P.
R914	*Alexander Pope: Tradition and Identity*

Works about Individual Works   If the library wishes to have individual works and critical works about them stand together on the shelf, a device may be used in the work mark for such an arrangement. The capital letter Z is inserted between the work mark for the work criticized and the work mark taken from the critic's surname, e.g.,

821.5	
P8115dZs	Sitter, J. E. *The Poetry of Pope's Dunciad.*
P8115dZw	Williams, A. L. *Pope's Dunciad: A Study of Its Meaning.*

This practice may be extended to include translations of literary works if one wishes to have the original work and the translations stand together, e.g.,

833.912	Thomas Mann
M317b	*Bekenntnisse des Hochstaplers Felix Krull*
M317bE	*Confessions of Felix Krull, Confidence Man.*

The letter *E* stands for an English translation.

In some libraries, the letter *x* is used as a work mark for an author's collected works, and the letter *y* for works such as bibliographies and concordances of individual authors, e.g.,

821.5	Pope, Alexander
P8115xb	*Complete Poetical Works*, edited by H. W. Boynton

> P8115xd   *Poetical Works*, edited by H. Davis.
>
> P8115ya   Abbott, E., comp. *A Concordance to the Works of Alexander Pope*.

The only problem in this practice is that an individual work with a title beginning with the letter *z* would then be separated from other individual works. An alternative is to use the letter *a* as a work mark for collected works, similar to the treatment of autobiographies. In this case, collected works of an author would precede individual works, an arrangement preferred by many libraries. Bibliographies and concordances would then be treated like other works about the author.

The works written by and about an individual author are therefore arranged in the following order:

> Collected works (arranged by date or by editor)
> Individual works (arranged alphabetically by title)
>> Original text
>> Translations (subarranged alphabetically by language and then by translators' names)
>> Critical appraisals (subarranged alphabetically by the critics' names)
> General critical appraisals not limited to a single work (subarranged by the critics' names)
> Serial publications devoted to the study of the author

For example,

833.912	Thomas Mann
M317a	*Gesammelte Werke*
M317t	*Der Tod in Venedig*
M317tE	*Death in Venice*
M317z	*Der Zauberberg*
M317zE	*The Magic Mountain*
M317zZm	Miller, R. D. *The Two Faces of Hermes: A Study of Thomas Mann's Novel, "The Magic Mountain."*
M317ze	Eichner, H. *Thomas Mann*
M317zs	Schröter, K. *Thomas Mann*
M317zz	*Blätter der Thomas Mann Gesellschaft.*

It should be noted that in filing, capital letters precede lowercase letters.

Shakespeare constitutes a special case because of the large number of editions and translations of his works and of works about him. In DDC, he has been given a special class number, <u>822.33</u>. Since no other author shares that class number, it would be redundant to take the Cutter number from his name. Therefore, a special scheme of Cutter numbers has been developed. It appears in the DDC schedules following the class number <u>822.33</u>.

In the case of anonymous classics, the Cutter number is based on the uniform title, and the work mark may be taken either from the title of the version being cataloged, or from the editor, translator, or the person most closely associated with the edition, e.g.,

> 821.1 Pearl (Middle English poem)
>
> P316c *The Pearl*; with an introductory essay by S. P. Chase
>
> P316g *Pearl*; edited by E. V. Gordon
>
> P316zk Kean, P. M. *The Pearl: An Interpretation*

For various versions of the Biblical text, since the class number already represents the Bible or the individual parts or books, it would be redundant to cutter under the title. The Cutter number is then taken from the name of the version, the name of the editor, or, lacking such, from the name of the publisher.

Edition mark

Many works appear in different editions, which share the same class and Cutter numbers. In order to create a unique call number for each edition, an edition mark in the form of a number added after the work mark or a date under the Cutter number is usually used, e.g.,

	025.431	025.431	025.431	025.431
	D515d$_{16}$	D515d$_{17}$	D515d$_{18}$	D515d$_{19}$
or				
	025.431	025.431	025.431	025.431
	D515d	D515d	D515d	D515d
	1958	1965	1971	1979

Some libraries use the dates as edition marks for all works; others use both methods in the catalog. The choice of method in each case depends on the appropriateness. Dates are usually used when the editions are not numbered. When there is more than one edition of a work within a year as is often the case with literary works, a letter is added arbitrarily to the date, e.g., 1976a, 1976b, 1976c, etc.

Copy and volume number

When a work is published in more than one volume or when the library has more than one copy of a work, a volume or copy number, or in some cases both, is added to the call number on the physical volume in order to provide a unique address in the collection, e.g.,

$$
\begin{array}{ll}
025.431 & 025.431 \\
D515d_{18} & D515d_{18} \\
v.2 & v.1 \\
 & copy\ 2
\end{array}
$$

The copy designation does not appear on the catalog entry, since the entry is for the entire work rather than an individual copy. The volume number may or may not appear there depending on whether the entry is for that particular volume or for the entire work.

Prefixes to Call Numbers

When a particular work is to be shelved in a special location or out of its ordinary place, a prefix is added to the call number. The most commonly used prefix is the letter R for books in the reference collection, e.g.,

R
031
En19

Prefixes are also used for large-size books, books in special collections, and nonbook materials.

SHELFLIST

The shelflist is a library catalog containing one record for each title in the library's collection. The records are arranged by call number. In other words, the order of the records in the shelflist corresponds exactly to that of the library materials on the shelves. Usually, the record in the shelflist is in the form of the main entry. In many libraries, additional information, such as accession number, source of acquisition, cost, etc., is also included. The shelflist record shows the number of volumes and copies of each title held by the library. This information is important, since the records in the library catalog do not normally show the number of copies, and the volumes held by the library may or may not correspond to that shown in the collation because of incomplete sets.

The shelflist is usually kept in the catalog department as a working tool. It is used most frequently as a tool for complete or partial inventory. Missing copies are recorded on the shelflist. It is an indispensable tool for assigning unique call numbers. In a number of libraries, the shelflist is made accessible to the public. Since it is arranged by class numbers, it is in effect a classed catalog and complements the dictionary catalog.

In most libraries, the shelflist is in the card form. A number of libraries have automated the shelflist and converted it into machine-readable form.

Exercise H

1. Complete the call numbers for the following titles:

92   Arthur, Sir G. *Concerning Winston Spencer Churchill* [1874–1965].

92   Ashley, M. P. *Churchill as Historian* [W. S. Churchill, 1874–1965].

92   Bullock, A. L. C. *Hitler: A Study in Tyranny.*

92   Churchill, Jennie Jerome, 1854–1921. *The Reminiscences of Lady Randolph Churchill.*

92   Churchill, Randolph Spencer, 1911–   *Winston S. Churchill* [1874–1965].

92   Churchill, Winston S., 1874–1965. *A Roving Commission: My Early Life.*

92   Churchill, Winston Spencer, 1874–1965. *Lord Randolph Churchill* [1849–1895].

92   Fishman, J. *My Darling Clementine* [wife of W. S. Churchill].

92   Gardner, B. *Churchill in Power* [W. S. Churchill, 1874–1965].

92   Graebner, W. *My Dear Mr. Churchill* [W. S. Churchill, 1874–1965].

92   Hackett, Francis. *What Mein Kampf Means to America.*

92   Hitler, Adolph. *Mein Kampf.*

92   Hitler, Adolph. *My Battle.*

92   James, R. R. *Lord Randolph Churchill* [1849–1895].

92   Kraus, R. *Young Lady Randolph* [Churchill, 1854–1921].

92   Leslie, Anita. *Jennie: The Life of Lady Randolph Churchill* [1854–1921].

92   Leslie, Anita. *Lady Randolph Churchill: The Story of Jennie Jerome* [1854–1921].

92   Martin, R. G. *Jennie: The Life of Lady Randolph Churchill* [1854–1921].

92   Smith, B. F. *Adolph Hitler: His Family, Childhood and Youth.*

2. Complete the call numbers for the following titles:

823.8   Brook, G. L. *The Language of Dickens.*

823.8   Churchill, R. C. *A Bibliography of Dickensian Criticism.*

823.8   Dickens, Charles. *Eine Geschichte von zwei Städte* [a German translation of *A Tale of Two Cities*].

823.8   Dickens, Charles. *Hard Times.*

823.8   Dickens, Charles. *Historia de dos Ciudades* [a Spanish translation of *A Tale of Two Cities*].

823.8   Dickens, Charles. *Paris et Londres en 1793* [a French translation of *A Tale of Two Cities*].

823.8   Dickens, Charles. *Les temps difficiles* [a French translation of *Hard Times*].

823.8   Dickens, Charles. *Schwere Zeiten* [a German translation of *Hard Times*].

823.8   Dickens, Charles. *A Tale of Two Cities.* 1934.

823.8   Dickens, Charles. *A Tale of Two Cities.* 1970.

823.8   Dickens, Charles. *Zwei Städte* [a German translation of *A Tale of Two Cities* by B. Dedek, 1924].

823.8   *Dickens Studies Newsletter.*

823.8   *The Dickensian: A Magazine for Dickens Lovers.*

823.8   Hayward, A. L. *The Dickens Encyclopedia.*

823.8   *Twentieth Century Interpretations of A Tale of Two Cities: A Collection of Critical Essays.*

CHAPTER 13
Library of Congress Classification

HISTORY

When the Library of Congress moved into its new building in 1897, the Jeffersonian classification system which had been used for organizing the Library of Congress collection since the early nineteenth century was found to be inadequate for the collection consisting of one and a half million volumes of books and other materials. Although both the Dewey Decimal Classification and Cutter Expansive Classification systems had been in use by libraries in the nation, neither was considered to be suitable for the Library of Congress. A new classification system, the Library of Congress Classification (LCC), was planned and constructed.

LCC consists of twenty-one classes displayed in over thirty separately published schedules. Unlike the other classification systems, the Library of Congress Classification was not the product of one master mind. The individual classes were developed by different groups of specialists under the direction of J.C.M. Hanson and Charles Martel. The schedules, each of which contains an entire class, a subclass, or a group of subclasses, have been developed and published separately. Therefore, it is sometimes thought of as "a coordinated series of special classifications."[1]

In developing the new classification system, Charles Ammi Cutter's Expansive Classification was selected as the chief guide, with considerable modifications in the notation. The outline to the sixth expansion of the Expansive Classification was used by Hanson in developing the outline of the new Library of Congress Classification scheme. Table 13-1 is a comparison of the two outlines. Hanson's outline was modified later (see Table 13-2 for the current outline).

For notation, it was decided to use one, or at most two, capital letters to indicate classes (see Table 13-2, page 276); arabic numbers, in integral— not decimal—sequence, for subdivisions; and Cutter num-

---

[1] Arthur Maltby. *Sayers' Manual of Classification for Librarians.* 5th ed. London: Andre Deutsch, 1975. P. 175.

TABLE 13-1 Comparison of Cutter's and Hanson's First Outlines

Cutter's Outline*		Hanson's First Outline (1899)†		
A	General works	A	1–200	Polygraphy; Encyclopedia; General Periodicals; Societies
B	Philosophy	A	201–3000	Philosophy
BR	Religion and religions (except the Christian and Jewish)	A	3001–B9999	Religion; Theology; Church history
C	Christian and Jewish religions			
D	Ecclesiastical history			
E	Biography	C	1–9999	Biography and studies auxiliary to history
F	History and allied subjects	D	1–9999	General history; periods; and local (except America) with geography
		E–F		American history and geography
G	Geography and travels	G		Geography, general, and allied studies (e.g., Anthropology; Ethnology)
H	Social sciences	H	1–2000	Political science
		H	2001–9999	Law
I	Sociology	I	1–8000	Sociology
J	Government; Politics			

	K	Legislation; Law; Woman; Societies	I	8001–9999	Women; Societies; clubs; etc.
			J	1–2000	Sports and amusements
			J	2001–9999	Music
			K		Fine arts
			L–M		Philosophy; Literature
	L	Science in general; Physical sciences (includes Science and **Arts treated in the same book**); Science (general works); Mathematics; Physics; Chemistry; Astronomy	N		Science; Mathematics; Astronomy; Physics; Chemistry
	M	Natural history in general; **Microscopy; Geology; Biology**	O		Natural history, general; Geology
	N	Botany	P		Zoology; Botany
	O	Zoology			
	Q	Medicine	Q		Medicine
	R	Useful Arts in general; Metric arts; Extractive and Productive arts; Chemical and Electrical arts; Domestic economy	R		Useful arts; Agriculture
	S	Engineering; Building	S		Manufactures
271	T	Manufactures; Handicrafts	T		Engineering

(Continued on page 272.)

TABLE 13-1   (Continued)

Cutter's Outline*		Hanson's First Outline (1899)†	
U	Defensive and preservative arts	U	Military, Naval science; Lighthouses; Life saving; Fire extinction
V	Recreative arts; Sports; Theater; Music	V–Y	Special collections
W	Fine Arts		
X	Language		
Y	Literature		
Z	Book Arts	Z	Bibliography (Book Arts)

*Charles Ammi Cutter. *Charles Ammi Cutter: Library Systematizer.* Francis L. Miksa, ed. Littleton, Colo.: Libraries Unlimited, 1977. Pp. 280–282.
†Leo E. LaMontagne. *American Library Classification with Special Reference to the Library of Congress.* Hamden, Conn.: The Shoe String Press, Inc., 1961. Pp. 228–229.

bers for individual books.[2] The decision not to use decimal numbers was later revised to allow decimal extensions as a means of expanding existing numbers or inserting new numbers.

For individual classes, Cutter's influence was most obvious in Class Z, Bibliography and Library Science, which was based on Cutter's Class Z, Book Arts.

Class Z was chosen as the first schedule to be developed because it would contain the bibliographical works necessary for the reclassification project. It was adopted by the Library of Congress in 1898 and published in 1902. An outline of the entire system appeared in 1904. By then, the classification of classes D, E–F, M, Q, R, S, T, U, and Z had been completed. Classes A, C, G, H, and V were in the process of development. By 1948, all schedules, with the exception of those for Class K, Law, had been completed and published. Class K is still being developed at the present. The first schedule of this class, containing the Subclass KF (United States law), was published in 1969. Schedules for the majority of the subclasses of law are still being developed and published as they are completed.

APPLICATION

Although designed mainly for the Library of Congress collection, LCC has been adopted by many academic and research libraries since the 1920s. A recent survey reveals that while 85.4 percent of all types of libraries in the United States and Canada use the Dewey Decimal Classification and 14.6 percent use the Library of Congress Classification,[3] among larger libraries (with a holding of more than 500,000 volumes) in the United States, 62.3 percent use LCC.[4] During the 1960s, in particular, there was a trend among the academic libraries using DDC to switch to LCC. The reasons for changing are said to be (1) the basic orientation of LCC toward research libraries and (2) the economic advantage offered by the LC cataloging services.

REVISION

Revision of LCC takes place continuously instead of at regular intervals. It usually takes the form of addition of new numbers or

[2]J.C.M. Hanson. "The Library of Congress and Its New Catalogue: Some Unwritten History." In *Essays Offered to Herbert Putnam by His Colleagues and Friends on His Thirtieth Anniversary as Librarian of Congress: 5 April 1929*. New Haven, Yale University Press, 1929. Pp. 186–187.

[3]John Comaromi et al. *A Survey of the Use of the Dewey Decimal Classification in the United States and Canada*. Albany, N.Y.: Forest Press Division, Lake Placid Education Foundation, 1975. P. 12.

[4]Ibid. P. 16.

revision of existing numbers. As the need arises in classifying the collection at the Library of Congress, new entries and changes are added to the existing scheme.

Revision is undertaken by subject catalogers at the Library of Congress. The Subject Cataloging Division is responsible for both the application and the development and maintenance of the LCC system.

Proposals for new numbers, submitted by LC subject catalogers, must be approved by an editorial committee of the division before they become official and are incorporated into the existing scheme. The additions and changes are published in *LC Classification—Additions and Changes* which appears quarterly. *Library of Congress Classification Schedules: A Cumulation of Additions and Changes,* issued periodically by the Gale Research Company of Detroit, contains cumulations of additions and changes which appear in the quarterly publication.

There is no regular timetable for issuing revised editions. New editions for individual schedules are prepared as needed and independently of one another. Class Q is in the sixth edition, while many of the P schedules are still in their first edition.

SCHEDULES

Library of Congress Classification schedules have been issued in four types of editions:

1. New schedules. This refers to a schedule for a class or subclass which has never been published before. Examples are the schedules for the subclasses of Class K, Law.

2. Reprint editions with additions and changes. When the stock of a particular schedule is exhausted, a reprint edition is issued which includes additions and changes up to the time of reprinting interfiled in one alphanumeric sequence which is separated from the main volume and index. Most of the older schedules which have been reissued appear in this format, e.g., the schedules for classes D, E–F, L, S, etc.

3. Cumulative editions. These are new editions which represent mainly a cumulation of the previous edition and the additions and changes incorporated into one file. The preparation of such an edition is normally performed by the editorial staff of the Subject Cataloging Division. Because relatively little revamping or rethinking of the classification is involved, the preparation is fairly mechanical and speedy. The recently published second edition of schedule PN, PR, PS, PZ and the third edition (1979) of schedule B–BJ were prepared in this manner. Other cumulative editions being prepared are the schedules for R and Z.

4. Revised editions. These are new editions which have undergone considerable revamping and revision. The process involves rethinking and reviewing of much of the entire schedule. Many numbers are changed and terminology updated. The preparation of such an edition involves not only individual catalogers but also the principal subject cataloger and his staff. Because of the thorough revision, it normally requires a great deal more time and effort to prepare such an edition. The recent editions of schedules Q, T, and M belong to this type and the schedule for Subclasses H–HJ is undergoing such a process.

Because different persons were responsible for the development of the individual schedules, there are often unique features in an individual schedule. The use of auxiliary tables and the degree and method for notational synthesis often vary from schedule to schedule. However, there are certain common features shared by all schedules, such as the notation, method and arrangement of form and geographic divisions, and a number of common auxiliary tables (to be discussed in detail later).

BASIC PRINCIPLES AND STRUCTURE

Like the other classification systems originating from the nineteenth century, the Library of Congress Classification is basically classification by discipline. The entire field of knowledge is divided into main classes corresponding to major academic disciplines. Because of the use of the letters as notation for representing main classes, there is a larger number of main classes in LCC than in the Dewey Decimal Classification. The main classes are divided into subclasses, which are further subdivided into form, place, time, and subject (or topical) aspects. The system thus forms a hierarchical structure, progressing from the general to the specific. (See Table 13-2.)

It should be borne in mind that the Library of Congress Classification was not designed as a general, universal system, but rather as a system specifically tailored for the Library of Congress collection. Later changes, expansions, and revisions of the system reflect to a large extent the development of that particular collection. Both the original design and later developments of LCC have been based on the "literary warrant" of the Library of Congress collection. In other words, details of the classification have been developed according to the needs of the library's collection. This explains partly the seemingly uneven distribution of notation, with a preponderance on social sciences, particularly history.

TABLE 13-2 Outline of Library of Congress Classification

A General works: Polygraphy
B Philosophy and Religion:
    B–BJ: Philosophy
    BL–BX: Religion
C History: Auxiliary sciences
D History: General and Old World
E–F History: America
G Geography; Anthropology; Folklore; etc.
H Social sciences:
    HA: Statistics
    HB–HJ: Economics
    HM–HX: Sociology
J Political science
K Law
L Education
M Music
N Fine arts
P Philology and Literature:
    P–PA: Philology: Classical philology and literature
    PB–PH: Modern European languages
    PG: Russian literature
    PJ–PM: Languages and Literatures of Asia, Africa, Oceania, America;
      Mixed languages; Artificial languages
    PN, PR, PS, PZ: Literature: General, English, American; Fiction and
      Juvenile literature
    PQ, part 1: French literature
    PQ, part 2: Italian, Spanish, Portuguese literatures
    PT, part 1: German literature
    PT, part 2: Dutch and Scandinavian literatures
Q Science:
    QA: Mathematics
    QB: Astronomy
    QC: Physics
    QD: Chemistry
    QE: Geology
    QH: Natural history (general)
    QK: Botany
    QL: Zoology
    QM: Human anatomy
    QP: Physiology
    QR: Microbiology
R Medicine
S Agriculture, etc.
T Technology:
    TA: Engineering (general); Civil engineering (general)
    TC–TH: Civil engineering
    TJ: Mechanical engineering and machinery

TABLE 13-2   (Continued)

TK: Electrical engineering; Electronics; Nuclear engineering
TL: Motor vehicles; Aeronautics; Astronautics
TN: Mining engineering; Metallurgy
TP: Chemical technology
TR: Photography
TS: Manufactures
TT: Handicrafts; Arts and crafts
TX: Home economics
U   Military science
V   Naval science
Z   Bibliography and Library science

Main Classes

The rationale of the arrangement of the main classes (see Table 13-2) has been explained by Charles Martel, [5] one of the persons responsible for the original planning and supervision of the development of the system. The class of general works (A), not limited to any particular subject, leads the scheme. It is followed by the class containing philosophy and religion (B) which sets forth the theory, or theories, of man concerning the universe. The following classes, history and geography (C–G), concern such ideas as man's abode and source of his means of subsistence, man as affected by and affecting his physical milieu, and mind and soul of man in transition from primitive to advanced culture. The next group, classes H–L, brings out the economic and social evolution of man. Classes M–P for music, fine arts, and language and literature concern the esthetic and intellectual development and state of man. Classes B–P form the group of the philosophico-historical and philological sciences. The second large group, classes Q–V, embraces the mathematico-physical, natural, and applied sciences. Bibliography, which in many libraries may be distributed through the different subject classes, is kept together in the Library of Congress and shares the same class (Z) with library science.

Subclasses

Each of the main classes, with the exception of classes E–F and Z, is divided into subclasses, representing disciplines or major branches of the main class. Class Q, for example, is divided into the following subclasses:

[5]LaMontagne. Op. cit. P. 254.

Q   Science (general)
QA   Mathematics
QB   Astronomy
QC   Physics
QD   Chemistry
QE   Geology
QH   Natural history (general)
QK   Botany
QL   Zoology
QM   Human anatomy
QP   Physiology
QR   Microbiology

Divisions

Each subclass is further divided into divisions representing components of the subclass. For example, the subclass chemistry has the
following divisions:

QD   *Chemistry*
23.3–26   Alchemy
71–142   Analytical chemistry
146–197   Inorganic chemistry
241–441   Organic chemistry
450–731   Physical and theoretical chemistry
901–999   Crystallography

Each of the divisions, in turn, has subdivisions specifying different
aspects of the subject, such as form, time, place, and further subject
subdivisions. Table 13-3 shows a portion of the subdivisions under
Inorganic chemistry.

TABLE 13-3   Portion of Subdivisions under Inorganic Chemistry

	QD Chemistry
	Inorganic Chemistry
	Cf. QD475, Physical inorganic chemistry
	QE351–399.2, Mineralogy
146	Periodicals, societies, congresses, serial collections, yearbooks
147	Collected works (nonserial)
148	Dictionaries and encyclopedias
149	Nomenclature, terminology, notation, abbreviations
	History
.5	General works
.7	By region or country, A–Z

TABLE 13-3   (Continued)

QD Chemistry
Inorganic Chemistry

150	Early works through 1800
	General works, treatises, and advanced textbooks
151	1801–1969
.2	1970–
.5	Elementary textbooks
152	Addresses, essays, lectures
.3	Special aspects of the subject as a whole
153	Study and teaching. Research
154	Problems, exercises, examinations
155	Laboratory manuals
.5	Handbooks, tables, formulas, etc.
156	Inorganic synthesis
157	Electric furnace operations
	Cf. QD277, Electric furnace operations (organic)
161	*Nonmetals*
162	Gases
163	Chemistry of the air
	Cf. TD881–890, Air pollution
165	Halogens: bromine, chlorine, fluorine, iodine
167	Inorganic acids
	Cf. QD477, General theory of acids and bases
169	Other, A–Z
	Heavy water, *see* .W3
	.W3 Water
	Metals
	Cf. TN600–799, Metallurgy
171	General works, treatises, and textbooks
172	By group, A–Z
	.A3 Actinide elements
	.A4 Alkali metals
	.A42 Alkaline earth metals
	.I7 Iron group
	.M4 Magnesium group
	.P8 Platinum group
	.R2 Rare earth metals. Rare earths
	.S6 Spinel group
	.T6 Transition metals
	.T65 Transplutonium elements
	.T7 Transuranium elements

Enumerative Display

The Library of Congress Classification is essentially an enumerative scheme in that compound subjects containing more than one concept, facet, or aspect, are enumerated in the schedules. Relatively little notational synthesis is required. Even form divisions and many common divisions are individually listed under each subject to which they are applicable. Auxiliary tables are included mainly as a device for saving space in the schedules. With few exceptions, they are used for pinpointing specific numbers within a range of given numbers provided in the main schedule, rather than for the purpose of providing additional notational segments to be added to the main number in order to render it more specific, as in the case of the Dewey Decimal Classification and other systems. As a result of enumeration, the schedules of the Library of Congress Classification are more voluminous than any of the other systems.

INDEXES

With very few exceptions, each schedule contains its own index. The Library of Congress has yet to produce a general index to all the schedules but two indexes compiled by groups not associated with the Library of Congress have appeared in recent years: *An Index to the Library of Congress Classification*[6] and *Combined Indexes to the Library of Congress Classification Schedules*.[7] *Library of Congress Subject Headings*,[8] which lists LCC numbers after many of the headings, has also been used as an alphabetical key to the classification schedules.

NOTATION

Symbols

The Library of Congress Classification uses a mixed notation of letters and arabic numerals. Main classes are represented by a single letter, e.g., Q (Science). Double or triple letters stand for subclasses, e.g., QD (Chemistry), DJK (Eastern Europe), and KFF (Law of Florida). The classes E, F, and Z, the earliest schedules, have not been subdivided into subclasses and only single letters are used.

[6]*An Index to the Library of Congress Classification*. J. McRee Elrod, Judy Inouye, and Ann Craig Turner, eds. Ottawa: Canadian Library Association, 1974.

[7]*Combined Indexes to the Library of Congress Classification Schedules*. Compiled by Nancy B. Olson. 15 vols. Washington, D.C.: U.S. Historical Documents Institute, Inc., 1974–

[8]Library of Congress, Subject Cataloging Division. *Library of Congress Subject Headings*. 9th ed. Washington, D.C.: Library of Congress, 1980.

Divisions within the subclasses are represented by arabic numbers from 1 to 9999 (as integers) with possible decimal extensions. Further subdivisions, if required, are achieved by means of Cutter numbers (a combination of a capital letter and a decimal number). A book number, also in the form of a Cutter number, and possibly the year of publication complete the call number. Typical forms of LC call numbers are:

		Class number
F	JF	One, two, or three capital letters
1765	529	Integer 1 to 9999
.2		Possible decimal extension
.W3	.M42	Book number *(aut. a mainentry)*
	1971	Year of publication
		Class number
HD	KDC	One, two, or three capital letters
9861	188	Integer 1 to 9999
.9		Possible decimal extension
.C68	.W5	Cutter number for further subdivision of subject
K54	B65	Book number
1974		Year of publication

Except the call numbers for maps, no LC call number contains more than two Cutter numbers. Certain call numbers for maps have triple Cutter numbers.

Using letters for main classes provides a much broader base for division than the notational system of the Dewey Decimal Classification, since there are twenty-six letters as opposed to the ten arabic numerals. One notable characteristic of the LCC notational system is that ample gaps have been left for future use. The letters I, O, W, X, and Y have not been assigned to any subjects. These can be used later when needed. For instance, the National Library of Medicine Classification Scheme, which is based on LCC, has used the letter W for Medicine. The same scheme also uses QS–QZ, which are vacant in LCC, for Preclinical sciences. There are also ample gaps left among the two-letter combinations for subclasses and arabic numbers for subdivisions throughout the system.

An important characteristic of LCC's notational system is that it is not consistently hierarchical. In other words, the notation does not necessarily reflect the hierarchical relationships among the subjects.

The LCC notation is much more hospitable than those used by other systems for several reasons. Expansion is usually achieved by using the vacant numbers. When this is not feasible, two other methods are used. Since LCC's notation is not hierarchical, decimal extensions can be used for coordinate subjects or even broader subjects. For example, TX724 represents Jewish cookbooks and TX725 other cookbooks. When a number was required for Oriental cookbooks between these two categories, the number TX724.5 was assigned. Because the notation is not hierarchical, the topic assigned to TX724.5 does not have to be a subdivision of that represented by TX724. Another method of subdivision is alphabetical arrangement of subtopics under the arabic number, e.g., TX723.5.A3–Z, other European cookbooks, by country, A–Z. In this case, the Cutter numbers .A3–Z represent geographic subdivision and form a part of the class number.

The notation of LCC has been criticized because it is not hierarchical and therefore does not express the structure of the scheme.[9] On the other hand, its advantage lies in the fact that the majority of class numbers are thereby kept relatively brief and are manageable for the purpose of shelving arrangement. Because the hierarchical structure and relationships can be ignored in the notation, it is much easier to accommodate new subjects or topics.

Mnemonics

LCC lacks the kind of mnemonics found in other systems that make use of the same notational symbols to represent form, geographical, or other subdivisions, which apply throughout the entire system. A limited amount of mnemonics is employed in Class A, where the second letter for the subclass is taken from the name of the subject covered, e.g., AC for Collections, AE for Encyclopedias, AS for Societies, etc.

EVALUATION OF LC CLASSIFICATION SYSTEM[10]
Merits

1. A practical system which has proved to be satisfactory. "It is a triumph for pragmatism."[11]
2. It is based on literary warrant and is particularly suited to the needs of academic and research libraries.

---

[9]Maltby. Op. cit. P. 180.

[10]Cf. Maltby. Op. cit. Pp. 187, 174–189; J. Mills. *A Modern Outline of Library Classification.* London: Chapman & Hall, Ltd., 1967. Pp. 89–102; and A. C. Foskett. *The Subject Approach to Information.* 3d ed. Hamden, Conn.: Linnet Books; London: Clive Bingley, 1977. Pp. 359–367.

[11]Maltby. Op. cit. P. 187.

3. It is largely an enumerative system and requires minimal notational synthesis.
4. Each schedule was developed by subject specialists rather than by a "generalist" who cannot be an expert in every field.

Weaknesses

1. Scope notes are inferior to those of DDC.
2. Much national bias in emphasis and terminology.
3. Failure to see subjects as compounds. Multitopical or multi-element works not yet enumerated cannot be classified with precision.
4. Alphabetical arrangements are often used in place of logical hierarchies.
5. Lack of clear and predictable theoretical basis for subject analysis.

INSTRUCTION ON USE

The following instruction and examples are based on the schedules H, KF, P, and Q.

Format of Schedules

Before one attempts to classify with the Library of Congress system, a familiarity with the format and physical characteristics of the schedules may be helpful. The scheme comprises over thirty separately published schedules which are similar in format. The following elements are usually found in each schedule:

1. Preface
2. Synopsis, listing the subclasses contained in the schedule (not included in some schedules)
3. Outline, giving details of the major divisions of the subclasses
4. Main schedule giving all the details of the classification of the subject
5. Tables, if any
6. Index
7. Supplementary pages of additions and changes (usually found in reissues of schedules which have not been revised for a considerable period of time)

Class Numbers

In classifying library materials with the Library of Congress Classification, the main task, after the subject content of the work has been determined and the principal concepts identified (see earlier discussion), is to choose the most appropriate number from the schedules. Among the general classification schemes, the LCC is the most enumerative. Under the majority of subjects, the form, period, geographic, and topical subdivisions are enumerated in the schedules, and no notational synthesis is required. In other cases, tables are provided in the schedules as means of selecting the appropriate number from a range of numbers listed in the main schedule. The use of tables will be discussed later.

Table 13-4 is an example taken from the schedule for Class Q, Science, illustrating the divisions of a subject.

TABLE 13-4   Divisions of a Subject: Class Q, Science

	QC Physics
	Descriptive and Experimental Mechanics
	Cf. QC73–73.8, Force and energy (general)
	QC176–176.84, Solid-state physics
	TA349–360, Applied mechanics
	For theoretical and analytical mechanics, *see* QA801–939
120	Periodicals, societies, congresses, serial collections, yearbooks
121	Collected works (nonserial)
.6	Dictionaries and encyclopedias
.8	Nomenclature, terminology, notation, abbreviations
	History
	For general history of mechanics, *see* QA802
122	General works
.2	By region or country, A–Z
123	Early works through 1800
	General works, treatises, and advanced textbooks
125	1801–1969
.2	1970–
127	Elementary textbooks
.3	Popular works
.4	Juvenile works
.6	Addresses, essays, lectures
128	Study and teaching. Research
129	Problems, exercises, examinations
131	Special aspects of the subjects as a whole
	Dynamics
	Cf. QA845–871, Analytic mechanics
133	General works, treatises, and textbooks

TABLE 13-4   (Continued)

QC Physics
Descriptive and Experimental Mechanics

135	Kinematics
136	Vibrations
	Cf. QA865–867.5; QA935–939, Analytic mechanics
	QC231–241, Sound
	TA355, Engineering
	Fluids. Fluid mechanics
	Including liquids
	Cf. QA901–930, Analytic mechanics
	TA357–359, Applied fluid mechanics
141	History
142	Early works through 1500
	General works, treatises, and textbooks
143	1501–1700
144	1701–1800
145	1801–1969
.2	1970–
.3	Handbooks, tables, formulas, etc.
.4	Special properties of liquids, A–Z
	.C6 Compressibility
	.D5 Diffusion
	.E9 Expansion
	.T5 Thermal properties
	.V5 Viscosity
.45	Special liquefied gases, A–Z
	.F5 Fluorine
	.H4 Helium

In Table 13-4, the numbers QC120–129 contain form, period, and geographic divisions of the subject, Descriptive and experimental mechanics. A periodical on mechanics is classed in QC120 and a current treatise on the subject is classed in QC125.2. Numbers beginning with QC131 provide topical divisions of the subject, such as Dynamics, Fluids. Each of the topical divisions may have its own subdivisions, depending on the amount of material on that subject in the Library of Congress collection. More elaborate subdivisions appear under Fluids and Fluid mechanics than under Dynamics. A handbook on Fluid mechanics is classed in QC145.3. When no form divisions are provided under a particular subject, the number designated for General works is used for all forms. A handbook on Dynamics is therefore classed in QC133.

Cutter Numbers

As mentioned earlier, the Cutter number is used in the Library of Congress Classification system for two purposes: as a further extension of the class number and as a book number. A Cutter number consists of a capital letter followed by an arabic number. The number is treated decimally and the decimal point precedes the letter, e.g., .R6.

The elaborate Cutter tables used with the Dewey Decimal Classification are not used with the Library of Congress Classification. Instead, a set of relatively simple Cutter tables are used. These are given below:[12]

1. After initial vowels

for the second letter:	b	d	l,m	n	p	r	s,t	u–y
use number:	2	3	4	5	6	7	8	9

2. After the initial letter S

for the second letter:	a	ch	e	h,i	m–p	t	u
use number:	2	3	4	5	6	7–8	9

3. After the initial letters Qu

for the third letter:	a	e	i	o	r	y
use number:	3	4	5	6	7	9

for names beginning Qa–Qt
   use: 2–29

4. After other initial consonants

for the second letter:	a	e	i	o	r	u	y
use number:	3	4	5	6	7	8	9

5. When an additional number is preferred

for the third letter:	a–d	e–h	i–l	m	n–q	r–t
use number:	2*	3	4	5	6	7

	u–w	x–z
	8	9

(*optional for third letter a or b)

Letters not included in the foregoing tables are assigned the next higher or lower number as required by previous assignments in the particular class.

The arrangements in the following examples illustrate some possible applications of these tables:

1. Names beginning with vowels:

Abernathy	.A2	Ames	.A45	Astor	.A84
Adams	.A3	Appleby	.A6	Atwater	.A87
Aldrich	.A4	Archer	.A7	Austin	.A9

2. Names beginning with the letter S:

Saint	.S2	Simmons	.S5	Steel	.S7
Schaefer	.S3	Smith	.S6	Storch	.S75
Seaton	.S4	Southerland	.S64	Sturges	.S8
Shank	.S45	Springer	.S66	Sullivan	.S9

3. Names beginning with the letters Qu:

Qadriri	.Q2	Quick	.Q5	Qureshi	.Q7
Quabbe	.Q3	Quoist	.Q6	Quynn	.Q9
Queener	.Q4				

4. Names beginning with other consonants:

Carter	.C3(7)*	Cinelli	.C5(6)	Cullen	.C8(4)
Cecil	.C4(2)	Corbett	.C6(7)	Cyprus	.C9(6)
Childs	.C45	Croft	.C7(6)		

*The number in parentheses is added if a two-digit Cutter number is desired.

5. When there are no existing conflicting entries in the shelflist, the use of a third letter author number may be preferred:

Cabot	.C3	Callahan	.C34	Carter	.C37
Cadmus	.C32	Campbell	.C35	Cavelli	.C38
Caffrey	.C33	Cannon	.C36	Cazalas	.C39

The numbers are decimals, thus allowing for infinite interpolation on the decimal principle.

Since the tables provide only a general framework for the assignment of numbers, it should be noted that the symbol for a particular name or work is constant only within a single class. Each entry must be added to the existing entries in the shelflist in such a way as to preserve alphabetical order in accordance with filing rules.

Cutter number as part of class number

In Table 13-4, the caption "By region or country, A–Z" indicates that Cutter numbers are used for geographic division of the subject. QC145.4 carries the caption "Special properties of liquids, A–Z." This means that individual properties are represented by Cutter numbers after the main class number. A work about the diffusion of fluids is classed in the following number:

QC   The double letters for the subclass,
      Physics

145.4 The arabic number meaning special properties
       of liquids

.D5   The Cutter number for diffusion

Cutter number as book number

Each call number contains a book number generally based on the main entry of the work. In this function, the LC Cutter number is similar to that used in the Dewey Decimal Classification. The main purpose is to distinguish different works on the same subject. A work about chemistry by J. E. Brady is assigned the number QD31.2.B7, and another work on the same subject by Eubanks is classed in QD31.2.E8. If the Cutter number taken from the tables has already been assigned to another work, it is adjusted for the work being classified. For example, a work about chemistry by F. Brescia received the call number QD31.2.B7$\underline{4}$. If the same author has written more than one work on a subject, the Cutter numbers are adjusted in a similar manner. For example,

	Hamlet, Peter
QD31.2.H35	*Introductory Chemistry: A New View*
QD31.2.H352	*Introductory, Organic, and Biochemistry: A New View*

Different editions or issues of the same work cataloged in separate entries are distinguished by adding the date of publication to the call number, e.g.,

	Embree, H. D.
QH345.E42	*Introduction to the Chemistry of Life*
QH345.E42 1975	*Introduction to the Chemistry of Life.* 2d ed. 1975

In order to place a translation of a work with the original text, the call number of the original work with an extension of the book number is assigned to the translation, for example,

	Higman, Bryan
QA76.7.H53	*A Comparative Study of Programming Languages*
QA76.7.H53$\underline{15}$	*Programmiersprachen: eine vergleichende Studie* (a German translation of the above title)

The following notations are used for translations unless there are specific instructions for subarranging translations in the schedules.

Table for Translations
.x   Cutter number of work in original language
.x13   English translation
.x14   French translation
.x15   German translation
.x16   Italian translation
.x17   Russian translation
.x18   Spanish translation

These notations may be adjusted to accommodate translations in other languages. For instance, for a Bulgarian translation, one may use .x12, or .x13 if the original work is in English.

Double Cutter numbers

When a class number includes a Cutter number as a subdivision, a second Cutter number is added as the book number, resulting in a double Cutter number.[13] For example, a work about scientific research in the United States by R. T. Arnold is assigned the following call number:

Q	The single letter meaning science in general
180	The arabic number meaning research, to be divided by region or country, A–Z
.U5	The first Cutter number for the United States
A77	The book number for the main entry, Arnold

Note that only one decimal point, preceding the first Cutter number, is required.

Call numbers for biography often contain double Cutter numbers, one for the biographee and one for the biographer, e.g., a biography of Einstein by Flückiger:

QC	The double letter for physics
16	The arabic number meaning an individual biography

[13]In rare instances, both Cutter numbers may be extensions of the class number and the call number will therefore not include a book number.

.E5   The first Cutter number for Einstein

F56   The second Cutter number for Flückiger

Successive Cutter numbers

Successive Cutter numbers are a series of Cutter numbers (e.g., .F3, .F4, .F5) or decimal extensions of a Cutter number (e.g., .F32, .F33, .F34, .F35) in an established sequence. They are used when certain works are to be grouped on the shelves in an established order. An example is the additional digits attached to a book number for a translation. In the schedules, instructions are sometimes given to use successive Cutter numbers. This occurs frequently in tables. (For an example, see page 296.)

A and Z Cutter numbers

In some cases, under a class number, a span of Cutter numbers at the beginning ("A" Cutter numbers) or at the end ("Z" Cutter numbers) of the alphabetical sequence are assigned special meanings. The "A" Cutter numbers are used most frequently for form divisions such as periodicals or official publications, and the "Z" Cutter numbers are often assigned to special divisions of the subject, for example, biography and criticism of a literary author, certain corporate bodies associated with the subject, etc.

UA	ARMIES: ORGANIZATION, DISTRIBUTION, ETC.
	By region or country
	Europe
	France
	Army
	Artillery
705.A1–5	Documents
.A6–Z4	General works
.Z5A–Z	Bataillons d'artillérie à pied
.Z6	Regiments. By number

QC	PHYSICS
174.4	**Quantum statistics**
.A1A–Z	Periodicals, societies, congresses, serial collections, yearbooks
.A2A–Z	Collected works (nonserial)
.A6–Z	General works, treatises, and textbooks

The Cutter numbers .A1 and .A2 are used for serial publications and nonserial collected works. .A3–.A5 are not used at the present. A treatise on quantum statistics by an author named Adams, which is normally assigned the Cutter number .A3 according to the Cutter tables, will receive a Cutter number greater than .A6.

Date in Call Numbers

Date as part of class number

In some cases, an LC call number contains a date as part of the class number. For example:

JK	Constitutional history—United States
1968	Statistics of elections and election returns
1972	Date of the election

In such cases, the book number follows the date to complete the call number.

Date as edition mark

The date of imprint or copyright following the book number is generally used as an edition mark in the Library of Congress Classification system. For example:

HG	Finance
655	Monetary policy of Canada
.C3	Book number based on the main entry, Cairns
1972	Imprint date of the second edition

If there is more than one edition of the same work published in the same year, a lowercase letter is added to the date for a variant edition. In general, the letters are assigned in the following manner:

[date]a	A facsimile or photocopy edition, the date being that of the original
[date]	Successive editions and reprints of the
[date]b	original in order of shelflisting.
[date]c	Such words as second edition, new edition,
[date]d	revised edition, improved edition, enlarged
etc.	edition, and first American edition, indicate that another edition exists. The date is the imprint or copyright date of the edition being classified.

Works entered under corporate headings[14]

A recent Library of Congress policy requires that the date of imprint be added to a work entered under a corporate heading, regardless of whether it is the first or a subsequent edition of the work. Under the same class number, all works entered under the same corporate heading (disregarding any subheadings) are assigned the same Cutter (book) number. The date is added to distinguish between different titles. If there is more than one work by the corporate body in the same year, successive work letters (i.e., [date]a, [date]b, etc.) are added to the imprint dates in the call numbers. To distinguish a serial publication from a monograph entered under the same corporate heading, successive work letters (i.e., a, b, c, etc.) are added to the Cutter (book) number. Examples:

xxxx .A8 1953	Auburn University. Agriculture Experiment Station. [Monographic title] 1953.
xxxx .A8 1953a	Auburn University. [Multivolume monographic title] 1953–1958.
xxxx .A8 1957	Auburn University. Labor Institute. [Open-entry multivolume monographic title] 1957–
xxxx .F3 1966	Farmacopee-Commissie. [Monographic title] 1966.
xxxx .F3 1966a	Farmacopee-Commissie. [Monographic title] 1966.
xxxx .F3a	Farmacopee-Commissie. [Open-entry serial title] 1969–
xxxx .F3b	Farmacopee-Commissie. [Closed-entry serial title] 1956–1968.
xxxx .N28 1949	National Research Council. [Monographic title] 1949.
xxxx .N32 1954	National Research Council (Canada). [Monographic title] 1954.

[14]*Cataloging Service*, **110**:6–8, Summer 1974.

xxxx .U3 1958	United States. Army. General Staff. [Monographic title] 1958.
xxxx .U3 1963	United States. Army. [Multivolume monographic title] 1963–1964.
xxxx .U3 1963a	United States. Army. Far East Command. [Monographic title] 1963.

Exercise A

Assign LC call numbers to the following works:

1. *Journal of Radioanalytical Chemistry* (main entry under title)
2. *Fossils of Rhinoceroses from Kenya* (main entry under Albert)
3. *Public Finance in Austria in the Twentieth Century* (main entry under Geld; original in German)
4. *Railroad Conductors* (main entry under Goodman)
5. *Geochemistry of Uranium* (main entry under Ranchin)
6. *History of the Harvard Law School* (main entry under Harvard Law School)
7. *Teaching Literature: A Guide for Teachers* (main entry under Learned)
8. *A History of the Theatre in Madrid* (main entry under Vare)
9. *Eighteenth-century English Drama: An Anthology* (main entry under title)
10. *Finance of Corporations* (main entry under Worre)

Tables

Tables represent recurring patterns of subdivision. Compared to other modern library classification schemes, the Library of Congress Classification relies to a lesser extent on the use of general auxiliary tables, because most of the subdivisions are enumerated in the schedules.

There is also a basic difference between the tables used in the Library of Congress Classification and those used in other systems. Tables used in the Dewey Decimal Classification, for instance, provide additional segments to be attached to a main class number in order to render it more specific. In the Library of Congress system, with the exception of tables containing subdivisions represented by Cutter numbers, the tables are a device to locate the desired number within a range of numbers given in the schedule. Usually, the number given in the table is *added* (in the arithmetic sense) instead of attached to the base number from the schedule. The main purpose of these tables is to save space in the schedules.

In the Library of Congress Classification, a table may occur within the schedule either before or after the range of numbers to which the table is applied. Such a table may be called an *internal table*. If the table is applied to an entire class or subclass, it appears at the end of the schedule immediately before the index. These may be called *auxiliary tables*.

The tables may contain notation in the form of arabic numbers or in the form of Cutter numbers. In a table that represents a numerical sequence, the following steps may be applied:

1. Find the range of numbers in the schedule which have been assigned to the subject in question.
2. Determine the appropriate table to be applied to the specific range of numbers.
3. Select the number in the table which represents the specific aspect appropriate to the document, and fit the number (usually by simple addition) into the range of numbers from the schedule.

In a table that contains Cutter numbers, the appropriate Cutter number is simply attached to the main number from the schedule.

The following examples illustrate the use of tables.

Internal tables

Tables used with specific spans of numbers are scattered throughout the schedules. Most of these are relatively brief. Table 13-5 is an example of an internal table (from Subclass HC).

In the schedule, Argentina is assigned the range of numbers HC171–180. Therefore, the call number assigned to a work on the current economic conditions of Argentina written by Ubertalli is HC175.U23, which is analyzed below:

HC	The double letters for the subclass, Economic history and conditions
175	The fifth number (under the 10 nos. column in Table 13-5, meaning a work covering a later period) in the span of numbers 171–180 assigned to Argentina
.U23	The book number based on the main entry, Ubertalli

A work about the economic conditions of Buenos Aires written by G. Bourdé is classed in the following manner:

TABLE 13-5   Internal Table

| HC | ECONOMIC HISTORY AND CONDITIONS | HC |

95–695 By country.
General works only; those on particular industries in HD, other special with subject.
Under each:

5 nos.	10 nos.	
1	1	Collections, including periodicals, societies and documents.
		.A1–3 Periodicals. Serial documents.
		Separate documents.
		.A4 Administrative documents.
		By date.
		Other documents to be classed with general works.
	2	Dictionaries. Directories.
2	3	General works.
		By period.
		Period divisions vary for different countries. Cf. corresponding divisions in HF3001–4040.
	4	Early.
	5	Later.
3		Local.
	7	By state, etc., A–Z.
	8	By city, A–Z.
		Annual (local) reviews of "Commerce," "Finance," "Trade," etc., HF3163 and HF3211–4040, subdivision (10) under each country; general, in HC14.
4	9	Colonies.
		Exploitation and economic conditions. Colonial administration and policy in JV.

HC	The double letters for the subclass, Economic history and conditions
178	The eighth number (under the 10 nos. column in the table, meaning a local subdivision by city) in the span of 171–180
.B9	The first Cutter number for the city, Buenos Aires
B68	The book number based on the main entry, Bourdé

Table 13-6 shows a portion of an internal table also found in Class H which contains another small table within it. For example, chemical industries are given the span of numbers HD9650–9660. Therefore, Table B is used with this topic. A general work on chemical industries in Italy entered under the title *Il Futuro dell'industria chimica in Italia* is classed as follows:

HD		The double letters meaning economic history
9656		The number (within the span 9650–9660) matching notation 6 in Table B, meaning chemical industries in a European country
	.I82	The Cutter number (.I8) for Italy and the decimal extension (2) based on the small table within Tables A and B, meaning a general work
	F87	The book number based on the main entry, *Il Futuro . . .*

The small table demonstrates the use of successive Cutter numbers. For Italy, the numbers matching those in the small table would be:

Other Countries
  Under each:
.I8   (1) Collections. Serials.
.I82   (2) General works.
.I83   (3) Local, A–Z.
.I84   (4) Firms, etc., A–Z.

Note that the first Cutter number is .I8 instead of .I81 because the use of a Cutter number ending in the digit "1" limits the possibility of interpolation and is therefore generally avoided.

Auxiliary tables

These tables are applicable to an entire class or subclass. They are often used in combination with internal tables. Most of these tables provide patterns for breaking down given ranges of numbers. Some provide alphabetical arrangements for geographical division by means of Cutter numbers. The following examples demonstrate the use of some of the auxiliary tables.

Example 1
The table "Regions and Countries in One Alphabet" provides alphabetical arrangement of countries by means of Cutter numbers. It is used whenever the schedule gives the instruction, "By country, A–Z"

TABLE 13-6   Portion of Internal Table, Containing Another Small Table

Tables of Subdivisions under Industries and Trades (HD9000–9999)

Under each:

A	B	
20 nos.	11 nos.	
0	0	General.
		By country.
	1	United States.
1	.1	Collections, associations, etc.
7	.7	By state, A–W.
8	.8	By city, A–Z.

		Other countries.
		Under each:
		(1) Collections. Serials.
		(2) General works.
		(3) Local, A–Z.
		(4) Firms, etc., A–Z.
14	5	America, A–Z.
15	6	Europe, A–Z.
19	10	Special, A–Z.

or "By region or country, A–Z." A portion of the table (from Class T) appears as Table 13-7. This table is printed in the schedules of classes C, D, E–F, H, T, U, and V (sometimes with the caption "Table of Countries in One Alphabet"). In fact, it is used throughout all classes in assigning Cutter numbers to countries. It should be noted that the Cutter number assigned to a particular country may sometimes vary under different class numbers, depending on what has already *existed* in the shelflist.

TABLE 13-7   Regions and Countries in One Alphabet (Portion)*

Abyssinia, *see* Ethiopia.		Haiti	.H2
Afghanistan	.A3	Holland, *see* Netherlands.	
Algeria	.A4	Honduras	.H8
Arabia, Saudi, *see*	.S33	Hong Kong	.H85
Argentine Republic ..	.A7	Iceland	.I2
Spain	.S7	Uruguay	.U8
Sweden	.S8	Venezuela	.V4
Switzerland	.S9	Yugoslavia	.Y8
Turkey	.T9		

*Details of the table are given in Appendix B of this book.

Table 13-7 is used in classifying the following works:

A history of astronomy in Poland, by V. S. Gubarev: QB33.P7G8

QB	Astronomy
33	History, by region or country, A–Z
.P7	Poland (according to the table of "Regions and Countries in One Alphabet")
G8	Gubarev

A work about old age pensions in Sweden, written by P. Gahrton: HV1481.S82G34

HV	Social pathology
1481	Assistance to the aged in Europe, A–Z
.S8	Sweden (according to the table of "Regions and Countries in One Alphabet")
2	General works (according to an internal table immediately preceding the number HV1475 in the main schedule)
G34	Gahrton

Two other tables also have universal application. These are "United States," a list of the states in alphabetical order (printed in schedules of classes G, H, T, U, and V, sometimes with the caption "Table of States"), and "Canada and Newfoundland—List of Provinces" (printed in schedule of Class T).[15] The following examples illustrate the use of these tables. For use of "United States":

A history of California labor by D. F. Selvin: HD8083.C2S4

HD	Economic history
8083	Labor in the United States, by state or region, A–W
.C2	California (according to the table "United States")
S4	Selvin

For use of "Canada and Newfoundland—List of Provinces":

A work about industrial promotion in Nova Scotia by R. E. George: HC117.N8G37

HC	Economic history and conditions
117	Canada (the number in the range HC 111–120 assigned to Canada in the

[15]Details of these tables are given in Appendix B of this book.

> main schedule, chosen according to the
> internal table under the numbers
> HC95–695), by state, etc., A–Z

.N8   Nova Scotia (according to the table
"Canada and Newfoundland—List of
Provinces")

G37   George

Example 2
"Tables of Geographical Divisions" (in Class H) are a group of ten tables providing detailed geographic divisions. They are used with spans of numbers given in the main schedule with specific instruction concerning which table is to be used in a particular case. For example, to classify a work about family patterns in Finland, by V. S. Heiskanen, the first step is to find the appropriate class number or numbers in the schedule.

HQ   The family
531–727   By country. Table II.

The instruction calls for the use of Table II. A portion of an updated version of the "Tables of Geographical Divisions" is reproduced as Table 13-8.

The number designated for Finland in Table II is 108.3. This number is added to the base number HQ530 to obtain the desired number, HQ638.3. Attaching the book number .H4 for Heiskanen yields the complete call number, HQ638.3.H4.

Example 3
Use of the tables of "Form Divisions" and the "Table of Subject Subdivisions for the Law of the States" in Subclass KF is illustrated in the following examples.

Compends of U.S. law on torts by W. A. Rutter: KF1250.Z9R8 1970

KF   United States law
1250   Torts, with indication that Table III
            is to be used
.Z9   Compends (according to Table III of
            "Form Divisions")
R8   Rutter
1970   Date of publication

TABLE 13-8   Tables of Geographical Divisions (Portion)   H

I	II	III	IV	V		VI	VII	VIII	IX	X
					Europe (continued)					
55	107–108	160–162	213–216	74–77	Russia	105–109	411–420	421–430	211–215	551–560
55.3	108.3	162.3	217	77.3	Finland	110	421–425	431–435	215.5	561–565
55.7	108.7	162.7	218	77.7	Poland	111	426–429.5	436–439.5	215.7	566–569.5
56	109–110	163–165	219–220	78	Scandinavia	113–114	430	440	216–220	570
57	111–112	166–168	221–224	79	Denmark	115–119	431–440	441–450	221–225	571–580
58	113–114	169–171	225–228	79.5	Iceland	120–124	441–450	451–460	226–230	581–590
59	115–116	172–174	229–232	80	Norway	125–129	451–460	461–470	231–235	591–600
60	117–118	175–177	233–236	81–84	Sweden	130–134	461–470	471–480	236–240	601–610
61	119–120	178–180	237–240	85–88	Spain	135–139	471–480	481–490	241–245	611–620
61.3	120.3	180.3	240.3	88.3	Andorra	139.3	480.3	490.3	245.3	620.3
61.5	120.5	180.5	240.5	88.5	Gibraltar	139.5	480.5	490.5	245.5	620.5
62	121–122	181–183	241–244	89	Portugal	140–144	481–490	491–500	246–250	621–630
63	123–124	184–186	245–248	90	Switzerland	145–149	491–500	501–510	251–255	631–640
64	125–126	187–189	249–252	91	Balkan States	150–154	501–510	511–520	256–260	641–650
64.5	126.5	189.5	252.5	91.4	Albania	154.4	510.5	520.5	260.5	650.5
65	127–128	190–191	253–254	91.5	Bulgaria	154.5	511–520	521–530	261–265	651–660
65.5	128.5	192–193	255–256	91.6	Yugoslavia	154.6	521–525	531–535	265.5	661–665
67	131–132	196–198	261–264	91.8	Romania	154.8	531–540	541–540	271–275	671–680
67.5	132.5	198.5	264.5	91.83	Greece	154.83	540.5	550.5	275.5	680.5
68	133	199	265	91.85	Asia	154.85	541–545	551–555	276	681
68.2	133.3	200	265.5	91.9	Middle East. Near East	154.9	546	556	276.5	682
68.25	133.4	200.5	265.7	91.93	Turkey	154.93	546.5	556.5	276.7	682.5
68.3	133.5	200.6	266	91.95	Cyprus	154.95	547	557	277	683
68.35	133.7	200.9	266.5	92	Syria	155	548	558	277.5	684
68.4	133.9	201	267	92.15	Lebanon	155.15	549	559	278	685
68.45	134	201.3	267.5	92.2	Israel. Palestine	155.2	550	560	278.5	686
68.5	134.3	201.6	268	92.25	Jordan	155.25	551	561	279	687
68.55	134.5	201.9	268.5	92.3	Arabian Peninsula. Arabia	155.3	552	562	279.5	688
68.6	134.7	202	269	92.35	Saudi Arabia	155.35	553	563	280	689
68.65	134.9	202.3	269.5	92.4	Yemen (Yemen Arab Republic)	155.4	554	564	280.5	690

The constitution of Hawaii as amended, 1968: KFH401 1968.A36

KFH (0–599)	Law of Hawaii
401	Particular constitutions (the base number 0 + 401 from the "Table of Subject Subdivisions for the Law of the States," KF, p. 225), by date of constitution
1968	Date of constitution
.A36	An official edition (cf. instruction under 401 on KF, p. 225)

Draftsman's manual to the Indiana Code of 1971 by J. M. Oddi and M. C. Attridge: KFI3421.5.B5O3

KFI (3000–3599)	Law of Indiana
3421.5	The base number 3000 + 421.5 (from the "Table of Subject Subdivisions for the Law of the States," KF, p. 226) meaning special topics with regard to legislative process
.B5	Special topic: Bill drafting
O3	Table VII (KF, p. 276) indicates that .A9–Z are used for treatises. O3 for Oddi falls within this range.

Example 4
Use of author tables in Class P is illustrated below. Works written by or about an individual literary author are classed together in the Library of Congress Classification. Each author is assigned a range of numbers, a number, or a Cutter number. The author tables provide patterns for subarrangement of works by and about the authors. These examples are based on the tables in the schedule for subclasses PN, PR, PS, PZ (second edition).

The Works of Mark Twain.   1972–   PS1300.F72

PS	American literature
1300	First number (according to Table II in subclasses PN, PR, PS, PZ) in the range of 1300–1348 assigned to Clemens, Samuel Langhorne (Mark Twain) for collected works
.F72	Book number (also according to Table II) for a work published in 1972

A work about Mark Twain by A. Henderson: PS1331.H4 1974b

PS	American literature
1331	A general biography-criticism (according to Table II), in the range of numbers assigned to Mark Twain
.H4	Henderson
1974b	Date of publication and the letter *b* indicating a variant edition (i.e. there is another edition of the same work also published in 1974)

An edition of *The Rape of the Lock* by Alexander Pope, edited by D. G. Lougee and R. W. McHenry: PR3629.A2L6.

PR3620–3638	Pope, Alexander (Table III*ª*)
PR3625–3630	Numbers for separate works according to Table III*ª*
PR3629	Number assigned to *Rape of the Lock*
.A2	Texts (Table X*ª* for separate works with one number)
L6	By editor

Exercise B

Assign LC call numbers to the following works:

1. *Labor Supply in West Germany* (main entry under Bonne)
2. *Railroad Conductors in France* (main entry under Jules)
3. *The Strange and the Beautiful World of Orchids* (main entry under Ebel)
4. *A Bibliography of Insurance Law* (main entry under Neal)
5. *Salt Industry in Austria* (main entry under Werner)
6. *A Concordance to the English Poems of George Herbert* (main entry under Little)
7. *Emerson Society Quarterly* (main entry under title)
8. *Commentary on Flaubert's Madame Bovary* (main entry under Bopp)
9. *West Virginia Child Labor Law and Regulations.* 1969 (main entry under West Virginia)
10. *Illinois Rules and Regulations for Fire Prevention and Safety, as amended June 4, 1964, and July 1, 1968.* 1970 (main entry under Illinois)

CHAPTER 14

Other Modern General Library Classification Systems

In addition to the Dewey Decimal Classification and the Library of Congress Classification, many other library classification systems, some for general collections and others for specialized collections or subject areas, have been developed in modern times. Following is a brief discussion of the principles and characteristics of a number of general library classification systems. They are presented in chronological order by date of publication of the first edition.

EXPANSIVE CLASSIFICATION BY CHARLES AMMI CUTTER (1837–1903)

Brief History

Expansive Classification (EC) was originally designed for the Boston Athenaeum. Cutter recognized later its value as a general library classification system and, with certain modifications and refinements, made it available to other libraries through the publication of the scheme in 1891–1893.[1]

The scheme consists of seven versions of the classification in varying degrees of fullness. The seventh classification was designed for a collection of ten million volumes. Unfortunately, Cutter died before its completion. There was no mechanism or organizational support for the updating of the scheme. Libraries have long ceased to adopt the system. The latest survey reveals that it is now used by only a dozen American and Canadian libraries, most of which are special or small public libraries.[2]

---

[1]C. A. Cutter. *Expansive Classification: Part I: The First Six Classifications.* Boston: C. A. Cutter, 1891–1893.

[2]Robert L. Mowery. "The Cutter Classification: Still at Work." *Library Resources and Technical Services,* 20:154–156, Spring 1976.

The major significance of Expansive Classification lies in the fact that it was used as the basis for the development of the Library of Congress Classification. A comparison of the outlines of the two systems reveals strong similarities in the main classes (see Table 13-1, pages 270–272).

Basic Principles

Recognizing that a village library and a national library have vastly different needs, Cutter decided to develop a system that can meet the needs of all sizes of libraries. Expansive Classification was therefore prepared in seven versions, called classifications, in increasing fullness of detail. The first classification has eight main classes with rather broad subdivisions. The second classification has fifteen main classes and the third through sixth classifications have twenty-seven (see Table 14-1). This idea of providing varying degrees of fullness to suit

TABLE 14-1   Outline of Expansive Classification

A	General works
B	Philosophy
Br	Religion (except the Christian and Jewish)
C	Christian and Jewish religions
D	Ecclesiastical history
E	Biography
F	History
G	Geography and travels
H	Social sciences
I	Sociology
J	Government; Politics
K	Legislation; Law; Woman; Societies
L	Science in general; Physical sciences
M	Natural history
N	Botany
O	Zoology
Q	Medicine
R	Useful Arts (technology)
S	Engineering; Building
T	Manufactures; Handicrafts
U	Defensive and preservative arts
V	Recreative Arts; Sports; Theater
Vv	Music
W	Fine Arts
X	Language
Y	Literature
Z	Book Arts

the needs of individual libraries is in keeping with Cutter's proposal of the full, medium, and short catalogs for libraries of different sizes. A similar principle, although to a lesser degree, was adopted by the Dewey Decimal Classification in issuing an abridged edition in addition to the unabridged. Universal Decimal Classification appears in three versions, the full, medium, and abridged editions.

In arranging the subdivisions of each main class, Cutter claims to have followed an evolutionary order; that is, placing the subdivisions of each subject in the order which the evolutionary theory assigns to their appearance in creation. For example, science proceeds from the molecular to the molar, from number and space, through matter and force, to matter and life. In book arts, the subdivisions follow the history of the book from its production through its distribution, to its storage and use in libraries, and ends with its description, i.e., bibliography.

Notation

To provide a broader base for division, Cutter adopted the letters in the Roman alphabet for main classes and subdivisions, e.g.,

X	Language
XDG	Grammar
XDHZ	Parts of speech
XDI	Noun
XDIW	Adjective

As a result of using letters, the notation is kept shorter than that in a system using arabic numerals only.

A table of common subdivisions, applicable throughout the system, lists form subdivisions represented by arabic numerals:

.1	Theory; Philosophy
.2	Bibliography
.3	Biography
.4	History
.5	Dictionaries; Encyclopedias
.6	Yearbooks; Directories
.7	Periodicals
.8	Societies
.9	Collections

For example,

XDG.4   History of grammar

For geographic subdivisions, a "local list" is provided, which is also applicable throughout the scheme. Following is an example from it:

21	Australia
211	W. Australia
212	N. Australia
213	Alexandra Land
214	S. Australia
215	Queensland, etc.
24	Asia and Africa
25	Asia and Europe
27	Europe and Africa
30	Europe
32	Greece
35	Italy
45	England, Great Britain
47	Germany
80	America
83	United States

For example,

IU	Schools
IU45	English schools
IU83	American schools

For subarrangement of books on the same subject, Cutter devised a system of author or book numbers to be used with the Expansive Classification. Ironically, this part of Cutter's system, which has become known as the Cutter numbers, has survived the classification itself and is now widely used with the Dewey Decimal Classification. Discussion and instruction on the use of Cutter numbers follow the chapter on DDC. A brief version of the Cutter number system is used with the Library of Congress Classification.

UNIVERSAL DECIMAL CLASSIFICATION
Brief History

Universal Decimal Classification (UDC) was an adaptation of Dewey Decimal Classification. UDC was originally developed for the purpose of compiling a classified index to a universal bibliography which would list all publications, including books and articles in periodicals. This project was initiated in 1895 by the Institut International de Bibliographie (IIB) located in Brussels, which later became the Fédération Internationale de Documentation (FID). Paul Otlet and Henri La Fontaine of Belgium, who were responsible for the initial development of UDC, decided to base the new system on DDC, which had become the most successful and best known library classification system by the end of the nineteenth century. As an indexing tool, it required much more detail and minute specifications. The IIB obtained Melvil Dewey's permission to expand and modify DDC to suit the purpose of a universal bibliography.

The first complete (international) edition in the French language was published in 1905 under the title *Manuel du répertoire bibliographique universel.*

Over the years, the project of the universal bibliography was abandoned, but the development of UDC as a general scheme for classification and indexing continued. It has been adopted widely in Europe. It now appears in three versions with varying details—full, medium, and abridged—and has been translated into over twenty languages. However, not all these are complete editions. Only parts of the English edition have been published.

The system is now maintained by the FID. A major difficulty has been the slow process in updating because of the very involved and complicated mechanism for revision, sometimes called a *hyperdemocratic procedure.* This mechanism ensures universal input but is extremely time-consuming.

UDC has also been known under various other names: Classification Internationale Décimale, the International Decimal Classification, the Expanded Dewey, and the Brussels Expansion of Dewey.

Developments in modern knowledge have placed a certain strain on a classification system such as DDC, which was originated in the nineteenth century. The same strain has been felt by UDC. New knowledge constantly comes into being. Existing knowledge is continuously redefined and realigned. Like DDC, UDC has also been making constant efforts to keep pace with knowledge while attempting to maintain a certain degree of stability.

In adopting the basic structure of DDC, UDC has also inherited its intrinsic weaknesses. Over the years, attempts have been made to rectify or mitigate some of the basic problems without uprooting the system. In addition to continuous expansion of details in order to keep pace with knowledge and proliferation of literature, many relocations have been made over the years. In recent years, a major relocation has been made by moving the language class to the literature class, a move resulting in a better collocation of related subjects and an entire vacant class for future use.

Recent Developments

Efforts have been made recently to demonstrate the applicability of UDC to computerized stores of information. Computerized applica-

TABLE 14-2   Outline of Universal Decimal Classification

0	Generalities of knowledge
1	Philosophy. Metaphysics. Psychology. Logic. Ethics
2	Religions. Theology
3	Social sciences
4	(Currently vacant. Formerly Linguistics; Philology)
5	Mathematics and Natural sciences
6	Applied sciences. Medicine. Technology
7	The Arts. Recreation. Entertainment. Sport
8	Linguistics. Philology. Literature. Belles-lettres
9	Geography. Biography. History

tions of UDC have been made in various countries including Canada, Britain, Germany, Denmark, and Switzerland.[3]

Concerning the immediate as well as the distant future of the system, two trends of thought have been reported.[4] One is to maintain the present framework of the system by making only routine amendments and extensions while at the same time employing new techniques of presentation and indexing. The other trend is toward a more thorough revamping of the system, even to the extent of creating a new universal classification scheme. It appears that while routine maintenance of the system follows more or less the first trend, efforts are also being made along the line of the second trend.

Basic Principles

An adaptation of DDC, UDC follows the basic outline of DDC in the main classes and major subdivisions (see Table 14-2). As a result, like DDC, UDC is also a general classification scheme covering all fields of knowledge. In subject subdivisions, the progression is from the general to the specific. Division is based on mutually exclusive classes, so far as this is possible. It also attempts to collocate related classes.

Because of its initial purpose and later requirements and developments, UDC has moved a long way from DDC in several aspects. An attempt has been made to remove all national biases. However, a western, or occidental, viewpoint is still detectable. To serve as an indexing tool, UDC is required to have many more detailed subdivisions than a scheme designed mainly for shelving purposes. There are many more detailed provisions in UDC than in DDC.

Over the years, UDC has adopted modern classification theory

[3]Malcolm Rigby. *Computers and the UDC: A Decade of Progress, 1960-1970.* Rockville, Md.: National Oceanic and Atmospheric Administration, Scientific Information and Documentation Division, 1970.

[4]Hans Wellisch. "UDC: Present and Potential." *Drexel Library Quarterly,* **10**:75–89, October 1974.

more readily than DDC and has become a more faceted scheme. It provides a greater degree of synthesis or combination of subjects and concepts by means of auxiliary devices. The common auxiliaries—such as form, period, and place—apply to all classes. Special auxiliaries apply to certain parts of the schedules. Subjects can be combined as required by means of connecting symbols to be discussed later.

Notation

A major reason for adapting DDC as the basis of UDC was the pure notation of arabic numerals, which provides both simplicity and infinite possibilities for expansion. The decimal system was also followed. However, UDC does not use the three-digit base number. In other words, UDC does not use the zero as a filler. For example, Religion is represented by 2 instead of 200, as in DDC. Divisions and subdivisions of main classes are represented by additional digits, e.g., 63 Agriculture, 633 Field crops. All numbers are read decimally. A decimal point is inserted after the third digit, e.g., 633.1 Cereal, corn, grain.

UDC is more capable than DDC of representing subject relationships. This is achieved through the use of facet indicators, or symbols, which identify the component parts of a class number. These are numerical, or nonverbal and nonnumerical signs; they are listed in Table 14-3. These common auxiliaries are applicable throughout the scheme. Through their use, UDC provides a much greater degree of notational synthesis than DDC. For example, the connecting symbols allow the combination of subjects not anticipated by the classificationist. The notation of UDC is both hierarchical and expressive.

TABLE 14-3   Facet Indicators in UDC

Symbol	Meaning
+	Combining two separate numbers
/	Combining two or more consecutive numbers
:	Relationships between two subjects
::	Similar to the colon sign
=	Language
(0 . . .)	Form
(1/9)	Place
(=0/9)	Race and nationality
" . . . "	Time
A/Z	Alphabetical subarrangement
.00 . . .	Point of view
=05 . . .	Persons

Following are examples of UDC numbers:

975.5 + 976.9	History of Virginia and Kentucky
975.5	History of Virginia
976.9	History of Kentucky
026:61 (058.7)	Directory of medical libraries
026	Libraries
61	Medicine
058.7	Directory
61 (038) =20=50	Italian-English dictionary of medicine
61	Medicine
038	Dictionary
20	English
50	Italian
850"19"	Twentieth-century Italian literature
850	Italian literature
19	Twentieth century

SUBJECT CLASSIFICATION
BY JAMES DUFF BROWN (1862–1914)

Brief History

The first edition of *Subject Classification* (SC) was published in 1906, followed by a second edition in 1917. The third and the latest edition (edited by J. D. Stewart) was published in 1939.

Prior to Subject Classification, Brown was responsible for two other schemes. The Quinn-Brown Classification (in collaboration with John Henry Quinn) was developed in 1894. It was modified by Brown and published in 1898 as *Adjustable Classification*.[5]

Toward the end of the nineteenth century, DDC was gradually gaining ground in Britain also. Brown, dissatisfied with the system because of its obvious American bias and other weaknesses, set out to devise a British system. However, Subject Classification failed to win over British libraries. Only a small number of libraries adopted it. The failure to keep the system up to date has contributed to its becoming obsolete.

Basic Principles

The arrangement of the main classes in SC follows an order of "scientific progression." Brown's theory is that in the order of things, matter and force came first, which gave rise to life, and life was

---

[5]James Duff Brown. *Adjustable Classification for Libraries, with Index*. London: Library Supply Company, 1898.

TABLE 14-4   Outline of Subject Classification

A	Generalia
	Matter and Force
B–D	Physical Science
	Life
E–F	Biological Science
G–H	Ethnology. Medicine
I	Economic biology. Domestic Arts
	Mind
J–K	Philosophy and Religion
L	Social and Political science
	Record
M	Language and Literature
N	Literary Forms. Fiction. Poetry
O–W	History and Geography
X	Biography

followed by mind. Finally, mind was followed by the making of its record. (See Table 14-4.)

Brown's famous "one-place theory" assumes that materials on a concrete subject are more useful grouped together in one place rather than scattered according to the author's standpoint or discipline. This is the major difference between this system and the other classification schemes such as DDC and LCC. The subject Iron may be treated from the standpoint of Metallurgy, Mineralogy, Inorganic Chemistry, Geology, Economics, Industry, etc. In SC, all materials on the subject Iron are grouped together. The location of each concrete subject is determined by the principle of placing each subject as near as possible to the science on which it is based. Hence, Iron is classed in Mineralogy, Apple is placed under Botany, and Music under Physics, as a subdivision of Acoustics. In such an arrangement, applications follow their theoretical base. Therefore, Chemical technology is placed after Chemistry, and Mining under Geology.

Notation

Brown adopts a simple mixed notation of one capital letter followed by arabic numerals. Main classes are represented by single capital letters as shown in Table 14-4. Subdivisions are denoted by arabic numerals, e.g.,

I	Economic Biology. Domestic Arts
I0	Agriculture. Dairy farming
I1	Veterinary medicine
I2	Milling. Gardening. Forestry
I3	Woodworking

Limited notational synthesis is provided by combining the main number with a number from the Categorical Table (for the subdivision of subjects) representing form or other divisions, e.g.,

.0	Generalia
.00	Catalogues. Lists
.01	Monarchs. Rulers
.02	Subdivisions for rearrangement
.1	Bibliography
.2	Encyclopaedias. Dictionaries
.10	History (for general use in all classes)

For example,

I229.10	History of gardening in England.

COLON CLASSIFICATION
BY SHIYALI RAMAMRITA RANGANATHAN
(1892–1972)

Brief History

Colon Classification (CC) was developed by S. R. Ranganathan, a prominent librarian from India and considered by many to be the foremost theorist in the field of classification. His writings on classification, the best known of which is *Prolegomena to Library Classification* (3d ed., 1967), form the basis of modern classification theory. Colon Classification is a manifestation of Ranganathan's theory. Although the Colon Classification has not been widely used even in India, Ranganathan's theory has influenced, in one way or another, all currently used classification and indexing systems.

The first edition of *Colon Classification* was published in 1933. The sixth edition[6] appeared in 1963, and the seventh has been in preparation for a number of years. Over the years, as Ranganathan refined and redefined his thinking about classification, each edition reflected the progress of his theory. Drastic changes took place between editions, and stability was sacrificed for the sake of keeping up with knowledge as well as classification theory.

Basic Principles

Knowledge is divided into more or less traditional main classes (see Table 14-5). However, the similarity between Colon Classification and other classification systems ends here.

Colon Classification is a faceted scheme. Each class is broken down

[6]S. R. Ranganathan. *Colon Classification*. 6th ed. Reprinted with amendments. Bombay: Asia Publishing House, 1963.

TABLE 14-5   Outline of Colon Classification, Main Classes

	Main Classes		
Z	Generalia	Δ	Spiritual experience and Mysticism
1	Universe of knowledge		
2	Library science	μ	Humanities and Social sciences
3	Book science		
4	Journalism	ν	Humanities
A	Natural sciences	N	Fine Arts
β	Mathematical sciences	NZ	Literature and Language
B	Mathematics	O	Literature
τ	Physical sciences	P	Linguistics
C	Physics	Q	Religion
D	Engineering	R	Philosophy
E	Chemistry	S	Psychology
F	Technology	Σ	Social sciences
G	Biology	T	Education
H	Geology	U	Geography
HZ	Mining	V	History
I	Botany	W	Political science
J	Agriculture	X	Economics
K	Zoology	Y	Sociology
KZ	Animal husbandry	YZ	Social work
L	Medicine	Z	Law
M	Useful Arts		

into its basic concepts or elements, according to certain characteristics, called *facets*. In isolating these component elements, Ranganathan has identified five fundamental categories: Personality, Matter, Energy, Space, and Time, often referred to as PMEST.

When classifying a document, the classifier identifies the component parts which reflect every aspect and element of the subject content and puts them together according to a structural procedure, called a *facet formula*, which has been individually designed for each main class. Thus, unlike enumerative classification schemes, Colon Classification does not list complete ready-made numbers in its schedules. A combination, or *synthesis*, of notation is tailored for each work being classified.

In addition to subject subdivisions in each main class, there are certain common subdivisions which can be applied throughout the entire scheme, e.g., form, space, time, and language subdivisions.

The basic ideas of facet analysis and synthesis had been present in the earlier classification schemes, notably in the form divisions of Dewey Decimal Classification, the common subdivisions and the local list in Cutter's Expansive Classification, and the categorical table in Brown's Subject Classification. But it was left to Ranganathan to systematize and formalize the theory. His Colon Classification fully manifests the theory of facet analysis and synthesis. His theory has also influenced other modern classification systems. Universal Decimal Classification shows a strong impact of Ranganathan's theory. Revision of Dewey Decimal Classification, particularly in recent editions, reflects the influence of facet analysis and synthesis, noticeably in the five new auxiliary tables established in edition 18. Even Library of Congress Classification, the most enumerative among modern systems, shows an increasing use of synthesis. For example, in the newly developed schedules for the K class, much more synthesis is required than in the schedules for the other classes developed earlier.

Notation

Notation for Colon Classification is extremely mixed and complex. It combines arabic numerals, capital and lowercase letters, some Greek letters, brackets, and certain punctuation marks.

The Generalia classes are represented by arabic numerals. Main classes are shown by capital letters of the Roman alphabet and certain Greek letters.

Basic concepts and elements under each main class are represented mainly by arabic numerals, e.g.,

L	Medicine
2	Digestive system
27	Large intestine
27219	Vermiform appendix

Common subdivisions, called common isolates, are shown in lowercase letters, capital letters, or arabic numerals, e.g.,

a	Bibliography
c	Concordance
d	Table
4	Asia
5	Europe
53	France
L	1700–1799 A.D.
N	1900–1999 A.D.

In formulating a class number, certain punctuation marks are used as facet indicators to show the nature of the element being presented. The following meanings have been assigned to the punctuation marks:

(,) connecting symbol for Personality
(;) connecting symbol for Matter

(:) connecting symbol for Energy
(.) connecting symbol for Space
(') connecting symbol for Time

Following are examples of class numbers from Colon Classification:

M7:8.56163'N66	Textile Printing in Lancashire in 1966.
M	Useful arts
M7	Textiles
:8	Textile printing
.56163	Lancashire
'N66	1966
TN3.44'N5	Basic schools in India to 1950
T	Education
TN3	Basic schools
.44	India
'N5	1950
V2,6:2'N5	Constitution of local bodies in India to 1950
V	History
2	India
,6	Local body
:2	Constitution
'N5	1950

BIBLIOGRAPHIC CLASSIFICATION
BY HENRY EVELYN BLISS (1870–1955)

Brief History

Henry Evelyn Bliss, for nearly half a century a librarian in the College of the City of New York, devoted over thirty years of his life to the study of classification and the development of Bibliographic Classification (BC). The publication of the scheme took thirteen years, from 1940 to 1953.

In the course of developing Bibliographic Classification, Bliss also produced numerous articles and books on classification. Among his best known works are *Organization of Knowledge and the System of the Sciences* (1929) and *Organization of Knowledge in Libraries and the Subject Approach to Books* (1933; 2d ed., 1939). The latter embodies the theory on which his classification scheme was based and includes an outline of the scheme. Before the full schedules were published, an expansion of the outline appeared in a one-volume work entitled *A System of Bibliographic Classification* (1935).

Bibliographic Classification was not widely adopted in the United States. However, it received much attention in Britain. In 1967 an abridged *Bliss Classification* was published there by the School Library Association. A Bliss Classification Association was formed in Britain, which has assumed responsibility for maintaining and updating the scheme. A second edition, under the editorship of J. Mills and V. Broughton, began publication in 1977.

In the new edition,[7] the editors have taken into consideration advances in modern classification theory developed since Bliss, particularly the principles of facet analysis, explicit citation orders, and explicit filing order, based on Ranganathan's work. While the main outline of the first edition was largely retained, many of the internal details have undergone radical revision. Each class has been given a fully faceted structure. Another aspect given thorough revision is the vocabulary, which has been revised and greatly enlarged and organized into explicitly named facets and arrays.

Basic Principles

Consensus

Bliss asserts that "knowledge should be *organized in consistency* with *the scientific and educational consensus,* which is *relatively stable* and tends to become more so as theory and system become more definitely and permanently established in general and increasingly in detail."[8] He believes that such an order would be the most helpful to library users. This scientific and educational consensus was followed by Bliss in arranging the main and subordinate classes (see Table 14-6).

The original Bliss Classification was essentially an "aspect" classification, or classification by discipline, in which information on individual "phenomena" is scattered over many disciplines and sub-disciplines, e.g., Iron is subordinated variously to Chemistry, Chemical technology, Mineralogy, Mining, Industrial economics, etc. The new edition provides at the beginning of the scheme classes for comprehensive works (called Generalia attributes, Generalia processes, and Generalia entities), but with the option of placing these works with the most suitable "aspect" or discipline.

Many new subjects have been added to the new edition, such as media science, recording and reproduction techniques, data processing, etc.

---

[7]J. Mills. "The New Bliss Classification." *Catalogue and Index,* **40**: 1, 3–6 Spring 1976.
[8]Henry Evelyn Bliss. *The Organization of Knowledge in Libraries.* 2d ed. New York: The H. W. Wilson Company, 1939. Pp. 42–43.

TABLE 14-6   Outline of Bibliographic Classification

2	Generalia: physical forms of documents
3	Generalia: forms of arrangement and presentation
	Phenomena
4	Attributes (e.g., structure, order, symmetry, color)
5	Activities and processes (e.g., organizing, planning, change, adaptation)
6	Entities (e.g., particles, atoms, molecules, minerals, organisms, communities, institutions, artefacts)
7	Universe of knowledge
	Communication and information
8	Data processing, Computer science
	Records, Documentation
9	Individual and mass communication
	Disciplines
A	Philosophy
AL	Logic
AM	Mathematics
AW	Statistics and probability
AX	Systemology, Organization theory, Management
AY	Science and technology
AZ	Science
B	Physics
BR	Technologies based primarily on physics (*Alternative* is UG)
C	Chemistry
CT	Materials science and technology (*Alternative* is UEV)
D	Astronomy
DG	Space science
DH	Earth sciences
E	Biology
EV	Microbiology
F	Botany
G	Zoology
H	Man, Anthropology
HA	Human biology
HH	Health sciences, Medicine
I	Psychology
J	Education
K	Social sciences
KA	Sociology
KY	Travel and description
L	History
L9	Biography
M	Europe
N	America

(*Continued on page 318.*)

TABLE 14-6   (Continued)

OA	Australia
OH	Asia
OS	Africa
P	Religion (*Alternative* is Z)
PX	The Occult
PY	Morals, Ethics
Q	Social welfare and administration
R	Political science
RO	Public administration
S	Law
T	Economics
TX	Management of enterprises
U	Technology, Useful Arts
UA	Agriculture and animal exploitation
UD	Mining technology
UE	Engineering and production technology
UO	Transport technology
US	Military science and technology
UY	Recreative arts
V	Arts, Fine Arts
VV	Music
VY	Performing Arts
W	Philology : language and literature
WA	Linguistics
WI	Individual languages and their literatures
YU	Literature : general and comparative
Z	Religion, Occult, Morals (*Alternative* is P)

Collocation of related subjects

Related subjects are brought together into close proximity. For example, certain pure sciences are collocated with the appropriate technology. This idea is similar to Brown's. However, Bliss did not carry it to the extreme as Brown did in Subject Classification. Bliss brings together only those pure sciences and technology which are most likely to be used together by the readers.

Subordination of special to general and gradation in specialty

In developing subclasses and subdivisions, Bliss ensures that relevant special subjects are subordinated to the comprehensive general subjects. In the ordering of coordinate topics in an array, Bliss employs the principle of gradation in specialty. The premise of this principle is that certain derivative subjects draw upon the findings of other subjects. In a classification scheme, the subject that borrows from another is considered to be more specialized than the latter and should follow it. For example, mathematics is a science that many other sciences draw upon and is therefore placed at the very beginning of the classification.

Alternative location

Bliss recognizes that frequently a subject may be placed with equal usefulness in two or more possible locations in the scheme. In order to render the system useful to the largest number of users, alternative locations are provided in the scheme for these subjects. For example, Economic history can be subordinated to General history or classed in Economics. There are a large number of alternative provisions in Bliss Classification. This feature is enhanced even further in the new edition. Alternative locations might be the placement of Religion between History and the Occult or at the end of the scheme, and the option to concentrate all Technology together in class U, as an alternative to subordinating the more science-oriented ones with the appropriate science (e.g., Chemical technology with Chemistry).

Alternative treatment

Bliss also realizes that in some cases, a body of material may be organized in different, but equally useful, ways. In such cases, he provides alternative treatment in the schedules. A notable example is the four modes of classifying literature:

1. Separating literary history from texts
2. Literary history and texts together
3. Combination of (1) for modern literature and (2) for earlier literature
4. Same as (3) except that modern texts are classed by form rather than by author

Notation

A simple notation is used. The Generalia classes are represented by arabic numerals. Subject classes are represented by single capital letters, and subclasses and subdivisions by a combination of capital letters, e.g.,

U	Technology, useful arts
UE	Engineering
UHC	Construction techniques
UHV	Architecture, planning and building
UJ	Architectural practice and design

Bliss constantly emphasized the desirability of brief notation. The wide base provided by the use of the letters in the alphabet and the nonexpressiveness of the notation contribute to its brevity. Letters provide twenty-six bases for combination as opposed to the ten bases of the arabic numeral system. The nonexpressiveness of the notation means that the notation for a narrow subject does not necessarily have to be longer than the one used for a broader subject. The new edition retains these notational features.

In the earlier edition, lowercase letters and arbitrary symbols were also used. These have been abandoned in the new edition. The notation now consists entirely of capital letters and numerals.

Auxiliary Schedules

There are six auxiliary schedules containing concepts which occur in some way or another in all or most subjects. They may be applied to any class in the system. The notation is similar to that used in the main schedules: arabic numerals, capital letters, or a combination thereof.

Table 14-7 contains excerpts from the auxiliary schedules.

The faceted structure of both the main schedules and the auxiliary schedules allows a great degree of synthesis. Following are examples of Bliss class numbers.

C	Chemistry
C5V	Bibliography
C6C	Chemical Research
C4C P	Chemist and society
P	Religion
POZ	Religion in individual countries
POZ RB	Religion in China
POZ Y	Religion in the U.S.
POZ YG	Religion in the south

TOPICS FOR DISCUSSION

1. In the second edition of DDC in which Dewey declared the policy of the "integrity of numbers," he assigned topics to all 100 divisions and to all but twenty-one of the 1,000 numbers in the 000–999 sequence. Nineteen of the twenty-one vacant numbers occurred in the 000 class, General works. Like his contemporaries, Dewey assumed that technology had reached its summit and there was nothing left to be invented. In establishing the scheme, he saw fit to use up the available numbers even in places where he did not need

TABLE 14-7 Excerpts from Auxiliary Schedules in Bibliographic Classification

Schedule			Divisions
1	Common subdivisions	2EN	Nonbook materials
		2WH U	Government publications
		5V	Bibliographies
		6C	Research in the subject
		7	History (see Schedule 4)
		8	Places, localities in the subject (see Schedule 2)
		9	Biography
1A	Persons	A	Persons in the subject
		CP	Relations to community, society
		JD	Minority groups
		NS	Families
		RC	Refugees
2	Place	AS	Regions by climate
		BAJ	Regions by land and resource use
		BC	Urban
		D	Europe
		O	Asia
		RB	China
		X	America
		Y	U.S.A.
3	Language	G	American aboriginal languages
		PB	Indo-European languages
		WB	Germanic
		X	German, Dutch, English
3A	Ethnic Groups	BS	Europiforms
		G	American aborigines
		KY	Northeast Asian groups
		L	Japanese
4	Periods of Time	DF	4000 B.C.
		EV	000 A.D.
		FX	1300
		GZ	1500
		Q	1900
		S	2000

to; for instance, he assigned 570, 580, and 590 to Biology, Botany, and Zoology respectively, making them coordinate topics, when the latter two should have been subsumed under 570 according to the hierarchical principle; 580 and 590 could have been left vacant and saved for future use. Find other similar examples of distorted hierarchy in the system and discuss the reasons and consequences of this irregular practice, particularly in terms of difficulties in maintaining logical collocation and inserting new subjects in later editions.

2. In the 800 (Literature) class of DDC, literary works by individual authors are scattered according to their literary form, e.g., T. S. Eliot's drama in 822.912, his poetry in 821.912, and his essays in 824.912. Discuss the advantages and disadvantages of such an arrangement. Also, consider the problems in classifying Eliot's collected works and criticism of his works in general.

3. In a hierarchical notational system, such as DDC, specificity entails long numbers. Yet in practice, particularly as a shelving device, long numbers create problems. Discuss some of these problems and possible solutions. Compare this aspect of DDC with the nonhierarchical notation of LCC.

4. During the 1960s, many libraries, particularly academic libraries, reclassified from DDC to LCC. Identify some of the reasons for the switch. One frequently-cited rationale is that LCC is more specific than DDC. Another claims that LCC is more stable than DDC. Evaluate some of these justifications.

5. Discuss the purpose and functions of unique call numbers.

6. Compare the Dewey Decimal Classification and the Library of Congress Classification in terms of the following topics: form subdivisions; geographic subdivisions; notation; Cutter numbers; treatment of a specific subject, e.g., library science, chemistry, literature, etc.

7. Using LCC as an example of an enumerative classification scheme and DDC as an example of a partially faceted scheme, compare the two kinds of classification systems in terms of application in libraries.

PART FIVE

Production and Organization of Cataloging Records

BASIC TOOLS

ALA Rules for Filing Catalog Cards. American Library Association, ALA Editorial Committee, Subcommittee on the ALA Rules for Filing Catalog Cards. 2d ed. Chicago: American Library Association, 1968.

ALA Rules for Filing Catalog Cards. American Library Association, ALA Editorial Committee, Subcommittee on the ALA Rules for Filing Catalog Cards. 2d abridged ed. Chicago: American Library Association, 1968.

Library of Congress. *Filing Rules for the Dictionary Catalogs of the Library of Congress.* Washington, D.C.: Processing Department, 1956.

Library of Congress. *The Library of Congress Author Catalog: A Cumulative List of Works Represented by Library of Congress Cards, 1948–1952.* Washington, D.C.: Library of Congress, 1953. 24 v.

Library of Congress. *The Library of Congress Catalog: A Cumulative Catalog of Books Represented by Library of Congress Printed Cards.* Washington, D.C.: Library of Congress, 1942. 167 v. Supplement, 1947. 42 v.

Library of Congress. *Library of Congress Name Headings with References.* Washington, D.C.: Library of Congress. Jan./Mar. 1974–

Library of Congress, MARC Development Office. *Books: A MARC Format.* 5th ed. Washington, D.C.: Library of Congress, 1972. (Also MARC formats for other types of materials.)

Library of Congress. *Monographic Series.* Washington, D.C.: Library of Congress. Jan./Mar. 1974–

The National Union Catalog: A Cumulative Author List Representing Library of Congress Printed Cards and Titles Reported by Other American Libraries. Washington, D.C.: Library of Congress, 1956–

Rather, John C. *Filing Arrangement in the Library of Congress Catalogs: An Operational Document.* Provisional version. Washington, D.C.: Library of Congress, 1971.

FURTHER READING

Avram, Henriette D. *MARC: Its History and Implications.* Washington, D.C.: Library of Congress, 1975.

Hoffman, Herbert H. *What Happens in Library Filing?* Hamden, Conn.: Linnet Books, 1976.

Library of Congress, MARC Development Office. *Information on the MARC System.* 4th ed. Washington, D.C.: Library of Congress, 1974.

Malinconico, S. Michael, and Fasana, Paul J. *The Future of the Catalog: The Library's Choices.* White Plains, N. Y.: Knowledge Industry Publications, 1979.

CHAPTER 15

Processing of Cataloging Records

PREPARATION OF CATALOGING RECORDS

Cataloging records are prepared for library materials as a means of bibliographic control. Each record is prepared by the methods outlined in previous chapters.

Definitions

The term *original cataloging* refers to the operation of preparing a cataloging record without the assistance of outside cataloging agencies. *Centralized cataloging* refers to the preparation of cataloging records by one agency, which are made available to libraries and information centers. *Cooperative cataloging* means cataloging records are contributed by two or more libraries or agencies and made available to each other. A cataloging record prepared by one agency to be used by others is called a *cataloging copy*.

Centralized and Cooperative Cataloging

The value of centralized cataloging has long been recognized by librarians. It would be most uneconomical for each library to perform original cataloging on all of its holdings. This would result in a great deal of duplication of efforts among libraries.

In 1901 the Library of Congress began distributing printed cards. This event marked a significant advance in centralized cataloging. Other types of centralized cataloging services became available later. Printed catalog cards designed for small libraries using a simplified form of descriptive cataloging, Sears subject headings, and abridged Dewey numbers were issued by the H. W. Wilson Company until 1975, when the service was discontinued. There are also many commercial and government-supported processing centers which provide precataloged books to libraries. Some of them create their own cataloging records; others adapt the Library of Congress's cataloging copies and make them available to libraries.

Processing centers offer a variety of services often tailored to the individual library's needs. Most provide catalog cards with books, and some process the materials (complete with markings, book pockets, and cards) which are ready to be shelved upon receipt. Other centers cater to specific types of libraries.

The Library of Congress has served as the de facto centralized cataloging agency for American libraries since 1901, when it began distributing printed cards to libraries. The card distribution service was later expanded to cover various other forms of disseminating cataloging data. These include proofsheets, printed catalogs, MARC tapes, and Cataloging in Publication (CIP) data.

Library of Congress printed cards may be ordered in sets for use in an individual library's catalog, or a library may enter a standing order to receive a copy of every LC cataloging record in the form of a main entry card for all titles cataloged by LC or for all titles within certain subject or form categories. Cross-reference cards are included. This service is called *proofsheet* or *proofslip*. Most libraries use only a small portion of the proofsheets received. It means that many of the records received by a particular library will not be used. The advantage of the service is to have the cataloging copy ready when or before an item is acquired by the library. As the titles cataloged by the Library of Congress proliferate, it becomes a great burden for a library simply to have the daily shipment of proofsheets filed properly. Many libraries have therefore abandoned the service in favor of commercial services which store the LC cataloging copies on microfiche which can be retrieved easily without the burden of filing.

In 1942, LC began publishing *The Library of Congress Catalog: A Cumulative Catalog of Books Represented by Library of Congress Printed Cards*, which makes available, en masse, the cataloging records of the vast holdings of the Library. The first set of catalogs includes entries for cards issued from August 1898 through July 1942. This was followed by a supplement covering the years 1942–1947 and *The Library of Congress Author Catalog, 1948-1952*. In 1953, the scope was enlarged to include cataloging entries of contributing North American libraries in addition to the LC entries. The title was changed to *National Union Catalog*. It is published by the Library of Congress regularly in nine monthly issues and cumulated quarterly, annually, and quinquennially. A subject catalog is published quarterly, also cumulated annually and quinquennially. In addition to the author catalog, there are also separate catalogs for other formats and media, such as motion pictures, filmstrips, and other materials for projection, manuscripts, microform masters, music, and newspapers. Two other recent Library of Congress publications also serve as valuable tools for catalogers:

Monographic Series and *Library of Congress Name Headings with References*, both issued serially. Catalogers use the LC catalogs to verify authors and titles and as sources for cataloging copies. When an LC entry is found for a work being cataloged, printed cards from the Library of Congress can be ordered, or cards can be reproduced from the printed catalog by means of photographic devices such as the Dennison copier and the Polaroid Land camera.

In March 1969, the Library of Congress began distributing cataloging data in machine-readable form for all monographs in English. Magnetic tapes containing LC cataloging records are distributed to subscribers weekly. By this means the entries are made available to users much more promptly than the printed cards or the printed catalogs. Libraries that have the necessary computer facilities can produce card sets or microform catalogs from the tapes. The coverage of LC MARC is being continuously enlarged.

The Cataloging in Publication (CIP) program was established on July 1, 1971, by the Library of Congress. The objective of the program is to provide cataloging information for a publication in the publication itself. It represents a cooperative effort between the Library of Congress and American publishers. There are now over 1,800 American publishers who participate in the CIP program. Currently, 75 to 85 percent of United States trade books are covered by CIP. Certain selected federal government documents are also included.

The publishers submit galleys of their books and a CIP data sheet to the CIP Office at the Library of Congress, where the material is processed through the regular cataloging channels. The cataloging data that require professional decisions—main entry, title proper, series statement, descriptive notes, subject headings, added entries, Library of Congress and Dewey Decimal Classification numbers—are prepared by catalogers at the Library of Congress and returned to the publisher for printing in the book. For children's materials, a summary and alternative subject headings are also provided. For medical books, National Library of Medicine subject headings and class numbers are also included.

The CIP data are displayed on the verso of the title page. Librarians working with the book in hand can then prepare a complete cataloging record by filling in the other title information, edition, imprint, and physical description. Other librarians may make use of the data for preliminary processing of the book while waiting for the arrival of the LC cards which have been ordered.

Another source of LC cataloging information is *Publishers' Weekly*. Its weekly publishing record contains LC cataloging data which are valuable because of their timeliness.

COMPUTER-PROCESSED CATALOGING RECORDS

Depending on the type of catalog—card catalog, book catalog, microform catalog, computerized catalog (see the discussion in Chapter 1)—used in the library, the cataloging records are displayed in the appropriate formats. Although the catalogs may be produced by traditional methods such as typing and printing, sometimes with modern equipment, this section will discuss a more recently developed method: the use of computers for processing cataloging records and producing catalogs.

Introduction

In recent years the term *on-line cataloging* has become a familiar one in technical services fields. The term refers to processing of cataloging records in an on-line mode (i.e., with instant feedback). The intellectual part of the cataloging process is still performed by human catalogers and is completed before the computer plays its part.

For nearly a century, the predominant form of displaying cataloging records has been the 3 by 5 catalog card. Except for the reproduction of multiple copies of the unit card, the cataloging process had been performed manually. With the advent of the computer and its application to library processes in the 1960s, a new technique for processing cataloging records was introduced, by which elements in the cataloging record are coded in machine-readable form and stored in a computerized data base. The resulting cataloging data in a central data base can be accessed through computer terminals and telecommunication by individual libraries. In the early 1970s, technology was developed to such an extent as to enable instant communication and feedback in the computerized cataloging access. This is called *on-line cataloging*.

To arrive at this stage, the first step was to develop a format by which the cataloging data are made machine-readable—in other words, a format[1] which enables the computer to recognize the elements and manipulate them for various purposes. Machine-readable cataloging data have been used for many purposes, among which are the production of catalog cards, book catalogs, microform catalogs, bibliographies, spine labels, book pockets, etc.

---

[1] A format is a method of organizing data so that the record and parts of the record can be identified. (Cf. Library of Congress, MARC Development Office. *Information on the MARC System.* 4th ed. Washington, D.C.: Library of Congress, 1974. P. 2.)

Library of Congress MARC System[2]

History

In the late 1950s, the Library of Congress began investigation of the possibility of using automated techniques for its internal operations. In the early 1960s, a study was made with financial support from the Council on Library Resources to determine the feasibility of applying automated techniques to the operations of LC. Another study was made of the possible methods of converting the data on LC cards to machine-readable form for the purpose of printing bibliographical products by computer. These studies generated a great deal of interest and enthusiasm. As a result, the Library of Congress, with a grant from the Council on Library Resources, initiated a pilot project in January 1966, to test the feasibility and utility of the distribution of cataloging data in machine-readable form from the Library of Congress to user libraries. The pilot project was named MARC (from *machine-readable cataloging*). The first few months of 1966 were devoted to the development of procedures and computer programs for the conversion, file maintenance, and distribution of MARC data, as well as programs to use the data at the participating libraries. For the pilot project, sixteen participating libraries of different types and geographic locations were chosen. Distribution of MARC tapes began in October 1966.

Between November 1966 and June 1968, approximately 50,000 cataloging records for English-language book materials were converted into the machine-readable form and distributed on magnetic tape to the participating libraries. The results of the MARC pilot project were sufficiently encouraging for the Library of Congress to proceed on a full-scale basis. The MARC Distribution Service was established in March 1969, to disseminate MARC records to subscribing libraries and institutions. Initially, the tapes included records for English-language monographic material currently cataloged by the Library of Congress.[3] Over the years, the coverage has been broadened to include other types of material and other languages. The original MARC format was refined and became the current MARC II format for books. LC MARC formats for other types of material have also been developed over the years under the direction of Henriette D. Avram. Some formats are still being designed.

---

[2]Henriette D. Avram. *MARC: Its History and Implications*. Washington, D.C.: Library of Congress, 1975. 49 pp.

[3]Library of Congress, MARC Development Office. *Information on the MARC System.* 4th ed. Washington, D.C.: Library of Congress, 1974. P. 1.

Collections of machine-readable records are also called data bases. The largest machine-readable cataloging (MARC) data bases in this country are the OCLC data base, the RLIN/BALLOTS data base, the WLN (Washington Library Network) data base, and the Library of Congress MARC data base, which is discussed below.

LC MARC data base

The LC MARC data base contains records created by the Library of Congress staff and those created by cooperating libraries and verified by the Library of Congress. Most of the records are for post-1966 publications. As a result of the previous RECON Project (retrospective conversion) and the COMARC Project (cooperative machine-readable cataloging) many earlier publications have also been converted into machine-readable form.

The LC MARC records are available to other libraries in the form of magnetic tapes. These records can be used to produce various products, such as catalog cards, book catalogs, bibliographies, spine labels, book pockets, etc. By far the major use of these records has been the production of catalog cards. With the planned closing of the card catalog by many libraries in the United States, it is expected that the display of the MARC records will take on more forms, such as records in an automated catalog or in a COM (computer-output microform) catalog.

LC MARC format[4]

Elements
A machine format for bibliographic records is an essential component of a machine-readable cataloging system. A machine format refers to the method of organizing data in order that the record and parts of the record can be identified and manipulated by the computer.

The data in a machine-readable cataloging record consist of a continuous string of characters. Different parts of the record, i.e., main entry, title, imprint, etc., are identified explicitly for computer manipulation.

A machine format generally consists of the following:

1. Data element—lowest unit of information, e.g., International Standard Book Number, etc.
2. Field—collection of data elements, e.g., a main entry consisting

[4]Library of Congress. MARC Development Office. *Information on the MARC System.* 4th ed. Washington, D.C.: Library of Congress, 1974. 48 pp.; and *Books: A MARC Format.* 5th ed. Washington, D.C.: Library of Congress, 1972. 106 pp.

of the data elements for the person's name and possibly a title of nobility or the dates of his birth and death; a field sometimes consists of only one data element, e.g., National Bibliography Number

a. Variable field—a field containing data elements, the lengths of which cannot be predetermined, e.g., a title statement that could vary in length

b. Fixed field—a field with data elements that are always expressed by the same number of characters, e.g., the coded form of a language is always three characters long

3. Record—collection of fields treated as a unit

Three elements form the basis for the MARC II format, currently used by LC and most of the libraries in this country: (1) Structure, (2) content designators, and (3) content.

1. The structure—the basic machine framework of the record, analogous to an empty container.
2. The content designators—the means by which elements in the record can be identified. These include the tag, indicators, and subfield codes (see explanation below).
3. The content—the data recorded in the fields.

Figure 15-1 shows a cataloging record in the LC MARC format.

Format structure

The MARC II format structure consists of: (1) leader, (2) record directory, and (3) variable fields (Figure 15-2).

1. Leader   Each MARC record begins with a leader consisting of the first twenty-four characters. It provides particular information about the ensuing record, such as the total length of the record, the type of record, and the bibliographic level. Some of the important information carried in the leader is as follows.

Length   The first item in the leader indicates the total length of the record expressed by an arabic numeral.

Record status   The second item (6th character) indicates record status. The symbols used are:

> n - New record
> c - Corrected or revised record
> d - Deleted record
> p - Previously CIP record

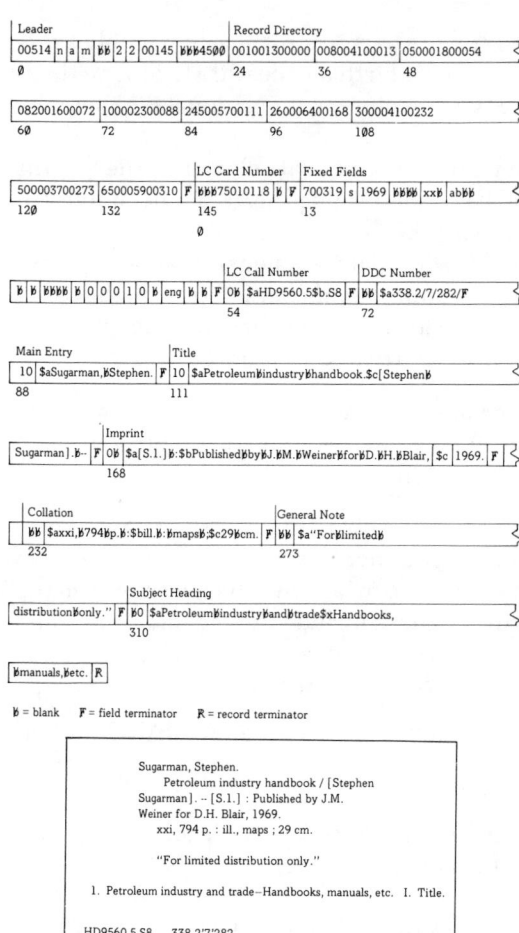

FIGURE 15-1 Sample cataloging record in the LC MARC format.

Leader	Record directory	Variable fields

FIGURE 15-2 MARC II communications format structure.

Type of record The type of record is indicated by a code which specifies the form of material described in the record. The following codes are used:

    a - Language materials, printed, e.g., books
    b - Language materials, manuscript
    c - Music, printed, e.g., sheet music

d - Music, manuscript
e - Maps and atlases, printed
f - Maps, manuscript
g - Film material, e.g., motion pictures,
        filmstrips, etc.
h - Microform publications
i - Sound recordings, nonmusical
j - Sound recordings, musical
k - Pictures, designs, other two-dimensional
        representations
l - Computer media, e.g., machine-readable data
x - Name authority file
y - Subject authority file

The type-of-record codes generally follow the categories provided in the Anglo-American Cataloguing Rules.

Bibliographic level   The bibliographic level is indicated by a code which denotes the relationship of the work described in the record to another bibliographic entity. The following codes are used:

m - Monograph (a work complete at the time issued or to
        be issued in a known number of parts)
s - Serial (a work issued in successive parts bearing
        numerical or chronological designations and intended
        to be continued indefinitely)
a - Analytic (a work that is part of a larger bibliographic
        entity and not issued separately, such as a chapter of a
        book, a journal article, or a single volume in a multi-
        volume set)
c - Collections (made-up collections of manuscripts,
        pamphlets, etc., that are gathered together and cat-
        aloged as a single unit)

2. Record Directory   Similar to the table of contents in a book which lists the chapters with the corresponding pages on which the chapters begin, the record directory lists entries which show what variable fields are in the record with their respective locations in the record.

The record directory consists of a series of fixed-length (twelve characters each) entries, one for each of the variable fields that contain cataloging information presented later in the record. The elements in each record directory entry are: the identification tag, the length, and the starting character position of each variable field.

Figure 15-3 shows the outline of record directory entries. The

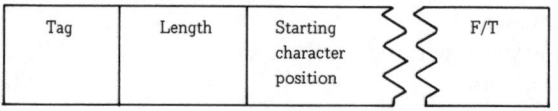

Tag	Length	Starting character position	F/T

F/T—Field Terminator

FIGURE 15-3 Outline of record directory entries.

record directory entries are arranged in sequential order. Consequently, it is not necessary to have the variable fields in sequential order as well. Updating of the record is facilitated because new fields can be added at the end of the record regardless of what the tags are.

3. Variable Fields The variable fields, which constitute the last part of the format structure, contain the essence of the record, i.e., cataloging information. Figure 15-4 shows the outline of a variable field and the corresponding record directory entry.

The parts of the record directory entry are described below.

Tag. The tag is three digits identifying a variable field. Tags in the LC MARC format are assigned by function according to cataloging usage, e.g., main entries beginning with a "1," series statements with a "4," subject headings with a "6," etc.

Table 15-1 gives examples of tags for the most frequently occurring fields in a cataloging record.

10	$a	Handel, Georg Friedrich,	$d	1685–1759	F/T

Indicator · Subfield code · Data · Subfield code · Data · Field Terminator

(a)

100	0042	00167

Tag · Length · Starting Character Position

(b)

FIGURE 15-4 (a) Outline of a variable field; (b) corresponding record directory entry.

TABLE 15-1   Tags for Frequently Occurring Fields

Tag	Name
Ø43	Geographic area code
Ø5Ø	LC call number
Ø82	Dewey Decimal Classification number
1ØØ	Main entry (personal name)
11Ø	Main entry (corporate name)
111	Main entry (conference or meeting)
13Ø	Main entry (uniform title heading)
245	Title
25Ø	Edition statement
26Ø	Imprint
3ØØ	Collation
4ØØ	Series statement (personal name-title)
41Ø	Series statement (corporate name-title)
44Ø	Series statement (title)
5ØØ	General notes
5Ø4	Bibliography note
5Ø5	Contents note
6ØØ	Subject added entry (personal name)
61Ø	Subject added entry (corporate name)
611	Subject added entry (conference or meeting)
65Ø	Subject added entry (topical subjects)
651	Subject added entry (geographic name)
7ØØ	Added entry (personal name)
71Ø	Added entry (corporate name)
73Ø	Added entry (uniform title)
74Ø	Added entry (title traced differently)
8ØØ	Series added entry (personal name-title)
81Ø	Series added entry (corporate name-title)
84Ø	Series added entry (title)

Length. This element consists of four digits indicating the total length of a variable field.

Starting Character Position. The starting character position is five digits representing the location of the field in the record, i.e., the character position at which this field begins.

A variable field can consist of the following parts.

Indicators   Indicators are two characters giving additional information about a field. In Figure 15-4, the main entry personal name field, tag 100, uses the first indicator position to specify the type of personal name according to the following codes:

    ø - Forename
    1 - Single surname
    2 - Multiple surname
    3 - Family name

The second indicator specifies whether the main entry is the same as the subject of the work:

    ø - Main entry is not the same as subject
    1 - Main entry is same as subject

Subfield codes   Subfield codes are two characters ($ and an alphabetic character) identifying each element in the field. For example, in the field of main entry in the form of a personal name, the following subfield codes are used:

Code	Subfield
$a	Name
$b	Numeration
$c	Titles and other words associated with the name
$d	Dates
$e	Relator
$k	Form subheading
$t	Title (of book)
$l	Language
$f	Date (of a work) } Not yet in MARC
$p	Part (of a work)

Data   Data are cataloging information contained in the field.

Field termination   The field terminator is a special character (Ⅎ) indicating the end of field. The end of each record is indicated by the record terminator "Ʀ".

On-line Cataloging

The availability of facilities for on-line processing of cataloging records has proved to be extremely helpful to libraries. By having access to a central data base, an individual library makes use of the existing records in the most efficient and effective way for its purposes. Following is a brief discussion of some of the processes involved in on-line cataloging.

Terminal

On-line cataloging is performed on a terminal which is connected to a central data base.

The terminal generally consists of two parts—a CRT (cathode ray tube) terminal, which looks like a television receiver, and an attached keyboard similar to that of a typewriter except that it contains special function keys for system use and special library characters. Many terminals are accompanied by line printers.

Searching

The main purpose of searching is to ascertain whether a particular record is in the data base.

Searching is generally performed by means of search keys. The search keys may consist of alphabetic characters, numeric characters, or both. The most commonly-used search keys are derived from the following elements in a record: name-title, name, title, subject entry, LC card number, ISBN, ISSN, and a special control number in the data base.

Frequently, a particular search key may call up more than one record, because the computer will respond with all the records containing the same search key. In such a case, a list of the items containing only brief information will be displayed and the searcher then decides which particular record in the list is to be displayed in full.

Once it is ascertained that a record is in the data base, it can then be used for whatever purpose is desired. For cataloging purposes, the next step is to compare the record with the item being cataloged. If they match without variations, the record then can be processed for cataloging purposes, i.e., cards can be printed from the record; and the record can be added to the library's own tape for producing COM catalogs; etc.

However, if the record varies in certain details from the item being cataloged, it can be modified or edited to suit individual purposes. The process of modifying a record in the data base is called *editing*.

Editing

Editing can be performed on-line. One great advantage of on-line cataloging is the instant feedback. In editing, the modification is made to the information displayed on the screen, and the modified or edited record will be shown instantly to ensure that all necessary modifications have been correctly processed.

Three basic methods are used in editing: overstriking, insertion, and deletion. Overstriking is used to substitute or replace existing characters in the record by others. When additional characters are required, insertion is made. Excessive characters are removed by means of deletion.

Inputting cataloging records

The inputting process is used to store cataloging data in machine-readable form in a data base. After the cataloging information has been identified and organized according to cataloging rules, the subject headings and call number have been assigned, and the individual elements have been encoded or tagged according to the MARC format, the record is then ready to be entered or input into the computerized data base.

The inputting process can also be performed in an on-line mode through the terminal. Results of input can be displayed immediately for proofreading and any necessary corrections.

CHAPTER 16

Filing

INTRODUCTION

To provide ready access to individual entries in a catalog, the entries must be arranged in an order comprehensible to the user. The process of arranging entries in a catalog is called *filing*.

The bases for the arrangement or organization of entries may differ in that an alphabetical, chronological, geographical, or classified (logical) sequence may be used. In the catalogs found in American libraries, which are predominantly in the form of the dictionary catalog, alphabetical filing is generally the basis for arrangement of cataloging entries, with various degrees of the other bases for filing interspersed in the strictly alphabetical system.

Filing alphabetically may appear simple and straightforward at first glance. In reality, many problems arise in filing which must be resolved. The problems multiply as the number of entries in a catalog increases. Over the years, a number of filing codes have been developed. Following is a discussion of the development of the filing codes and some of the most common problems encountered in filing.

FILING CODES

Many libraries do not adhere strictly to one filing code. Local modifications are common phenomena. However, there is one basic feature which is common to all the codes and generally followed by libraries. The alphabetical order is based on word-by-word filing rather than letter-by-letter filing. The latter is not uncommon in reference works such as directories, dictionaries, and encyclopedias. There is a basic difference between the two methods. In the word-by-word filing, "New Jersey" precedes "Newcastle," while in letter-by-letter filing, the reverse is true.

In word-by-word filing, the blank between words has a filing value preceding any letter or character, a practice often referred to as "nothing before something."

Cutter

Charles Ammi Cutter's *Rules for a Dictionary Catalog*[1] contains rules for filing. These rules were developed in correspondence with his idea of the dictionary catalog. The basic principle of arrangement is the alphabetical sequence and the interfiling of author, title, and subject entries. Occasionally, certain features of the classified groupings were introduced, resulting in departures from the strictly alphabetical order.

ALA (1942)

The first edition of the *ALA Rules for Filing Catalog Cards* is essentially a summary of various acceptable methods of filing as practiced in American libraries at the time. Because there was no real consensus, alternatives were given in 60 percent of the rules. Many of the rules provide classified subgroupings within the alphabetical sequence. As a result, librarians found the code difficult to use.

LC (1956)

The *Filing Rules for the Dictionary Catalogs of the Library of Congress* were developed for use in the Library of Congress but, like other LC services, they are also made available in published form to other libraries. There is considerable departure from the strictly alphabetical order, particularly in the interfiling of different kinds of entries and in the grouping of subject headings.

ALA (1968)

In view of the new developments in cataloging rules in the 1960s and constant pleas from librarians for a simplified filing code, a second edition of the *ALA Rules for Filing Catalog Cards* was issued. This edition stresses the importance of correlation between the formation of headings and the filing order. The headings are to be filed as written, without resorting to mental insertions, deletions, or transpositions. The basic principle is the straight alphabetical order (disregarding punctuation) with only a few exceptions. The major exception is that personal surname entries are grouped together and filed before other entries bearing the same word or combination of words.

---

[1]Charles Ammi Cutter. *Rules for a Dictionary Catalog.* 4th ed. Washington, D.C.: Government Printing Office, 1904. First published under the title *Rules for a Printed Dictionary Catalogue* in 1876.

ALA Abridged (1968)

This is an abridgment of the preceding code. It contains the same basic rules as the full version, but with most of the specialized and explanatory material omitted. It was designed for the catalogs of small and medium-sized general libraries.

LC (1971)

Because the 1956 rules were developed specifically for card catalogs and are not amenable to computer filing, a new set of filing rules was developed at the Library of Congress by John C. Rather with the aim that the new code should be hospitable to various kinds of uses: searching for a known item with perfect information; searching for an item with incomplete or inexact information; and browsing. A provisional version was issued in 1971, but the document has not yet been officially published.[2] The basic principles underlying this code are: (1) elements in a heading should be taken in exactly the form and order in which they appear; (2) related entries should be kept together if they would be difficult to find when a user did not know their precise form; and (3) a standard set of fields should be established for each major type of filing entry. This code is currently being used at the Library of Congress in a number of its computer-produced files and catalogs, e.g., *Library of Congress Subject Headings* and *Library of Congress Catalogs: Film and Other Materials for Projection.*[3]

PROBLEMS IN FILING

Although the alphabetical sequence appears to be a simple and straightforward principle, there are many situations encountered in the arrangement of catalog entries which call for certain modifications of the basic principle in order to make the catalog useful. Nonalphabetical characters also appear in headings and cannot be handled by the simple instruction of alphabetical arrangement. Following is a discussion of the major problems in filing. Each code mentioned above seeks to resolve these problems, sometimes in different ways. No attempt will be made to enumerate the provisions of each code under each of the problems.

[2]An abridged version appeared in John C. Rather. "Filing Arrangement in the Library of Congress Catalogs." *Library Resources and Technical Services,* 16:249–256, Spring 1972.

[3]Library of Congress, Subject Cataloging Division. *Library of Congress Subject Headings.* 9th ed. Washington, D.C.: Library of Congress, 1980; and *Library of Congress Catalogs: Film and Other Materials for Projection.* Washington, D.C.: Library of Congress, 1953–

Different Kinds of Entries
Beginning with the Same Word or Words

Frequently, headings representing different kinds of entries (author, title, subject, cross-references) begin with the same word or words. For example, the words "London," "Rose," "Love," etc., may appear as the entry word of any of the three kinds of entry. In such a case, the question is whether it would be useful from the user's point of view to file them in a strictly alphabetical order, or whether it might be more useful to group them by kind of entry first and then alphabetize within each group. This is the area where the different codes vary greatly in their treatment. The problem is further complicated by the fact that among the author entries or subject entries, there are different kinds of names—personal, corporate, and geographic—which may begin with the same word.

Even among personal names alone, the question of useful arrangement arises because of the different kinds of personal name headings: compound names, names with prefixes, given names (without surnames), titles of addresses and nobility, etc.

Abbreviations

Initials are generally filed as separate one-letter words. Acronyms, on the other hand, are often filed as words rather than initials. The problem arises when, in some cases, it is not exactly clear whether a group of letters written together are meant to be initials or an acronym.

Numerals

These may be filed numerically in a separate sequence from the alphabetical file or filed as if spelled out (normally in the language of the entry), i.e., 1,200 as twelve hundred and 1,002 as one thousand two. The latter is a more common practice. However, exceptions must be made in some cases: e.g., **Henry II** and **Henry V** are filed as *Henry 2* and *Henry 5* instead of "Henry the Second" and "Henry the Fifth."

Diacritical Marks

The treatment of diacritical marks such as umlauts, accents, diereses, etc., varies. They are disregarded in most cases. In some cases, they may have a filing value. For example, *ü* may be filed as *u* or *ue*.

Signs and Symbols

Nonalphabetical and nonnumerical signs, including punctuation marks, must be taken into consideration. A decision must be made with regard to how they should be filed. The codes again vary in their treatment.

Subject Headings

Methods of interfiling subject headings beginning with the same word also vary. The following headings taken from *LC Catalogs: Subject Catalog*[4]

> Cookery—History
> Cookery—Periodicals
> Cookery (Horse meat)
> Cookery, American
> Cookery, French
> Cookery for diabetics

are not filed in a strictly alphabetical order. The same headings, according to the ALA rules, are arranged in the following order:

> Cookery, American
> Cookery for diabetics
> Cookery, French
> Cookery—History
> Cookery (Horse meat)
> Cookery—Periodicals

Exercise

1. Choose one of the problems encountered in filing discussed in this chapter and compare the treatment given to this problem in two or more of the existing filing codes.
2. The following list of entries is taken from *Filing Rules for the Dictionary Catalogs of the Library of Congress*. Rearrange these entries according to one of the other filing codes.

   Stone, Thomas (person as author)
   Stone, Thomas (added entry)

[4]Library of Congress, Subject Cataloging Division. *Library of Congress Catalogs: Subject Catalog*. Washington, D.C.: Library of Congress, 1950–   .

STONE, THOMAS (person as subject)
*Stone, Pa. (place alone as corporate author)
*Stone, Pa. (added entry)
*Stone, Pa. Dept. of Education (place as corporate author with official subheading)
*Stone, Pa. Dept. of Education (added entry)
*STONE, PA. DEPT. OF EDUCATION (subject)
*Stone, Pa. Fire Dept. (corporate author)
*STONE, PA. WATER COMMISSIONERS (subject)
*STONE, PA. (place as general subject without subject subdivision)
*STONE, PA.—BIOGRAPHY
*STONE, PA.—HISTORY
*STONE, PA.—WATER SUPPLY
STONE (i.e., a thing as subject)
STONE, see also BUILDING STONES
STONE, ARTIFICIAL
The Stone Age in North America (title of a book)
Stone and Webster, Boston
STONE AND WEBSTER, BOSTON

GLOSSARY[1]

Access point. A name, term, code, etc., under which a bibliographic record may be searched and identified. *See also* Heading.

Added entry. An entry, additional to the main entry, by which an item is represented in a catalog; a secondary entry. *See also* Main entry.

Alphabetical subject catalog. A catalog containing subject entries based on the principle of specific and direct entry and arranged alphabetically. Cf. Alphabetico-classed catalog; Classed catalog; Dictionary catalog.

Alphabetico-classed catalog. A subject catalog in which entries are listed under broad subjects and subdivided hierarchically by topics. The entries on each level of the hierarchy are arranged alphabetically. Cf. Alphabetical subject catalog; Classed catalog; Dictionary catalog.

Analytical entry. An entry for a part of an item for which a comprehensive entry has been made.

Analytical subject entry. A subject entry for part of a work.

Analytico-synthetic scheme. A classification scheme which identifies subjects by their component parts and requires fitting together the appropriate parts in order to provide a class mark for a work. For example, the Colon Classification is an analytico-synthetic scheme, while the Dewey Decimal Classification is partially so.

Anonymous. Of unknown authorship.

Area. A major section of the bibliographic description, comprising data of a particular category or set of categories.

Array. A group of coordinate subjects on the same level of a classification structure, e.g., oranges, lemons, limes, but not citrus fruit.

Artefact. Any object made or modified by a human being.

Author. *See* Personal author.

---

[1]The following works have been used in compiling this glossary: *Anglo-American Cataloguing Rules.* 2d ed. Michael Gorman and Paul W. Winkler, eds. Chicago: American Library Association, 1978; Lois Mai Chan. *Library of Congress Subject Headings: Principles and Application.* Littleton, Colo.: Libraries Unlimited, 1978; Melvil Dewey. *Dewey Decimal Classification and Relative Index.* 19th ed. 3 vols. Edited under the direction of Benjamin A. Custer. Albany, N.Y.: Forest Press, Division of Lake Placid Education Foundation, 1979; David Judson Haykin. *Subject Headings: A Practical Guide.* Washington, D.C.: Government Printing Office, 1951.

Author number. A combination of letters or figures, or both, representing the name of an author in a call number. *See also* Book number.

Author-title added entry. *See* Name-title added entry.

Author-title reference. *See* Name-title reference.

Authority record. *See* Name authority record; Subject authority record.

Bibliographic control. The operation by which recorded information is organized or arranged and thereby made readily retrievable.

Bibliographic record. A record containing details with regard to identification and physical and other characteristics of a document.

Binder's title. The title lettered on the cover of an item by a binder, as distinguished from the title on the publisher's original cover.

Biographical heading. A subject heading used with biographies which consists of the name of a class of persons with appropriate subdivisions, e.g., **Physicians—California—Biography; Poets, American—19th century—Biography.**

Book number. That portion of a call number which designates a specific individual work within its class. May consist of author number or other elements, or both, e.g., a work mark or an edition mark.

Broad classification. (1) A classification scheme which does not provide for minute subdivision of topics. (2) Arrangement of works in conformity with the provisions of such a scheme.

Call number. A composite symbol consisting of the class number and the book number and sometimes the volume number, the edition mark or the copy number, or both, which provides identification of an individual item and its shelf location.

Caption title. The title of a work given at the beginning of the first page of the text or, in the case of a musical score, immediately above the opening bars of the music.

Cartographic material. Any material representing, wholly or in part, the earth or any celestial body at any scale; includes two- and three-dimensional maps and plans; aeronautical, navigational, and celestial charts; globes; block diagrams; sections; aerial, satellite, and space photographs; atlases; bird's-eye views, etc.

Catalog. (1) A list of library materials contained in a collection, a library, or a group of libraries, arranged according to some definite plan. (2) In a wider sense, a list of materials prepared for a particular purpose, e.g., an exhibition catalog, a sales catalog.

Cataloging. The process of preparing entries for a catalog.

Cataloging copy. A cataloging record prepared by an agency to be used by other agencies or libraries.

Cataloging record. A basic unit in a catalog, containing cataloging data—bibliographic description, subject headings, and call number—of a particular item. The record may be displayed in different forms, the most common being a catalog card.

Centralized cataloging. The preparation of cataloging records by one agency to be used by other agencies or libraries.

Chain. A string of subjects each of which is subordinate to the one before it in a classification scheme, e.g., **Zoology—Vertebrates—Amphibians—Frogs.**

Characteristic of division. Any of the various ways in which a given subject may be divided. Example: division of literature by nationality/language, form, and period.

Chart. (1) An opaque sheet that exhibits data in graphic or tabular form, e.g., a wall chart. (2) In cartography, a special-purpose map generally designed for the use of navigators (e.g., an aeronautical chart, a nautical chart), although the word is also used to designate other types of special purpose maps, e.g., a celestial chart, i.e., a "star map."

Chief source of information. The source of bibliographic data to be given first preference as the source from which a bibliographic description (or portion thereof) is prepared.

Chronological subdivision. *See* Period subdivision.

Citation formula. An established sequence of facets to be used in representing a particular subject.

Citation order. The order by which the facets of a subject are arranged.

Class. (*noun*) A group of objects exhibiting one or more common characteristics, usually identified by a specific notation. (*verb*) To assign a class number to an individual work. *See also* Classify, Classification(2).

Class entry. A subject entry consisting of a string of hierarchically related terms beginning with the broadest term leading to the subject in question, in the form of a chain.

Class number. A notation assigned to a subject in a classification scheme. It constitutes a portion of the call number.

Classed catalog. A subject catalog consisting of class entries arranged logically according to a systematic scheme of classification. Also called *Class catalog, Classified subject catalog, Systematic catalog.* Cf. Alphabetical subject catalog; Alphabetico-classed catalog; Dictionary catalog.

Classification. (1) An arrangement in some logical order of the whole field of knowledge, or of some specified portion thereof. (2) The art of arranging books or other objects in conformity with such a scheme.

Classificationist. A person who designs or develops a classification system or one who engages in the philosophy and theory of classification.

Classifier. A person who applies a classification system to a body of knowledge or a collection of documents.

Classify. To arrange a collection of works according to the provisions of a classification scheme. *See also* Class (*verb*).

Close classification. (1) A classification providing for minute subdivision of topics. Also called *bibliographic classification*. (2) Arrangement of works in conformity with the provisions of such a scheme. Cf. Broad classification.

Coextensive heading. A heading which represents precisely (no more general or specific than) the subject content of a work.

Collaborator. One who works with one or more associates to produce a work; all may make the same kind of contribution, as in the case of shared responsibility, or they may make different kinds of contributions, as in the case of collaboration between an artist and a writer. *See also* Joint author; Mixed responsibility; Shared responsibility.

Collection. If by one author: three or more independent works or parts of works published together. If by more than one author: two or more independent works or parts of works published together and not written for the same occasion or for the publication in hand.

Collective biography. A work consisting of two or more life histories. Cf. Individual biography.

Collective title. A title proper that is an inclusive title for an item containing several works.

Colophon. A statement at the end of an item giving information about one or more of the following: the title, author or authors, publisher, printer, date of publication or printing; it may include other information.

Colored illustration. An illustration in two or more colors.

Compiler. One who produces a collection by selecting and putting together matter from the works of various persons or bodies. Also, one who selects and puts together in one publication matter from the works of one person or body. Cf. Editor.

Compound surname. A surname consisting of two or more proper names, often connected by a hyphen, conjunction, or preposition.

Conference. (1) A meeting of individuals or representatives of various bodies for the purpose of discussing and acting on topics of common interest. (2) A meeting of representatives of a corporate body that constitutes its legislative or governing body.

Continuation. (1) A supplement (q.v.). (2) A part issued in continuance of a monograph, a serial, or a series.

Conventional name. A name, other than the real or official name, by which a corporate body, place, or thing has come to be known.

Conventional title. *See* Uniform title.

Cooperative cataloging. The preparation by one of several participating agencies or libraries of a cataloging record which is made available to the other participating agencies or libraries.

Corporate body. An organization or group of persons that is identified by a particular name and that acts, or may act, as an entity. Typical examples of corporate bodies are associations, institutions, business firms, nonprofit enterprises, governments, government agencies, religious bodies, local churches, and conferences.

Cover title. A title printed on the original cover of an item. *See also* Binder's title.

Cross classification. A situation in which a given work deals with two or more subdivisions of a subject, with each subdivision representing a different characteristic of division. Such a situation creates the possibility of inconsistent classification. Example: a work on weaving cotton cloth deals with two subdivisions of textile technology, cotton (material) and weaving (process), and may be classed with either. *See also* Citation order.

Cross-reference. *See* Reference.

Descriptive cataloging. That part of cataloging consisting of the presentation of bibliographic description and the determination of access points through authors' names and titles.

Dictionary catalog. A catalog in which all the entries (author, title, subject, series, etc.) and the cross-references are interfiled in one alphabetical sequence. The subject entries in a dictionary catalog are based on the principle of specific and direct entry. The term, when used in reference to the subject entries, is sometimes used interchangeably with the term, *alphabetical subject catalog*. Cf. Alphabetical subject catalog; Alphabetico-classed catalog; Classed catalog.

Direct subdivision. Geographic subdivision of subject headings by name of a local place without interposition of the name of a larger geographic entity. Cf. Indirect subdivision.

Discipline. An organized field of study or branch of learning dealing with specific kinds of subjects or subjects considered from specific points of view, or both.

Duplicate entry. (1) Entry of the same subject heading in two different forms, e.g., **United States—Foreign relations—France** and **France—Foreign relations—United States.** (2) Assignment of two subject headings to bring out different aspects of a work. Frequently, one of the headings is a specific heading and the other is a general (also called generic) heading subdivided by an aspect, e.g., **Poa** and **Grasses—Scandinavia** for a work about Poa in Scandinavia.

Edition.   (1) In the case of books and booklike materials, all those copies of an item produced from substantially the same type image, whether by direct contact or by photographic methods. (2) In the case of nonbook materials, all the copies of an item produced from one master copy and issued by a particular publishing agency or a group of such agencies. Provided the foregoing conditions are fulfilled, a change of identity of the distributing body or bodies does not constitute a change of edition. *See also* Issue; Reprint.

Editor.   One who prepares for publication an item not his own. The editorial labor may be limited to the preparation of the item for the manufacturer, or it may include supervision of the manufacturing, revision (restitution), or elucidation of the text, and the addition of an introduction, notes, and other critical matter. For certain works it may involve the technical direction of a staff of persons engaged in writing or compiling the text. Cf. Compiler.

Element.   A word, phrase, or group of characters representing a distinct unit of bibliographic information and forming part of an area (q.v.) of the description.

Entry.   A record of an item in a catalog. *See also* Heading.

Entry word.   The word by which an entry is primarily arranged in the catalog, usually the first word (other than an article) of the heading. Cf. Heading.

Enumerative scheme.   A classification scheme which lists subjects and their subdivisions and provides ready-made class marks for them.

Explanatory reference.   An elaborated *see* or *see also* reference that explains the circumstances under which the headings involved should be consulted.

Facet.   A term denoting a component (based on a particular characteristic) of a compound subject, e.g., geographical facet, language facet, literary form facet.

Facet analysis.   The division of a subject into its component parts (facets). Each array of a facet consists of parts based on the same characteristic, e.g., English language, French language, German language, etc.

Faceted scheme.   *See* Analytico-synthetic scheme.

Festschrift.   A collection of two or more essays, addresses, or biographical, bibliographical, and other contributions published in honor of a person, an institution, or a society, usually on the occasion of an anniversary or birthday celebration.

Filmstrip. A length of film containing a succession of images intended for projection one at a time, with or without recorded sound.

Fixed location. System of marking and arranging library materials by shelf and book marks so that their absolute position in room, tier, and on shelf is always the same.

Form heading. A heading representing the physical, bibliographical, artistic, or literary form of a work, e.g., Encyclopedias and dictionaries; Essays; Short stories; String quartets.

Form subdivision. A division of a subject heading which brings out the form of the work, e.g., **—Periodicals; —Bibliography; —Collected works.**

Format. In its widest sense, any particular physical presentation of an item.

Free-floating subdivision. A subdivision which may be used by a cataloger at the Library of Congress under any existing appropriate subject heading for the first time without establishing the usage editorially.

General material designation. A term indicating the broad class of material to which an item belongs, e.g., sound recording. See *also* Specific material designation.

General reference. A blanket reference to a group of headings rather than a particular heading. Example:

> *Nicknames*
>   *sa subdivision* Nicknames *under subjects,* e.g., Kings and rulers—Nicknames; *also special nicknames,* e.g., Hoosier (nickname), Uncle Sam (nickname).

Cf. Specific reference.

Geographic qualifier. The name of a larger geographic entity added to a local place name, e.g., Cambridge (**Mass.**); Toledo (**Spain**). Cf. Qualifier.

Geographic subdivision. A subdivision by the name of a place to which the subject represented by the main heading is limited. Cf. Direct subdivision; Indirect subdivision.

Half title. A brief title of a publication appearing on a leaf preceding the title page.

Heading. A name, word, or phrase placed at the head of a catalog entry to provide an access point in the catalog.

Hierarchy. The arrangement of disciplines and subjects in an order ranging from the most general to the most specific.

Indirect subdivision. Geographic subdivision of subject headings by name of country, constituent country (Great Britain), state (United States), province (Canada), or constituent republic

(U.S.S.R.), with further subdivision by name of state (other than United States), province (other than Canada), county, city, or other locality. Cf. Direct subdivision.

Individual biography. A work devoted to the life of a single person. Cf. Collective biography.

Integrity of numbers. The policy of maintaining the stability of numbers in a classification scheme. Such a policy is opposed to revision, especially when the relocation of a subject is involved.

International Standard Book Number (ISBN). *See* Standard number.

International Standard Serial Number (ISSN). *See* Standard number.

Issue. (1) In the case of books and booklike materials, those copies of an edition forming a distinct group that is distinguished from other copies of the edition by more or less slight but well-defined variations; most commonly a new impression for which corrections or revisions have been incorporated into the original type images. (2) In the case of nonbook materials, those copies of an edition of an item forming a distinct group that is distinguished from other copies by well-defined variations. *See also* Edition; Reprint.

Item. A document or set of documents in any physical form, published, issued, or treated as an entity, and as such forming the basis for a single bibliographic description.

Joint author. A person who collaborates with one or more other persons to produce a work in relation to which the collaborators perform the same function. *See also* Shared responsibility.

Key title. The unique name assigned to a serial by the International Serials Data System (ISDS).

Kit. An item containing two or more categories of material, no one of which is identifiable as the predominant constituent of the item; also designated *multimedia item*.

Leaf. One of the units into which the original sheet or half sheet of paper, parchment, etc., is folded to form part of a book; each leaf consists of two pages, one on each side, either or both of which may be blank.

Literary warrant. The principle which allows a category to exist in a classification or thesaurus only if a work exists for that category. The use of an actual collection or holdings of a library or actual published works as the basis for developing a classification scheme or thesaurus.

Local subdivision. *See* Geographic subdivision.

Macroform. A generic term for any medium, transparent or opaque, bearing images large enough to be easily read by the naked eye. *See also* Microform.

Main entry. The complete catalog record of an item, presented in the form by which the entity is to be uniformly identified and cited. The main entry may include the tracings of all other headings under which the record is to be represented in the catalog. *See also* Added entry.

Main heading.   The first part of a heading that includes a subheading.

MARC.   A system in which cataloging records are prepared in a format which enables the computer to recognize the elements and manipulate them for various purposes.

Microfiche.   A sheet of film bearing a number of microimages in a two-dimensional array.

Microfilm.   A length of film bearing a number of microimages in linear array.

Microform.   A generic term for any medium, transparent or opaque, bearing microimages. *See also* Macroform.

Mixed authorship.   *See* Mixed responsibility.

Mixed notation.   A notational system using a combination of two or more kinds of symbols, e.g., letters and numerals.

Mixed responsibility.   A work of mixed responsibility is one in which different persons or bodies contribute to its intellectual or artistic content by performing different kinds of activities, e.g., adapting or illustrating a work written by another person. *See also* Shared responsibility.

Mnemonics.   Recurring concepts denoted by the same notational symbols in a classification scheme.

Model heading.   A subject heading which serves as a model of subdivisions for headings in the same category, i.e., subdivisions listed under a model heading may be used whenever appropriate under other headings in the same category, e.g., **Shakespeare, William, 1564–1616,** as a model heading for literary authors; **Piano** as a model heading for musical instruments. Also called *Pattern heading.*

Monograph.   A nonserial item, i.e., an item either complete in one part or complete, or intended to be completed, in a finite number of separate parts.

Monographic series.   *See* Series(1).

Multimedia item.   *See* Kit.

Multipart item.   A monograph complete, or intended to be completed, in a finite number of separate parts.

Name authority record.   A record which shows a personal or corporate heading in its established form, cites the authorities consulted in determining the choice and form of name, and indicates the references made to the heading.

Name-title added entry.   An added entry consisting of the name of a person or corporate body and the title of an item.

Name-title reference. A reference in which the refer-from line, the refer-to line, or both consist of the name of a person or a corporate body and the title of an item.

Notation. Numerals, letters, and/or other symbols used to represent the main and subordinate divisions of a classification scheme.

Notational synthesis. *See* Number building.

Number building. The process of making a number more specific through addition of segments taken from other parts of the classification.

Object. A three-dimensional artefact (or replica of an artefact) or a specimen of a naturally occurring entity. *See also* Realia.

Original cataloging. The preparation of a cataloging record without the assistance of outside cataloging agencies.

Other title information. Any title borne by an item other than the title proper or parallel titles; also any phrase appearing in conjunction with the title proper, parallel titles, or other titles, indicative of the character, contents, etc., of the item or the motives for, or occasion of, its production or publication. The term includes subtitles, avant-titres, etc., but does not include variations on the title proper, e.g., spine titles, sleeve titles, etc.

Parallel title. The title proper in another language or script or both.

Part. (1) One of the subordinate units into which an item has been divided by the author, publisher, or manufacturer. In the case of printed monographs, generally synonymous with *volume;* it is distinguished from a fascicle by being a component unit rather than a temporary division of a work. (2) As used in the physical description area, the word *part* designates bibliographic units intended to be bound several to a volume.

Pattern heading. *See* Model heading.

Period subdivision. A subdivision which shows the period or span of time treated in a work or the period during which the work appeared. Also called *Chronological subdivision.*

Personal author. The person chiefly responsible for the creation of the intellectual or artistic content of a work. For example, writers of books and composers of music are the authors of the works they create; compilers of bibliographies are the authors of those bibliographies; cartographers are the authors of their maps; and artists and photographers are the authors of the works they create. In addition, in certain cases performers are the authors of sound recordings, films, and videorecordings.

Phoenix schedule. A term used in the Dewey Decimal Classification meaning a completely new development of the schedule for a specific discipline. Except by chance, only the basic number for the discipline remains the same as in previous editions; all other numbers are freely reused.

Phonorecord. *See* Sound recording.

Plate. A leaf containing illustrative matter, with or without explanatory text, that does not form part of either the preliminary or the main sequences of pages or leaves.

Portfolio. A container for holding loose materials, e.g., paintings, drawings, papers, unbound sections of a book, and similar materials, consisting of two covers joined together at the back; the covers are usually tied with tapes at the fore edge, top, and bottom.

Predominant name. The name or form of name of a person or corporate body that appears most frequently (1) in the person's works or works issued by the corporate body; or (2) in reference sources, in that order of preference.

Preliminaries. The title page or title pages of an item, together with the verso of each title page, any pages preceding the title page or title pages, and the cover.

Pseudonym. A name assumed by an author to conceal or obscure his or her identity.

Pure notation. A notational system using one kind of symbol only, e.g., arabic numerals or letters.

Qualifier. A term (enclosed in parentheses) placed after a subject heading for the purpose of distinguishing between homographs or clarifying the meaning of the heading, e.g., **Indexing (Machine-shop practice); PL/I (Computer program language); Mont Blanc (Freighter); Novgorod (Russia : Duchy).** Cf. Geographic qualifier.

Realia. Actual objects (artefacts, specimens) as opposed to replicas. *See also* Object.

Refer from reference. An indication of the terms or headings *from* which references are to be made to a given heading. It is the reverse of the indication of a *see* or *see also* reference and is represented by the symbols *x* (*see* reference from) and *xx* (*see also* reference from).

Reference. A direction from one heading or entry to another.

Reference source. Any publication from which authoritative information may be obtained. Not limited to reference works.

Related body. A corporate body that has a relation to another body other than that of hierarchical subordination, e.g., one that is founded but not controlled by another body; one that only receives financial support from another body; one that provides financial or other types of assistance to another body, such as "friends" groups, or both; one whose members have also membership in or an association with another body, such as employees' associations and alumni associations.

Relative location.   The arrangement of library materials according to their relations to each other and regardless of their locations on the shelves.

Relocation.   An adjustment in the schedules resulting in the shifting of a topic between successive editions from one number to another.

Reprint.   (1) A new printing of an item made from the original type image, commonly by photographic methods. The printing may reproduce the original exactly (an impression) or it may contain more or less slight but well-defined variations (an issue). (2) A new edition with substantially unchanged text. *See also* Edition; Issue.

Running title.   The title, or abbreviated title, of the book repeated at the head of each page or at the head of the versos.

Secondary entry.   *See* Added entry.

***See also* reference.**   A reference from a heading to a less comprehensive or otherwise related heading. It is indicated in *Library of Congress Subject Headings* by the symbol *sa*.

***See* reference.**   A reference from a term or name not used as a heading to one that is used.

Segmentation.   The practice of breaking down a long class number into shorter segments. Libraries that decide to use shorter numbers can then cut off the long number at designated points, e.g., 574.1'92'05.

Serial.   A publication in any medium issued in successive parts bearing numerical or chronological designations and intended to be continued indefinitely. Serials include periodicals; newspapers; annuals (reports, yearbooks, etc.); the journals, memoirs, proceedings, transactions, etc., of societies; and numbered monographic series. *See also* Series(1).

Series.   (1) A group of separate items related to one another by the fact that each item bears, in addition to its own title proper, a collective title applying to the group as a whole. The individual items may or may not be numbered. (2) Each of two or more volumes of essays, lectures, articles, or other writings, similar in character and issued in sequence, e.g., Lowell's *Among my books*, second series. (3) A separately numbered sequence of volumes within a series or serial, e.g., *Notes and queries*, first series, second series, etc.

Shared authorship.   *See* Shared responsibility.

Shared responsibility.   Collaboration between two or more persons or bodies performing the same kind of activity in the creation of the content of an item. The contribution of each may form a separate and distinct part of the item, or the contribution of each may not be separable from that of the others. *See also* Joint author; Mixed responsibility.

Shelflist.   A file of cataloging records arranged by call number.

Sine loco (s.l.).   Without place, i.e., without the name of the place of publication.

Sine nomine (s.n.).   Without name, i.e., without the name of the publisher.

Sound recording.   A recording on which sound vibrations have been registered by mechanical or electrical means so that the sound may be reproduced.

Specific entry.   Entry of a work under a heading which expresses its special subject or topic as distinguished from an entry for the class or broad subject which encompasses that special subject or topic.

Specific material designation.   A term indicating the special class of material (usually the class of physical object) to which an item belongs, e.g., sound disc. *See also* General material designation.

Specific reference.   A reference from one heading to another. Cf. General reference.

Split files.   Separate files of subject entries in a catalog under headings represented by current and obsolete terms which refer to the same subject. The device has been adopted by the Library of Congress recently to facilitate updating of terminology.

Standard number.   The International Standard Number (ISN), e.g., International Standard Book Number (ISBN), International Standard Serial Number (ISSN), or any other internationally agreed upon standard number, that uniquely identifies an item.

Standard title.   *See* Uniform title.

Statement of responsibility.   A statement, transcribed from the item being described, relating to persons responsible for the intellectual or artistic content of the item, to corporate bodies from which the content emanates, or to persons or corporate bodies responsible for the performance of the content of the item.

Subdivision.   The device of extending a subject heading by indicating one of its aspects—form, place, period, topic. Cf. Form subdivision; Geographic subdivision; Period subdivision; Topical subdivision.

Subject.   The theme or topic treated by the author in a work, whether stated in the title or not.

Subject analysis.   The process of identifying the intellectual content of a work. The results may be displayed in a catalog or bibliography by means of notational symbols as in a classification system, or by verbal terms such as subject headings or indexing terms.

Subject analytic. *See* Analytical subject entry.

Subject authority record. A record of a subject heading which shows its established form, cites the authorities consulted in determining the choice and form of the heading, and indicates the cross references made to and from the heading.

Subject catalog. A catalog consisting of subject entries only. The subject portion of a divided catalog.

Subject entry. An entry in a catalog or a bibliography under a heading which indicates the subject of an item.

Subject heading. The term (a word or a group of words) denoting a subject under which all material on that subject is entered in a catalog.

Subject-to-name reference. A reference from a subject heading to a name heading for the purpose of directing the user's attention from a particular field of interest to names of individuals or corporate bodies that are active or associated in some way with the field. Current Library of Congress policy requires only subject-to-corporate-name references. Also called *Red-to-Black* reference.

Subordinate body. A corporate body that forms an integral part of a larger body in relation to which it holds an inferior hierarchical rank.

Subseries. A series within a series; that is, a series which always appears in conjunction with another, usually more comprehensive, series of which it forms a section. Its title may or may not be dependent on the title of the main series.

Supplement. An item, usually issued separately, that complements one already published by bringing up-to-date or otherwise continuing the original or by containing a special feature not included in the original; the supplement has a formal relationship with the original as expressed by common authorship, a common title or subtitle, and/or a stated intention to continue or supplement the original.

Supplied title. The title provided by the *cataloger* in the case of an item that has no title proper on the chief source of information or its substitute. It may be taken from elsewhere in the item itself or from a reference source, or it may be composed by the cataloger.

Syndetic device. The device used to connect related headings by means of cross references.

Synthesis. The process of composing a class number, subject heading, or indexing term by combining various elements in order to represent a complex subject. *See also* Number building.

Text. (1) A term used as a general material designation to designate printed material accessible to the naked eye (e.g., a book, pamphlet, or broadside). (2) The words of a song, song cycle, or, in the plural, a collection of songs.

Title. A word, phrase, character, or group of characters, normally appearing in an item, naming the item or the work contained in it. *See also* Caption title; Cover title; Running title; Supplied title; Title proper; Uniform title.

Title frame. A frame containing written or printed material not part of the subject content of the item.

Title page. A page at the beginning of an item bearing the title proper and usually, though not necessarily, the statement of responsibility and the data relating to publication. The leaf bearing the title page is commonly called the *title page* although properly called the *title leaf.*

Title proper. The chief name of an item, including any alternative title but excluding parallel titles and other title information.

Topical subdivision. A subdivision which represents an aspect of the main subject other than form, place, or period. Cf. Form subdivision; Geographic subdivision; Period subdivision.

Tracing. (1) The record of the headings under which an item is represented in the catalog. (2) The record of the references that have been made to a name or to the title of an item that is represented in the catalog.

Transparency. A sheet of transparent material bearing an image and designed for use with an overhead projector or a light box. It may be mounted in a frame.

Uniform heading. The particular heading by which a subject or person that may be represented by different names or different forms of a name is to be listed in the catalog.

Uniform title. (1) The particular title by which a work that has appeared under varying titles is to be identified for cataloging purposes. (2) A conventional collective title used to collocate publications of an author, composer, or corporate body containing several works or extracts, etc., from several works, e.g., complete works, several works in a particular literary or musical form.

Verso. The left-hand page of a book, usually bearing an even page number.

Verso of the title page. The back side of the title page.

Videorecording. A recording on which visual images, usually in motion and accompanied by sound, have been registered; designed for playback by means of a television set.

Volume.   (1) In the bibliographic sense, a major division of a work, regardless of its designation by the publisher, distinguished from other major divisions of the same work by having its own inclusive title page, half title, etc. (2) In the material sense, all that is contained in one binding, portfolio, etc., whether as originally issued or as bound after issue. The volumes as a material unit may not coincide with the volume as a bibliographic unit.

APPENDIX A[1]

Policies of the Library of Congress Relative to AACR 2

OPTIONS TO BE FOLLOWED BY THE LIBRARY OF CONGRESS

Below is a compilation of the Library of Congress decisions relative to all the options in AACR 2. . . .

The compilation covers only the provisions in AACR 2 that are explicitly labeled "optional," or "optionally" plus four cases of "alternative" rules. There are as many unlabeled options or choices that must be made by a cataloger, a cataloging department, or a library administration. Perhaps the majority of these choices would be covered by provision 0.9 in the general introduction to AACR 2, meaning that no advance word is desirable or possible: these matters are properly in the hands of the cataloger responding to specific cases. Some of the choices not covered by provision 0.9 are candidates for rule interpretation. *Cataloging Service Bulletin* during 1980 will provide advance notice of Library of Congress decisions in this regard.

1.1C.	For the display of GMDs, apply selectively. See subrule .1C for each chapter.
1.1E5.	Generally apply.
1.2B4.	Do not apply.
1.4C7.	Apply when there is no ISBN or ISSN and the information is given in the item being cataloged or is otherwise readily available without special research.
1.4E.	Apply on a case-by-case basis.
1.4F5.	Apply whenever the copyright date is different from the publication date.

[1]From *Cataloging Service Bulletin*, No. 8 (Spring 1980), pages 8–14.

1.4F8.	Apply.
1.4G4.	Apply on a case-by-case basis.
1.5A3.	Apply.
1.5B5.	Apply.
1.5E1.	Apply on a case-by-case basis.
1.8B2.	Apply.
1.8D.	Apply for current items.
1.8E1.	Apply.
2.1C.	Do not apply.
2.2B3.	Do not apply.
2.4E.	Apply on a case-by-case basis.
2.4G2.	Apply on a case-by-case basis.
2.5B21.	Apply to early printed books whenever the particular case seems to warrant it.
2.5E1.	Apply on a case-by-case basis.
2.8C.	Apply for current items.
2.8D2.	Apply.
2.16E.	Generally apply.
2.16G.	Generally apply.
2.16H.	Apply.
2.17B.	Apply whenever the information seems important for the particular book.
2.18C.	Apply whenever the edition being cataloged is listed in one of the following: *Bristol, BAL, Evans, STC,* or *Wing* (use the forms shown here). Also apply whenever the edition (including a facsimile) being cataloged is found in any other list or bibliography and the citation provides useful information (e.g., to distinguish editions or to substantiate the cataloger's conclusions).
3.1C.	Do not apply.
3.2B3.	Do not apply.
3.3B2.	Apply.

3.3C2.	Apply.
3.3D.	Apply both the option that is the whole of 3.3D and the specific option in 3.3D1.
3.4D1.	Apply.
3.4G2.	Apply on a case-by-case basis.
3.5D1.	Do not apply.
3.5D3.	Apply.
3.5D5.	Apply.
3.5E1.	Apply on a case-by-case basis.
3.8D.	Apply for current items.
4.1C.	Do not apply.
4.1F2.	Apply.
4.4B1.	Apply whenever the information is readily available.
4.5B1.	Do not apply.
4.5B2.	Apply both options.
4.5D2.	Apply.
5.1C.	Do not apply.
5.2B3.	Do not apply.
5.4D1.	Apply.
5.4E.	Apply on a case-by-case basis.
5.4G2.	Apply on a case-by-case basis.
5.5E1.	Apply on a case-by-case basis.
5.8D.	Apply for current items.
6.1C.	Apply.
6.2B3.	Do not apply.
6.4D1.	Apply.
6.4E.	Apply on a case-by-case basis.
6.4G2.	Apply on a case-by-case basis.
6.5B1.	Do not apply.

6.5C8.	Apply whenever the information would be needed for selecting playback equipment.
6.5E1.	Apply on a case-by-case basis.
6.8D.	Apply for current items.
7.1B2.	Apply on a case-by-case basis.
7.1C.	Apply.
7.2B3.	Do not apply.
7.4E.	Apply on a case-by-case basis.
7.4F2.	Apply.
7.4G2.	Do not apply.
7.5B1.	Do not apply.
7.5E1.	Apply on a case-by-case basis.
7.8D.	Apply for current items.
8.1C.	Apply.
8.2B3.	Do not apply.
8.4E.	Apply on a case-by-case basis.
8.4G2.	Apply on a case-by-case basis.
8.5B1.	Apply.
8.5C7.	Apply whenever the information seems important for the particular item being cataloged.
8.5E1.	Apply on a case-by-case basis.
8.8D.	Apply for current items.
9.1C.	Apply.
9.2B3.	Do not apply.
9.4E.	Apply on a case-by-case basis.
9.5D1.	Apply whenever the information is readily available.
9.5D2.	Apply whenever the information is readily available.
9.7B4.	Apply.
9.8D.	Apply for current items.

10.1C.	Apply.
10.2B3.	Do not apply.
10.4E.	Apply on a case-by-case basis.
10.4G3.	Apply on a case-by-case basis.
10.5B1.	Do not apply.
10.5B2.	Apply on a case-by-case basis.
10.5E1.	Apply on a case-by-case basis.
10.8D.	Apply for current items.
11.1C.	Apply.
11.2B3.	Do not apply.
11.4E.	Apply on a case-by-case basis.
11.5B1.	Do not apply.
11.5E1.	Apply on a case-by-case basis.
11.8D.	Apply for current items.
11.7B10.	Apply on a case-by-case basis.
12.1C.	Do not apply.
12.2B3.	Apply.
12.4E.	Apply on a case-by-case basis.
12.4G.	Apply on a case-by-case basis.
12.5E1.	Apply on a case-by-case basis.
12.7B7c.	Apply whenever the information is readily available.
12.7B7e.	Do not apply.
12.7B7f.	Apply both options whenever the information is readily available.
12.8D.	Do not apply.
12.8E1.	Apply.
21.0D.	Do not apply.
21.18B.	Do not apply.
21.27.	Do not apply.

21.28A.	Apply the alternative rule.
21.29G.	Do not apply.
21.30L.	Apply.
21.36C1–C3.	Do not apply.
21.36C5–C9.	Do not apply.
22.3C2.	Apply the alternative rule.
22.16A.	Apply whenever the information is readily available.
22.18.	Apply whenever the information is readily available.
23.4B.	Apply the first option to the names of cities, towns, etc. Apply it also to the names of larger places below the national level except to

      (1) the names of the states, provinces, and territories of Australia, Canada, and the United States;

      (2) the names of counties, regions, and island areas in the British Isles (other than the counties of Northern Ireland);

      (3) the names of the constituent states of Malaysia, the Soviet Union, and Yugoslavia; and

      (4) the names of islands.

> Tyrone (Northern Ireland)
> Bangkok (Thailand)
> Masindi (Uganda)
> Port Said (Egypt)
> Quito (Ecuador)
> Tokyo (Japan)
> Trondheim (Norway)
> Seine-et-Oise (France)
> Uttar Pradesh (India)

but:
> Humberside
> Kelantan
> Kirghiz S.S.R.
> New South Wales
> Pennsylvania
> Réunion
> Saskatchewan

> Slovenia
> Strathclyde

Apply the second option if the name of a larger place being added to a particular place name is in one of the categories specified above.

> Bucks County (Pa.)
> Hull (Humberside)
> Entre-Deux (Réunion)
> Frunze (Kirghiz S.S.R.)
> Kota Baharu (Kelantan)
> Ljubljana (Slovenia)
> Lanark (Strathclyde)
> Philadelphia (Pa.)
> Regina (Sask.)
> Sydney (N.S.W.)

24.1A.	Do not apply the alternative rule.
24.3A.	Do not apply the alternative rule.
24.4C1.	Apply on a case-by-case basis.
24.7B2.	Apply.
25.2A.	Apply.
25.5E.	Apply.
26.2D2.	Do not apply.
26.3A4.	Decision deferred.
26.4A2.	Do not apply.
26.5A.	Do not apply.

PARAGRAPHING CERTAIN PARTS OF A BIBLIOGRAPHIC DESCRIPTION

AACR 2, rule 1.0C, says that each area of a description may be separated from a previous area (including each occurrence of a note) either by the standard punctuation (. —) or by paragraphing. The Library of Congress will continue its current practice of paragraphing, with a period at the end of each paragraph unless the paragraph already ends with a closing mark of punctuation (a question mark, exclamation point, parenthesis, bracket); in such a case, the period is omitted.

SPACING AFTER INITIALS

The Library of Congress has been studying its policies that govern spacing after initials and has made the following decisions, which will be implemented beginning January 2, 1981:

(1) Personal Names

Separate adjacent initials in personal names used in headings by one space.

> Manchester, P. W.
> Flam, F. A. (Floyd A.)
> H. D.
> D. S., Master
> i. e., Master
> Morrow, W. W.

Otherwise, close up adjacent initials in personal names used in other areas of the catalog record:

> / by W.W. Morrow . . .
> New York : W.W. Morrow, 1980

(2) Corporate Names

For initials both in headings and other areas of the catalog record, do not separate adjacent initials with a space, including those cases in which a personal name forms part of a corporate name.

> W.W. Morrow Foundation
> DR Service
> TEE Consulting Services Inc.
> U.S.D.A. Symposium . . .
> F & H Denby
> > (*the ampersand is treated as a word*)

APPENDIX B

Tables in Library of Congress Classification

REGIONS AND COUNTRIES IN ONE ALPHABET

The numbers in this list are intended to be used as a guide for the best distribution of numbers and not necessarily as a fixed standard. Considerable latitude may be used in cases where the countries are arranged in continental groups.

Abyssinia, *see* Ethiopia	
Afghanistan	.A3
Africa, South	.A35
Algeria	.A4
Arabia, Saudi, *see* .S33	
Argentine Republic	.A7
Australia	.A8
Austria	.A9
Bangladesh	.B3
Belgium	.B4
Bolivia	.B5
Borneo	.B54
Botswana	.B57
Brazil	.B6
British Guiana, *see* .G95	(.B7)
British Honduras	.B8
Bulgaria	.B9
Cambodia	.C16
Cameroon	.C17
Canada	.C2
Central Africa	.C42
Ceylon, *see* .S73	
Chile	.C5
China	.C6
Colombia	.C7

Congo (Brazzaville)	.C75
Costa Rica	.C8
Cuba	.C9
Czechoslovak Republic	.C95
Denmark	.D4
Dutch East Indies, *see* .I5	
Dutch Guiana, *see* .S75	(.D8)
East Africa	.E18
Ecuador	.E2
Egypt	.E3
Ethiopia	.E8
Formosa, *see* .T28	
France	.F8
French Guiana	.F9
French-speaking Equatorial Africa	.F82
French-speaking West Africa	.F83
Gabon	.G23
Germany. Federal Republic	.G3
Democratic Republic	.G35
Ghana (Gold Coast)	.G4
Great Britain	.G7
Greece	.G8
Greenland	.G83
Guatemala	.G9
Guinea	.G92
Guyana	.G95
Haiti	.H2
Holland, *see* .N4	(.H7)
Honduras	.H8
Hong Kong	.H85
Iceland	.I2
India	.I4
Indonesia	.I5
Iran	.I7
Israel	.I75
Italy	.I8
Japan	.J3
Jordan	.J6
Korea	.K8
Korea, North	.K83
Kuwait	.K85

Laos	.L28
Lebanon	.L4
Lesotho	.L45
Liberia	.L7
Libya	.L74
Luxemburg	.L9
Macao	.M2
Madagascar	.M28
Malawi	.M3
Malaya	.M318
Malta	.M33
Mauritania	.M39
Mauritius	.M4
Mekong River Valley	.M45
Mexico	.M6
Morocco	.M8
Mozambique	.M85
Netherlands	.N4
Nicaragua	.N5
Nile River Valley	.N6
North Sea	.N67
Northern Rhodesia, *see* .Z3	
Norway	.N8
Nyasaland, *see* .M3	
Pakistan	.P18
Palestine, *see* .I75	
Panama	.P2
Paraguay	.P3
Persia, *see* .I7	(.P4)
Peru	.P5
Philippine Islands	.P6
Poland	.P7
Portugal	.P8
Romania	.R6
Russia	.R9
Rwanda	.R93
Sahel	.S18
Salvador	.S2
Santo Domingo	.S3
Saudi Arabia	.S33
Senegal	.S38
Siam, *see* .T5	(.S5)

Singapore	.S53
Somalia	.S59
South Africa, *see* .A35	
Spain	.S7
Sri Lanka	.S73
Sudan	.S74
Surinam	.S75
Swaziland	.S79
Sweden	.S8
Switzerland	.S9
Syria	.S94
Taiwan	.T28
Tanzania	.T35
Thailand	.T5
Togo	.T64
Trucial States, *see* .U54	
Tunisia	.T8
Turkey	.T9
Uganda	.U4
United Arab Emirates	.U54
United States	.U6
Upper Volta	.U66
Uruguay	.U8
Venezuela	.V4
Vietnam (Democratic Republic)	.V53
Yugoslavia	.Y8
Zambia	.Z3

UNITED STATES

Alabama	.A2
Alaska	.A4
Arizona	.A6
Arkansas	.A8
California	.C2
Colorado	.C6
Connecticut	.C8
Dakota (Territory)	.D2
Delaware	.D3

District of Columbia	.D6
Florida	.F6
Georgia	.G4
Hawaii	.H3
Idaho	.I2
Illinois	.I3
Indian Territory	.I4
Indiana	.I6
Iowa	.I8
Kansas	.K2
Kentucky	.K4
Louisiana	.L8
Maine	.M2
Maryland	.M3
Massachusetts	.M4
Michigan	.M5
Minnesota	.M6
Mississippi	.M7
Missouri	.M8
Montana	.M9
Nebraska	.N2
Nevada	.N3
New Hampshire	.N4
New Jersey	.N5
New Mexico	.N6
New York	.N7
North Carolina	.N8
North Dakota	.N9
Ohio	.O3
Oklahoma	.O5
Oregon	.O7
Pennsylvania	.P4
Rhode Island	.R4
South Carolina	.S6
South Dakota	.S8
Tennessee	.T2
Texas	.T4
Utah	.U8
Vermont	.V5
Virginia	.V8
Washington	.W2
West Virginia	.W4
Wisconsin	.W6
Wyoming	.W8

CANADA AND NEWFOUNDLAND— LIST OF PROVINCES

Alberta	.A3
Assiniboia	.A6
Athabasca	.A8
British Columbia	.B8
Franklin	.F8
Keewatin	.K3
Labrador	.L2
Mackenzie	.M2
Manitoba	.M3
New Brunswick	.N5
Newfoundland	.N6
Northwest Territories	.N7
Nova Scotia	.N8
Ontario	.O6
Prince Edward Island	.P8
Quebec	.Q3
Saskatchewan	.S2
Ungava	.U6
Yukon	.Y8

CUTTER NUMBERS FOR INDIVIDUAL BIOGRAPHY[1]

The following table is used as a guide in formulating Cutter numbers for autobiography, individual biography, etc., in all classes except N (Fine Arts) and P (Language and Literature). Consult the appropriate LC schedules for tables for Class N and Class P.

.x	Cutter number for individual
.xA2	Collected works. By date of imprint
.xA25	Selected works. Quotations. By date of imprint
.xA3–39	Autobiography, diaries, etc.
.xA4	Letters. By date of imprint
.xA42–49	Letters to an individual. By correspondent, A–Z
.xA5–59	Speeches, etc.
.xA6–Z	Biography and criticism

[1]This table is a revised and updated version of the one published in *Cataloging Service*, **107**:5–6 (December 1973).

APPENDIX C

First Level of Description

This appendix contains cataloging records for the items appearing on pages 30–47 prepared according to the rule for the first level of description (1.0D1). The examples below show the differences in the formal description (i.e., title proper through physical description) between the first and second levels of description. AACR 2 does not specify any differences between the two levels with regard to notes or the standard number. Furthermore, there is no indication in the rules of any differences between the levels with regard to choice of access points or forms of headings.

1. Politella, Joseph, 1910-
   Religion in education. — 1st ed. — American Association of Colleges for Teacher Education, c1956.
   x, 90 p.
2. Minneapolis-St. Paul street map. — Scale [1:47,520]. — Rand McNally, [1970]
   1 map.
3. Eliot, T.S. (Thomas Stearns), 1888–1965.
   The waste land/and other poems. — Caedmon, c1971.
   1 sound disc (48 min.)
4. There's something about a story. — Produced and distributed by Connecticut Films, [197-?]
   1 film reel (27 min.)
5. School library quarters planned to meet the needs of an expanding education program / produced by Virginia McJenkin. — American Library Association, c1952.
   1 filmstrip (98 fr.)
6. Using the card catalog. — Hammond, c1969.
   16 transparencies.
7. New chances / prepared for the United States Office of Education by the Leadership in Library Education Institute, Florida State University. — Association for Educational Communications and Technology, c1975.
   1 filmstrip (80 fr.)

8. Scott, Edith, 1918-
   J.C.M. Hanson and his contribution to twentieth
   century cataloging. — Department of Photoduplication,
   University of Chicago, 1970.
   1 microfilm reel.
9. Bailey, Frederick Randolph, 1871-1923.
   Bailey's Text-book of histology. — 13th ed. —
   Williams & Wilkins, 1953.
   xviii, 775 p.
10. Theories for teaching / by Joe Park . . . [et al.]. —
    Dodd, Mead, 1974.
    x, 177 p.
11. Dewey, Melvil, 1851-1931.
    Dewey decimal classification and relative index. —
    Ed. 19. — Forest Press, 1979.
    3 v.
12. Wittgenstein, Ludwig, 1889-1951.
    Philosophical grammar. — University of California
    Press, 1974.
    495 p.
13. The Cambridge history of Poland from Augustus II to
    Pilsudski (1697-1935) / edited by W.F. Reddaway . . .
    [et al.]. — 1st ed. — [Cambridge] University Press,
    1941.
    xvi, 630 p.
14. Conference on Education in Science for the
        Undergraduate Non-science Concentrator (1962 :
        Oakland University)
    Science in the college curriculum / [edited by] Robert
    Hoopes. — [s.n.], 1963.
    x, 211 p.
15. Rangnekar, S.B.
    Imperfect competition in international trade. —
    Oxford University Press, 1947.
    xvi, 187 p.
16. Library resources & technical services / American
    Library Association, Resources and Technical Services
    Division. — Vol. 1, no. 1 (winter 1957)–   . — [S.n.],
    1957–
        v.

BIBLIOGRAPHY

"AACR 2: Background and Summary." *Library of Congress Information Bulletin,* **47**:640–652, October 20, 1978.

ALA Catalog Rules: Author and Title Entries. Preliminary American 2d ed. Chicago: American Library Association, 1941.

ALA Cataloging Rules for Author and Title Entries. 2d ed. Clara Beetle, ed. Chicago: American Library Association, 1949.

ALA Rules for Filing Catalog Cards. 2d ed. Prepared by the ALA Editorial Committee, Subcommittee on the ALA Rules for Filing Catalog Cards, Pauline A. Seely, Chairman and Editor. Chicago: American Library Association, 1968.

ALA Rules for Filing Catalog Cards. 2d abridged ed. Prepared by the ALA Editorial Committee, Subcommittee on the ALA Rules for Filing Catalog Cards, Pauline A. Seely, Chairman and Editor. Chicago: American Library Association, 1968.

Allerton Park Institute. *Major Classification Systems: The Dewey Centennial.* Papers presented at the Allerton Park Institute. Sponsored by Forest Press, Inc., University of Illinois Graduate School of Library Science, and University of Illinois Office of Continuing Education and Public Service, held November 9-12, 1975, Allerton Park, Monticello, Illinois. Urbana-Champaign: University of Illinois Graduate School of Library Science, 1976.

Anderson, Dorothy. *Universal Bibliographic Control: A Long Term Policy—A Plan for Action.* Munich: Verlag Dokumentation, Pullach, 1974.

Angell, Richard S. "Library of Congress Subject Headings—Review and Forecast." In Hans (Hanan) Wellisch and Thomas D. Wilson, eds., *Subject Retrieval in the Seventies.* Westport, Connecticut: Greenwood, 1972.

Anglo-American Cataloging Rules. Prepared by the American Library Association, the Library of Congress, the Library Association, and the Canadian Library Association. North American text. Chicago: American Library Association, 1967. Reprinted in 1970 with supplement of additions and changes.

Anglo-American Cataloging Rules. North American Text. Chapter 6: *Separately Published Monographs.* Chicago: American Library Association, 1974.

Anglo-American Cataloging Rules. North American Text. Chapter 12 Revised: *Audiovisual Media and Special Instructional Materials.* Chicago: American Library Association, 1975.

Anglo-American Cataloging Rules. North American Text. Chapter 14 Revised: *Sound Recordings.* Chicago: American Library Association, 1976.

Anglo-American Cataloguing Rules. 2d ed. Prepared by the American Library Association, the British Library, the Canadian Committee on Cataloguing, the Library Association, the Library of Congress. Michael Gorman and Paul W. Winkler, eds. Chicago: American Library Association, 1978.

Austin, Derek. "The Development of PRECIS, and Introduction to its Syntax." In Hans H. Wellisch, ed., *The PRECIS Index System: Principles, Applications, and Prospects, Proceedings of the International PRECIS Workshop.* Sponsored by the College of Library and Information Services of the University of Maryland, October 15–17, 1976. New York: The H. W. Wilson Company, 1977.

Austin, Derek. *PRECIS: A Manual of Concept Analysis and Subject Indexing.* London: Council of the British National Bibliography, 1974.

Austin, Derek. "The Semantics of PRECIS: Vocabulary Control and RIN System." In Hans H. Wellisch, ed., *The PRECIS Index System: Principles, Applications, and Prospects, Proceedings of the International PRECIS Workshop.* Sponsored by the College of Library and Information Services of the University of Maryland, October 15–17, 1976. New York: The H. W. Wilson Company, 1977.

Austin, Derek, and Jeremy A. Digger. "PRECIS: The Preserved Context Index System." *Library Resources and Technical Services,* **21**:13–30, Winter 1977.

Avram, Henriette D. *MARC: Its History and Implications.* Washington, D.C.: Library of Congress, 1975.

Bakewell, K. G. B. *A Manual of Cataloguing Practice.* Oxford: Pergamon Press, 1972.

Bliss, Henry Evelyn. *Bliss Bibliographic Classification.* 2d ed. J. Mills and Vanda Broughton, eds., with the assistance of Valerie Lang. London: Butterworths, 1977–

Bliss, Henry Evelyn. *The Organization of Knowledge in Libraries.* 2d ed. New York: The H. W. Wilson Company, 1939.

Bliss, Henry Evelyn. *Organization of Knowledge and the System of the Sciences.* New York: The H. W. Wilson Company, 1929.

Bliss, Henry Evelyn. *A System of Bibliographic Classification.* 2d rev. ed. New York: The H. W. Wilson Company, 1936.

British Museum. Department of Printed Books. *Rules for Compiling the Catalogues of Printed Books, Maps and Music in the British Museum.* Rev. ed. London: British Museum. Printed by order of the Trustees, 1936.

Brown, James Duff. *Adjustable Classification for Libraries, with Index.* London: Library Supply Company, 1898.

Brown, James Duff. *Subject Classification for the Arrangement of Libraries and the Organization of Information, with Tables, Indexes, etc., for the Subdivision of Subjects.* 3d ed. Revised and enlarged by J. D. Stewart. London: Grafton & Co., 1939.

Catalog Rules: Author and Title Entries. American ed. Chicago: American Library Association, 1908.

Cataloging Service. Washington, D.C.: Library of Congress, Processing Department, 1–125, June 1945–Spring 1978.

Cataloging Service Bulletin. Washington, D.C.: Library of Congress, Processing Services, 1– , Summer 1978– .

Chan, Lois Mai. *Immroth's Guide to the Library of Congress Classification.* 3d ed. Littleton, Colo.: Libraries Unlimited, 1980.

Chan, Lois Mai. *Library of Congress Subject Headings: Principles and Application.* Littleton, Colo.: Libraries Unlimited, 1978.

Classification in the 1970s: A Second Look. Maltby, Arthur, ed. Rev. ed. London: Clive Bingley, 1976.

"Classification: Theory and Practice." Ann F. Painter, ed. *Drexel Library Quarterly,* vol. 10, no. 4. Philadelphia: Drexel University, 1974.

Comaromi, John Phillip. *The Eighteen Editions of the Dewey Decimal Classification.* Albany, N.Y.: Forest Press Division, Lake Placid Education Foundation, 1976.

Comaromi, John P., Mary Ellen Michael, and Janet Bloom. *A Survey of the Use of the Decimal Classification in the United States and Canada.* Albany, N.Y.: Forest Press Division, Lake Placid Education Foundation, 1975.

Combined Indexes to the Library of Congress Classification Schedules. Compiled by Nancy B. Olson. 15 vols. Washington, D.C.: U.S. Historical Documents Institute, Inc., 1974–

Cutter, Charles A. *C. A. Cutter's Three-Figure Author Table. (Swanson-Swift revision 1969)* Chicopee, Mass.: H. R. Huntting Company, 1969[?].

Cutter, Charles A. *C. A. Cutter's Two-Figure Author Table. (Swanson-Swift revision 1969)* Chicopee, Mass.: H. R. Huntting Company, 1969[?].

Cutter, Charles A. *Cutter-Sanborn Three-Figure Author Table. (Swanson-Swift revision 1969)* Chicopee, Mass.: H. R. Huntting Company, 1969[?].

Cutter, Charles A. *Expansive Classification: Part I: The First Six Classifications.* Boston: C. A. Cutter, 1891–1893.

Cutter, Charles A. *Rules for a Dictionary Catalog.* 4th ed. Washington, D.C.: Government Printing Office, 1904. Republished, London: The Library Association, 1953. (First published under the title *Rules for a Printed Dictionary Catalogue* in 1876.)

Daily, Jay E. "Subject Headings and the Theory of Classification." *American Documentation,* 7:269–274, October 1957.

Dewey, Melvil. *Abridged Dewey Decimal Classification and Relative Index.*

Ed. 11. Edited under the direction of Benjamin A. Custer. Albany, N.Y.: Forest Press, Division of Lake Placid Education Foundation, 1979.

Dewey, Melvil. *Dewey Decimal Classification and Relative Index.* Ed. 19. Edited under the direction of Benjamin A. Custer. Albany, N.Y.: Forest Press, Division of Lake Placid Education Foundation. 1979.

Dunkin, Paul S. *Cataloging U.S.A.* Chicago: American Library Association, 1969.

Encyclopedia of Library and Information Science. Allen Kent and Harold Lancour, eds. William Z. Nasri, asst. ed. New York: Marcel Dekker, Inc. 1968–   .

Foskett, A. C. *The Subject Approach to Information.* 3d ed. Hamden, Conn.: Linnet Books; London: Clive Bingley, 1977.

Frarey, Carlyle J. "Subject Headings." *The State of the Library Art.* Vol. 1, part 2. New Brunswick, N. J.: Graduate School of Library Science, Rutgers State University, 1960.

Freedman, Maurice J. "Automated Network Catalog Products and Services." *Journal of Library Automation,* 9:145–155, June 1976.

Gorman, Michael. "The Anglo-American Cataloguing Rules, Second Edition." *Library Resources and Technical Services,* 22:209–226, Summer 1978.

Hamdy, M. Nabil. *The Concept of Main Entry as Represented in the Anglo-American Cataloging Rules: A Critical Appraisal with Some Suggestions: Author Main Entry vs. Title Main Entry.* Littleton, Colo.: Libraries Unlimited, 1973.

Hanson, J. C. M. "The Library of Congress and Its New Catalogue: Some Unwritten History." In *Essays Offered to Herbert Putnam by His Colleagues and Friends on His Thirtieth Anniversary as Librarian of Congress: 5 April 1929.* New Haven: Yale University Press, 1929.

Haykin, David Judson. *Subject Headings: A Practical Guide.* Washington, D.C.: Government Printing Office, 1951.

Henderson, Kathryn Luther. "'Treated with a Degree of Uniformity and Common Sense:' Descriptive Cataloging in the United States—1876–1975." *Library Trends,* 25:227–271, July 1976.

Hoffmann, Herbert H. *What Happens in Library Filing?* Hamden, Conn.: Linnet Books, 1976.

Horner, John. *Cataloguing.* London: Association of Assistant Librarians, 1970.

Hunter, Eric. *AACR 2: An Introduction to the Second Edition of Anglo-American Cataloguing Rules.* London: Clive Bingley; Hamden, Conn.: Linnet Books, 1979. (A programmed text.)

An Index to the Library of Congress Classification. J. McRee Elrod, Judy Inouye, and Ann Craig Turner, eds. Ottawa: Canadian Library Association, 1974.

International Conference on Cataloguing Principles, Paris, 1961. *Report of International Conference on Cataloguing Principles.* A. H. Chaplin and Dorothy Anderson, eds. London: Organizing Committee of the International Conference on Cataloguing Principles, National Central Library, 1963. London: Bingley on behalf of IFLA, 1969.

International Conference on Cataloguing Principles, Paris, 1961. *Statement of Principles.* Annotated ed. with commentary and examples by A. H. Chaplin and Dorothy Anderson. Provisional ed. Sevenoaks (Kent): International Federation of Library Associations Secretariat, 1966.

International Federation of Library Associations. Working Group on the General International Bibliographic Description. *ISBD(G): General International Standard Bibliographic Description: Annotated Text.* London: IFLA International Office for UBC, 1977.

International Federation of Library Associations. *ISBD(M): International Standard Bibliographic Description for Monographic Publications.* 1st standard ed. London: IFLA Committee on Cataloguing, 1974.

International Federation of Library Associations. *ISBD(S): International Standard Bibliographic Description for Serials.* Recommended by the Joint Working Group on the International Standard Bibliographic Description for Serials set up by the IFLA Committee on Cataloguing and the IFLA Committee on Serial Publication. London: IFLA Committee on Cataloguing, 1974.

International Federation of Library Associations. *International Standard Bibliographic Description (for Single and Multi-Volume Monographic Publications).* London: IFLA Committee on Cataloguing, 1971.

Jewett, Charles C. *Smithsonian Report on the Construction of Catalogs of Libraries, and Their Publication by Means of Separate, Stereotyped Titles, with Rules and Examples.* 2d ed. Washington, D.C.: Smithsonian Institution, 1853. Reprinted, Ann Arbor, Mich.: University Microfilms, 1961.

Kelm, Carol R. "The Historical Development of the Second Edition of *Anglo-American Cataloguing Rules.*" *Library Resources and Technical Services,* **22**:22–33, Winter 1978.

Koel, Åke I. "Can the Problems of Corporate Authorship Be Solved?" *Library Resources and Technical Services,* **18**:348–354, Fall 1974.

LaMontagne, Leo E. *American Library Classification with Special Reference to the Library of Congress.* Hamden, Conn.: The Shoe String Press, Inc., 1961.

Lancaster, F. W. *Vocabulary Control for Information Retrieval.* Washington, D.C.: Information Resources Press, 1972.

Langridge, Derek. *Approach to Classification for Students of Librarianship.* Hamden, Conn.: Linnet Books; London: Clive Bingley, 1973.

Library of Congress Classification Schedules: A Cumulation of Additions and Changes. Detroit: Gale Research Company, 1974–

Library of Congress. *Filing Rules for the Dictionary Catalogs of the Library of Congress.* Washington, D.C.: Processing Department, 1956.

Library of Congress. *The Library of Congress Catalog: A Cumulative Catalog of Books Represented by Library of Congress Printed Cards.* Washington, D.C.: Library of Congress, 1942. 167 v. Supplement, 1947. 42 v.

Library of Congress. *Library of Congress Name Headings with References.* Washington, D.C.: Library of Congress. Jan./Mar. 1974–

Library of Congress. *Monographic Series.* Washington, D.C.: Library of Congress. Jan./Mar. 1974–

Library of Congress. *Rules for Descriptive Cataloging in the Library of Congress.* Adopted by the American Library Association. Washington, D.C.: Library of Congress, 1949.

Library of Congress, MARC Development Office. *Books: A MARC Format: Specifications for Magnetic Tapes Containing Catalog Records for Books.* 5th ed. Washington, D.C.: Library of Congress, 1972.

Library of Congress, MARC Development Office. *Information on the MARC System.* 4th ed. Washington, D.C.: Library of Congress, 1974.

Library of Congress, Processing Department. *Studies of Descriptive Cataloging: A Report to the Librarian of Congress by the Director of the Processing Department.* Washington, D.C.: Government Printing Office, 1946.

Library of Congress, Subject Cataloging Division. *Classification.* 34 vols. Washington, D.C.: Library of Congress, 1901–

Library of Congress. Subject Cataloging Division. *LC Classification—Additions and Changes.* Washington, D.C.: Library of Congress. List 1–   Mar./May 1928–

Library of Congress, Subject Cataloging Division. *Library of Congress Subject Headings.* 9th ed. Washington, D.C.: Library of Congress, 1980. (With quarterly supplements accumulated annually. Also available in microform with the entire list cumulated quarterly.)

List of Subject Headings for Use in a Dictionary Catalog. Prepared by a Committee of the American Library Association. Boston: Published for the ALA Publishing Section by the Library Bureau, 1895.

Lubetzky, Seymour. *Cataloging Rules and Principles: A Critique of the ALA Rules for Entry and a Proposed Design for Their Revision.* Washington, D.C.: Library of Congress, 1953.

Lubetzky, Seymour. *Code of Cataloging Rules, Author and Title Entry: An Unfinished Draft.* Chicago: American Library Association, 1960.

Malinconico, S. Michael, and Fasana, Paul J. *The Future of the Catalog: The Library's Choices.* White Plains, N.Y.: Knowledge Industry Publications, 1979.

Maltby, Arthur. *Sayers' Manual of Classification for Librarians.* 5th ed. London: Andre Deutsch, 1975.

Manuel du répertoire bibliographique universel: organisation, travaux, règles, classification. Bruxelles: Institut International de Bibliographie, 1905.

Merrill, William Stetson. *Code for Classifiers.* 2d ed. Chicago: American Library Association, 1939.

Metcalfe, John. *Information Retrieval, British and American, 1876–1976.* Metuchen, N.J.: Scarecrow, 1976.

Mills, J. *A Modern Outline of Library Classification.* London: Chapman & Hall, Ltd., 1960.

Mills, J., "The New Bliss Classification." *Catalogue and Index,* **40**:1, 3–6, Spring 1976.

Mowrey, Robert L. "The Cutter Classification: Still at Work." *Library Resources and Technical Services,* **20**:154–156, Spring 1976.

National Union Catalog: A Cumulative Author List Representing Library of Congress Printed Cards and Titles Reported by Other American Libraries. Washington, D.C.: Library of Congress, 1956–

Needham, C. D. *Organizing Knowledge in Libraries: An Introduction to Information Retrieval.* 2d ed. London: Andre Deutsch, 1971.

Osborn, Andrew D. "The Crisis in Cataloging." *Library Quarterly,* **11**: 393–411, October 1941.

Palmer, Bernard I. *Itself an Education: Six Lectures on Classification.* 2d ed. London: Library Association, 1971.

Panizzi, Sir Anthony, et al. "Rules for the Compilation of the Catalogue." *Catalogue of Printed Books in the British Museum.* London: British Museum. Printed by order of the trustees, 1841. Vol. 1, pp. v–ix.

Pettee, Julia. *Subject Headings: The History and Theory of the Alphabetical Subject Approach to Books.* New York: The H. W. Wilson Company, 1947.

Prospects for Change in Bibliographic Control. Abraham Bookstein, Herman H. Fussler, Helen F. Schmierer, eds. Chicago: University of Chicago Press, 1977.

The Prussian Instructions: Rules for the Alphabetical Catalogs of the Prussian Libraries. Translated from the 2d ed., authorized August 10, 1908, with an introduction and notes by Andrew D. Osborn. Ann Arbor, Mich.: University of Michigan Press, 1938.

Ranganathan, S. R. *Colon Classification.* 6th ed. Reprinted with amendments. Bombay: Asia Publishing House, 1963.

Ranganathan, S. R. *Prolegomena to Library Classification.* 3d ed. Assisted by M. S. Gopinath. London: Asia Publishing House, 1967.

Rather, John C. *Filing Arrangement in the Library of Congress Catalogs: An Operational Document.* Provisional version. Washington, D.C.: Library of Congress, 1971.

Rather, John C. "The Future of Catalog Control at the Library of Congress." *Journal of Academic Librarianship,* 1:4–7, May 1975.

Reader in Classification and Descriptive Cataloging. Ann F. Painter, ed. Washington, D.C.: Microcard Editions, 1972.

Richmond, Phyllis A. "AACR 2—A Review Article." *Journal of Academic Librarianship,* 6 (no. 1) : 30–37, March 1980.

Rigby, Malcolm. *Computers and the UDC: A Decade of Progress, 1960–1970.* Rockville, Md.: National Oceanic and Atmospheric Administration, Scientific Information and Documentation Division, 1970.

Sears, Minnie Earl. *List of Subject Headings for Small Libraries, Compiled from Lists Used in Nine Representative Small Libraries.* New York: The H. W. Wilson Company; London: Grafton & Co., 1923.

Sears List of Subject Headings. 11th ed. Barbara M. Westby, ed. New York: The H. W. Wilson Company, 1977.

Shera, Jesse H., and Margaret Egan. *The Classified Catalog: Basic Principles and Practices.* Chicago: American Library Association, 1956.

Simonton, Wesley. "An Introduction to AACR 2." *Library Resources and Technical Services,* 23:321–339, Summer 1979.

Simonton, Wesley. "Author Catalog." *Encyclopedia of Library and Information Science.* New York: Marcel Dekker, Inc., 1969. 2:127–132.

Subject Headings for Children's Literature. 2d ed. Washington, D.C.: Library of Congress, 1975.

Subject Retrieval in the Seventies: New Directions: Proceedings of an International Symposium. Held at the Center of Adult Education, University of Maryland, College Park, May 14 to 15, 1971. Hans (Hanan) Wellisch, Thomas D. Wilson, eds. Westport, Conn.: Greenwood Publishing Company, published in conjunction with the School of Library and Information Services, University of Maryland, 1972.

The Use of the Library of Congress Classification: Proceedings of the Institute on the Use of the Library of Congress Classification. Richard H. Schimmelpfeng and C. D. Cook, eds. Sponsored by the American Library Association, Resources and Technical Services Division, Cataloging and Classification Section, New York City, July 7–9, 1966. Chicago: American Library Association, 1968.

Vatican Library. *Rules for the Catalog of Printed Books.* Translated from the 2d Italian ed. by the Very Rev. Thomas J. Shanahan, Victor A. Schaefer, and Constantin T. Vesselowsky. Willis E. Wright, ed. Chicago: American Library Association, 1948. (3d ed. in Italian appeared in 1949.)

Verona, Eva. *Corporate Headings: Their Use in Library Catalogues and National Bibliographies: A Comparative and Critical Study.* London: IFLA Committee on Cataloguing, 1975.

Weintraub, D. Kathryn. "*AACR 2:* A Review Article." *Library Quarterly,* 49:435–443, October 1979.

Wellisch, Hans H. "UDC: Present and Potential." *Drexel Library Quarterly,* 10:75–89, October 1974.

Index

Index

COMARC Project (cooperative machine-readable cataloging), 330
Comaromi, John P., 208, 217n., 273n.
Commentaries, 92
(*See also* Biographical/critical works)
Common subdivisions:
Library of Congress Subject Headings, 145
(*See also* Free-floating subdivisions)
Sears List of Subject Headings, 175
Compilers, 59, 85, 90, 97
Compound surnames, 104, 342
Computer-output microform (COM), 6–7, 330, 337
Computer terminals, 336–337
Computerized catalog, 4–5, 330
Conditions of authorship, 18, 90
Conferences, congresses, and meetings:
entry for, 94
example, 42
headings for, 42, 112
Congresses (*see* Conferences, congresses, and meetings)
Content designators, 331
Contents note, 31, 32, 39–41, 43–46, 76, 78
Context dependency, 189, 190
"Continued by" note, 74
"Continues" note, 74
Cooperative cataloging, 325
Cooperative machine-readable cataloging (COMARC Project), 330
Copy number, 266
Copyright date, 64
examples, 31, 32, 35–37
Cooperative authorship, 14, 18, 88–89
(*See also* Corporate bodies)
Corporate bodies:
added entries under, 34, 35, 37, 41, 42, 47, 97
headings for, 108–113
examples, 34, 35, 37, 41, 42, 47
filing of, 342
references for, 119–120
spacing after initials in, 368
main entry under, 42, 93–94, 292–293
in statement of responsibility, 37, 47, 59
as subject headings, 154, 179
Critical works (*see* Biographical/critical works)
Cross references (*see* References)
CRT (cathode-ray-tube) terminal, 337

Custer, Benjamin A., 207, 220
Cutter, Charles A., 9, 18, 52, 87, 124, 207, 258, 273, 303, 306
cataloging rules of, 12–13
classification by, 303–306
filing rules of, 340
subject cataloging rules, 127, 128, 131
(*See also* Cutter numbers; Expansive Classification)
Cutter numbers, 207, 258–265, 306
in Library of Congress Classification, 281, 286–291, 293–299, 301–302, 369–374
Cutter tables, 207, 258
for Library of Congress Classification, 286–287

Data bases, 328, 330
Data element, 330
Dates:
added to headings, 106, 112, 113
examples, 31, 32, 39, 40, 42–45
in call numbers, 265, 292, 302
as edition mark, 265, 291
of publication and distribution, 63–64
examples, 31–47
uncertain, 31, 34, 64
DDC (*see* Dewey Decimal Classification)
Description, 25–83
areas of, 48, 55–77
examples, 30–47
levels of, 48, 52–54, 375–376
Descriptive cataloging, 9–122
definition, 11
Descriptive cataloging codes (*see* Cataloging codes)
Dewey, Melvil, 207, 217–218
(*See also* Dewey Decimal Classification)
Dewey Decimal Classification (DDC), 7, 125, 167, 209, 210, 212, 217–257, 262, 293, 306, 307, 313, 314, 327
abridged, 220–221, 248–255, 325
history of, 217–220
notation of, 226–228, 281
outline of, 224
principles, 223–226
revision of, 221–223
Dictionary catalog, 7, 97, 126–132, 181, 267, 339
Dimensions, 69–70
examples, 31–47, 70–71
Direct geographic subdivisions, 150–152